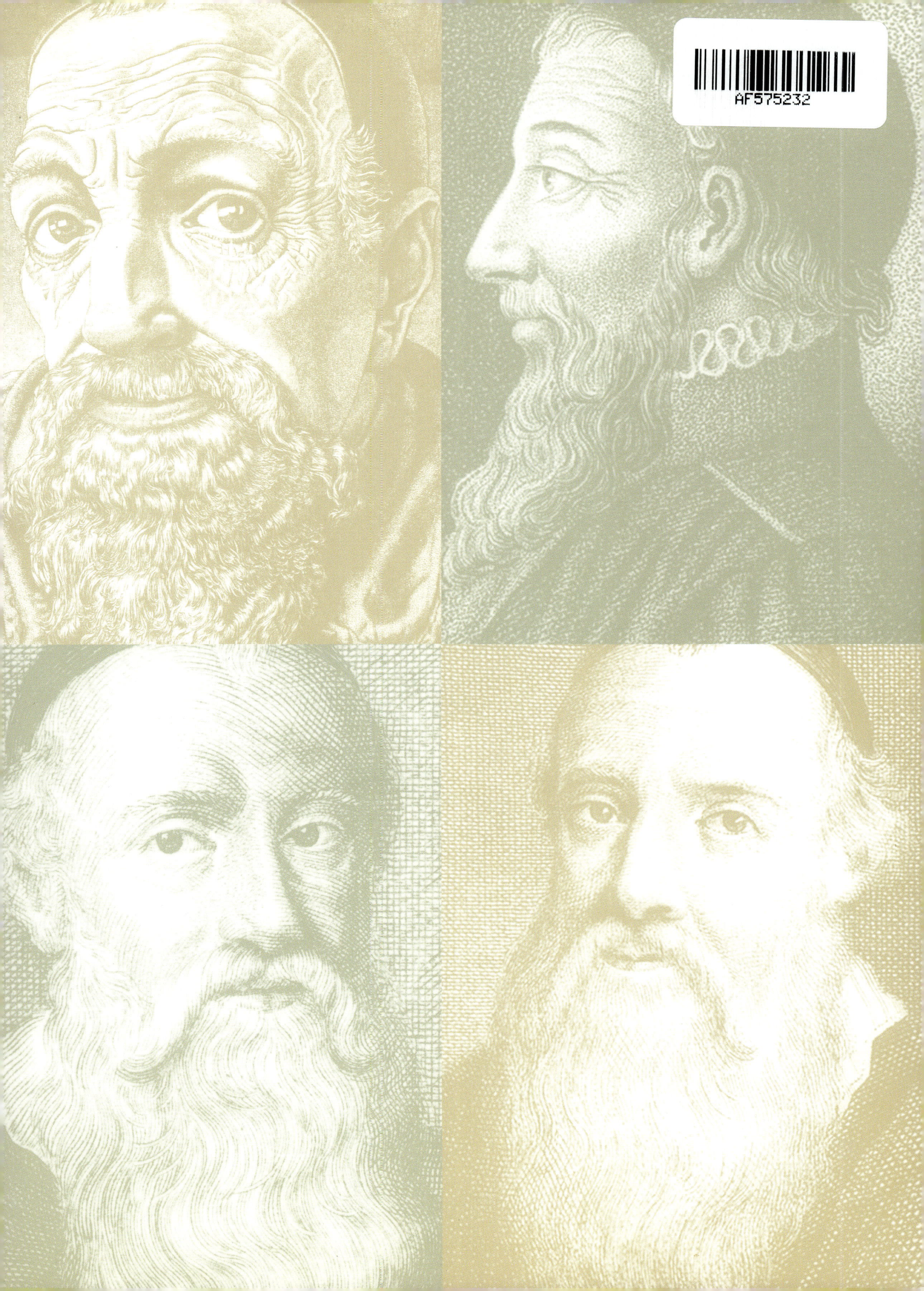

♦

♦ MENNO SIMONS ♦

♦

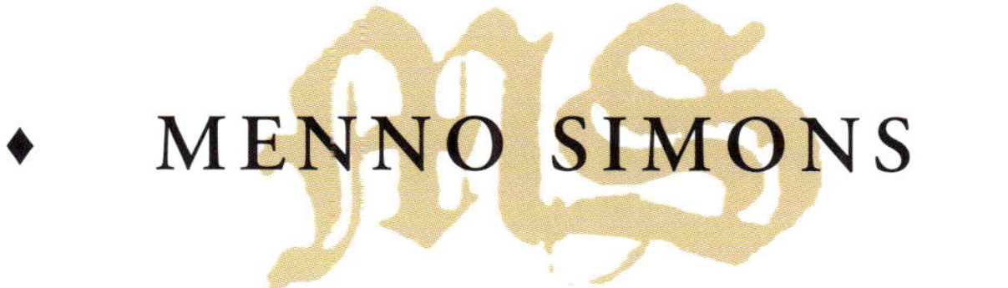

MENNO SIMONS

Places, Portraits and Progeny

PIET VISSER
MARY S. SPRUNGER

with assistance from
ADRIAAN PLAK

translation
GARY K. WAITE

photography
IMAN HEYSTEK
ESTHER VAN WEELDEN

KNIJNENBERG ♦ KROMMENIE ♦ THE NETHERLANDS
FRIESENS ♦ ALTONA ♦ MANITOBA ♦ CANADA
MASTHOF PRESS ♦ MORGANTOWN ♦ PA ♦ U.S.A.
KÜMPERS-VERLAG ♦ HAMBURG-ALTONA ♦ GERMANY
in cooperation with
UNIVERSITY LIBRARY OF AMSTERDAM ♦ THE NETHERLANDS
EASTERN MENNONITE UNIVERSITY ♦ HARRISONBURG ♦ VA ♦ U.S.A.

Library of Congress Cataloging-in-Publication Data
Menno Simons: Places, Portraits and Progeny/Piet Visser, Mary S. Sprunger, Adriaan Plak. Illustrated.
Includes bibliographical references and index. p. cm.
ISBN 1-55056-462-5 (also published in an Dutch and German Edition)
1. The Netherlands-Mennonites-History-ca. 1530-1740
I. Visser, Piet. II Sprunger, Mary S. III Plak, Adriaan

Canadian Cataloguing in Publication Data
Visser, Piet (Pieter), 1949- & Sprunger, Mary S. (Mary Susan), 1962-
Menno Simons: Places, Portraits and Progeny
Illustrations.
Bibliography: p.
Includes index.
ISBN 1-55056-462-5 (also published in a Dutch and German edition)
1. History-Mennonites-The Netherlands I. Title

ISBN of the English edition: 1-55056-462-5
(ISBN Dutch edition: 90-70353-07-5/CIP, ISBN German edition: 3-930435-20-9)

Publisher of the English edition:
Friesens, One Printer's Way, Altona, Manitoba R0G 0B0, Canada
Distributor in the U.S.A.:
Masthof Press, Route 1, Box 20, Morgantown, PA 19543-9701

Printed in Canada

♦ CONTENTS

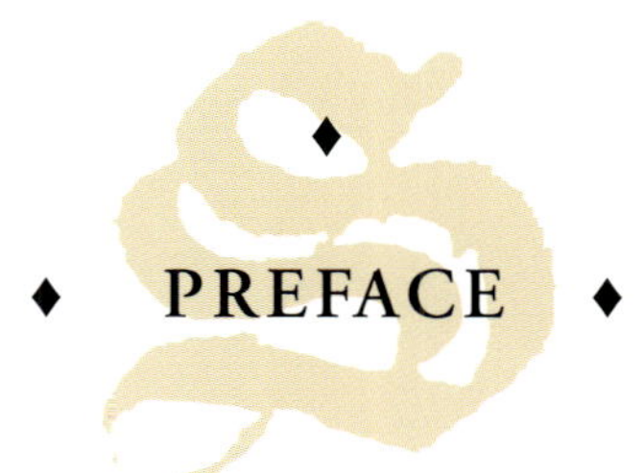

PREFACE

Menno Simons, who was born in 1496 in Witmarsum, Friesland, and died in 1561 near Bad Oldesloe in Northern Germany, was the only Reformer native to the Netherlands. Constantly seeking refuge from the persecution that took the lives of thousands of his followers, Menno shaped the religious movement called the Mennonites or *doopsgezinden* (baptism-minded). Setting up its own New Testament norms and values this diverse Anabaptist-Mennonite community has been both marked and purified by intolerance for centuries, though at the cost of great suffering. Sixteenth-century Dutch refugees found asylum in the Vistula Delta in Poland. In time many of them were forced to create a new existence in the Ukraine, Russia. When the situation there also became unbearable, many emigrated to the United States of America and Canada. Swiss Mennonites were also mercilessly persecuted in the sixteenth and seventeenth centuries. After a temporary stay in the Palatinate and Alsace-Loraine, these homeless people, together with many South Germans, set sail for Pennsylvania in the New World. Both ethnic groups spread from there throughout the United States, Canada, Mexico, Paraguay and Brazil, always in search of a life of unlimited religious freedom.

Always and everywhere the Mennonites have asked and still ask the same two questions: will we be accepted as we are and can we accept the society that tolerates us? The spiritual descendents of Menno Simons who would survive in the Netherlands have found the most remarkable answers to these questions. On the wings of the new spirit of the young Dutch Republic, which wrested sovereignty from the Spanish and headed for its Golden Age, they rose out of the dark swamps of death and oppression to the shining summits of peace and prosperity.

This book attempts to trace back the footsteps of Menno's life by text and image, to record his many faces iconographically, and to portray the changing image of his Dutch spiritual descendents to about 1740. This triptych, which also deals with survival, art and the art of life, could not have been accomplished without the devotion of many people. The Mennonite printer Kees Knijnenberg at Krommenie (The Netherlands) has been, materially and immaterially, the great stimulator of this project, together with his colleague David Friesen in Altona, Manitoba (Canada). Mary Sprunger, Eastern Mennonite University, Harrisonburg, Virginia (USA), was in charge of the third part. Adriaan Plak, Amsterdam University Library, has described the Menno prints of Part II. We are much indebted to Daniel Horst, Rijksprentenkabinet Amsterdam, for his introduction to the second part. For the text of the first part we express our gratitude to Marja Keyser who made available her short chronology of Menno's life which was updated by Sjouke Voolstra. Most of the historical scenes and documents were photographed by Iman Heystek. Those materials were supplied by the Amsterdam University Library and its permanent loan, the *Doopsgezinde Bibliotheek* (Mennonite Historical Library) without charging the customary reproduction fees. Esther van Weelden made the photographs of the modern scenery of Menno's past. Assisted by Sher Doruff, she is also responsible for the design of the book. Piet Visser composed and edited the images and text of the book.

We are very grateful to Martje Postma at Hamburg (Germany) and Gary K. Waite at Fredericton, New Brunswick (Canada), who made the German and English translations respectively. Finally, we thank private owners, museums, libraries and their staffs, who made available the remaining visual materials, as well as other people who contributed in one way or the other. Without intentionally doing injustice to anyone unmentioned, they are: F.D.F.M. Aalbers (Rijksmuseum Amsterdam, Neth.), Ch. van Beurden (Amsterdam Historical Museum, Neth.), J.C. Bierens de Haan (Arnhem, Neth.), L. Bowman (Menno Simons Historical Library, EMU, Harrisonburg, VA, USA), D.C. de Clercq (Amsterdam, Neth.), A.R.A. Croiset van Uchelen (Amsterdam University Library, Neth.), P.J. Foth, (Hamburg, Germ.), J. Gleysteen (Goshen, IN, USA), S.S. Hesselink ('t Goy-Houten, Neth.), T. Kootte (Museum Catharijne Convent, Utrecht, Neth.), C.J.M. Kordes (Rijksdienst Beeldende Kunst, The Hague, Neth.), A. Leerintveld (Royal Library, The Hague, Neth.), J.C. Nix (Atlas van Stolk, Rotterdam, Neth.), G. Pol-Visser (Ruinen, Neth.), M. Polder (Knijnenberg bv, Krommenie, Neth.), M.P.A. Schlecht (Dutch Mennonite Conference, Amsterdam, Neth.), C. Schuckman (Hollstein Project Amsterdam, Neth.), J. Springer (Mennonite Historical Library, Goshen College, IN, USA), W.G. Voltman-Vaags (Amsterdam, Neth.), S. Voolstra (Landsmeer, Neth.), G.J. Waltner (Mennonite Research Institute, Weierhof, Germ.), H. de Wit (Zaan Historical Museum, Zaandijk), as well as the board of directors of Eastern Mennonite University and the University Library of Amsterdam.

Amsterdam / Harrisonburg
30 June 1996 *Mary Sprunger & Piet Visser*

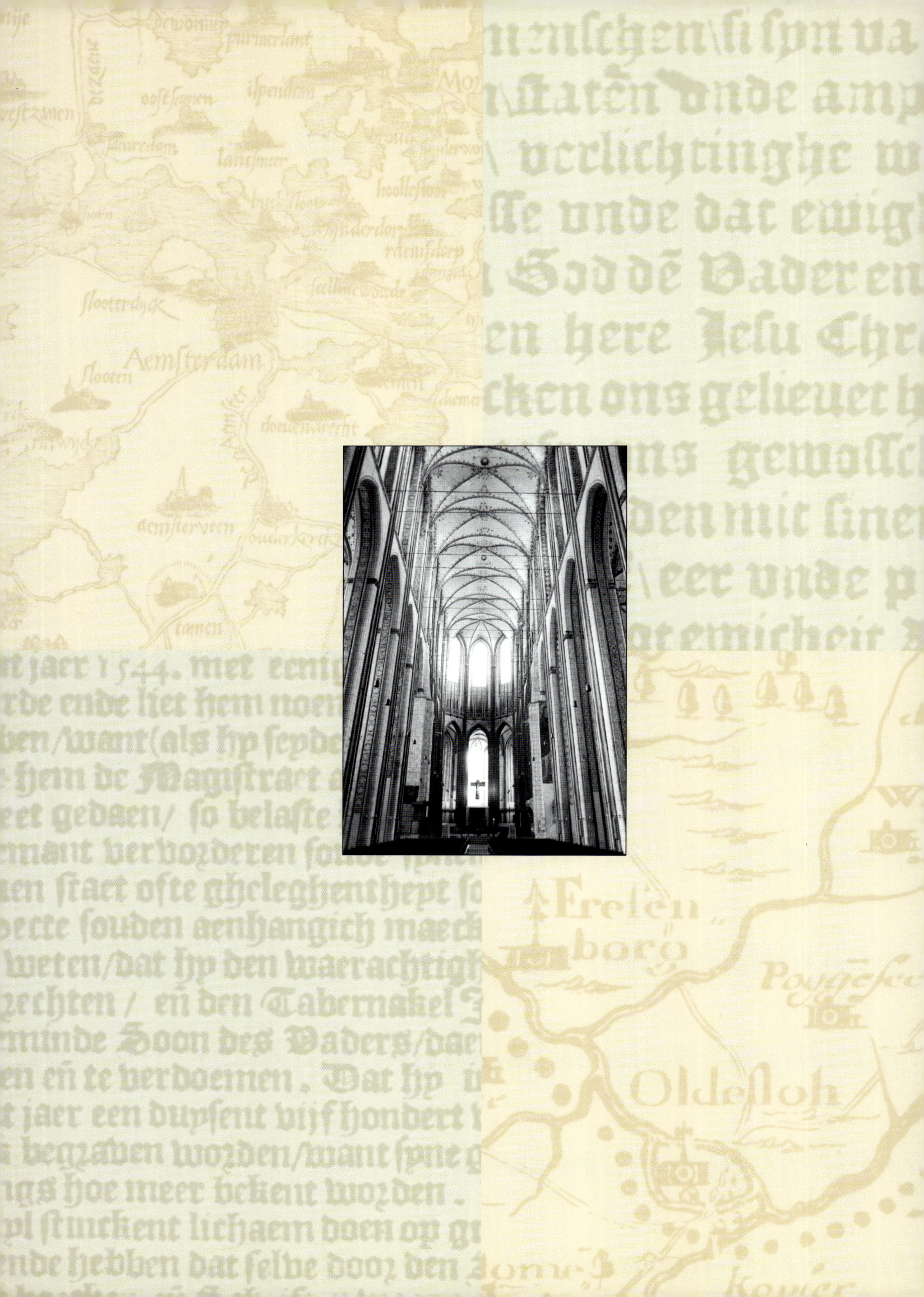

purmerlant
oostsanen
ilpendam
saerdam
lantsmeer
hoollesloot
ransdorp
slooterdyck
Aemsterdam
slooten
doeuenarecht
aemsterveen
verlichtinghe
unde dat ewig
God dē Vader en
en here Jesu Chr
cken ons gelieuet
eer unde
t jaer 1544. met eeni
rde ende liet hem noen
ben/want (als hy seyde
hem de Magistraet
eet gedaen/ so belaste
emant verbozderen soude
aen staet ofte gheleghentheyt so
secte souden aenhangich maeck
weten/dat hy den waerachtigh
zechten / en den Tabernakel
eminde Soon des Vaders/dae
en en te verdoemen. Dat hy
t jaer een duysent vijf hondert
s begraven worden/want syne
ngs hoe meer bekent worden.
yl stinckent lichaem doen op g
ende hebben dat selve door
Erefen borg
Oldesloh

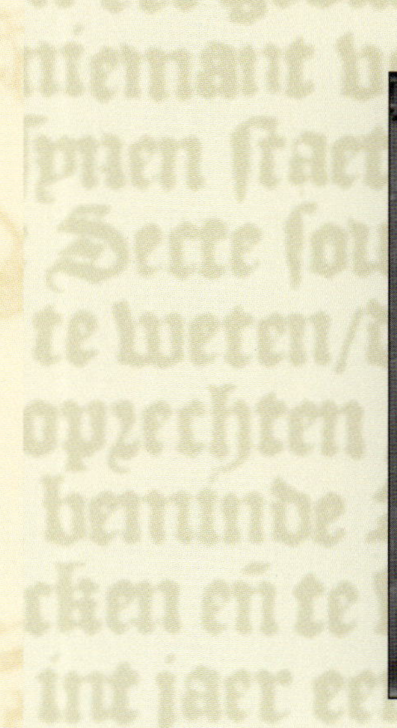

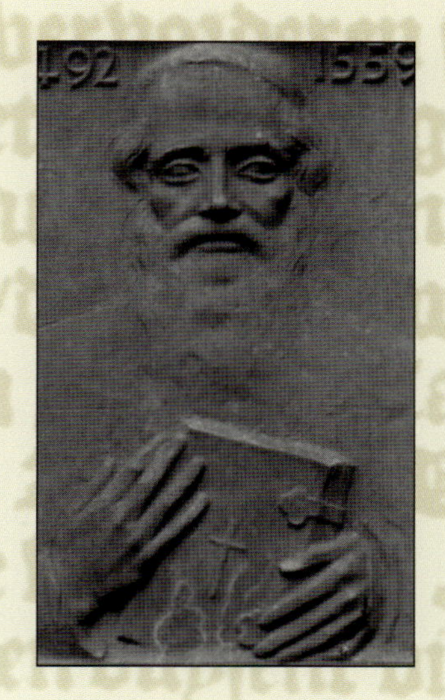

I

♦ IN THE FOOTSTEPS ♦
OF
MENNO

♦

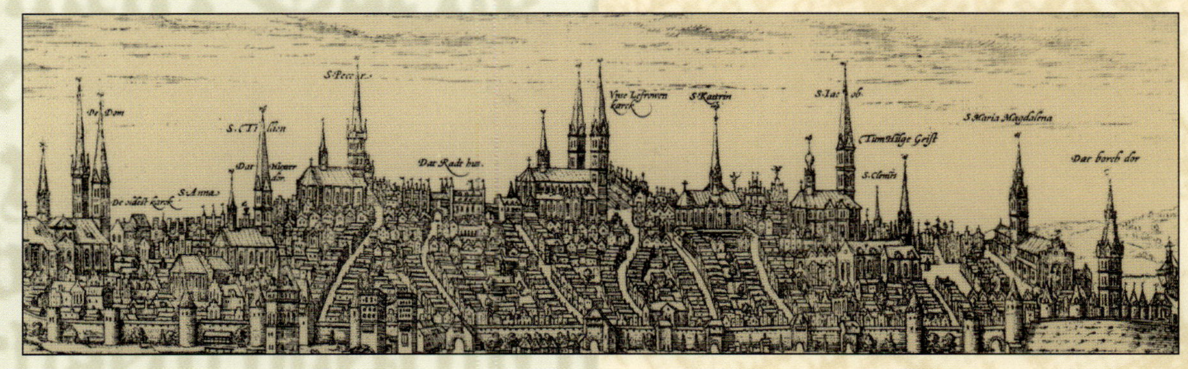

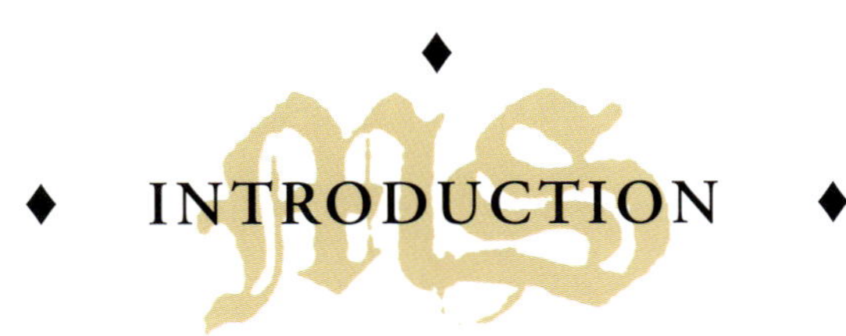

INTRODUCTION

'His father, of peasant background, moved with the family to Mansfeld shortly after Martin's birth, where he became active in the copper mines and achieved a certain prosperity. Martin was able to pass through the Latin school and begin law studies at the university at Erfurt (1501-1505)'. So begins the entry about Martin Luther in the sixth part of the *Moderne Encyclopedie van de Wereld-literatuur* (*The Modern Encyclopedia of World Literature*). In these two sentences alone are compressed many biographical details; more than we could ever gather together about Menno's life. Moreover, Menno Simons does not appear once in the above mentioned work, no more, for that matter, than Zwingli or Calvin.

We know that Luther was born on the 10th of November 1483, but of Menno all we have is an estimation that he must have seen the light of day sometime during January 1496. And even that year was disputed until the beginning of this century, just as was the date of his death. When previous generations of Netherlanders first celebrated a centennial of Menno's birth, the fourth, the commemoration date was not 1896 but 1892! If 1492 was then regarded as his year of birth, his year of death was generally fixed at 1559. The discrepancy in dates was resolved in 1914, to the credit of Karel Vos, Menno's first real biographer. Not much has been added to this pioneering work since, except for those details which have appeared from archival material discovered later. In other words, whoever attempts to chart Menno's life can do little more than take Vos's hand and make a rather circuitous movement in a landscape full of blindspots.

The irony of Menno's history – if fortunate for us – is that it is precisely his opponents who are to be thanked for providing us with the best information about his life as a priest. In 1554 at Wismar, Menno completed a written defence against Gellius Faber, *Een klare beantwoordinge, over een schrift Gellii Fabri* (*A Clear Reply to Gellius Faber*). This Faber alias Jelle Smit, a former priest of Jelsum, Friesland, who left the Catholic Church in the same year as Menno had fiercely attacked the Anabaptists in a booklet written two years earlier. He upbraided them for not basing the calling of their teachers, including Menno, upon the true church of God; instead, he argued, they proceeded directly from the heretical sects of Melchior Hoffman and the Münsterite rebels. Menno, as leader of the peaceful Mennonites, could not let this pass unnoted. He set out to deny each of the Münsterite suspicions. For this reason in the *Klare beantwoordinge* he took up a detailed description of the beginning of his pastoral career. It is dedicated to his gradual discovery of the falseness of Catholic doctrine, to his reformist reading, his constantly maturing Anabaptist sympathies and his preaching against and resistance to Münsterite fanaticism. Not until much later would this long passage be printed as a separate booklet under the title *Wtganck: ofte bekeeringe van Menno Symons* (*Menno's Renunciaton of Rome*) (Hoorn, 1621). This authentic source brings us closest to the beginning of Menno's

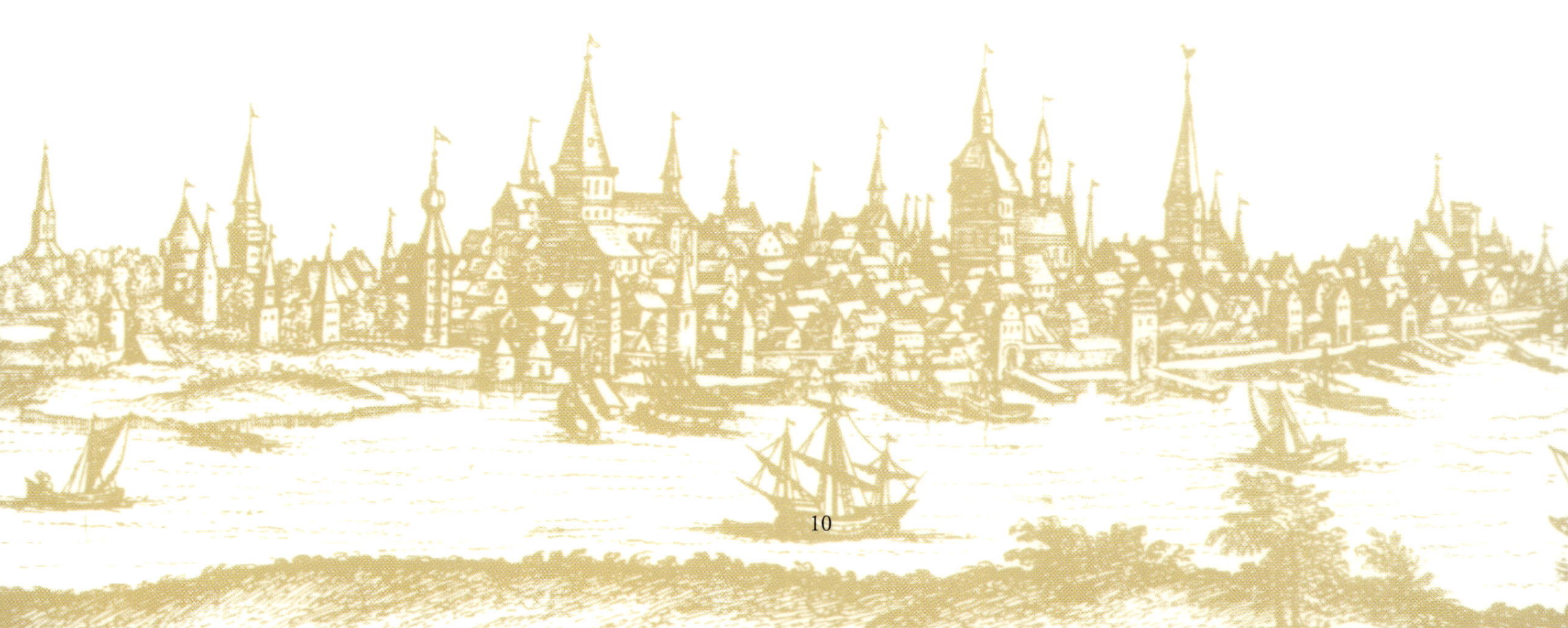

career, in about 1536. At the same time we must remember that it was at least eighteen years after that date when Menno composed this memoir, drawing primarily from his own memory. How much more could he have told? What further details has he concealed? Each so-called ego-document gives occasion for personal coloration and distortion of reality, if not in a premeditated fashion. So too with Menno's writing. He perceived only one need; to present a clean slate, bleached of all Münsterite stains and dirt. For the biographer the question remains of how blindly one can sail upon these prefurnished facts. However, this appears above all to be an academic question for there are no other sources, let alone objective ones, neither for checking, nor for amplification. Out of sympathy for him we grant Menno the benefit of the doubt as an informant.

And is this objection also not true for the rest of the scarce data regarding his later career? Just as for all writers of the recorded history of Dutch Anabaptism, Menno's chronicler is dependent upon reports of supporters and especially of opponents. His fellow covenanters practically never dared, for the sake of preserving life, to take up the pen. For each name of a brother or sister, of a house or a street committed to paper, could have resulted in death. His adversaries, cold inquisitors and exasperating priests, preferred to dip their pens in poison in order to exterminate Anabaptism. There is then, nothing left to us except to gather together from left and especially from right the loose ends of Menno's eventful life – of this recourse there is no doubt. Even the scarce reports from his own entourage are colored by subjectivity. We might be able to form an image of the true historical Menno somewhere between his being abused on the one hand as a liar and weathervane, and on the other admired for his remorse over bad decisions.

And what methodology holds for his activities, applies at the very least to his wanderings. The roads that he walked between Pingjum and Oldesloe, with or without crutch; the waters upon which he sailed, lying down or standing; the villages and towns which he called at as a fugitive or where he was able to stay for longer periods with wife and children; the fields, barns or cellars wherein he hid or where he prayed and preached or debated differences with others, form merely vague lines and coarse points upon the map of the sixteenth-century Low Countries.

This chronicle of his life thus forces us to be conveyed through the hazy landscape of his time, which did not grant even to him and his company a clear light. Nevertheless, text and image in this first part, endeavor to rescue from the obscurity of four or five centuries his weighty activities and compulsive wandering. With a sleuth's eye and with all possible good will and restrained imagination, a trace of Menno can still be recovered, despite all of the footprints that have been erased by time, envy and conflict.

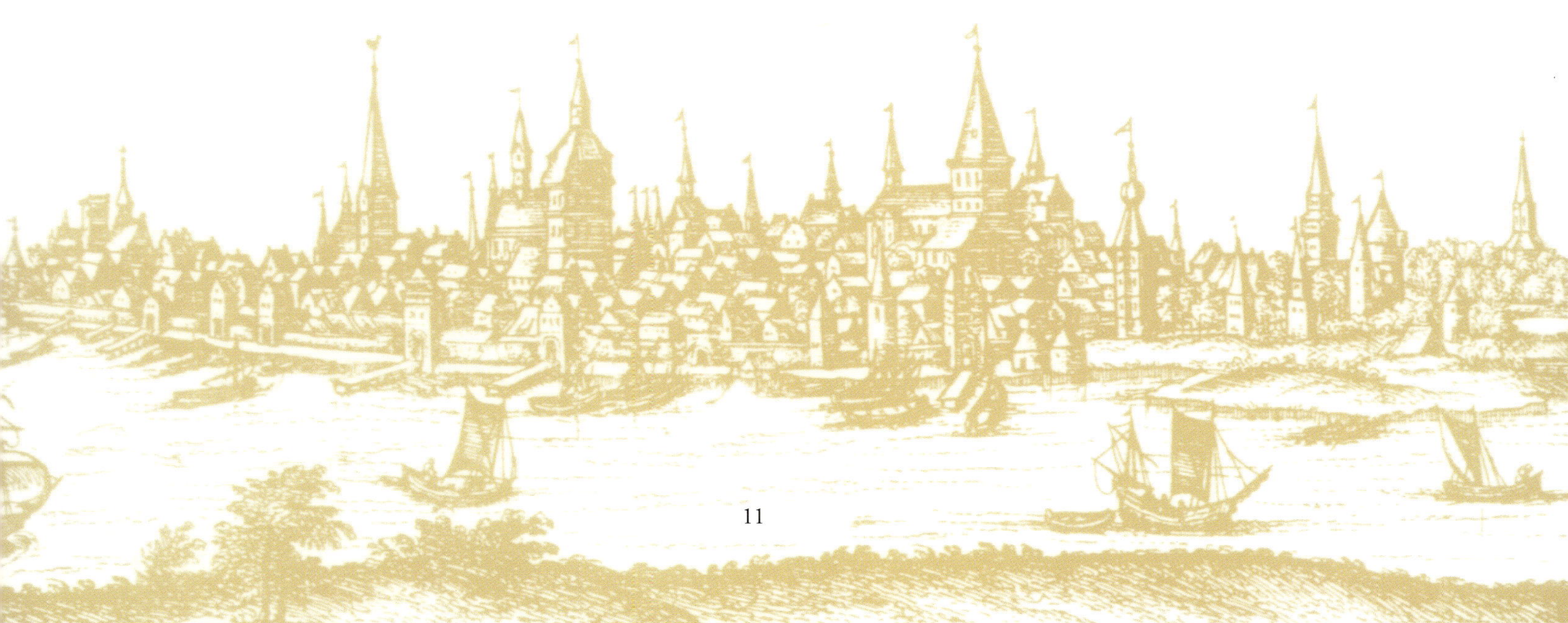

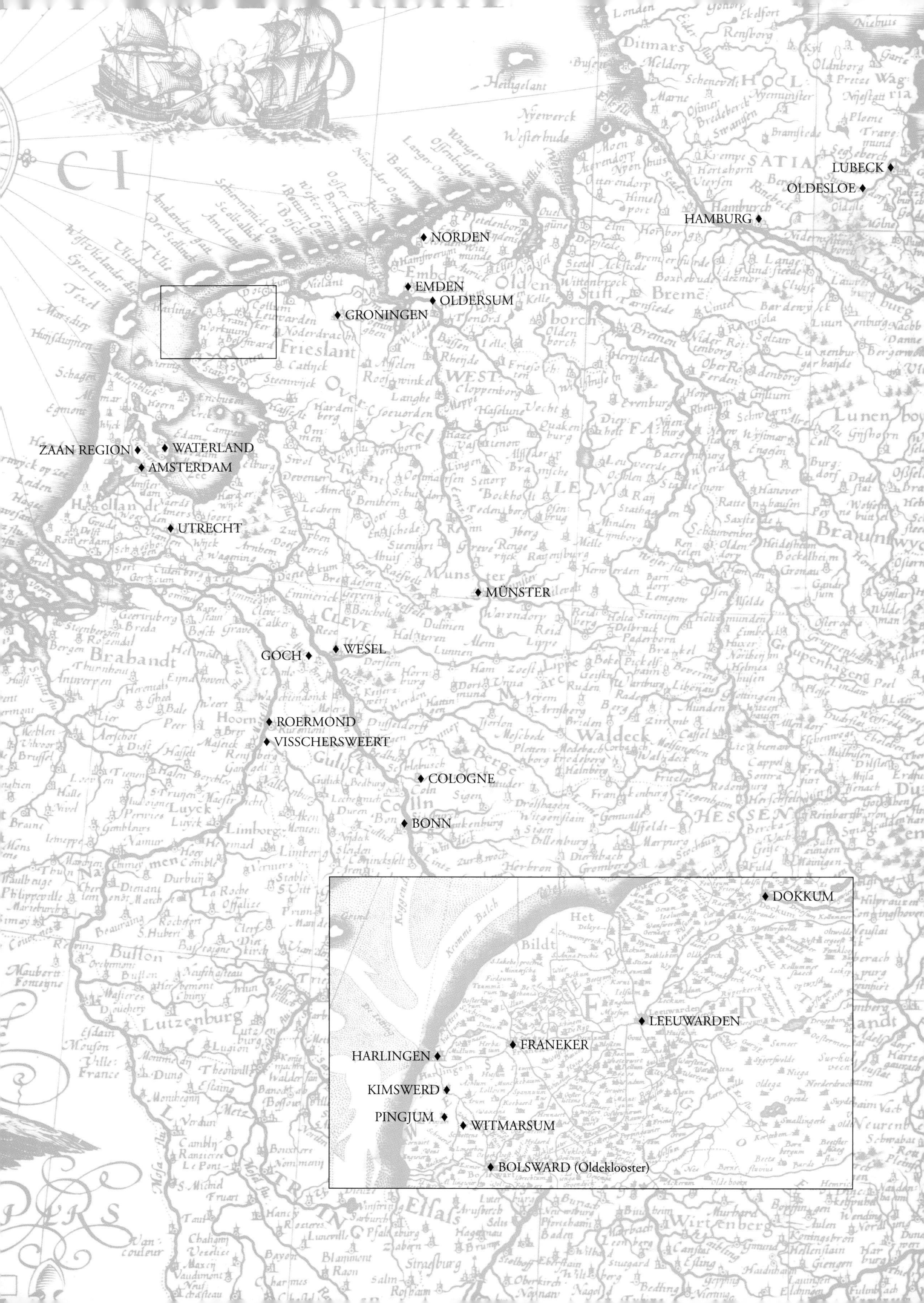

LUBECK
OLDESLOE
HAMBURG
NORDEN
EMDEN
OLDERSUM
GRONINGEN
ZAAN REGION
WATERLAND
AMSTERDAM
UTRECHT
MÜNSTER
GOCH
WESEL
ROERMOND
VISSCHERSWEERT
COLOGNE
BONN
DOKKUM
LEEUWARDEN
FRANEKER
HARLINGEN
KIMSWERD
PINGJUM
WITMARSUM
BOLSWARD (Oldeklooster)

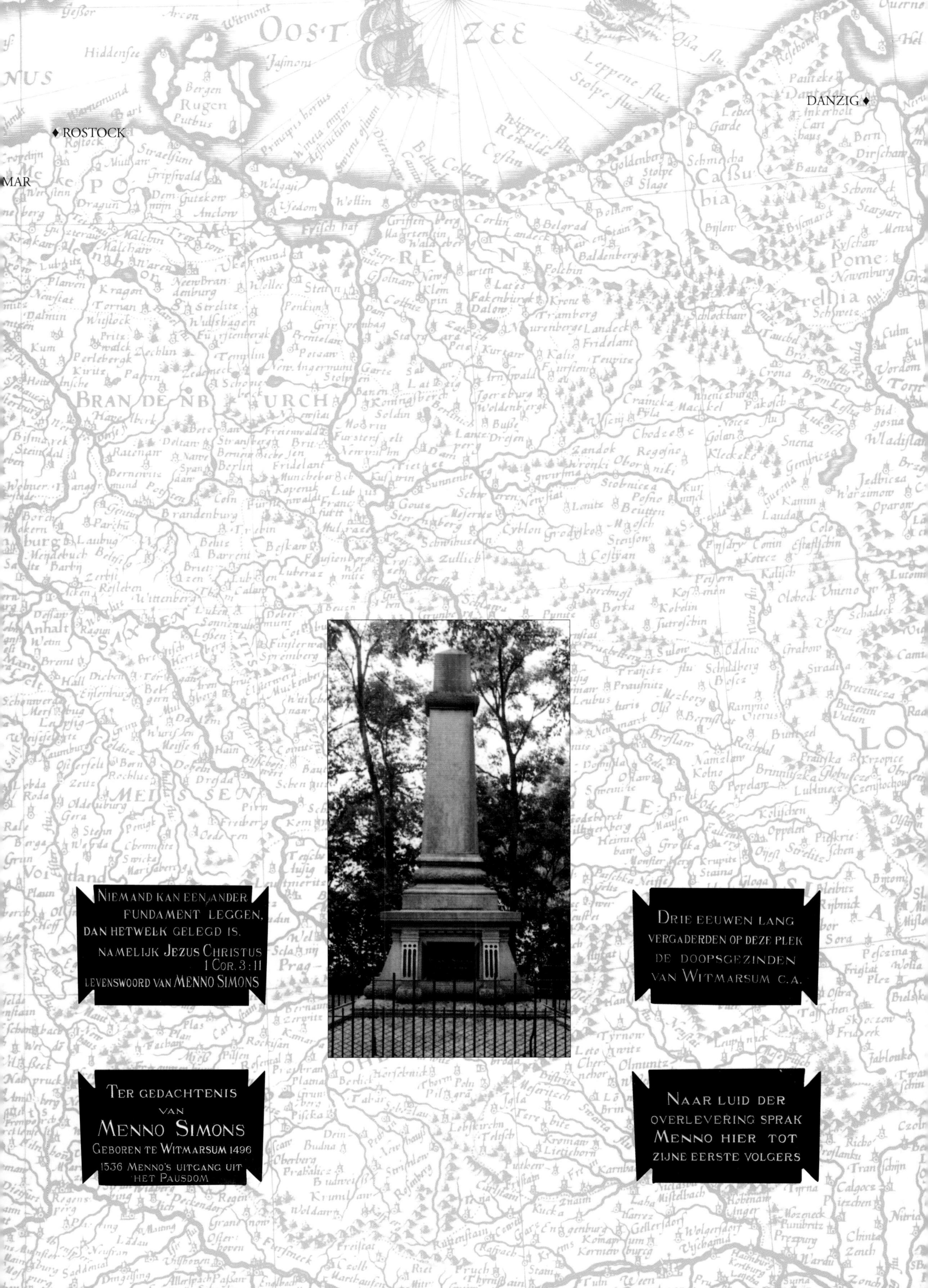
ROSTOCK
DANZIG
MAR
OOST ZEE
Niemand kan een ander
fundament leggen,
dan hetwelk gelegd is,
namelijk Jezus Christus
1 Cor. 3 : 11
Levenswoord van Menno Simons
Drie eeuwen lang
vergaderden op deze plek
de doopsgezinden
van Witmarsum c.a.
Ter gedachtenis
van
Menno Simons
Geboren te Witmarsum 1496
1536 Menno's uitgang uit
het Pausdom
Naar luid der
overlevering sprak
Menno hier tot
zijne eerste volgers

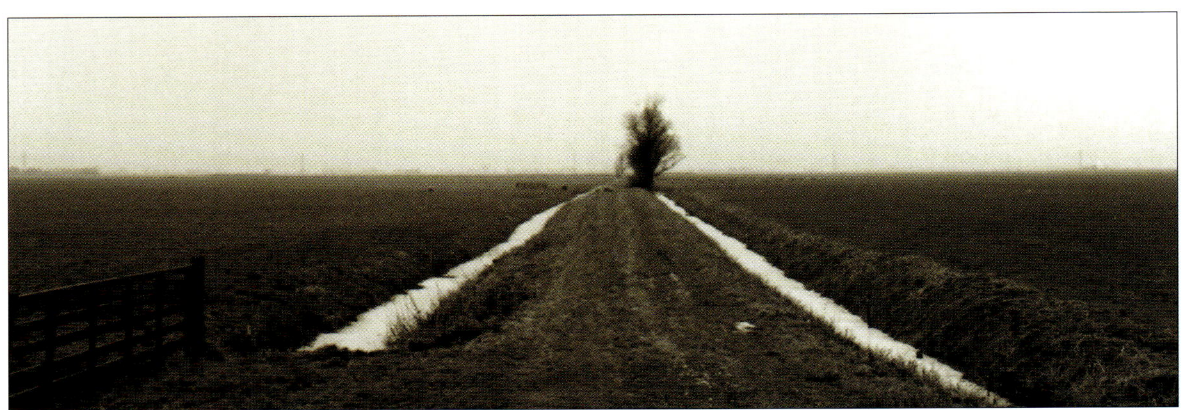

1a. *Winter near Witmarsum* - EVW

WITMARSUM

1 ♦ 1496 - 1523

And be no servant of men. (Menno)

In January 1496 is born in the wide, wintry land of Friesland, in the village of Witmarsum, a boy, Minne or Menno, the son of Simon. The family of this peasant Simon, which later resided in neighboring Pingjum, apparently numbers three other boys: Peter, Tijde, and Jan, who would die young. The heavy clay district of Westergo belongs to the most fertile region of Friesland. The Catholic church, with one of the richest parishes here, has ruled religious life for centuries. For many generations the noble family Aylva has wielded the secular sceptre. But in Menno's early youth many of these types of certainties evaporate. Outside his playground of farmyard and village there ignites a severe conflict over Frisian freedom between the Schieringers and Vetkopers. In 1515 the domain of Sjoerd van Aylva near Witmarsum is devastated. In 1524 Friesland is forced to submit to the authority of the Habsburg empire of Charles V. The young Menno witnesses from close by the results of warfare and plunder. He learns that men enslave their fellows, or even worse. And thereafter it is in the incomprehensible power of God, that his Frisian land is put to the test with drought and floods, pestilence and cattle disease.

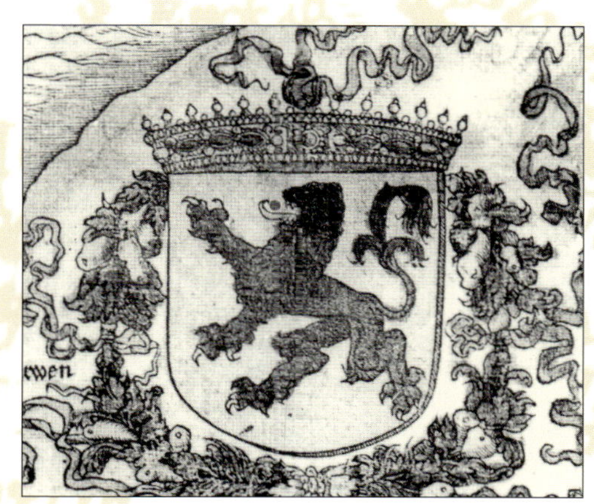

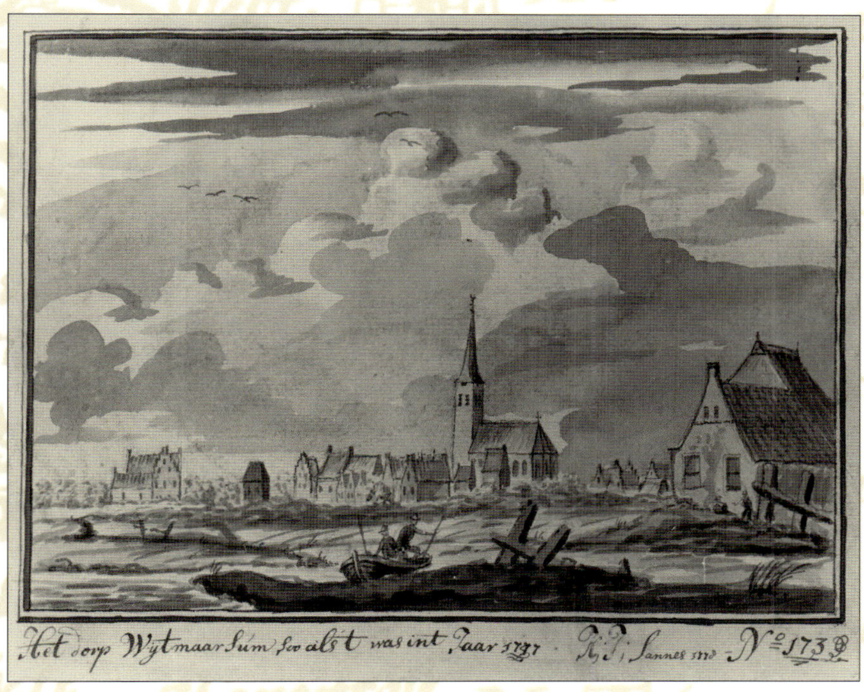

1b. K.P. Sannes,
Witmarsum (1777) - FML

1c. Deventer,
Detail of a map of Friesland (1558) - UBA

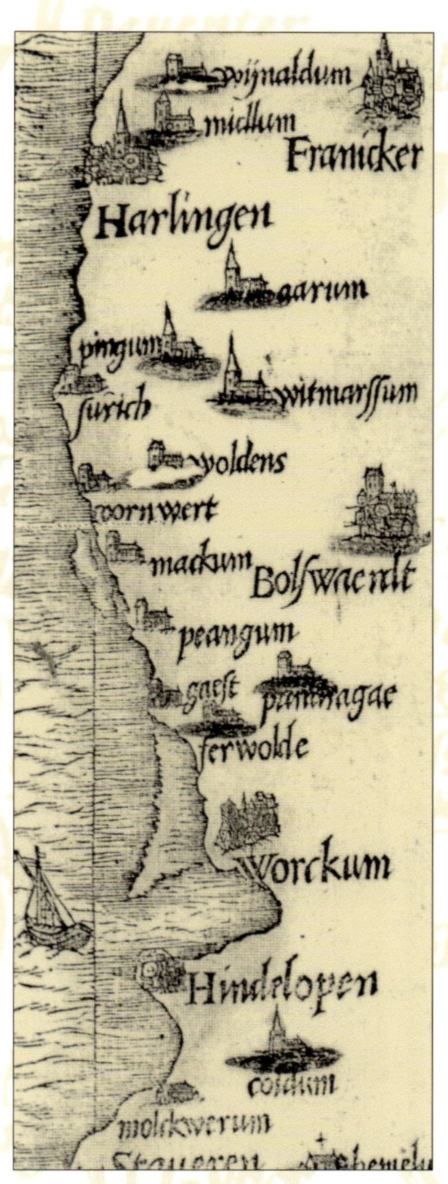

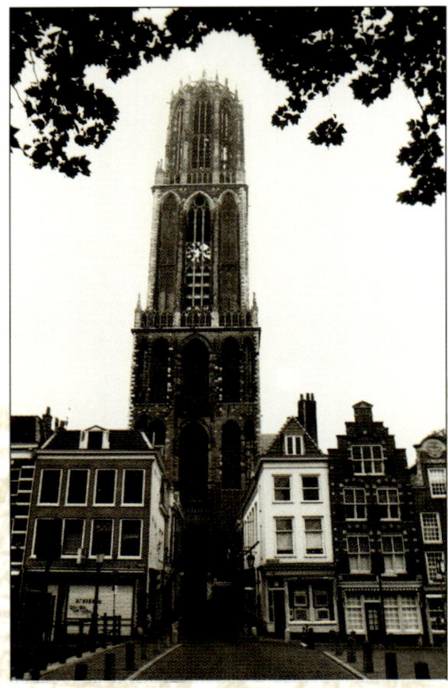

2a. *Cathedral tower at Utrecht* - EVW

UTRECHT

2 ♦ 1524

It happened in the year 1524, the twenty-eighth of my life, that I assumed the duties of a priest in my paternal village called Pingjum. (Menno)

The young Menno still refuses to hear that all the world now expects the end of the world. He is 28 years old when on the 26th of March he is ordained a priest. He completes his exams, his demeanor is judged to be good, and he convinces the bishop that he has satisfactory means by which to carry on his priestly office. The trip to the bishopric of Utrecht is an especially high point, when he is installed as vicar of Pingjum. The parishioners themselves have nominated him – a special right of the Frisian Catholics.
As vicar he assists the priest with the mass and the other ministerial tasks. He receives some 60 guilders per year. Along with this he is still the prebend who, for a fee, reads specially ordered masses for marriages or deaths. Menno's calling is rather late. Commonly Frisian priests were ordained as priests sometime after their twentieth birthday. Menno wraps himself in silence about this, just as he reveals nothing about his education. Did he have private lessons from a parish priest, who imparted to him the Vulgate-Latin, the reading of the mass and the doctrine of Rome? Did he attend a cloister school, two of which were in Bolsward, near Witmarsum? The priest and the prebend of Pingjum had attended the university of Rostock - Menno is the only one without academic education.

2b. Deventer, *Wonseradeel / Friesland* (1558) - UBA

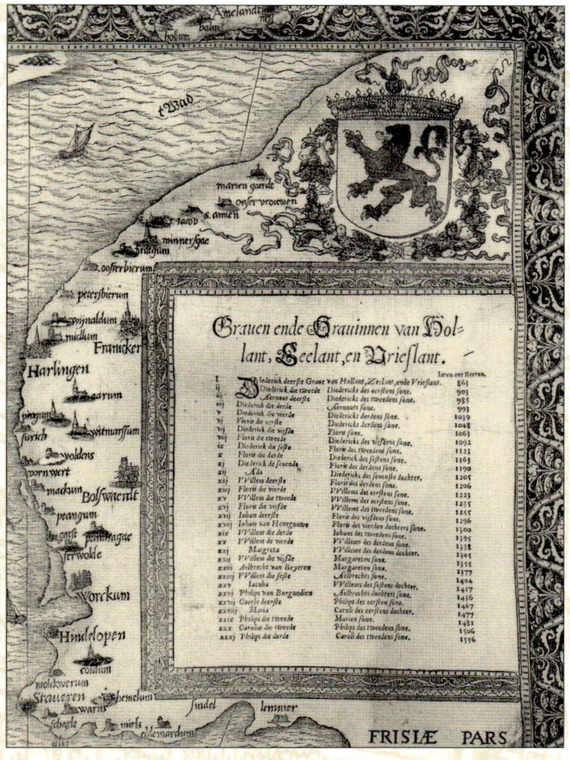

2c. J.G. Visscher, *Pingjum* (1778) - FML

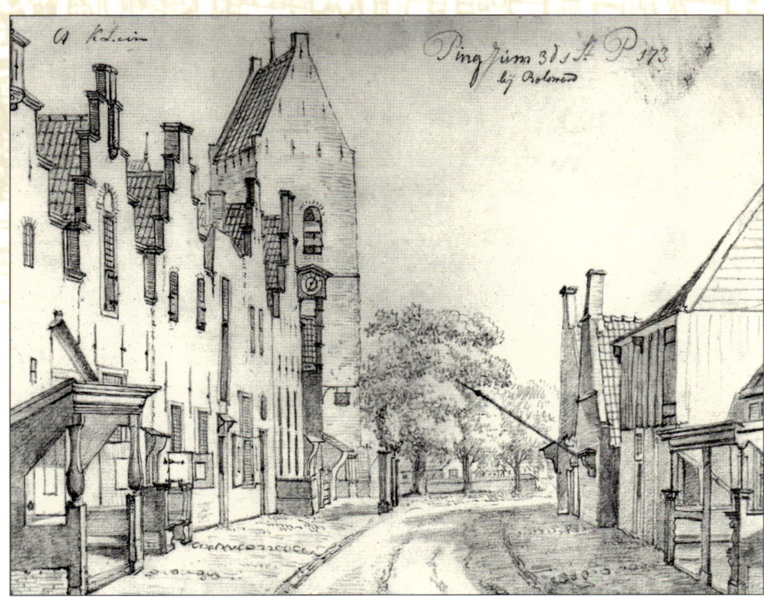

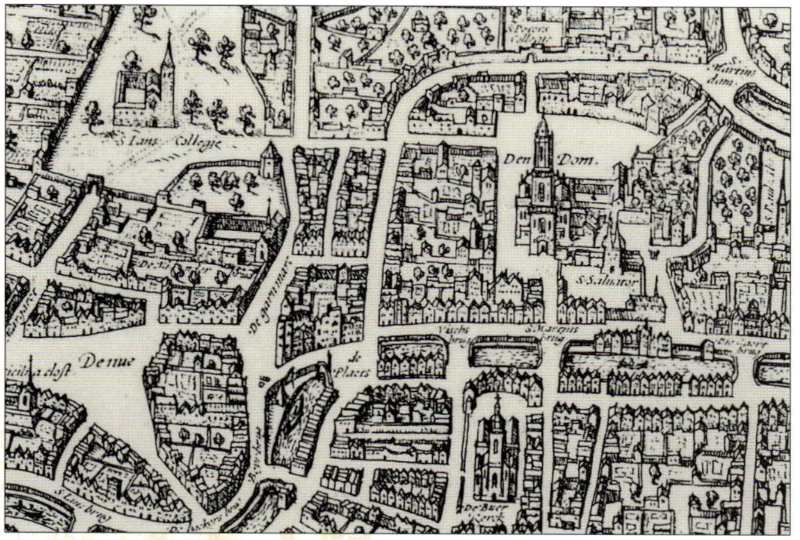

2d. B&H I, *Utrecht* (1572) - UBA

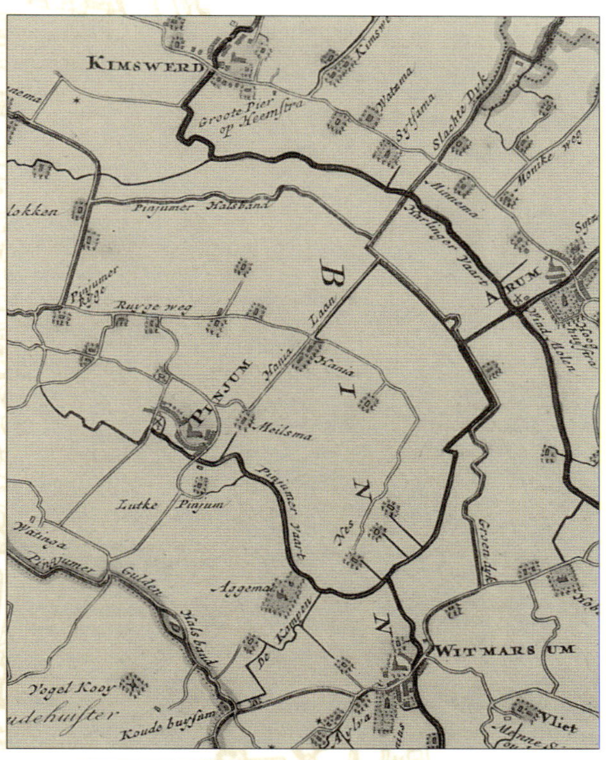

2e. *Wonseradeel county (*1664) - FML

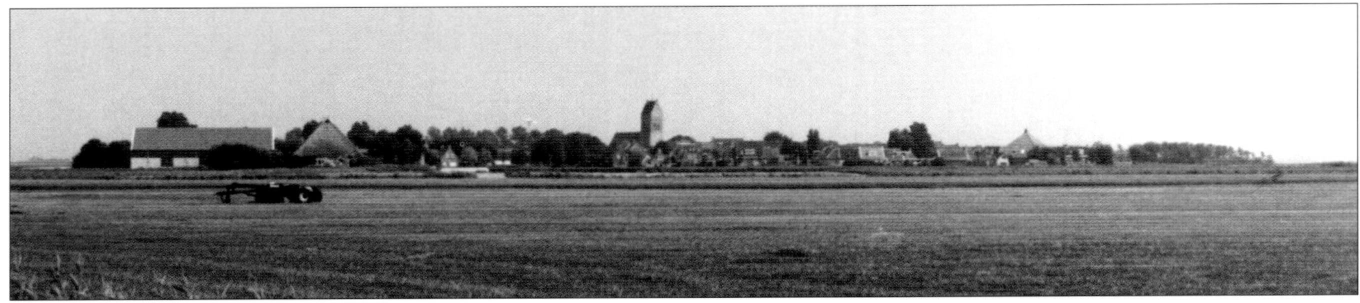

3a. *View of Pingjum / church of Pingjum* - EVW

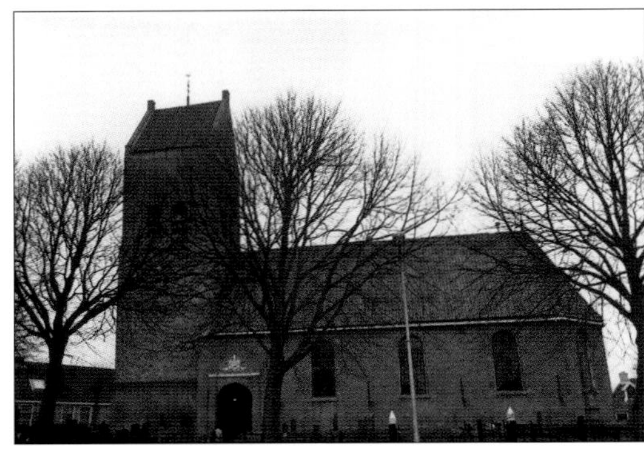

PINGJUM

3 ♦ 1526 - 1531

The two young men mentioned earlier and I spent our time emptily in playing [cards] together, drinking, and in diversions as, alas, is the fashion and usage of such useless people. (Menno)

From the beginning vicar Menno is tormented by the devil, for every time he conducts the celebration of the eucharist, he asks himself if the host and wine are truly changed into Christ's flesh and blood. The doubt is fed by the sharp criticism of the church, which is continuously and clearly audible. Monks and priests are scolded as good-for-nothings and exploiters; as well, the veneration of images is ridiculed.
A number of lay people, called sacramentarians, are criticizing the doctrine of transubstantiation which is celebrated in the mass. The biblical humanism of Erasmus, which revealed that a number of practices were not biblically based, finds a hearing in broader circles. Luther's critique of the doctrine of salvation through good works and his break with the church, penetrates Friesland as well, thanks to the book printers. His sola fide and sola scriptura provoke Menno's curiosity. Around 1526 he is able to lay his hands on a New Testament in Luther's translation. If previously the bible 'had not touched his daily life', now bible study teaches him how far 'we were deceived'. At the end of 1527 in the neighboring pastorate of Witmarsum, the writings of Luther and other heretical publications are seized on command of lord Tjaard van Aylva. Then around 1530 Menno hears that there are even more ideas being spread by messengers of a Melchior Hoffman, by people who are baptized anew.

3b. M. Hoffman, *Weyssagung* (1530) - UBA-DG

Weyssagung auß Heiliger Gotlicher geschrifft.

Von den trübsalen diser letsten zeit.

Von der schweren hand vnd straff gottes über alles gottloß wesen.

Von der zůkunfft des Türckischen Thirannen/vnd seines gantzen anhangs.

Wie er sein reiß thůn/vnd volbringen wirt/vnnd zů einer straff/vnnd růdten.

Wie er durch Gottes gwalt sein niderlegung vnnd straff entpfahen wirt.ꝛc.

Melchior Hoffman.

1530.

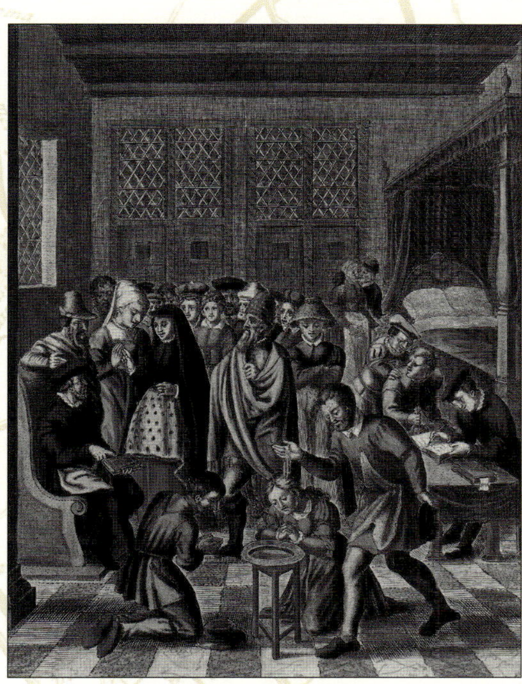

3c. *Baptismal scene*, in: Hortensius - UBA-DG

3d. *The Roman Catholic Angler, satirical print against the sale of indulgences* (ca. 1523) - AVS

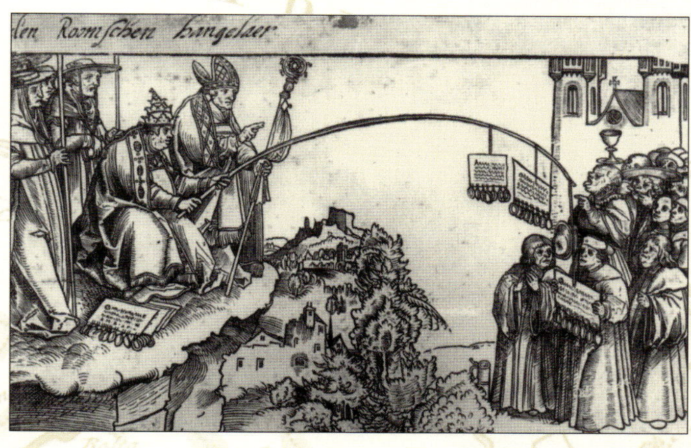

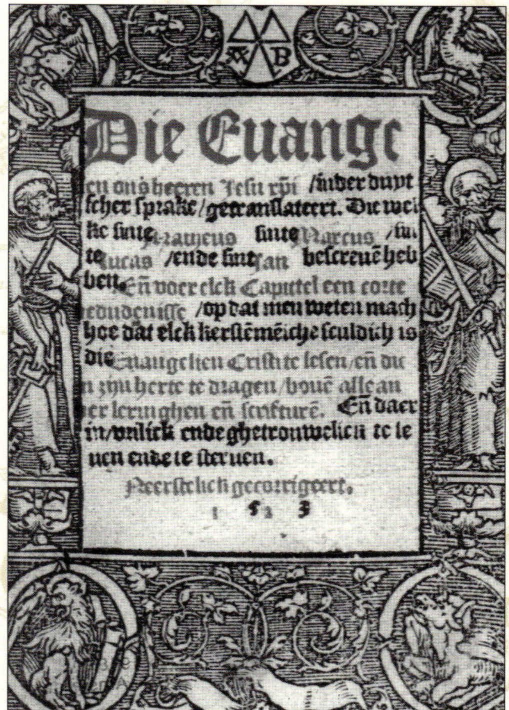

Die Euange
lien ons heeren Jesu christi / in der duyt
scher sprake / getranslateert. Die wel
cke sinte Matheus sinte Marcus / sin
te Lucas / ende sint Jan bescreuen heb
ben. En voer elck Capittel een corte
inhoudenisse / op dat men weten mach
hoe dat elck kerstē mēsche sculdich is
die Euangelien Christi te lesen / en die
in zijn herte te dragen / bouē alle an
der leringhen en scrifturē. En daer
in vrilick ende ghetrouwelick te le
uen ende te steruen.
Neerstelick gecorrigeert.
1 5 2 3

3e. *Luther-testament: The Gospel* (1523) - UBA

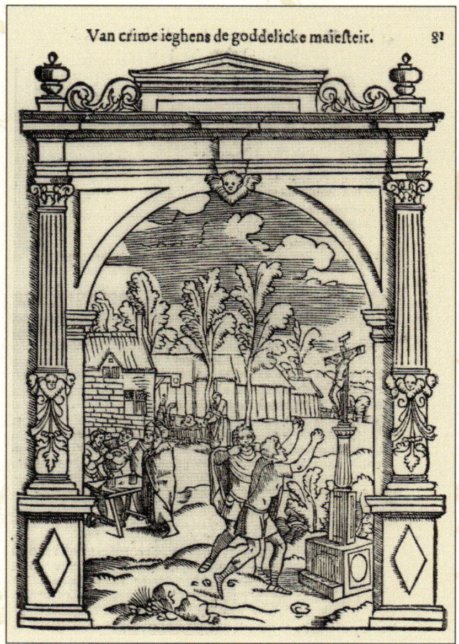

Van crime ieghens de goddelicke maiesteit. 81

3f. *Blasphemy* (1555), in: Damhoudere - UBA

4a. H. Tavernier, *Witmarsum* (1785) - FML

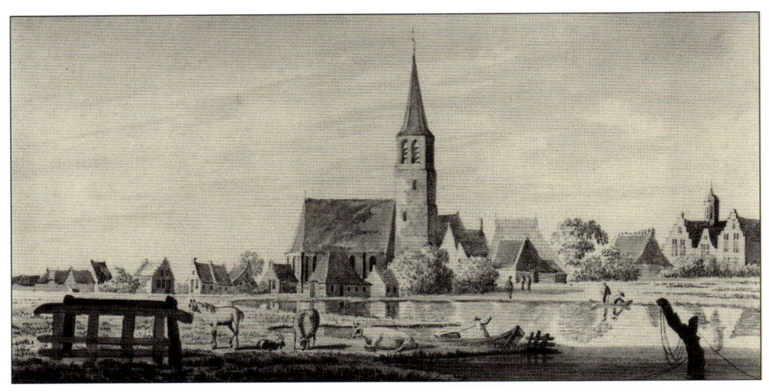

WITMARSUM

4 ♦ 1531 - 1533

Although I had now acquired considerable knowledge of the Scriptures, yet I wasted that knowledge through the lusts of my youth in an impure, sensual, unprofitable life, and sought nothing but gain, ease, favor of men, splendor, name and fame, as all generally do who sail that ship. (Menno)

Menno is well liked, he is regarded as a 'fine Man'. He puts up with one and all: 'Everyone sought and desired me; the world loved me and I loved the world'. In March 1531 he hears of the beheading of Sicke Frericksz Snijder at Leeuwarden, a man who had renewed his baptism. That makes him even more curious about this modern conception of baptism. On that point he studies the church fathers and Luther, Bucer and Bullinger. His conclusion is again 'that we were deceived in regard to infant baptism'. For the present he does nothing with the knowledge, waiting instead for an honourable cause: the appointment to priest in the rich parish of Witmarsum at the end of 1532. As village priest he has prestige. Among his new parishioners he would find willing ears for his growing critique of Rome and increasingly evangelical preaching. At the end of 1533 in Leeuwarden he is told by Anabaptist messengers that the baker Jan Matthijs from Haarlem is teaching that the tyrants will be punished by God and the New Jerusalem is expected on earth. The report that the Westphalian city of Münster is chosen for this, also reaches Menno. That he has a weakness for the Anabaptist teaching escapes no one, but for him the Münsterite fanaticism goes too far. He advises prudence to those of his parishoners interested in the new ideas. However, the gas is now out of the bottle; his own brother Peter is already completely under the spell of the realization of this disastrous ideal.

4b. C. van Sichem I, *Melchior Hoffman* (1607) - UBA-DG

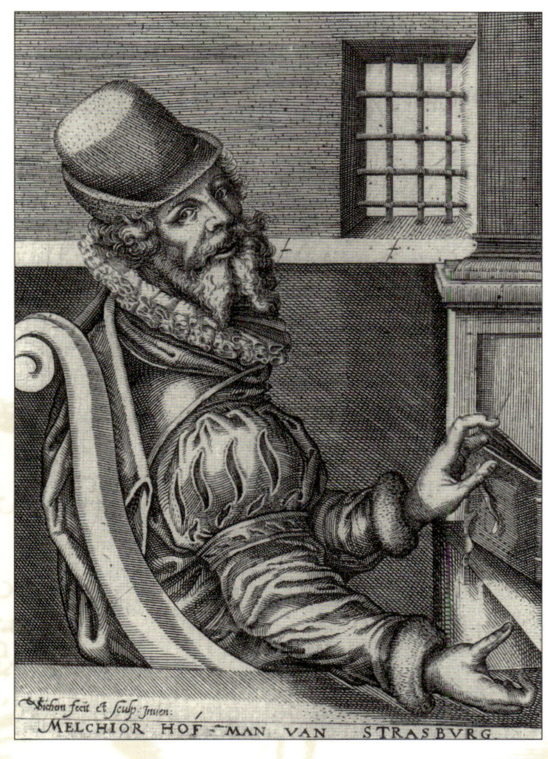

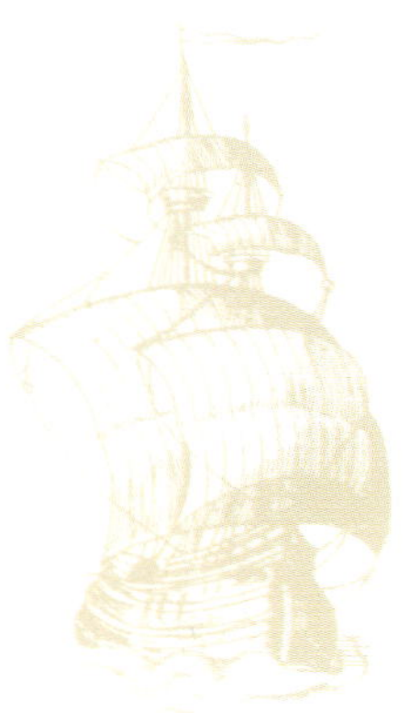

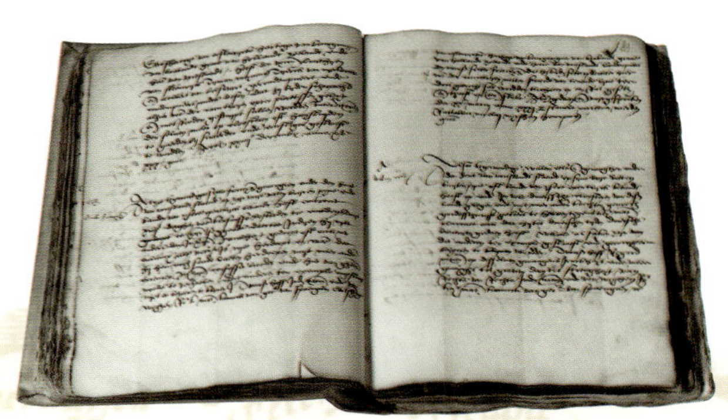

4d. *Book of Criminal Sentences, showing the sentence of Sicke Fericksz Snijder* (1531) - FML

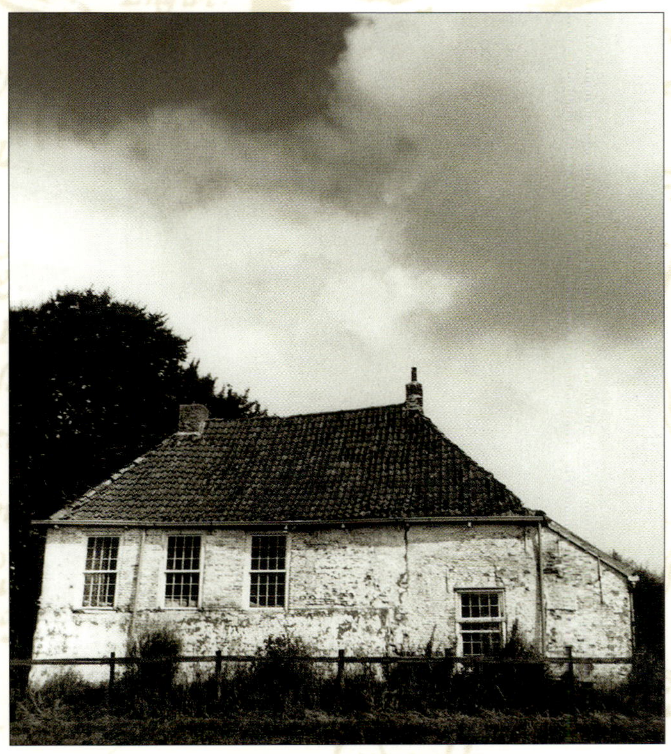

4c. *The White House near Witmarsum, where according to popular tradition Menno lived and preached* - EVW

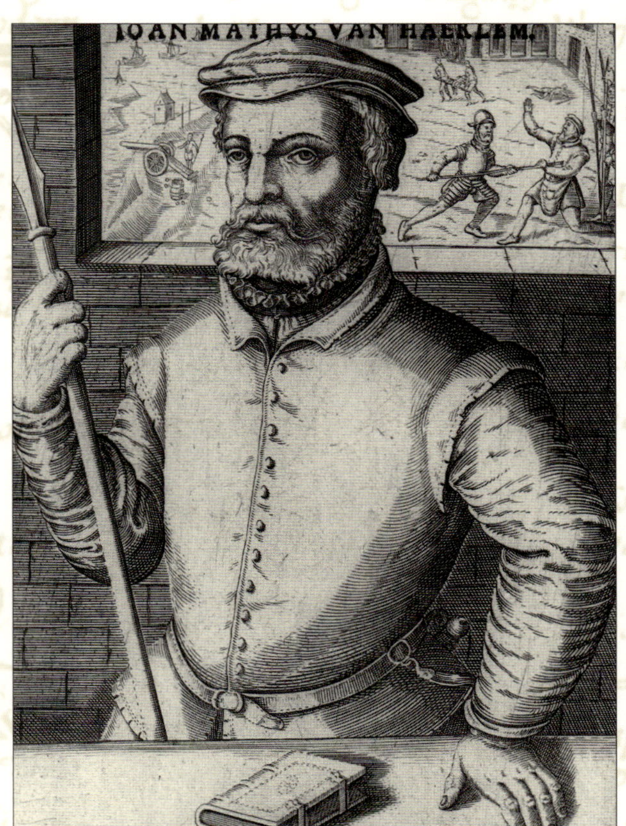

4e. C. van Sichem I, *Jan Matthijs* (1607) - UBA-DG

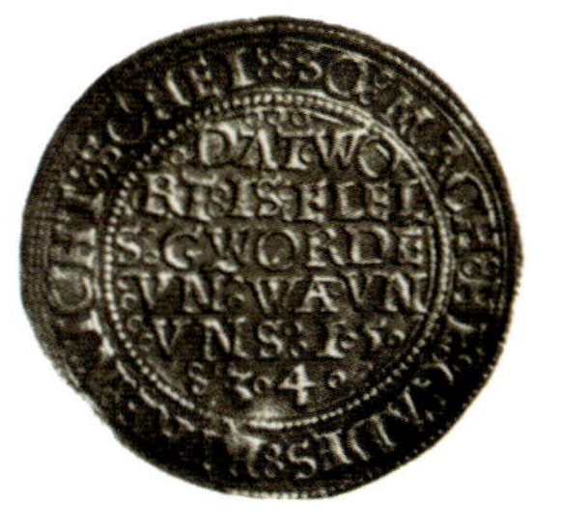
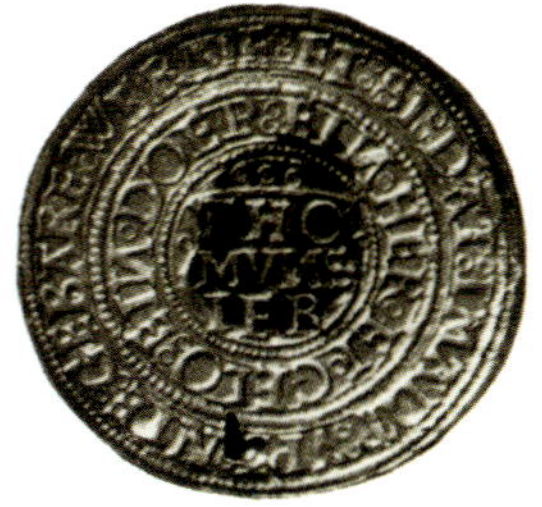
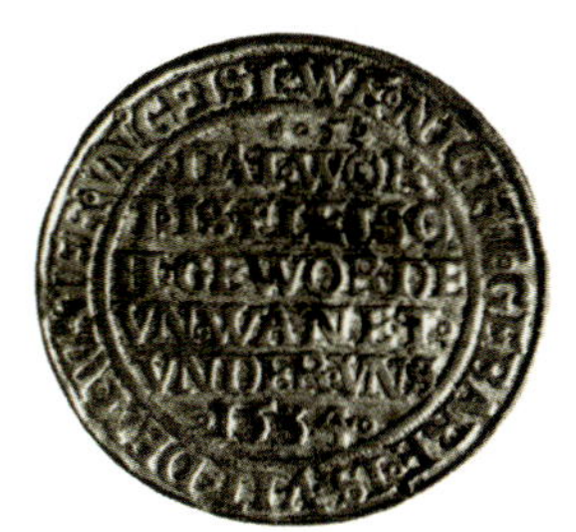
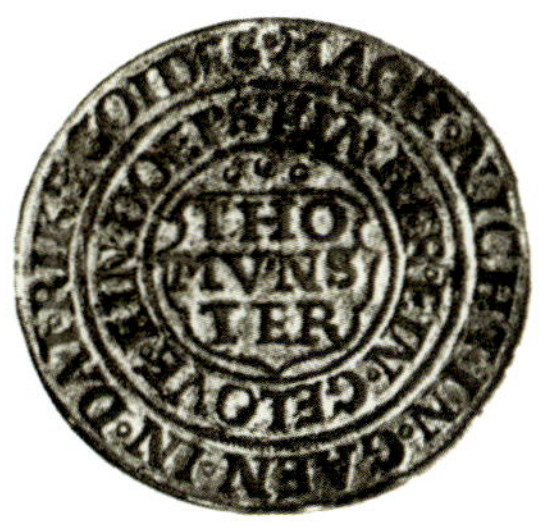

5a. *Coins of the Münsterites:*
Taler and half Taler (1534) - FML

WITMARSUM LEEUWARDEN

5 ♦ 1534

Next in order the sect of Münster made its appearance, by whom many pious hearts in our quarter were deceived ... my admonition did not help, because I myself still did that which I knew was not right. (Menno)

On the 27th of February 1534 the expulsion of the 'godless' from Münster begins, whereby Anabaptist radicals defy the might of church and state. The authorities are thrown into a commotion as a result of which they issue severe placards in Friesland, Groningen, everywhere. But Münster has a strong power of attraction, for it seemed possible to overthrow centuries-old vested authority structures. Hundreds of people set off for the New Kingdom. All of Holland and Friesland remain turbulent, despite all of the ordinances against unruly Anabaptists. Menno is divided, for in his heart he knows the appeal of the singular, biblically-grounded Anabaptist teaching, but he abhors the use of blind force. He plays a double role. In the summer he attends a meeting of the Frisian religious in the Franciscan church at Leeuwarden. In that anti-heretical bulwark they plan how to help carry out the imperial placards. At the end of the year Menno secretly debates with certain itinerant Münsterite propagandists. He can silence them, it is said, but it is of no use.

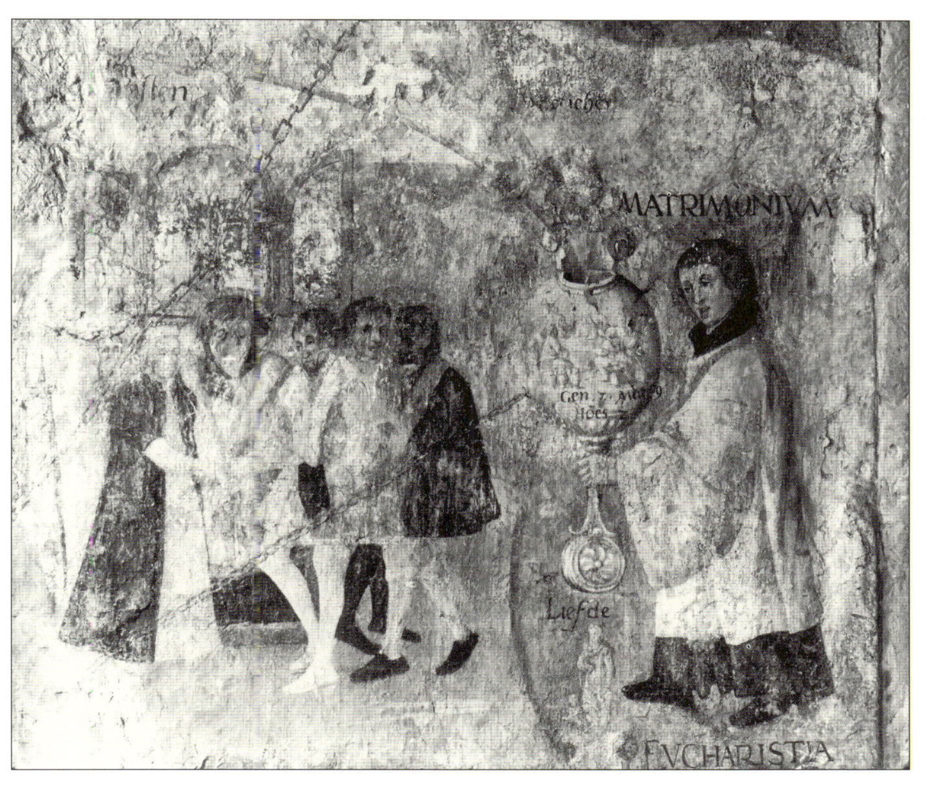

5d. *The Sacraments, wall painting from a Leeuwarden monastry* (ca. 1500) - FML

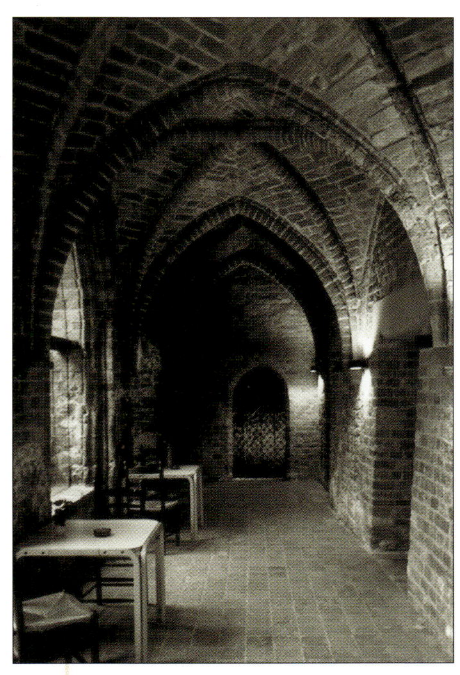

5b. *Vaulted cloister of the Jacobines' Church, Leeuwarden* - EVW

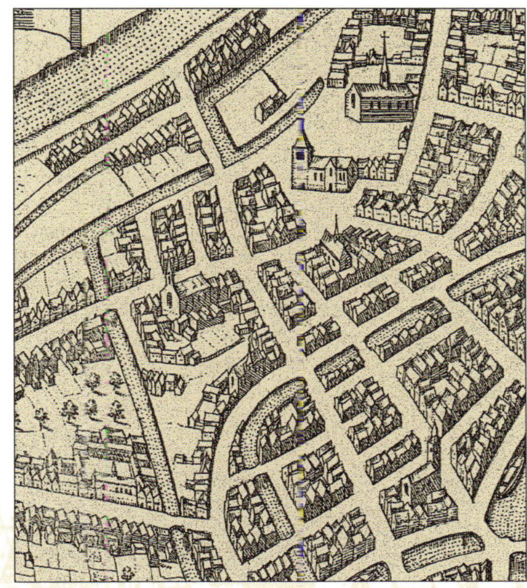

5e. B&H III, *Detail of Leeuwarden* (1580) - UBA

5c. B&H I, *Münster* (1572) - UBA

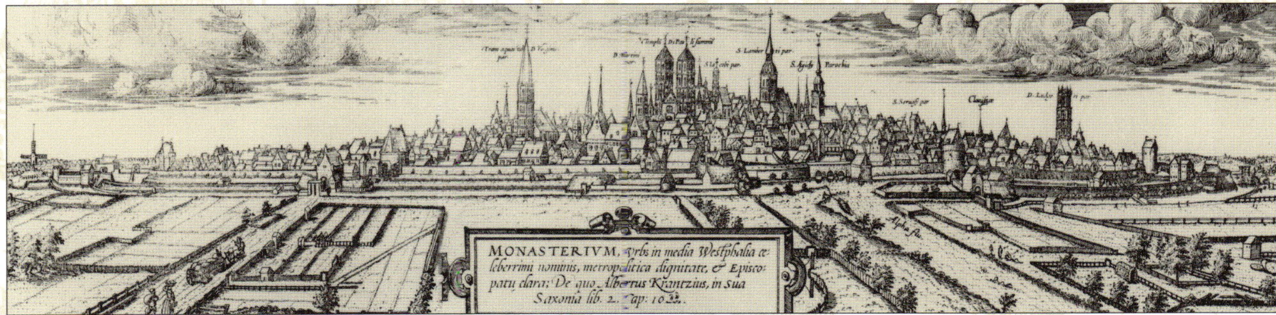

6a. *Behind the trees stood once the Oldeklooster (Old Cloister) / nameplate of Old Cloister road* - EVW

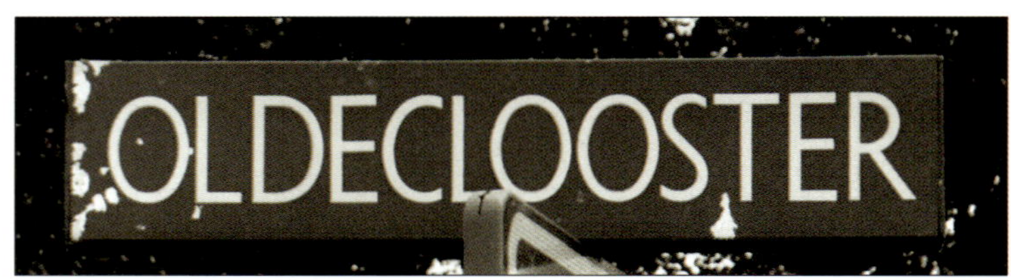

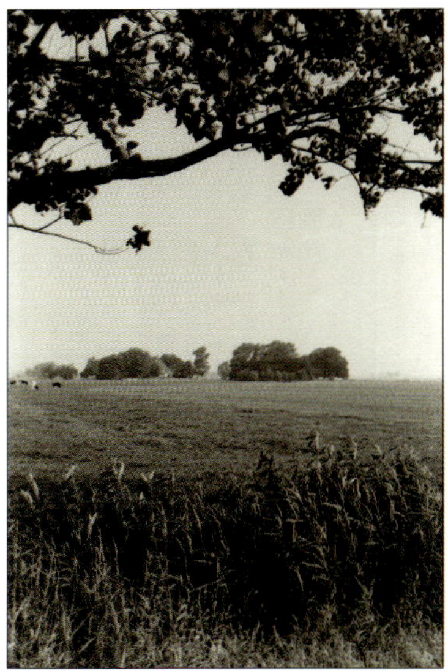

WITMARSUM OLDEKLOOSTER

6 ♦ March - April 1535

Afterwards the poor straying sheep who wandered as sheep without a proper shepherd, after many cruel edicts, garrotings, and slaughters, assembled at a place near my place of residence called Oude klooster. And, alas! through the ungodly doctrines of Münster ... they drew the sword to defend themselves. (Menno)

Menno, dissembling with Rome and his conscience, is powerless. He knows that just before Easter some parishioners are gathering with hundreds of other Anabaptists near Franeker under the leadership of the Münsterite emissary Jan van Geelen. From there they march to the Old Cloister near Bolsward. At the end of March they occupy it by a ruse. Among them is his own brother Peter, who had worked his way up in the Münsterite kingdom of king Jan van Leyden to stewart of queen Divara. For scarcely a week the Anabaptists fancy themselves as ruling the world around Bolsward, but then they are cruelly roused out of their dream. With a show of military might Stadtholder Schenck van Toutenburg by imperial command, evacuates the Frisian mini-Münster. Many victims fall; Menno's brother perishes. Some manage to escape, such as Jan van Geelen. Others are captured and are almost immediately executed in Leeuwarden. Menno is appalled over both so much blind faith and such a measureless show of force.

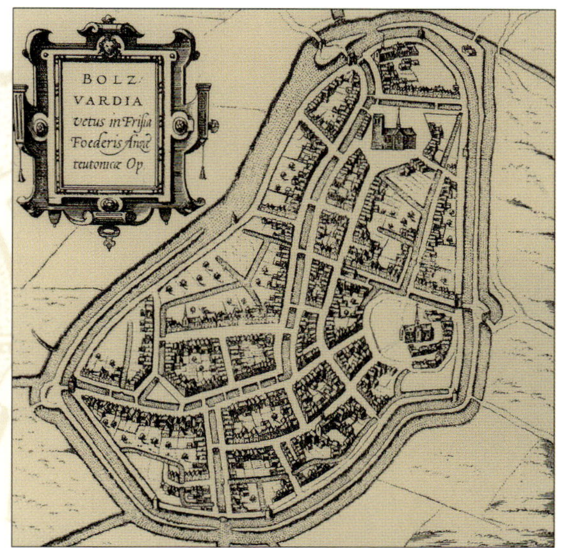

6b. B&H IV, *Bolsward* (1580) - UBA

6d. *Facade of the Broere Church, a former monastic church at Bolsward* - EVW

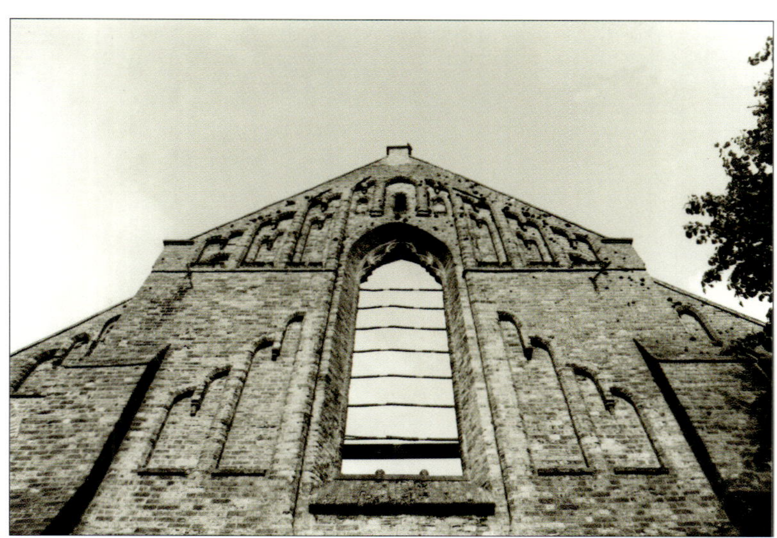

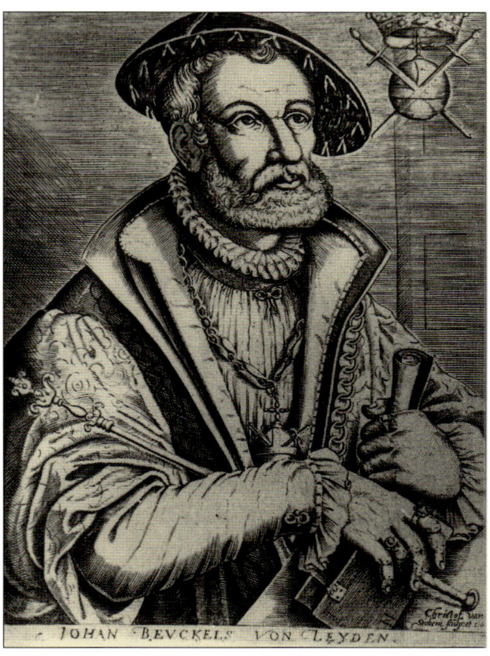

6e. C. van Sichem I,
Jan van Leyden (1607) - UBA-DG

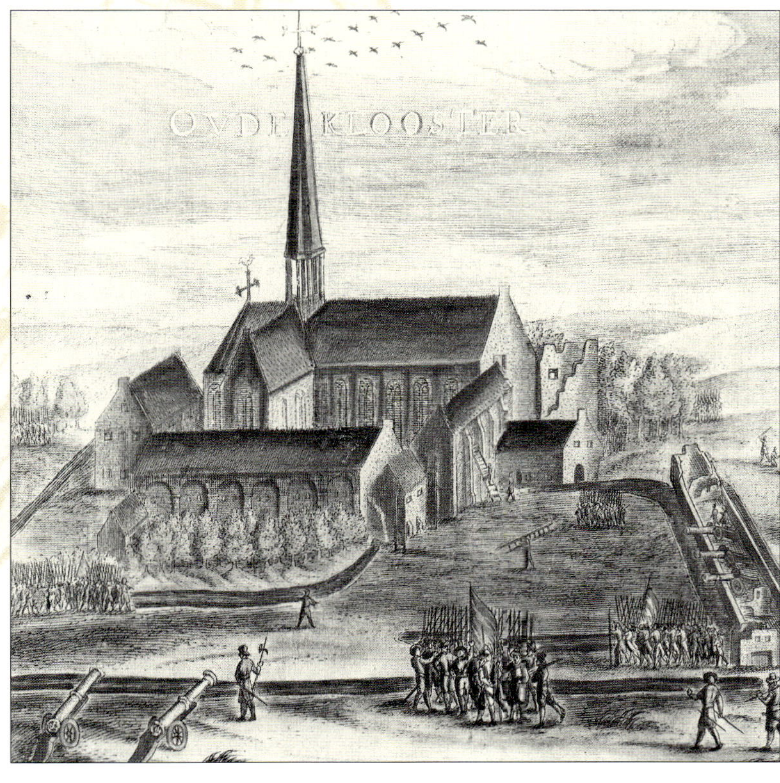

6c. *Relief of Oldeklooster, Bolsward*,
in: Hortensius - UBA-DG

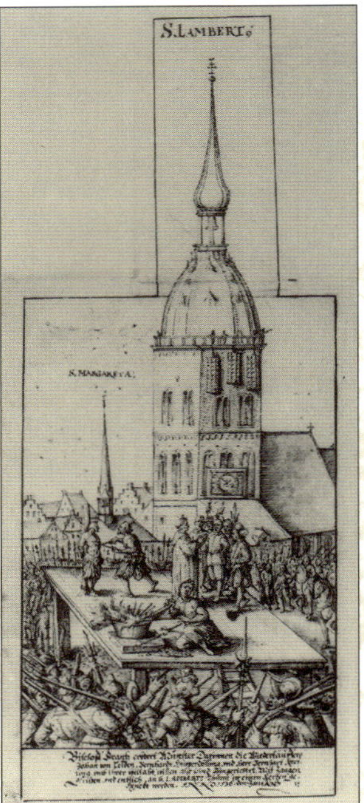

7a. *Execution of the Anabaptist leaders at Münster* (1536) - UBA-DG

WITMARSUM
AMSTERDAM

7 ♦ May - June 1535

Everybody defended himself by a reference to me, no matter who. I saw plainly that I was the stay and defense of the impenitent who all leaned on me. ... And I was one of those who had disclosed to some of them the abominations of the papal system. But I myself continued in my comfortable life and acknowledged abominations. (Menno)

The Münsterite monster still continues to rage unwearyingly. Jan van Geelen knew many people whom he could mobilize in the Anabaptist bulwark of Amsterdam to seize power there as well. They run naked through the streets as new Adams and Eves to warn their neighbors of the end of time. During the night of May 10/11 they occupy the City Hall on the Dam Square, but this Münsterite grasp for power is easily nipped in the bud. Dozens of Anabaptists perish in the fight. In the days following, one after another are executed at the place of the calamity. Like dogs they are hung upside down and flung onto the wheel at the gallows field north of the IJ river. Every burgher, traveller or uninvited guest with sinister plans could learn their lesson here. Things proceed no differently at Münster, for on the 25th of June the city is retaken after more than a year. The degenerate rule of king Jan van Leyden and his many wives is pulverised. The leaders are gruesomely dispatched and, as an eternal example, their remains hoisted high up in iron cages – like heavenly thrones – on the spire of St. Lambert's church. The authorities show no more pity, for from now on the Anabaptist heresy must be destroyed. Life and goods of the rebaptized are declared forfeit by the imperial placard of the 10th of June 1535.

7c. *Naked runners of Amsterdam,* in: Hortensius - UBA-DG

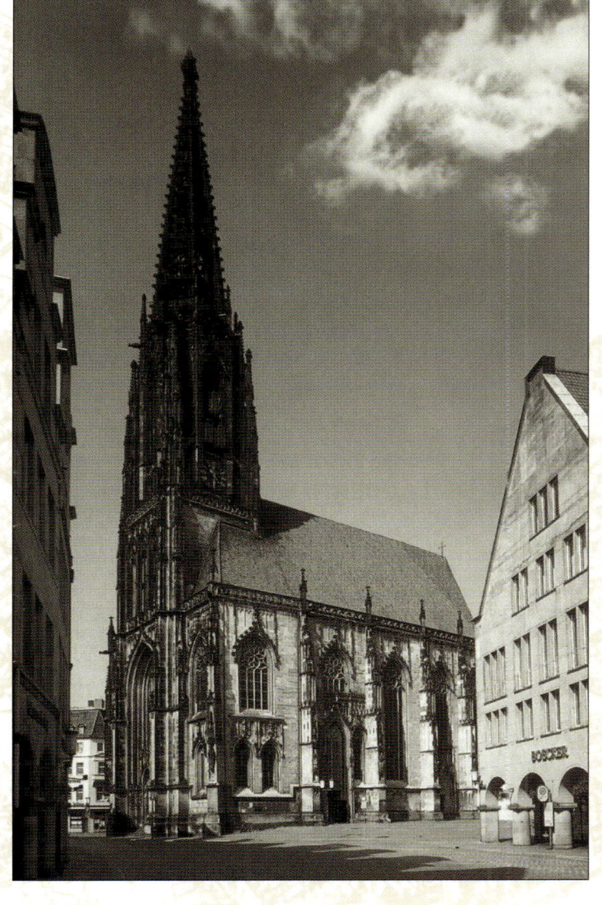

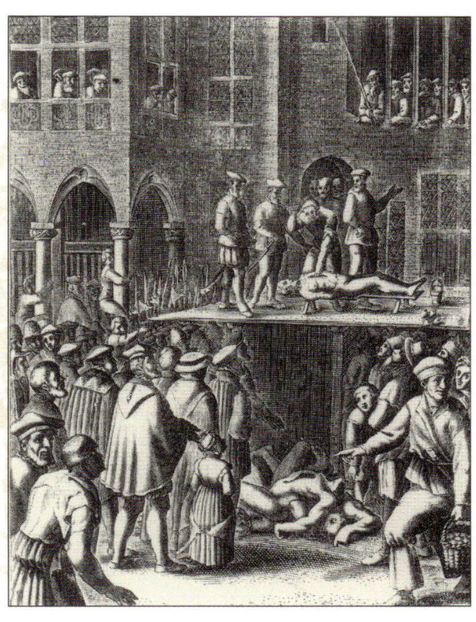

7d. *Execution of the occupiers of the Amsterdam City Hall,* in: Hortensius - UBA-DG

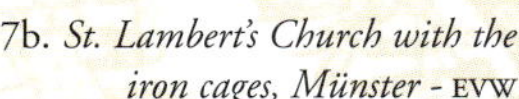

7b. *St. Lambert's Church with the iron cages, Münster* - EVW

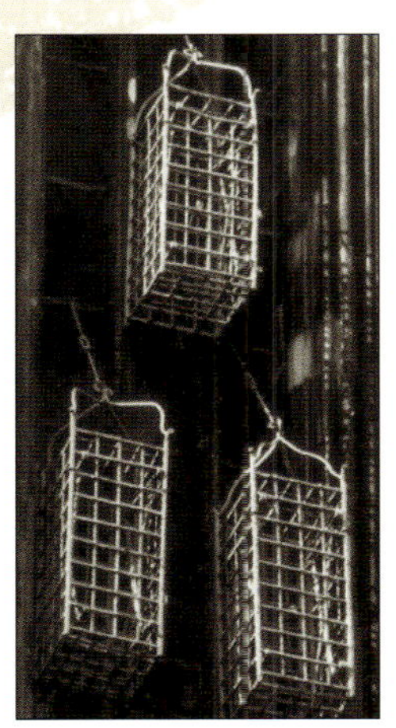

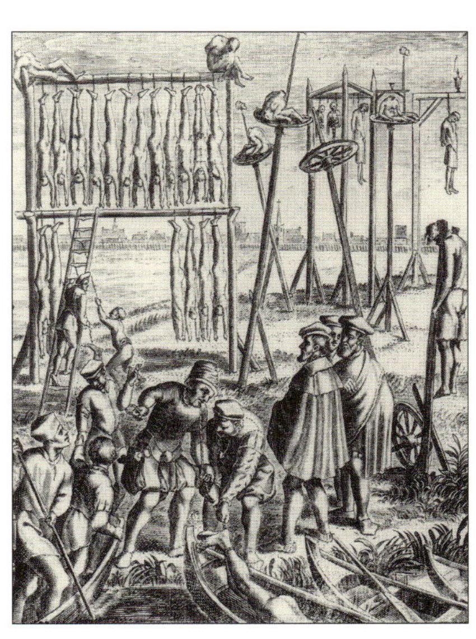

7e. *Hanging of the corpses at the place of execution Volewijk, Amsterdam,* in: Hortensius - UBA-DG

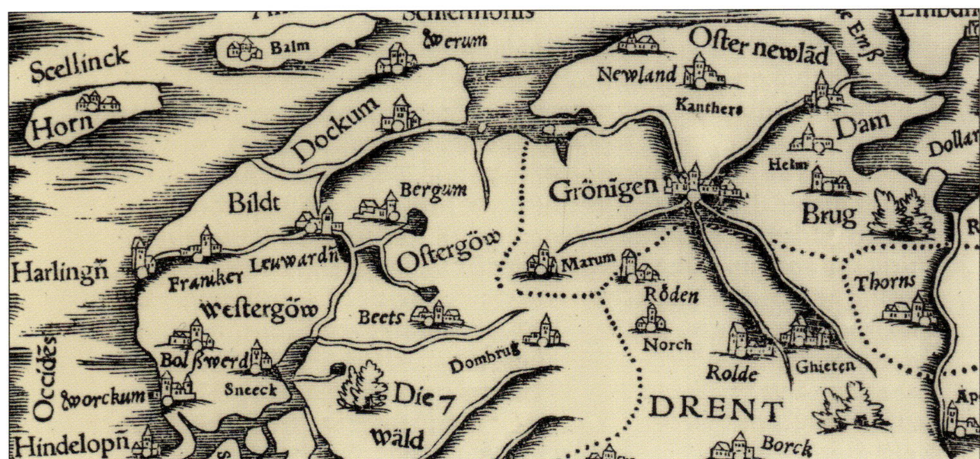

8a. Münster, *Friesland and Groningen* (1550) - UBA

WITMARSUM

8 ♦ January 1536

I also faithfully warned everyone against the abominations of Münster ... After about nine months or so, the gracious Lord granted me His fatherly Spirit, help, and hand. (Menno)

Meanwhile the frocked priest of Witmarsum mumbles rosaries in a state of deepest distress. The forty-year old Menno is in a crisis. For twelve years he has served the false God, the whore of Babel. However, as far as his employer is concerned, he still appears to be a faithful Saul. His good name and fame, his fine and comfortable life dissemble under a false habit. All the time he really knows better and airs his growing doubts. He preaches publicly from the gospel and calls for true repentence; he explains to his flock the meaning of baptism and the Lord's Supper. The tract which he composed against the Münsterite Anabaptist kingdom, however, can be returned to the drawer; for the sudden demise of king Jan has deprived the first fruit of his pen of any topicality. Menno appears not to be able to choose between the muzzled servant and the courageous man. And the man in him also awakens, for have not his eyes fallen on a Beguine, Geertruyd? Finally, after a long conflict of conscience, the true Paul in him stands up in the New Year of 1536 and in January he departs from 'Popedom'. He says farewell to the rich Romish life, but as a result he must leave his Frisian fatherland, at least for the present.

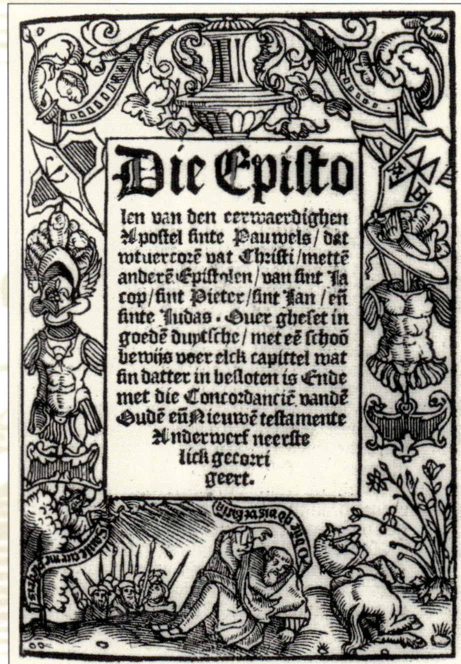
Die Episto
len van den eerwaerdighen
Apostel sinte Pauwels/ dat
wtuercorē vat Christi/ mettē
anderē Epistolen/ van sint Ja
cop/ sint Pieter/ sint Jan/ eñ
sinte Judas. Ouer ghesiet in
goedē duytsche/ met eē schoō
bewijs voer elck capittel wat
sin datter in besloten is Ende
met die Concordanciē vandē
Oudē eñ Nieuwē testamente
Anderwerf neerste
lick gecorri
geert.

8b. *Luther-testament: Letters of Paul* (1523) - UBA

8d. *Commermorative plaque of the Menno monument near Witmarsum* - EVW

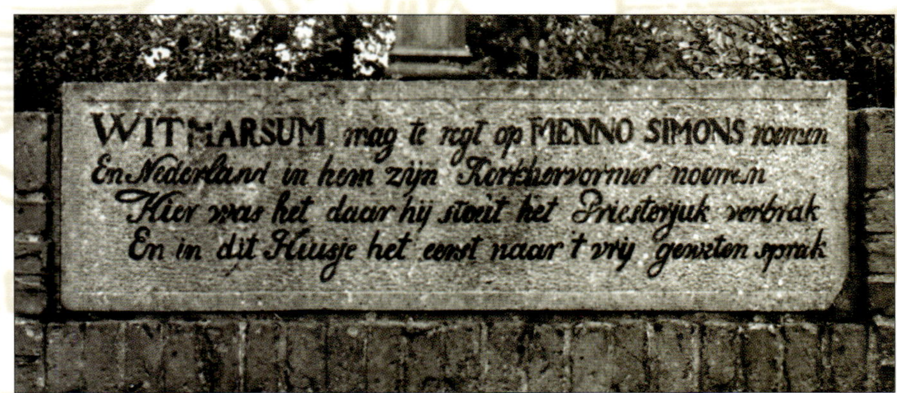

Een
Gantz duidelijck ende klaer bewijs/ uyt die H. Schrifture/ dat Jesus Christus/ is de rechte belovede David inden geest/ een Koninck aller Koningen een Heer aller Heerē/ ende de rechte geestelijcke Koninck over dat geestelicke Israhel/ dat is zijn gemeynte/ die hy mit syn eyghen bloedt ghecoft: ende verworven heft.

Eertijts geschreven aen allen waren Broeders ende Bondtgenoten/ hier ende daer verstroeyt.

Door

Menno Symons.

Tegens

De grouwelijcke ende grootste blasphemie van Jan van Leyden/

Die hem uytgaff voor een blyde Coninck over al/ ende der elender vroude geworden, hem settende in de stede Gods.

Nopt voor desen Ghedruckt/

1. Corinth. 3. 13.

Daer en mach gheen ander fondament ghelecht worden / dan datter gelecht is / 't welck is Christus Jesus.

8e. Menno, *Tract against Jan van Leyden, ca. 1535* (1627) - UBA-DG

8c. *A farewell to the herd of Witmarsum* - EVW

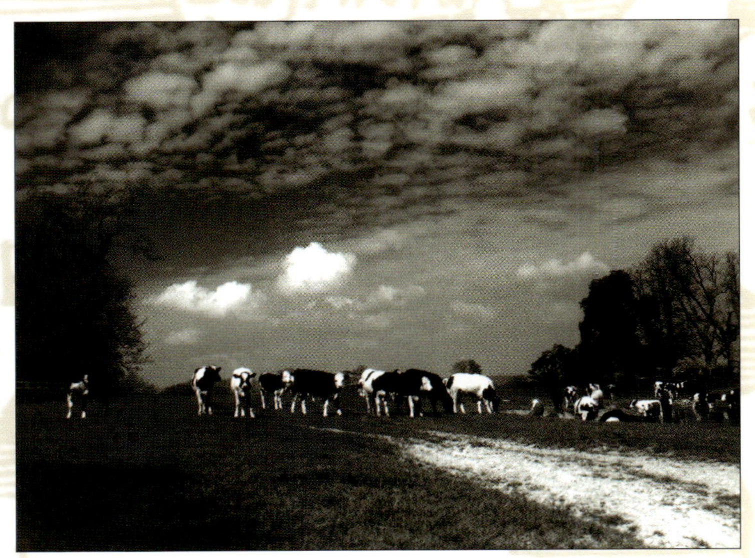

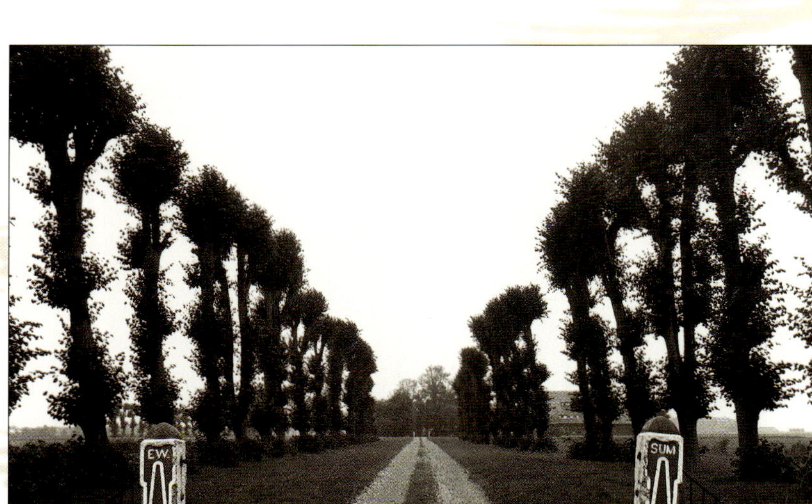

9a. *Entrance to the site where the former Euwsum castle was built in 1472, Oosterburen* - EVW

GRONINGEN

9 ♦ 1536

I willingly submitted to distress and poverty under the heavy cross of Christ ... I was secretly exercising myself in the Word of God by reading and writing.

(Menno)

Menno flees in the direction of East Frisia, which lies outside of Emperor Charles' sphere of influence. He probably hides first in the Groningen countryside, at some address of the lord of Euwsum. This district still buzzes with Anabaptist heresies. In the spring of 1535 the Münsterite prophet Herman Schoenmaker had led a turbulent gathering near 't Zand and had baptized a minimum of 300 people. Menno must have made the necessary contacts with peaceful Anabaptists already in Witmarsum, such as the Leeuwarden brothers Obbe and Dirk Philips who take an interest in him and help him here. For the present he dedicates himself to his studies, although he does undertake certain secret missions. For example, in the autumn of 1536, together with Dirk Philips, he converts the priest of Eppenhuizen and conducts disputations assisted by another ex-priest, Hugo Claes. That same year Menno is also mentioned in Witmarsum when two inhabitants are accused of having provided shelter for 'Mr. Mynno Simonsson former priest at Witmarsum'. Did Menno during this sojourn marry Geertruyd?

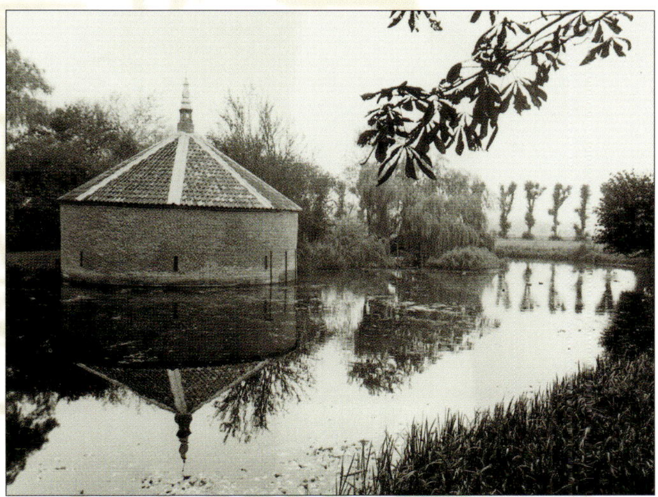

9b. *Gun turret of the former Euwsum castle, Oosterburen* - EVW

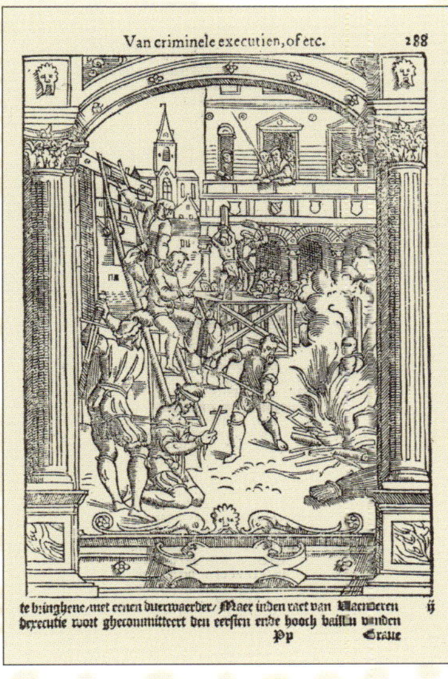

9c. *Various methods of execution* (1555), in: Damhoudere - UBA

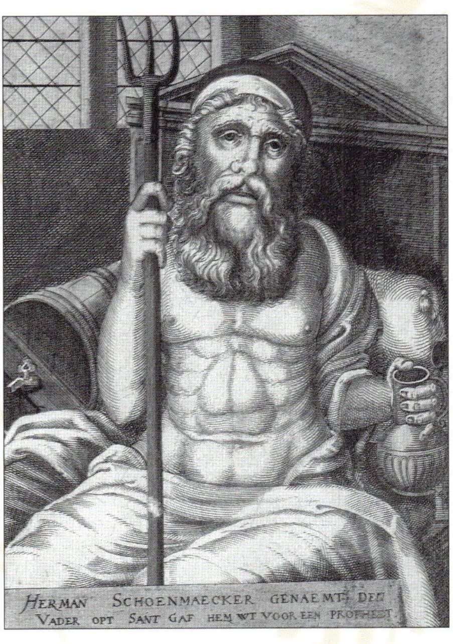

9d. C. van Sichem I, *Herman Schoenmaker* (1607) - UBA-DG

9e. J. de Pundere, *Viglius van Aytta, Frisian nobleman, member of the Secret Council and persecutor of the Anabaptists* (1564) - FML

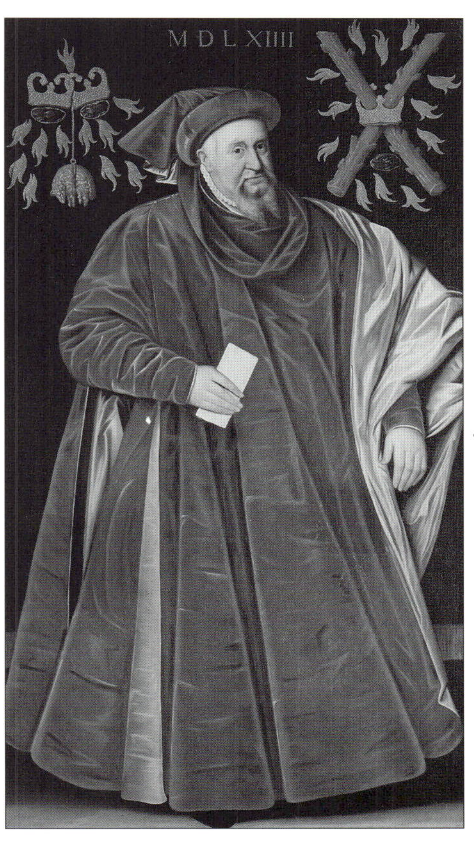

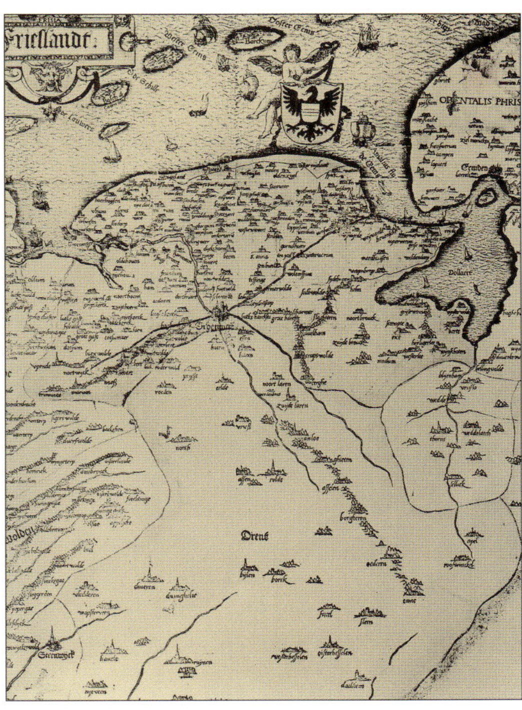

9f. Deventer, *Groningen* (1558) - UBA

10a. David Joris,
Beginning of a handwritten tract
(16th. century) - UBA-DG

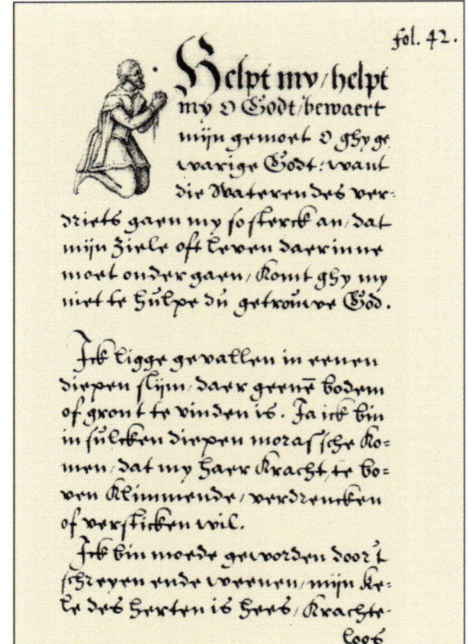

GRONINGEN
OLDERSUM
KIMSWERD

10 ♦ 1537 - 1539

It happened about one year after this ... that some six, seven, or eight persons came to me ... and ... prayerfully requested me to make the great sufferings and need of the poor oppressed souls my concern.. (Menno)

At the beginning of 1537 Menno is requested to take over leadership of the peaceful persuasion of the Anabaptists. In Groningen city he is ordained an elder by Obbe Philips. Menno is astonished that others perceive leadership qualities in him. But could he not always make friends as a priest? He is considered authoritative and is not burdened with the Münsterite stain in defending Anabaptist teaching to outsiders. It appears certain that during the spring Menno chooses the East Frisian Oldersum as a fixed dwelling place. There he enjoys the protection of nobleman Hero of Oldersum and Gödens. In his new capacity as leader Menno writes his first tract, *Een claer onderwysinghe ... van die gheestelicke verrysenisse* (*A clear Teaching ... concerning Spiritual Resurrection*). It is not published until much later. Dirk Philips becomes his friend and fellow worker. His leadership, however, is not widely recognized and even less is said of Anabaptist unity. The Münsterite ghost still haunts in the person of Jan van Batenburg, whose followers travel about plundering and robbing in the name of the Lord and heaven throughout East Frisia and the eastern Netherlands. From the outset David Joris also belongs to the peaceful camp, but this eloquent glasspainter from Delft receives visions and constitutes himself as a prophetic leader, the third David. To the annoyance of Menno, he turns away from the external church, its worship and sacraments. Many come to hate the David Jorists, abundantly represented in East Frisia, because of their 'dissembling with the world'. Menno undertakes various journies. In 1538 he lodges in Friesland at Kimswerd with Tjaard Renicx, whose hospitality, however, is repaid with death by the authorities in January 1539. That year Menno baptizes, possibly in the house of his brother Tijde at Pingjum, Quirijn Pietersz van Kruiningen.

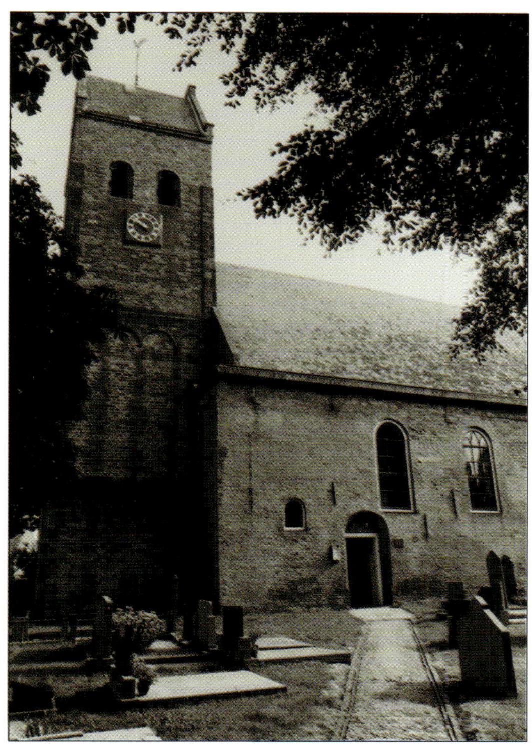

10b. *St. Laurence Church at Kimswerd* - EVW

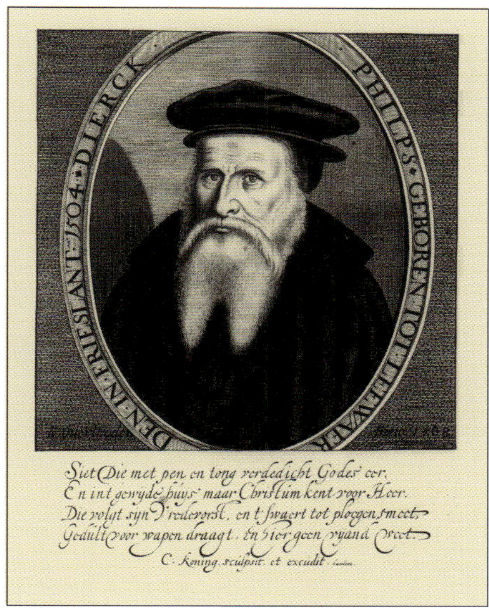

10d. C. Koning, *Dirk Philips* (ca. 1630) - UBA-DG

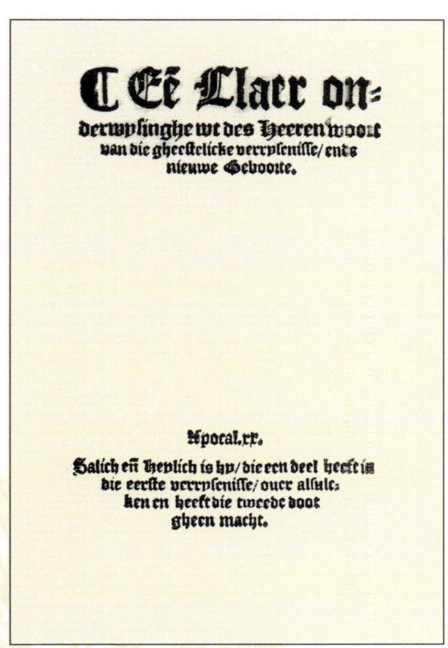

C Eē Claer on-
derwysinghe wt des Heeren woort
van die gheestelicke verrysenisse/ ent's
nieuwe Gheboorte.

Apocal.xx.

Salich eñ heylich is hy/ die een deel heeft in
die eerste verrysenisse/ over alsulc-
ken en heeft die tweede doot
gheen macht.

10c. Menno, *A clear Teaching, 1539* (1554-55) - UBA-DG

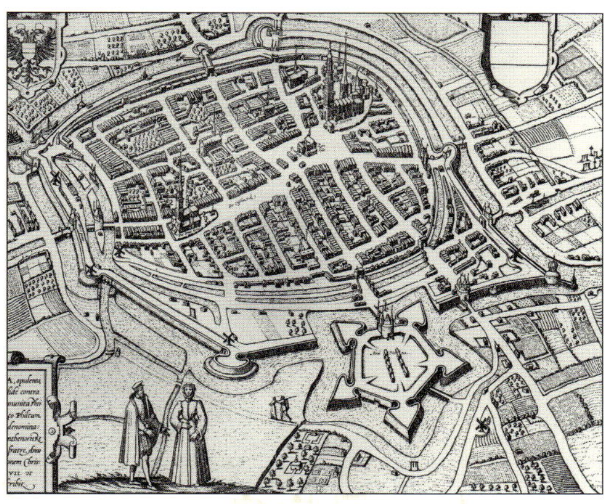

10e. B&H I en II, *City of Groningen* (ca. 1580) - UBA

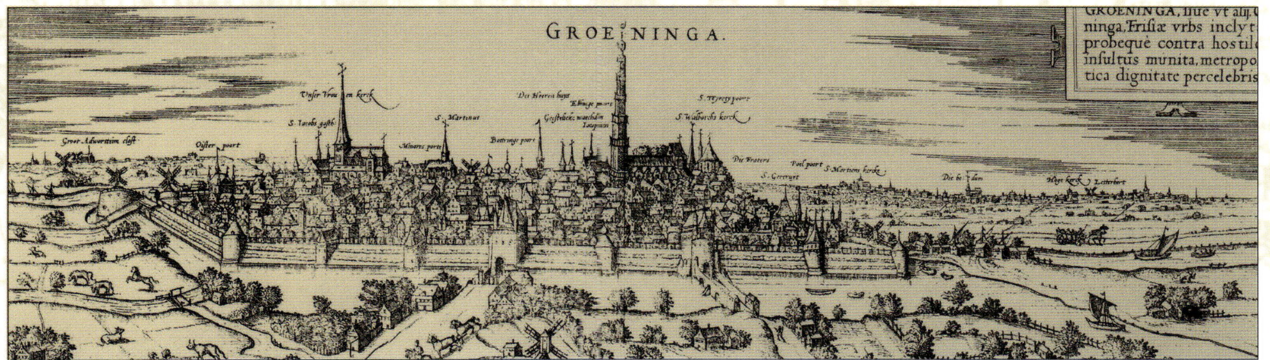

11a. *Coat of arms of Oldersum* - EVW

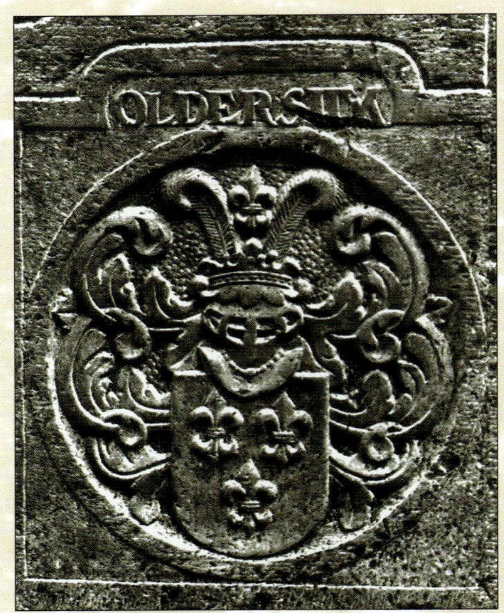

OLDERSUM

11 ♦ 1539 - 1541

A Mr. Minne Simonsson [is] ... one of the most principal of the aforementioned sect ... in order to capture and apprehend this one we have made diverse attempts and promised much money. (Court of Friesland)

In 1539 and 1540 some of Menno's writings are disseminated for the first time in print: the *Verclaringhe des chrystelycken doopsels* (*Explanation of Christian Baptism*) and *Die oorsake waerom dat ick M.S. niet af en late te leeren, ende te schrijven* (*The Reason Why I Do Not Cease Teaching and Writing*). They are printed in the greatest secrecy at Antwerp by Matthias Crom. Furthermore, from an anonymous printer in the eastern Netherlands appears the *Leringhen op den 25. Psalm* (*Meditation on the Twenty-Fifth Psalm*), *Van die weder-geboorte* (*The New Birth*) and his most important writing, *Dat fundament des christelycken leers* (*The Foundation of Christian Doctrine*). Therein he endeavors to convince the authorities that the Anabaptist teaching is purely evangelical and has nothing in common with Münsterite violence. In the meantime the movement suffers a great loss. In 1540 a frustrated Obbe Philips, outstripped as a leader by Menno, turns away from the movement and goes over to the spiritualists. This forces Menno to reformulate his vision of the visible church and congregational discipline. How can the church be a fellowship without spot or wrinkle? How might it purify itself of the radical and more mystical elements? He writes *Van dat rechte christen gheloove* (*The True Christian Faith*), which will be printed ca. 1542/43 in Antwerp, and his first book on the ban, Een lieffelijcke vermaninghe van *dat schouwen der valscher broederen* (*A Kind Admonition on Shunning False Brethren*). He gets mixed up in the abduction of the wife of priest Feddo Hommes, over which the increasingly contested disciplinary measures of marital separation will soon cast a dark shadow.

Dat funda-
ment des Christelyke leers
doer [illegible] op dat al-
der corste gescreuen.
Menno Simons
Ten eersten
Van den tydt der genaden.
Ten anderen
Van ware penitentie.
Ten derden
Van den geloue.
Ten veerden
Van den doepe.
Ten vyften
Van den Auentmael.
Ten sesten
Van den midinghe Babels.
Ten seuensten
Een langhe besluyt reden.
Daer mach gheen ander fundament ge-
lecht worden behaluen datter gelecht is
het welcke is Jesus Christus. 1.Cor.3.
Menno

11b. Menno,
Foundation Book.
An opponent has replaced
Menno's name for that of
brother Dirck (?) - UBA-DG

Voele goede
und Chrystelycke leringhen
op den 25. Psalm doer Menno Simons in een maniere van bid-
den gescreuen.

Fundamentum aliud nemo potest
ponere preter id quod positum
est quod est Jesus Christus.
1.Corinth.3.

Anno M. D.
XXXIX.

11d. Menno,
Meditation on
the Twenty-Fifth Psalm
(1539) - UBA-DG

1. Corinth. 3.
Daer en mach gheen ander Funda-
ment ghelept worden / behaluen datter ghelept
is/ het welcke is Christus Jesus.

Dat Funda-
ment des Christelycken leers
Door Menno Simons op dat al-
der corste gescreuen.

Anno. M. D.
XXXIX.

Dat funda-
ment des Christelyke leers
doer Menno Simons op dat al-
der corste gescreuen.
Ten eersten
Van den tydt der genaden.
Ten anderen
Van ware penitentie.
Ten derden
Van den geloue.
Ten veerden
Van den doepe.
Ten vyften
Van den Auentmael.
Ten sesten
Van den midinghe Babels.
Ten seuensten
Een langhe besluyt reden.
Daer mach gheen ander fundament ge-
lecht worden behaluen datter gelecht is
het welcke is Jesus Christus. 1.Cor.3.
Menno

Menno Si-
mons die wunschet dē geordi-
neerde Oeuericheit sampt allen menschen\ si syn van wat na-
men\ staten unde ampten dat si
syn\ verlichtinghe ware ken-
tenisse unde dat ewighe leuen
van God dē Vader ende unsen
lieuen here Jesu Christo\ den
welcken ons gelieuet heeft\ unde heeft ons gewosschen van
unsen sonden mit sinen bloede\
hem si loff\ eer unde prys\ van
ewicheit tot ewicheit Amen.
A ij Dit

11c. Menno, *Foundation Book, with the table of contents*
(1539/1540) - UBA-DG

Een Lieffelijcke
Vermaninge ofte Onderwij-
singe wt Gods Woort/ Door Men.
Sy. Hoe dat een Christen sal geschickt zijn/ende van
dat schouwen ofte affsijden der valscher Broederen ende Susteren/ ofte die met Ketterschen
Leeringhen verleydt zijn/ ofte die een
Wlepschelick schandighe Leuen
voeren.

1. Corinth. 3.
Daer en mach gheen ander Funda-
ment ghelept worden / behaluen datter ghelept
is/ het welcke is Christus Jesus.

Ecclesiasti. 1.
Die Liefde Gods is eerlicke VVijsheyt.

Int laer onses Heeren duysent vijf-
hondert ende. XLI.

11e. Menno, *The first book on the ban:*
A Kind Admonition, 1541
(ca. 1575) - UBA-DG

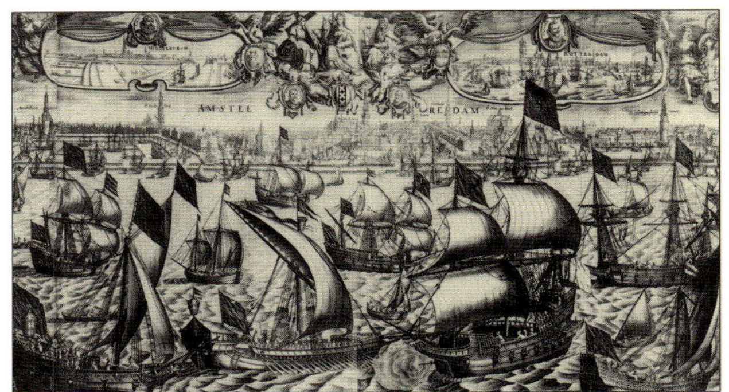

12a. A. de Koninck (exc.), *Harbour of Amsterdam* (1623) - UBA-DG

AMSTERDAM ZAAN REGION LEEUWARDEN

12 ♦ 1542

Syouck Haeyes ... has publicly confessed, that he recently ... had been outside of this city of Leeuwarden in a field near the Zwette and there with a Mr. Minne Simonsson ... contaminated with diverse heresies and on account of which a fugitive from this land, has spoken, communicated and listened to his preaching.

(Criminal Sentences, Leeuwarden)

In addition to David Jorists and Batenburgers, the authorities conduct a fierce hunt for Mennonites. In 1542 the death sentence is ordered for the publication, dissemination and reading of Menno's writings. On top of this a price of 100 Carolus guilders is promised to anyone who hands over Menno as 'the principal' Anabaptist. For friend and enemy Menno is now the only, but not undisputed, leader. Hundreds of men and women offer up their lives as martyrs of the Mennonite cause. In spite of the considerable danger Menno preaches in Amsterdam and the Zaan region. On 14 November Syouck Hayes is forbidden to leave Leeuwarden for six years and ordered to pay a fine of 50 guilders, for the simple reason that he had heard Menno preach outside of the city and had chatted with him. Again and again Menno is able to escape his persecutors and betrayers. Above all, wherever he preaches and baptizes, he endeavors to improve the organization of church life by installing local leaders or bishops. Thus Adam Pastor and Hendrik van Vreeden are named elders for Westphalia, Anthonius van Keulen and Gillis van Aken for the Rhineland and Frans Reines Kuiper for Friesland.

12d. *The Zwette river, east of Leeuwarden* - EVW

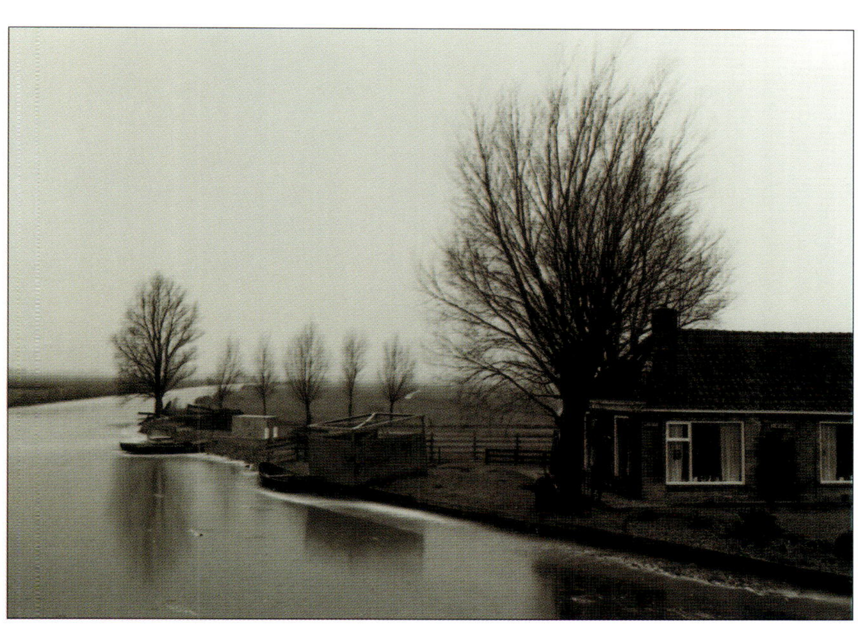

12b. C. van Sichem I, *Adam Pastor* (1607) - UBA-DG

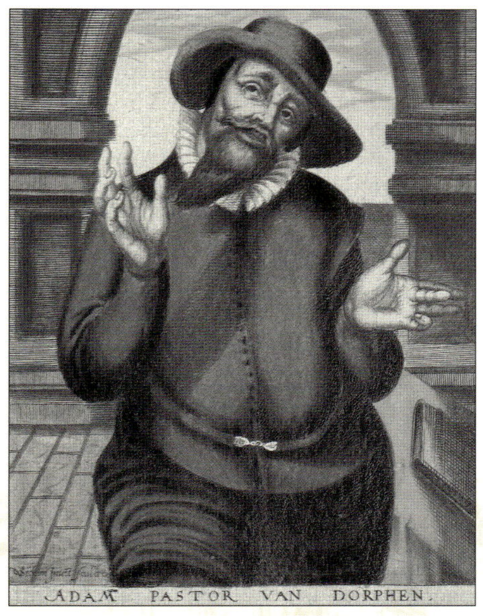

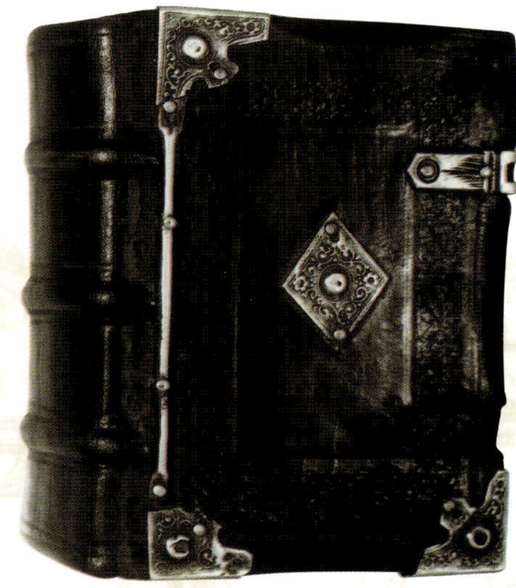

12e. *16th-century Anabaptist book binding* - UBA-DG

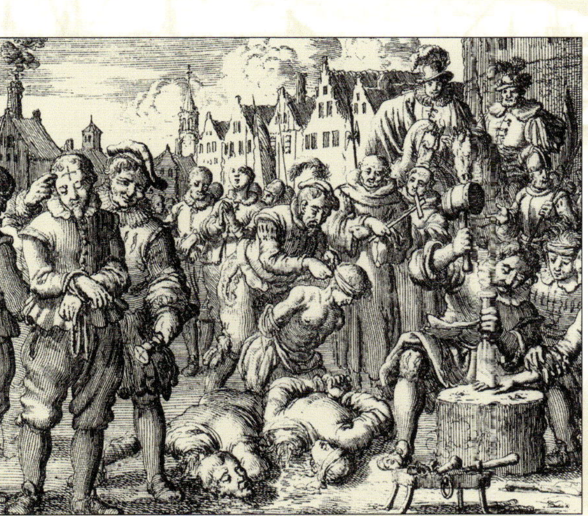

12c. J. Luyken, *Anabaptist Martyrs* in: Braght - UBA-DG

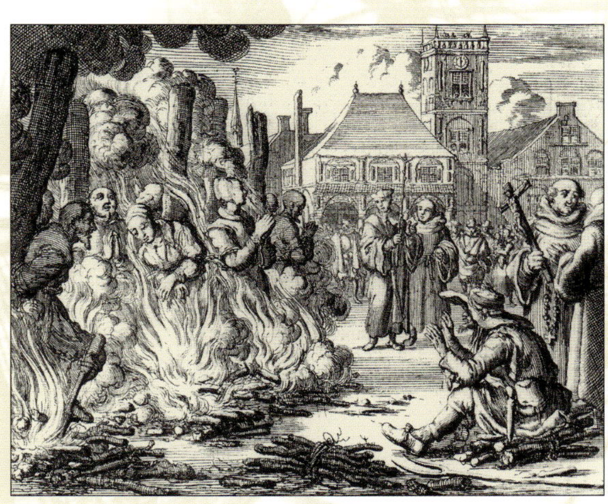

12f. J. Luyken, *Female Anabaptist Martyrs* in: Braght - UBA-DG

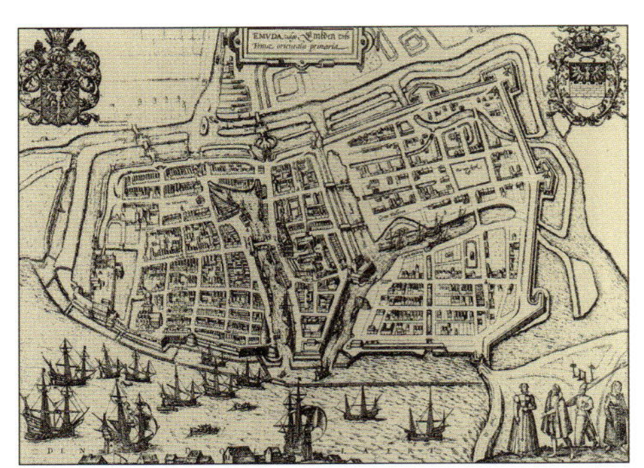

13a. B&H II, *Emden* (ca. 1580) - UBA

EMDEN
OLDERSUM

13 ♦ 1543 - 1544

So that to this hour I could not find in all the country ... a cabin or hut ... in which my poor wife and our little children could put up in safety for a year or two. (Menno)

Countess Anna van Oldenburg, who was well-disposed to the heretics, is forced by governess Mary of Hungary to take harsher action against them. It seems that the relative peace in East Frisia has ended for Menno and Geertruyd. They have children; probably a son named Jan, and two daughters, of whom only one will survive Menno and later live in Hoorn. Moreover, in the doctrinal realm Menno has even more to endure. David Joris challenges him to a written defence of his teaching. In his *Fundament*-book, Menno primarily has Joris in mind when he opposes the 'damned sects'. In his response, Menno predicts the same lot for Joris as had befallen Jan van Leyden. Many do not thank him for this, for in East Frisia there is much sympathy for David and his following there is large. Menno's leadership is put to a further test when the Polish Johannes A Lasco, superintendent of the fugitive Protestant church in Emden, announces at the end of 1544 his desire to enter into a debate with Menno. The confrontation is to be held the following year from January 28 to 31 inclusive, in the church of the Franciscan cloister at Emden. On the agenda are: the doctrines of original sin, salvation, and baptism, as well as the calling of ministers and the doctrine of the incarnation of Christ. The last three topics remain major points of dispute, over which Menno is to provide a written clarification. Without his knowledge his opponents publish his rushed work – not his best writing. Not until seven years later will Menno publish his response, wherein he still complains about this discourteous proceeding.

13b. David Joris, *Allegorical print of the Bride of God, in the Wonderboeck* (ca. 1582) - UBA-DG

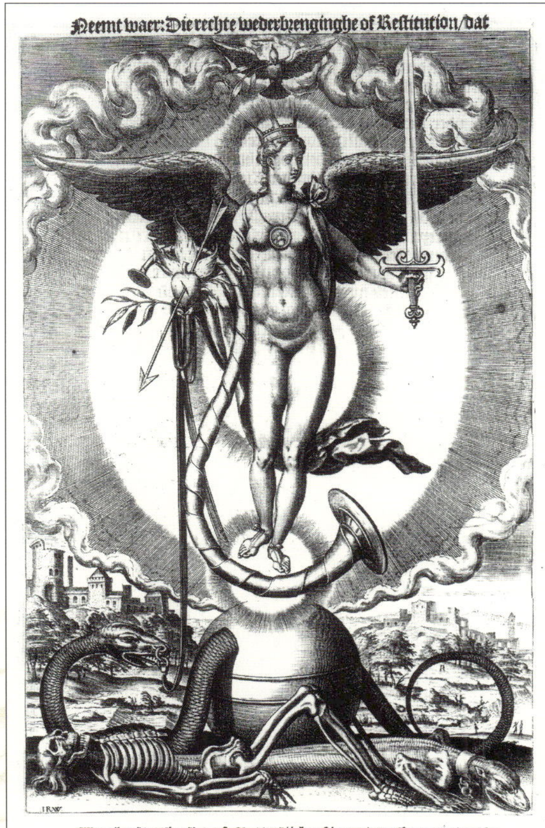

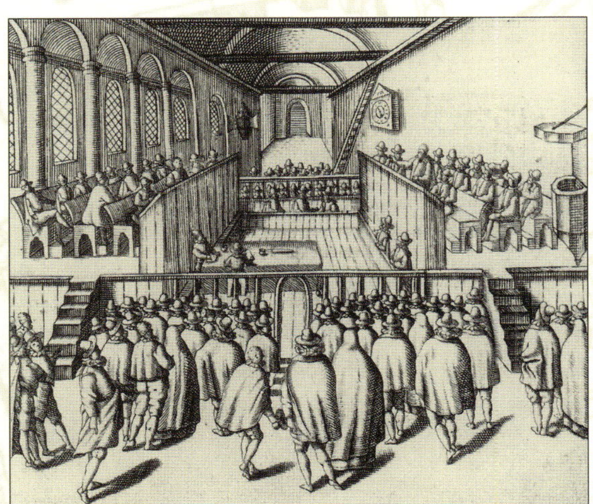

13c. *Religious dispute between Mennonites and Dutch Reformed* (1597) - UBA-DG

13d. *The Great Church at Emden which at present houses the Johannes A Lesco Library* - EVW

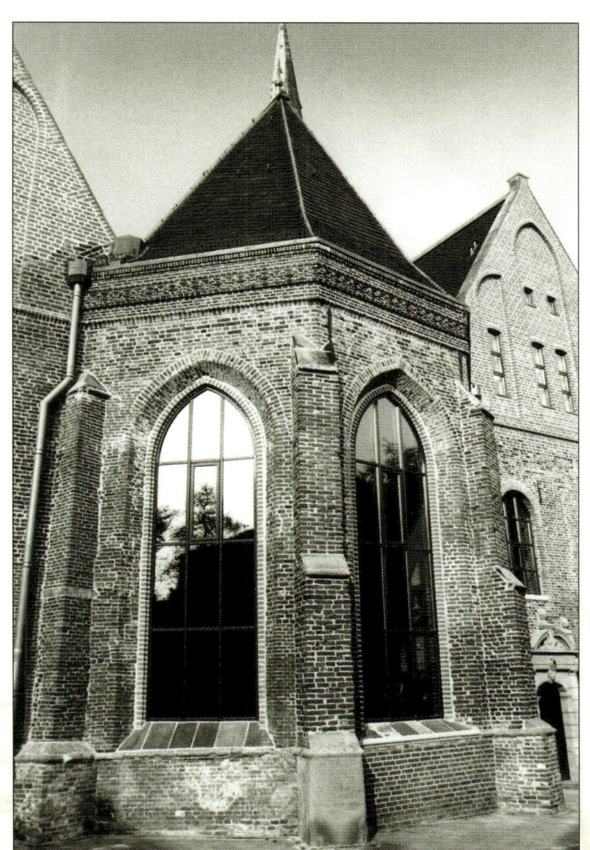

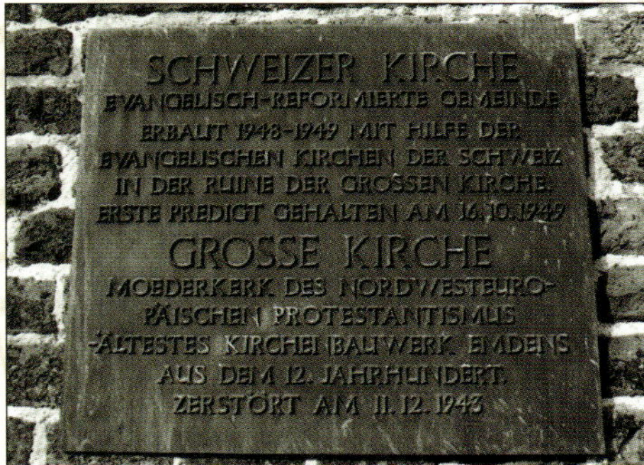

13e. *Commemorative Plaque, Great Church at Emden* - EVW

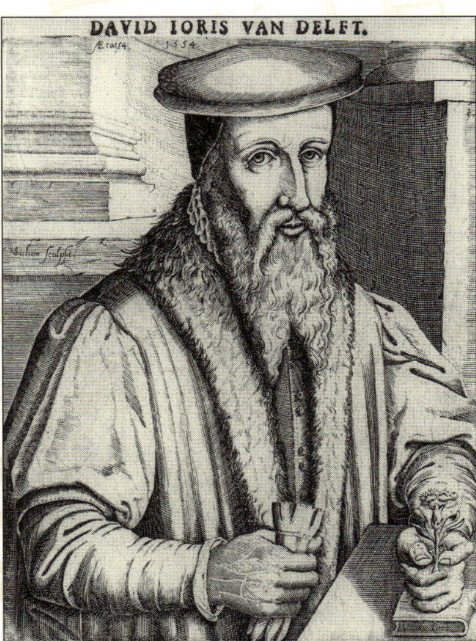

13f. C. van Sichem, *David Joris* (1607) - UBA-DG

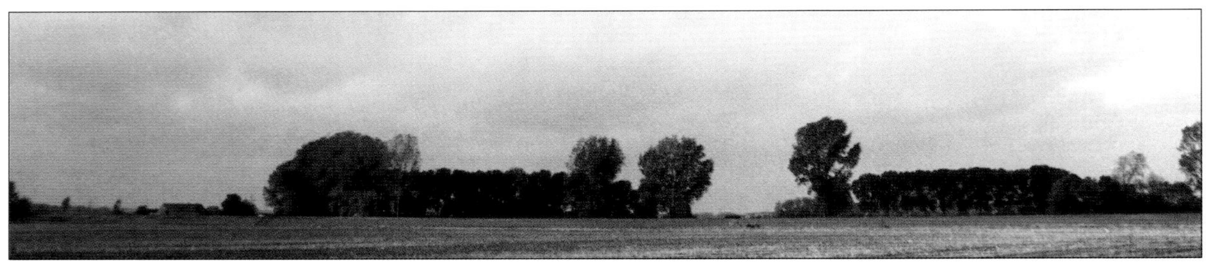

14a. *Pasture near Visschersweert* - EVW

BONN WESEL ROERMOND VISSCHERSWEERT

14 ♦ 1544 - 1545

When they are greeted as doctors, lords, and teachers by everyone, we have to hear that we are Anabaptists, bootleg preachers, deceivers, and heretics ... where they are gloriously rewarded for their services with large incomes and good times, our recompense and portion must be fire, sword, and death. (Menno)

On the 19th of January, Jan Claesz, a bookprinter, is beheaded on the Dam Square in Amsterdam. He was arrested because he had sold Menno's *Van dat rechte Christen gheloove* (*The True Christian Faith*), which had been secretly printed in Antwerp. From Brussels the regent issues a warning not to allow Menno to slip back into the Netherlands. The East Frisian asylum no longer provides solace. David Joris leaves for good to Basel, where he establishes himself as the gentleman Jan van Brugge. Accompanied by Dirk Philips Menno departs for the Rhineland, where the prince-bishop of Cologne is inclined to tolerate the reform-minded. Menno preaches and baptizes in places such as Bonn, Wesel and Roermond and consults with the local elders. In 1550 Jan Neulen from Visschersweert, captured at the Maas near Roermond, confesses that five years earlier Menno had preached at night in a pasture and thereafter disappeared. From him is the description of Menno's appearance: 'A stout, fat, heavy man, broken or rough of face and a brown beard, could not walk well'. Menno therefore now suffers the burden of lameness, the result of an accident along the way. As 1546 approaches the moderate Cologne prince-bishop must retire from the field, and Menno thus is forced to seek his safety elsewhere. The Low Countries remain too dangerous, for on top of the frequently renewed placards, since February 28, 1545 the inquisition is vigilent there.

14b. *The stairs leading to the Maas river at Visschersweert, where Menno would have boarded a ship* - EVW

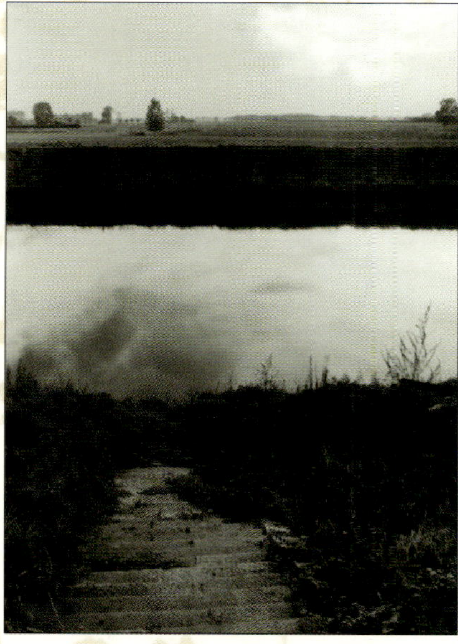

14e. J. A Lasco, *Polemical writing against Menno* (1545) - UBA-DG

DEFENSIO
VERAE SEMPERQVE
IN ECCLESIA RECEPTAE DO-
ctrinæ De Christi Domini incarnati-
one, Aduersus Mennonem Simonis
Anabaptistarum Doctorem, per
IOANNEM à LASCO Po-
loniæ Baronem, Ministrum
Ecclesiarum Phrisiæ
Orientalis.

HEBRAE. II.

Postea quam pueri cõmunionem habent carnis & sanguinis, et ipse similiter particeps factus est eorundem, ut per mortem aboleret eum qui mortis habebat imperium.

BONNAE
Ex officina Laurentii Mylii.
ANNO. M. D. XLV.

14c. B&H I, *Cologne* (ca. 1580) - UBA

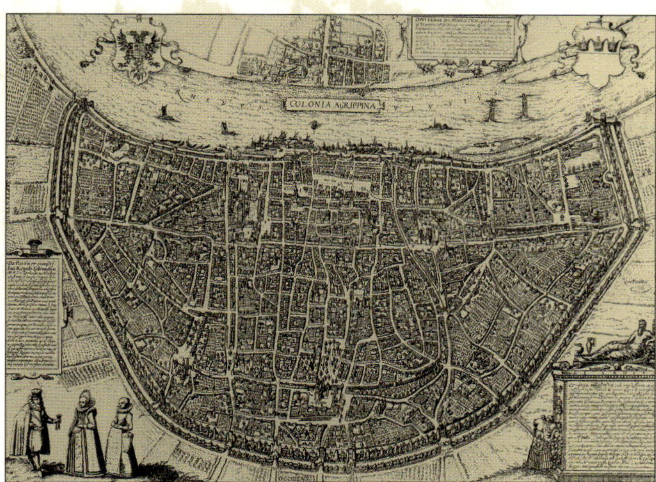

14d. Van Blesdijk: *Polemical Jorist writing against Gellius Faber* 1545 (1607) - UBA-DG

Weder-antwoort
Nicolaes Mey-
naertsz. van Bleesdijck op ze-
keren Brief by Gellium onderteec-
kent/ waer in hy syne meyninge unde oordeel
stelt op eenich Tractaet geintituleert Een
Christlijcke verantwoordinghe unde
billijcke wederlegginghe etc.
Geschreuen in't Jaer
1545.

Prouerb. Cap.13. vers.3.
Wie synen Mont bewaert, die bewaert sijn Ziele: Maer wie mit sijnen Mont onbehoorlijck
wtvaert, die sal verschricken.

Ghedruckt int Jaer 1607.

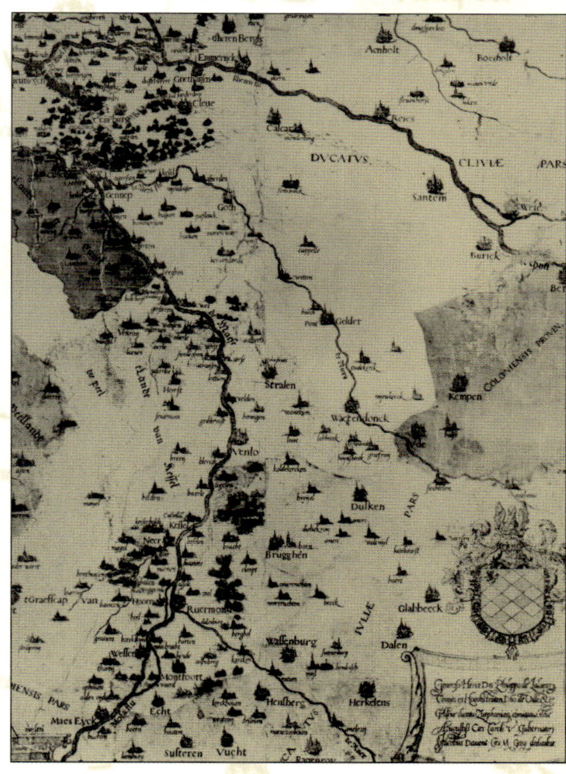

14f. Deventer, *Detail of the Maas and Rhine regions* (1558) - UBA

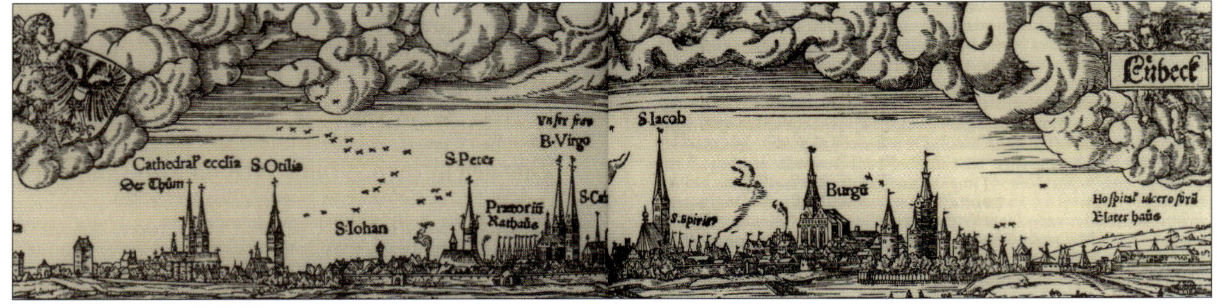

15a. Münster, *Lübeck (*1550) - UBA

LÜBECK EMDEN GOCH

15 ♦ 1546 - 1547

For during the last four years, alas, Christian love and peace have become pretty thin with some, on account of much pernicious arguing and bickering. (Menno)

Menno now travels to the Hanseatic cities on the Baltic coast. The increasingly strong rivalry of the David Jorists in this region compel him to a debate to finish airing out their mutual feelings. In Lübeck, Menno, Dirk Philips, Adam Pastor, Lenaert Bouwens and Gillis van Aken sit down at the table with a Jorist deputation led by David's son-in-law Nicolaes Meyndertsz van Blesdijk. The point of discussion is above all baptism, which according to the Jorists may also be ministered to children. Their rejection of the external church likewise remains an abomination for Menno. The debate certainly leads to no rapprochement, and the paths remain permanently divided. In the meantime there is new commotion in Menno's own circle. The doctrine of incarnation, which Menno had taken over from Melchior Hoffman, comes under fire from Adam Pastor and Frans Kuiper. On top of this they express strong doubts about the trinity. In 1547 the questions get a chance at discussion at a large meeting in Emden, but nothing comes of it. Menno pursues the matter in private. Later that year a second gathering is convened in Goch. When Pastor cannot be moved from his anti-trinitarian position, Dirk Philips cuts the Gordian knot. Without consultation he pronounces the ban over Adam. Above all this will impute a rigorous zealotry to Menno. The Adamites in the Rhine region maintain their devotion to their elder and Adam Pastor proceeds tirelessly with his preaching and baptizing. Kuiper still conforms to the Mennonite vision, but not for long.

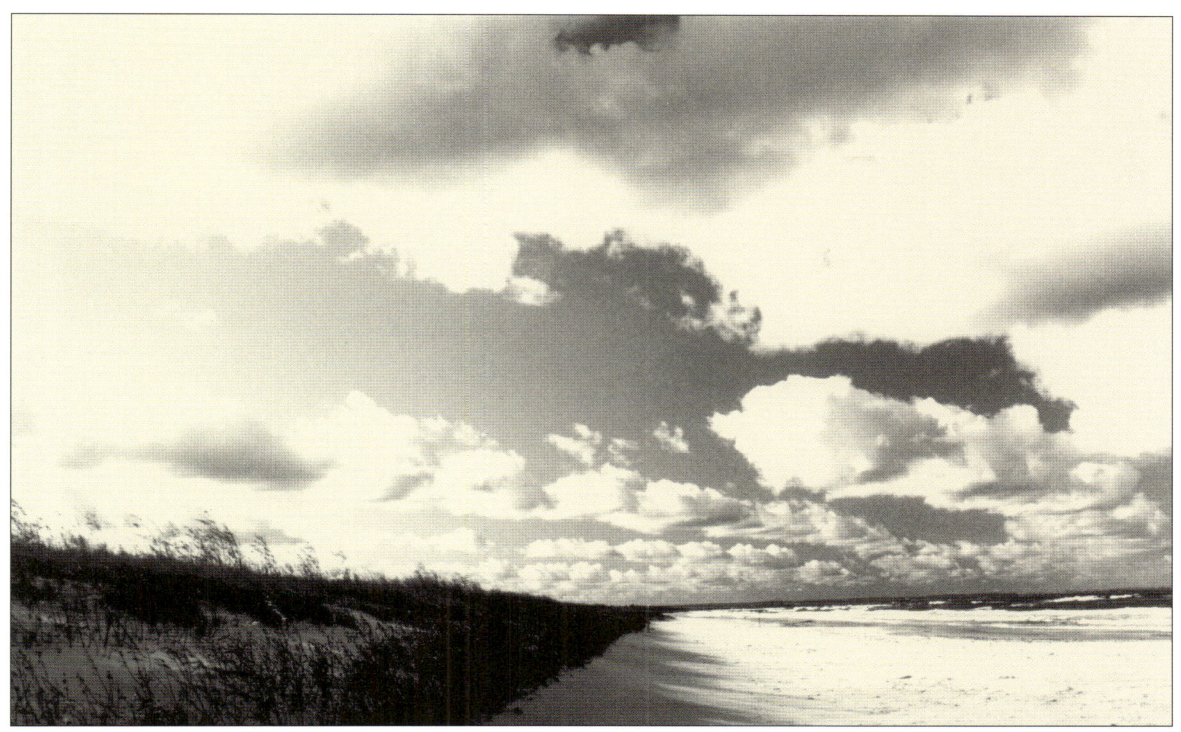

15b. *The Baltic sea shore* - EVW

15c. *The so-called 'House at the Five Rings' at Goch* - EVW

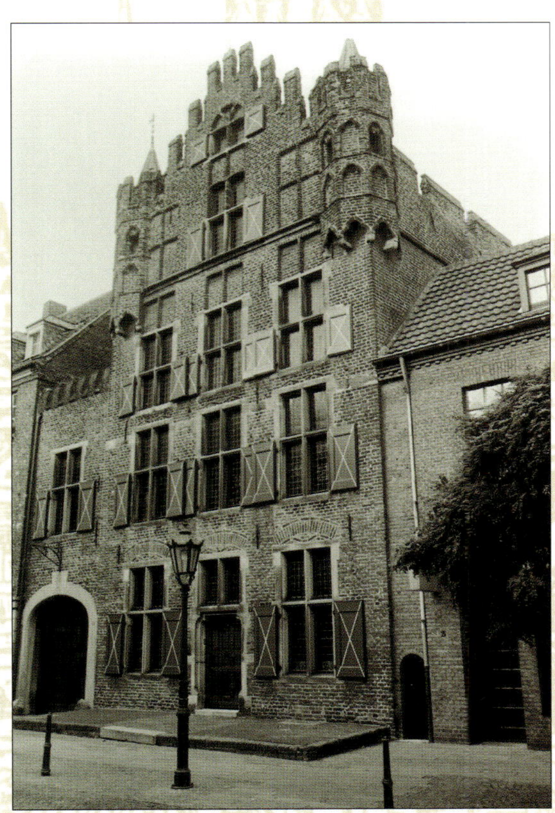

Chriſtelijcke Verant-
woordinghe,

Ende billijcke ne=
derlegginge des valſchen onghe=
grondeden Oordeels / Laſterens ende
Scheldens : By Menno Symonſz. in eenen
Sendtbrief wtgegeuen / tegens etlijcke Liefheb-
bers ende Navolghers der warer gherechticheyt
Chriſti / om dat ſy ſo ſuperſtitieus in ſommighe
Ceremonien te onderholden / niet bevonden
werden/als hy. Allen die de middel-ſtrate
ende Godtlijcke billijckheyt te be-
vlytighen luſt hebben/ zeer
nut ende dienſt-
lijck.

Prouerb. xix. verſ. 2.

Waer gheen beſcheydenheyt is / daer heeft het een Ziele
niet goet : ende die ſnel van voeten is / die ſtoot hem
lichtelijck.

Pſal. Cap.71.7.

Veele menſchen vloden voor my / recht of Ick een wonder-
lijcken grouwel gheweeſt waer: Maer ghy/O Heere/
gaeft my een zeer vaſt betrouwen.

Ghedruckt in't Jaer xvj^c ende Seuen.

15d. Van Blesdijk, *Polemical Jorist writing against Menno* (1546) - UBA-DG

16a. *The Vistula* - EVW

DANZIG EMDEN FRIESLAND GRONINGEN

16 ♦ 1549 - 1551

Claes Janszoon alias Brongers ... confesses ... to have had made by him forbidden books of Menno Simonsson ... together with having received the same Menno Simonsson ... inside his house and to have remained with him as a companion, without bringing the same to the local officer.

(Criminal Sentences, Leeuwarden)

Outside, the enemy spies; inside, discord rules. Again the devil tosses Menno to and fro. Menno writes his second book on the ban; *Een claer bericht ... van der excommunicatie* (*A Clear Account ... of Excommunication*). In 1549 he stays some weeks in Danzig in order to settle the various differences. The city and the neighboring Vistula Delta are very popular among the persecuted Dutch brothers and sisters and in this relative peace thousands of Mennonites are able to construct a new existence. Also in this year Menno abides for a time in Emden where he speaks with Flemish refugees, thereafter he travels to Friesland. There Claes Jansz is beheaded because he had provided shelter for Menno instead of handing him over to the authorities, for which Claes, playing double jeopardy, already had received a reward. Menno's writings are put on the Louvain *Index* of March 26, 1550. To the Groningen Mennonites he sends a letter with his confession *van den drie eenighen eeuwighen God* (*of the Triune Eternal God*); a defence against Adam Pastor. Hendrik van Vreeden and Anthonius van Keulen, two other elders, separate from Menno. In 1551 Lenaert Bouwens is named, without Menno's knowledge, elder of Groningen and Friesland because Menno now resides elsewhere. In May of that year Menno is seen 'in the the land of Groningen' with the lord of Euwsum.
In the south the Mennonites lose elder Theunis van Hasthenrath, who is burned on 30 July.

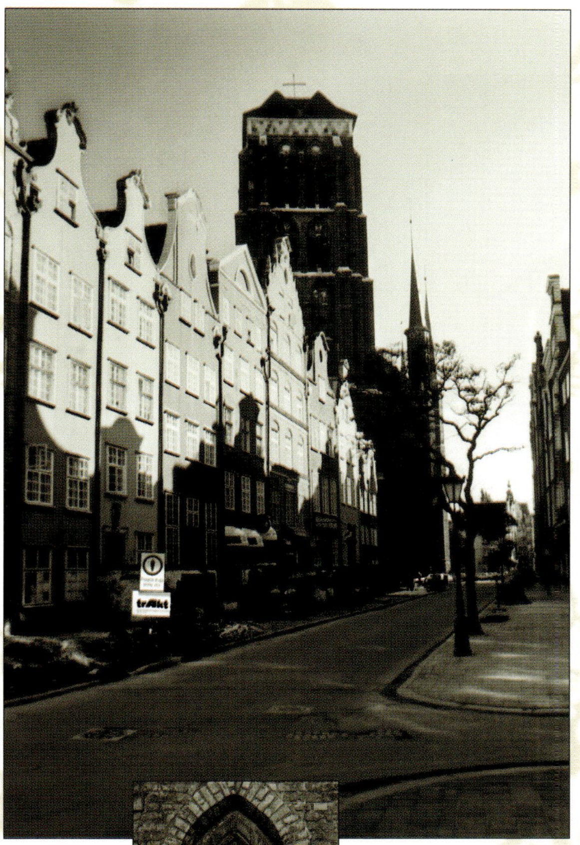

16b. *The Piwna Street at Danzig with St. Mary's Church* - EVW

16c. *A door of St. Marys Church* - EVW

16e. B&H II, *Danzig* (ca. 1580) - UBA

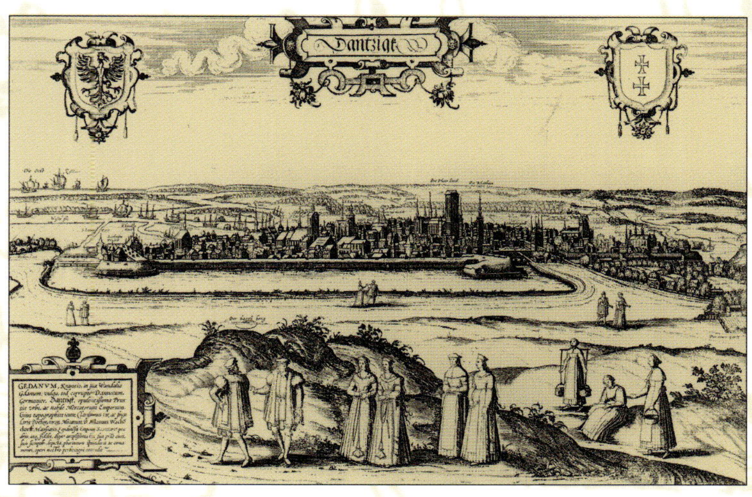

ANABAPTISTICÆ HÆRESEOS CONFVTATIO, ET VERE CHRISTIANI BAPTISMI, ac potißimum pædobaptiſmatis aſſertio in duos libros diuiſa, quorum prior ueram Christiani baptiſmi energiam declarat, poſterior pædobaptiſmatis Christianam inſtitutionem ex ſacris literis demonſtrat, contra Mennonis Simonis Friſij anabaptiſticæ prauitatis ſummi antiſtitis uirulentas blaſphemias, authore Martino Duncano Kempenſi Guormarianæ Eccleſiæ in Hollandia paſtore.

Item quod neque ex teſtimonio proprię conſcientiæ quãtumuis iuſtæ, neq; ex ſcriptura, certò ſcire poſſumus, ſine peculiari reuelatione, nos nunc eſſe iuſtos, & cælo dignos, quanquam id firmiter ſperare oporteat futurum. Præterea quæ ſit vera Chriſti Eccleſia, ex ſacris literis demonſtratio, cum multis alijs hoc ſeculo omnibus Chriſtianis valde neceſſarijs.

Prouerb. 22.
Ne tranſgrediaris terminos antiquos, quos poſuerunt patres tui.

ANTVERPIÆ,
Imprimebat Iohannes Grauius Typographus à Cæſ. Maieſt. admiſſus, Anno 1549.

Cum gratia & priuilegio.

16f. Duncanus, *Polemical writing against the Anabaptists by the priest of Wormer (Holland)* (1549) - UBA-DG

16d. Münster, *Northern Germany / Mecklenburg and Pommerania* (1550) - UBA

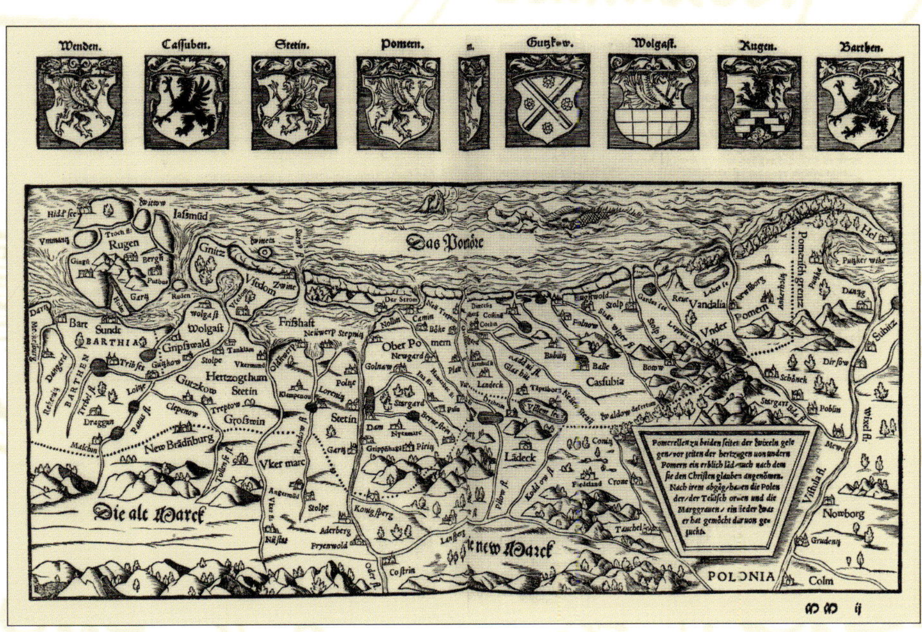

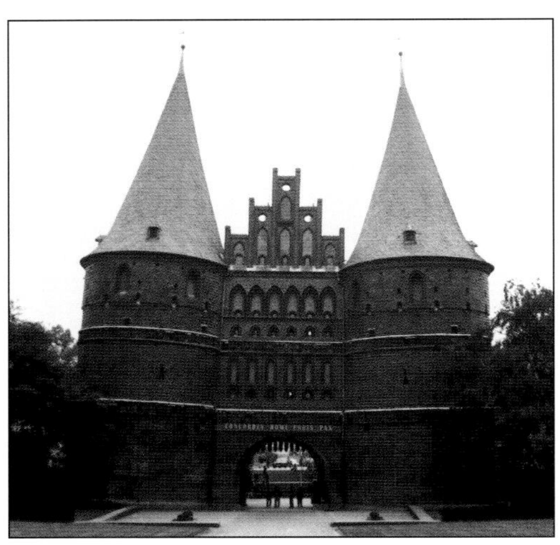

17a. *Holsentor, the city gate of Lübeck* - EVW

LÜBECK

17 ♦ 1552 - 1553

Duo hodie inter Anabaptistas quasi in civili bello praecipui duces extiterunt, Simon Menno et Adam Pastoris. (Among the Anabaptists have now appeared, just as in a civil war, two chief ringleaders: Simon Menno en Adam Pastor). (Cassander)

Between all these trips and activities, Menno takes advantage of the opportunity to publish at least three compositions. In these he attempts to convince 'all authorities' and 'theologians' to exercise greater moderation regarding his denounced folk. He provides his own rank and file with further explanation of a number of doctrines. He probably lives for a time in Lübeck, where in 1552 there is held a new meeting of the most important elders, once again on the agenda is the matter of Adam Pastor who has not cared a whit for his ban. The opinions are irreconcilably opposed, so that the ban remains vindicated. However, Pastor grasps his pen in 1553 and publishes two writings, making the matter public. Menno and his fellows wrap themselves in quiet and maintain a dead silence about the Mennonite heretic. Once again he is caught up in a tiresome question. Gillis van Aken, the very active elder in the Rhineland who also has much influence in Flanders, is suspected 'of leading an entirely unchaste, fleshly life, fornicating with some of the young women whom he has baptized'. Menno can do nothing other than to remove Gillis as well from his office. When the city of Lübeck promulgates a mandate forbidding in the strongest terms any Anabaptists from remaining within the city walls, Menno must again pack up his travel chest.

17e. Menno, *Letter of comfort to some widows (beginning of the 1550's) - the only original writing of Menno extant* - UBA-DG

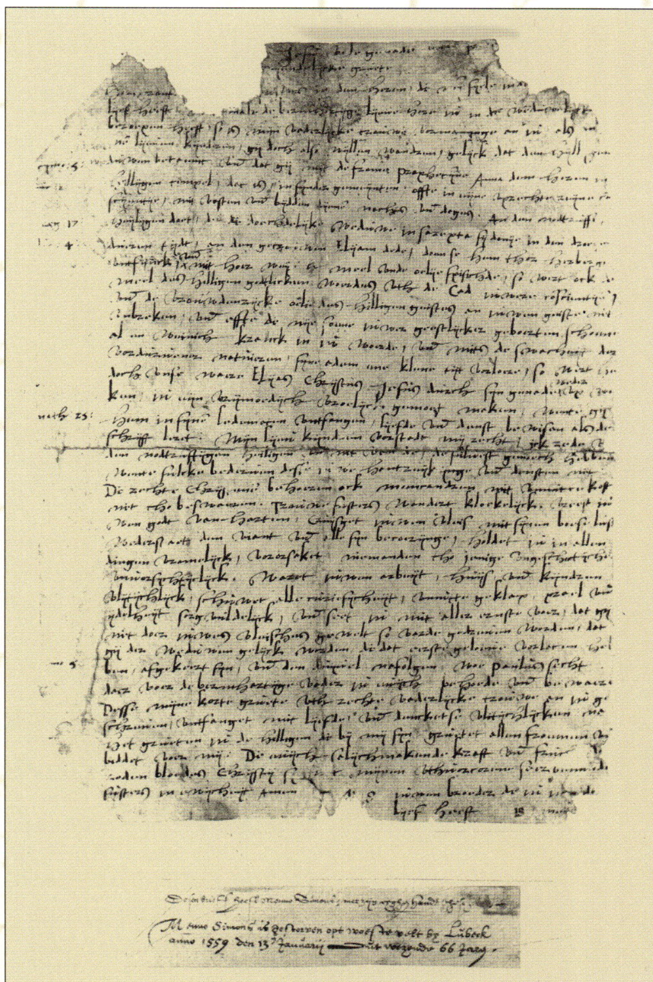

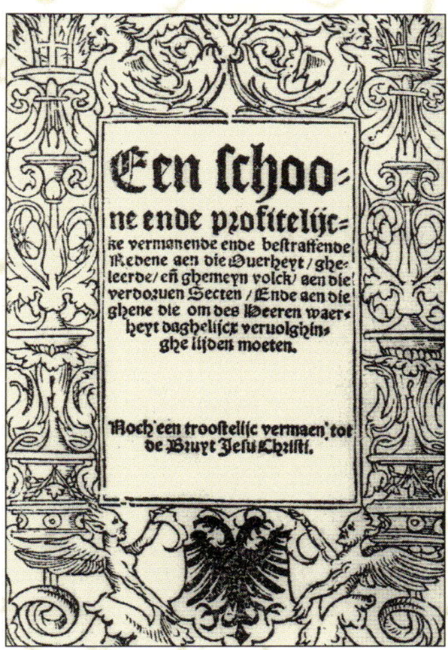

Een schoo-ne ende profitelijc-ke vermanende ende bestraffende Redene aen die Overheyt / ghe-leerde / en ghemeyn volck / aen die verdorven Secten / Ende aen die ghene die om des Heeren waer-heyt dagheliicx veruolghin-ghe lijden moeten.

Noch een troostelijc vermaen tot de Bruyt Jesu Christi.

17b. Menno, *Tract to the authorities – the double eagle also decorates the Lübeck coat of arms* (ca. 1552) - UBA-DG

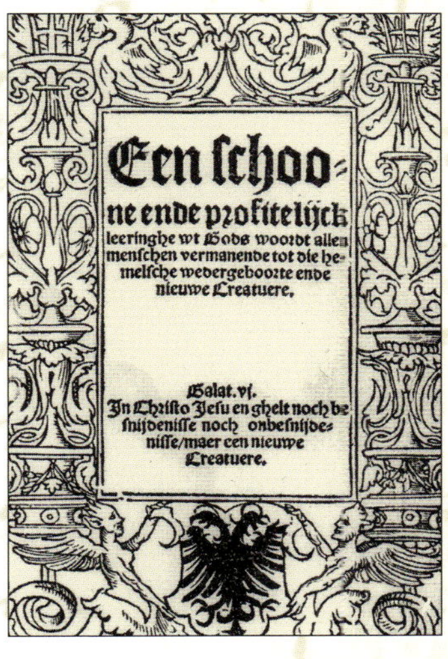

Een schoo-ne ende profitelijck leeringhe wt Gods woordt allen menschen vermanende tot die he-melsche wedergeboorte ende nieuwe Creatuere.

Galat. vj.
In Christo Jesu en ghelt noch be-snijdenisse noch onbesnijde-nisse / maer een nieuwe Creatuere.

17c. Menno, *Tract about the New Birth* (ca. 1552) - UBA-DG

17d. *The cathedral of Lübeck near the Mühlenteich* - EVW

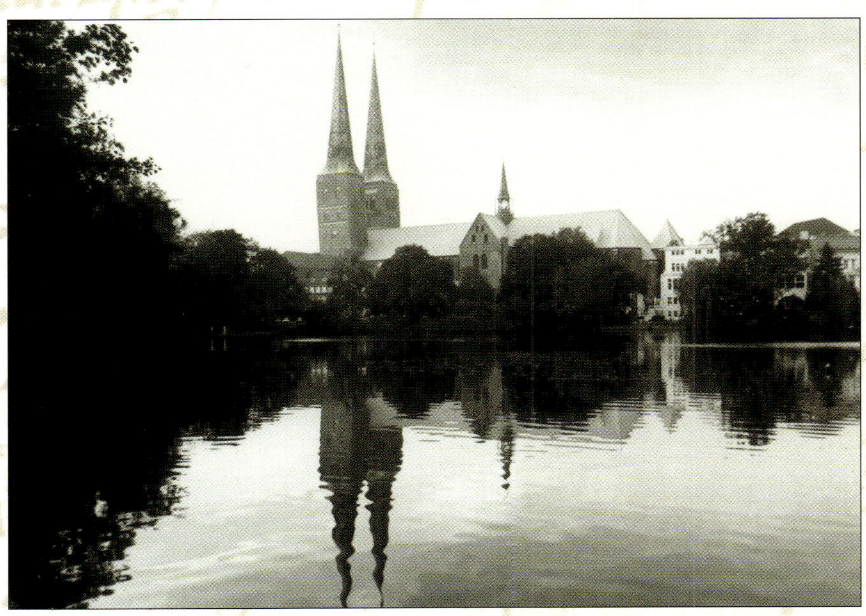

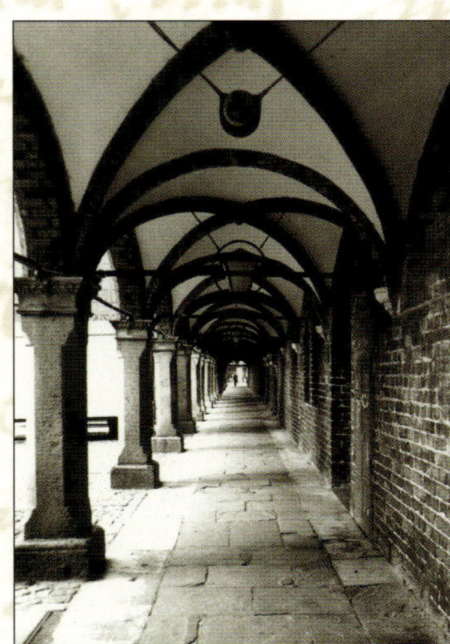

17f. *Vaulted passage of the Lübeck City Hall (1240-50)* - EVW

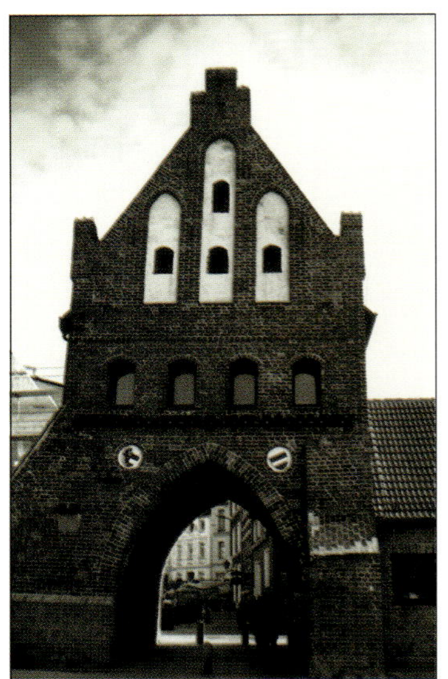
18a. *The Water gate of Wismar* - EVW

WISMAR

18 ♦ 1553 - 1554

Now that Menno is deprived of his distorted and offensive writings, and must roam the fields as if defenceless, he resolves to use as his excuse some drawbacks or improprieties which are supposed to follow from our teaching (as he says). (Martin Mikron)

In the autumn of 1553 Menno secretly finds shelter in Wismar. There he begins his *Klare beantwoordinge* (*Clear Reply*) to Gellius Faber, the ex-priest Jelle Smit from Jelsum in Friesland, now preacher at Emden, who had published an *Antwert ... up einen bitter hönischen breef der Wedderdöper* (*Reply ... to a Nasty Letter by the Anabaptists*). Into this work Menno inserts his autobiographical *Renunciation of Rome.* Then on the 21st of December a ship full of reformed refugees from London and Denmark becomes stuck in the ice near the coast. With the permission of the municipality the Mennonites help the shipwrecked with provisions and shelter, actions prompted by the desire to win them over to the Anabaptist cause. On the day after Christmas elder Hermannus Backereel, quite recovered but provoked by this zealous mission, calls for a disputation with Menno. The famous issues such as the incarnation doctrine, baptism and calling of preachers once again stand high on the agenda. From February 6th to the 15th the discussion is led by the more eloquent Martin Mikron, leader of the Emden refugee church. Menno becomes exhausted from these long sessions, having to tie himself in all manner of knots and catch himself in lies. The disputes result in an endless round of abuse and insinuations. On February 15th the debate becomes locked in a great dissension, for Mikron and his party are literally worked out of the Anabaptist house. At a convent 'in a secret place in the land of Mecklenburg' seven elders take up the evaluation of this harsh confrontation. It is decreed that *buitentrouw* (marriage with non-Mennonites) will be punished by the ban and shunning, but that marital shunning needs to be handled with caution. The previously banned Gillis van Aken is again allowed back into the fellowship 'with a confession of guilt'. Now, just as the Lübeck authorities had done earlier, so too the Wismar authorities declare all Protestants to be undesirable persons. Menno moves once again.

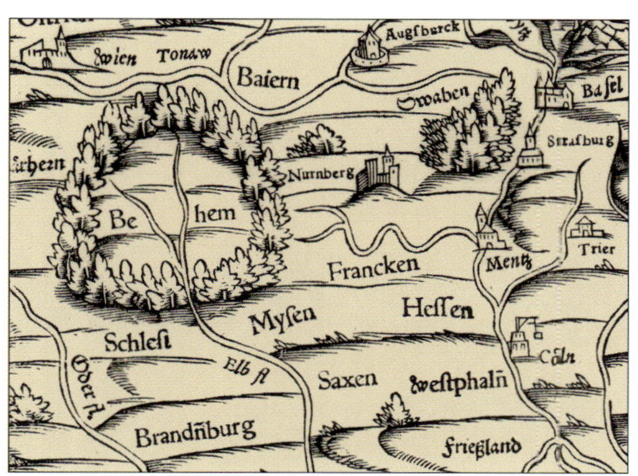

18b. Münster, *Mecklenburg* (1550) - UBA

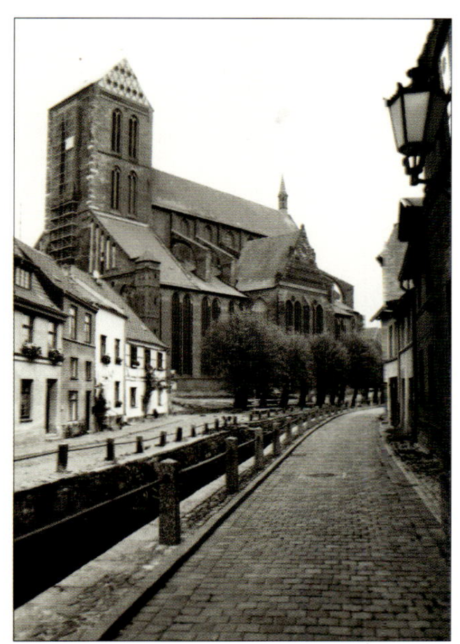

18c. *St. Nicolas Church at Wismar* - EVW

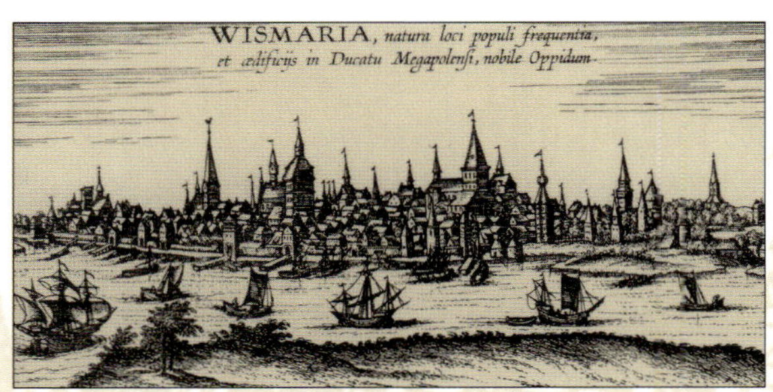

18d. Münster, *Wismar* (1550) - UBA

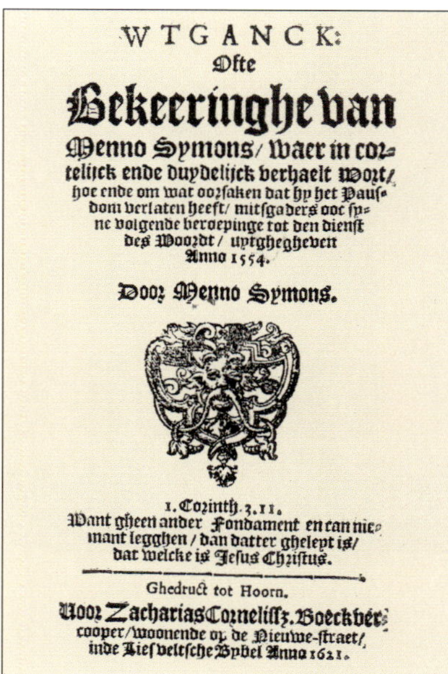

WTGANCK:
Ofte
Bekeeringhe van
Menno Symons/ waer in cor-
telijck ende duydelijck verhaelt wort/
hoe ende om wat oorsaken dat hy het Pausdom verlaten heeft/ mitsgaders oock syne volgende beroepinge tot den dienst
des Woordt/ uytghegheven
Anno 1554.

Door Menno Symons.

1. Corinth. 3. 11.
Want gheen ander Fondament en can nie-
mant legghen / dan datter ghelept is/
dat welcke is Jesus Christus.

Ghedruckt tot Hoorn.
Voor Zacharias Cornelisz. Boeckver-
cooper/ woonende op de Nieuwe-straet/
inde Liefvelsche Bybel Anno 1621.

18e. Menno's *Renunciation of Rome, included in the defence against Gellius Faber in 1553* (1621) - UBA-DG

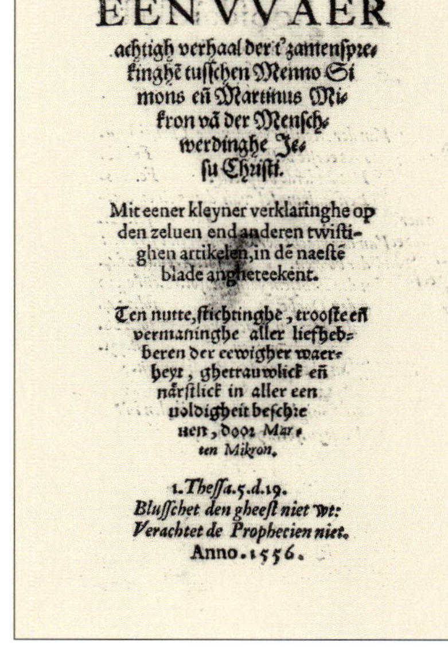

EEN VVAER
achtigh verhaal der t'zamenspre-
kinghe tusschen Menno Si-
mons en Martinus Mi-
kron vā der Mensch-
werdinghe Je-
su Christi.

Mit eener kleyner verklaringhe op
den zeluen end anderen twisti-
ghen artikelen, in dē naeste
blade angheteekent.

Een nutte, stichtinghe, troostē
vermaninghe aller liefhebberen der eewigher waer-
heyt, ghetrauwlick en
nārstlick in aller een
voldigheit beschre
ven, door Mar-
ten Mikron.

1. Thessa.5.d.19.
Blusschet den gheest niet: Verachtet de Prophecien niet.
Anno.1556.

18f. M. Mikron, *Report of the dispute with Menno in 1553* (1556) - UBA-DG

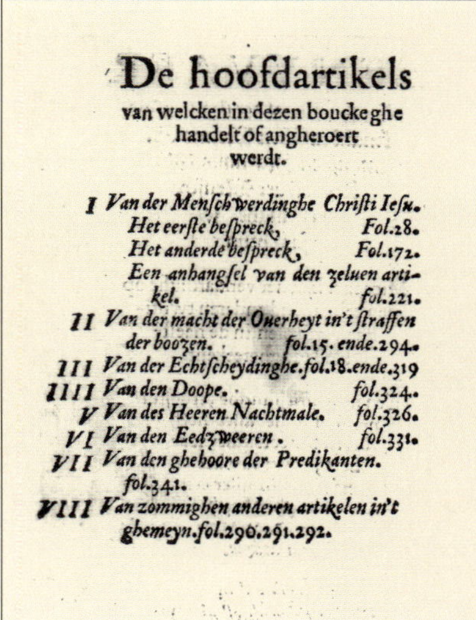

De hoofdartikels
van welcken in dezen bouckeghe
handelt of angheroert
werdt.

I Van der Menschwerdinghe Christi Iesu.
Het eerste besprek, Fol.28.
Het anderde besprek, Fol.172.
Een anhangsel van den zeluen arti-
kel. fol.221.
II Van der macht der Ouerheyt in't straffen
der boozen. fol.15. ende.294.
III Van der Echtscheydinghe.fol.18.ende.319
IIII Van den Doope. fol.324.
V Van des Heeren Nachtmale. fol.326.
VI Van den Eedzweeren. fol.331.
VII Van den ghehoore der Predikanten.
fol.341.
VIII Van zommighen anderen artikelen in't
ghemeyn.fol.290.291.292.

18g. Idem, *Survey of the discussed matters* - UBA-DG

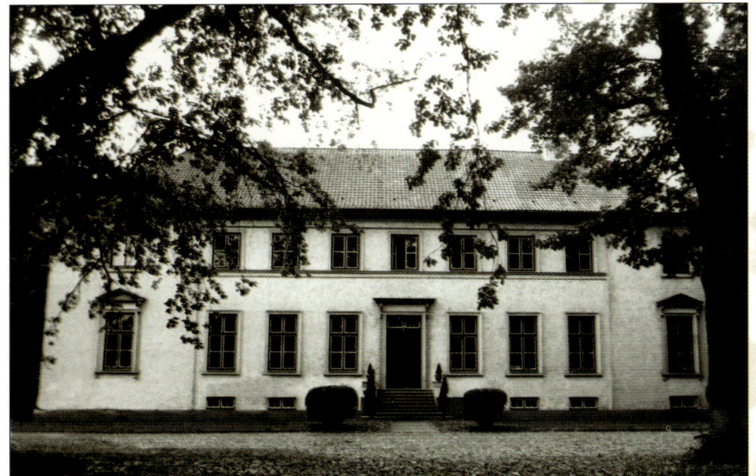

19a. *The present-day Fresenborg near Bad Oldesloe* - EVW

19b. J. de Clerck (exc.), *King Christian III of Denmark* (ca. 1612) - UBA

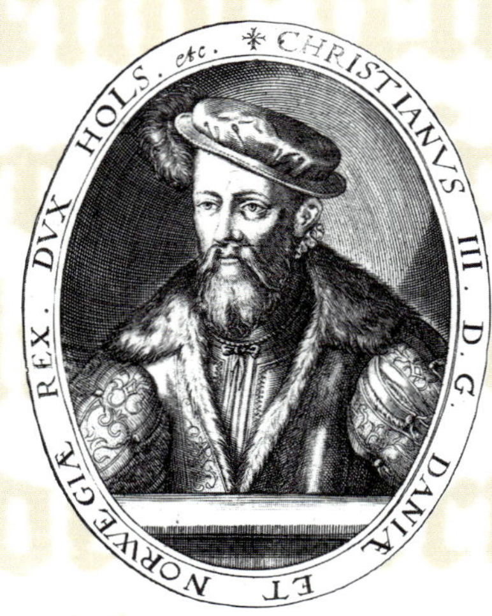

OLDESLOE

19 ♦ 1554 - 1555

Money and riches I do not have. Nor do I desire them, although some alas, from a perverted heart, say that I eat more roasted than they do seethed; and that I drink more wine than they do beer. (Menno)

In Wüstenfelde on the Fresenborg estate of Bartholomaeus von Ahlefeldt near Bad Oldesloe, between Hamburg and Lübeck in Holstein, the increasingly ailing Menno and his family find a secure shelter. Since 1543 von Ahlefeld has been allowing Anabaptists upon his domain, very much against the will of king Christian III of Denmark. With his help a printshop is established in what would later be called the Mennokate (cottage). Within works a printer for Menno known solely by his initials B.L. Four titles see the light of day here, among which are three drastically revised older texts. The Fresenborg press also publishes Menno's account of the dispute with Martin Mikron. Does the November 28th, 1554 report of the Danish court concerning the arrest of an Anabaptist and his printers near Oldesloe mean the end of the Fresenborg press? The accused were coming from Lübeck, in possession of ten wooden barrels of Dutch bibles and concordances; fourteen similar barrels had already been sent to Amsterdam. Between Menno and his friend of the first hour Dirk Philips, residing now in Danzig, there develops an even wider estrangement over the question of discipline. In an uninhibited fashion Dirk holds forth both orally and in writing his harsh position over the ban and shunning. Not only his people, but Menno's own body and limbs are increasingly working against him. At times he can be moved only by sitting on a wagon or lying in a ship.

Eyne Troestelijke Vermaninge van dat lijden/Cruyze/vñ Veruolginge der Heyligen/umme dat woort Godes/vñ zijne getuichenisse.
Menno Simons.

Salich zijn ghi
wen iuw de luyde umme mijnent wyllen schenden vñ veruolghen/vñ reden allerleye quaet wedder iuw/soo se daeranne liegen/Weset frolijck/unde hebbet eynen goeden moet/Idt wert iuw im Hemmel wol belonet werden/wente alsoo hebben se veruolghet de Propheten/de voor iuw ghewesen zijn. Matth. 5.

Daer en mach
gheen ander Fundament ghelecht worden/behaluen datter ghelecht is/welcker is Christus Jesus. 1. Corin. 3.

Eyne seer Lieflijcke Meditation vñ Godtsalige Oeffeninge/mit vele Christelijke Leeringen/voor eyne bedroefde bekummerde Conscientie/de van der werelt/vant vleesch/Helle/sunde/doot/vñ Duyuel bestreden wert (Op den. 25. Psalm. Ad te leuaui animã meã int Latijn genoemet) bedesscher wijse veruatet. Menno Symons.

Jck roepe thoe
dem Heeren in mijner noodt/unde he verhoort mij. Heere redde mijne Siele van den loeghenhafftigen Munden vñ van den valschen Tunghen. Psalm. 120.

Eyne ander
Grunt kan nyemant leggen dan allene de/de ghelecht is/Christus Jesus. 1. Cori. 3.

Ein Fundament vñ klare Anwisinge/van de heylsame vñ Godtsellyghe Leere Jesu Christi/uth Godes woort mit gueder corte veruatet/vñ wederumme mit grooter vlyte auergheleesen unde ghebetert. Menno Symons.

☞ Thom. i. Van de tijt der Ghenaden.
☞ Thom. ij. Van de ware Boete.
☞ Thom. iij. Van den Ghelouen.
☞ Thom. iiij. Eyn vormanende Supplicatie an der Oeuerichept.
☞ Thom. v. Van der Doepe.
☞ Thom. vi. Van des Heeren nachtmael.
☞ Thom. vij. Van de mydinge Babels.
☞ Thom. viij. Eyn besluytende vormaninge/an der Oeuerichept/Gheleerden/Gemeyne volcke/Secte/vñ an de Huyt Stadt/vñ Ghemeynte Christi.

☞ Eyne ander Grundt kan nyemandt leggen/dan allene de/de ghelecht is/welcker ys Jesus Christus. i. Corin. iij.
Godt die Vader ghetuiget vã Christo vñ spricht. Dit is mijn gelieuede Sone/an dẽ welckeren ic ein guet geuallen hebbe/hem hoeret. Mat. xvij.

19c. Menno, *Three revised works, printed by B.L. on the Fresenborg press in the Mennokate* (ca. 1554) - UBA-DG

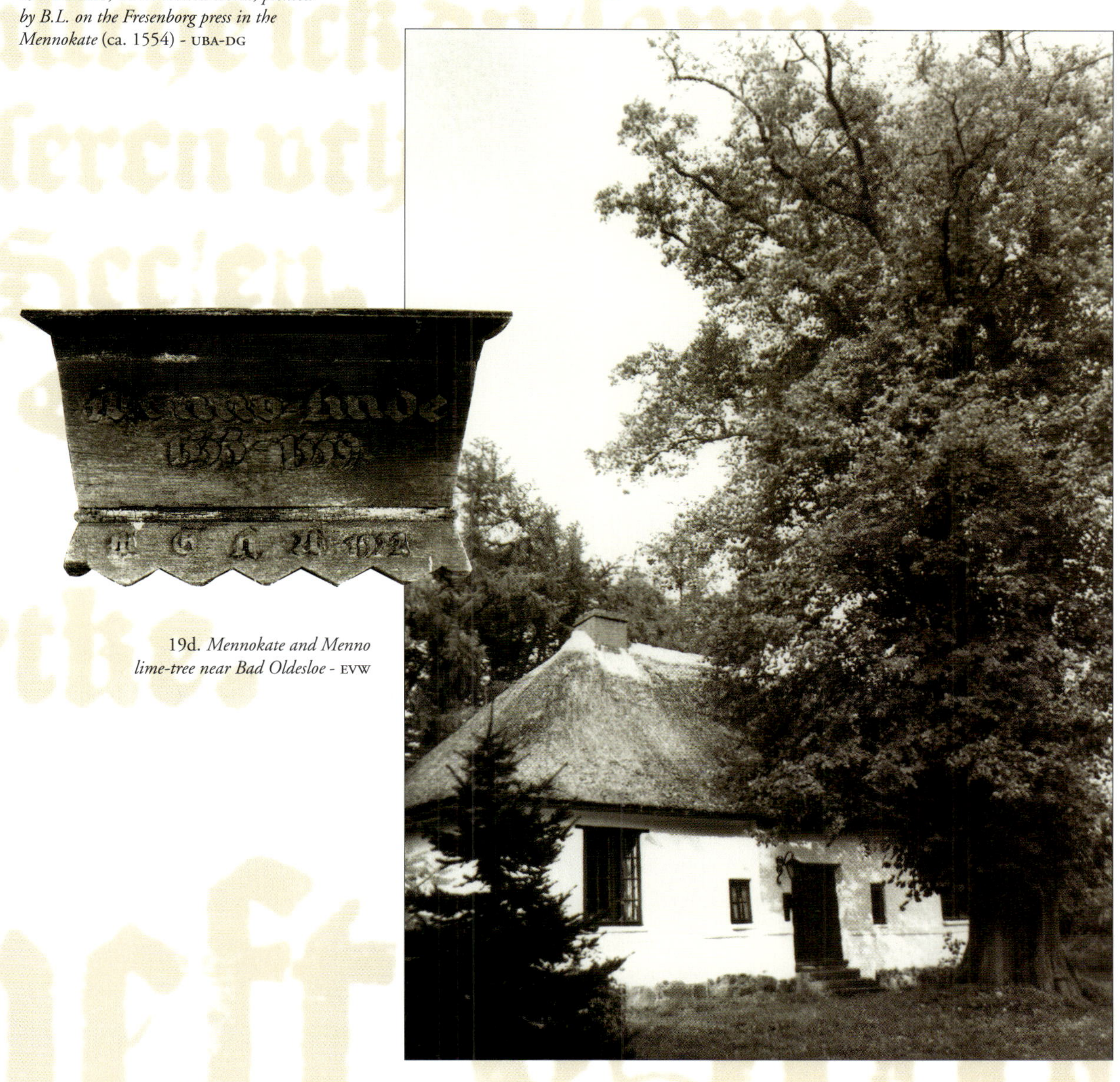

19d. *Mennokate and Menno lime-tree near Bad Oldesloe* - EVW

Anno. 1555.

Ondergheschreuen by my den Cruppel / uwe Broeder ende Dienaer / den 13. Nouembris.

20a. Menno, *Subscription of one of his printed letters* - UBA-DG

OLDESLOE WATERLAND

20 ♦ 1555 - 1556

In such fear, poverty, misery, and danger of death have I, wretched man [... with my poor, weak wife and children ...] performed to this hour, without alteration, the service of the Lord. And I hope through His grace to perform it to His glory as long as I linger in this tabernacle. (Menno)

Menno must passively look on while the rank and file becomes even more divided. The much younger Lenaert Bouwens, elder at Emden and filled with a great missionary zeal — he will baptize during his itinerant life more than 10,000 people — turns out to be strict with the ban as well. Gillis van Aken, now restored again to his office, brings about similar unrest in the Waterland. Menno must travel again, for twice he is described as being north of Amsterdam restoring the peace. Thanks to the moderate Jan Jacobsz Scheedemaker from De Rijp he finds the congregations there still standing upon the 'old foundation'. When on November 13 Menno writes the brothers in Franeker about the ban, he signs it 'Menno the lame'. It is a response to an alarming letter over a Swaen Rutgers, who was banned by Lenaert because she refused to shun her sinning husband. In April of 1556 Menno invites some fellow-elders to Wüstenfelde for a discussion over the discipline question. Dirk Philips is absent, but Zylis and Lemmeken are there on behalf of the High German churches, as well as Hendrick Naeldeman who represents the Franeker Mennonites. Despite finding Swaen's excommunication too rough, Menno tries to defend marital shunning as biblical, but he finds little understanding for it among his colleagues. The matter gnaws at him even more, because the sympathetic Franekers have just arranged for a Utrecht printer, Jan Hendricksz van Schoonrewoerd, to establish himself in their city. This person publishes, naturally anonymously, a number of Anabaptist writings including those of Menno.

Een ganz duyt lijck/ende bescheyde-
woordt. An°.1556.wt waerheyt ende ex.
der heylighen godlicken schrift grondt-
ken veruaetet/op Martini Mikrons A. M.:
christische leere ende onwaerachtighe valsche verhael van den handel ofte bispreck.
An°.53. minder ghetal / tusschen hem ende
my van die alderheylichste menschwerdinghe onses Heeren Jesu Christi voor veele ge
tuyghen gheschien. Met noch eene hardt
grondtlicke scherpe sendebrief ofte vermae
ninge an hem seluen/om hem seluē
recht tho leren kennen/ dat
hy boete doe / ende
eewich sae-
lich wer
de.

M. S.

Dat is dat eewich leuen/ dat sy di(o vader)
alleene bekennen eenen waeren God/ende
den du gesent heefst/Christum
Jesum. Johann.17.

Daer mach gheen ander Fondament ghelecht worden. behaluen datter gelecht
is/ Christus Jesus .1. Corinth.3.

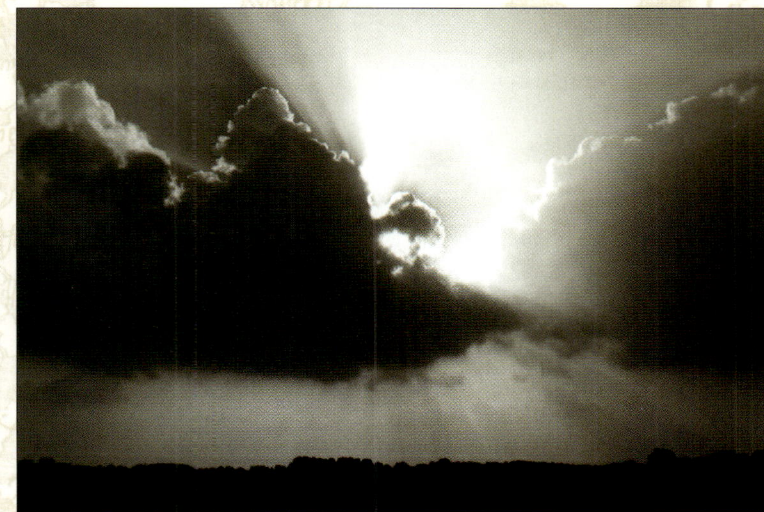

20c. *Clouds over Oldesloe* - EVW

Van het rechte Christen gheloove/ dat des
menschen harte omkeert/verandert/ God-
vresende/oprecht/nieuw/ vreedich/ vrolick/
eñ salich maecket/met sijn rechte natuerlic-
ke eygenschappē /aert/natuere/werckingē
ende crachten. An° .1556. wederom-
me met groter vlite doorghe-
sien/eñ wat formlijc
ker gheset-
tet.

M. S.

Wie an mi ghelooft (spreect Christus) die
sal leuen/al waert oock dat hy storue. Ende
die daer leeft ende gelooft an mi
die sal in ewicheyt niet
steruen. Jo-
ā.11.

Daer mach gheen ander Fundament ghelecht worden/behaluen datter ge
lecht is/Christus Je-
sus.1.Cor.
.3.

eenen gheeste ghedoopt, so veruullet myne
vruechde, ende weest eender ey met ghesint
na Christum Jesum, bouwet ende en breeckt
niet. De eene onderwijse der anderen in der
liefde, schuert noch en rijtet niet, op dat de
godsalige vrede/onder al en kinderen Gods
bestae/ende onghebroken by ons allen blijue
tot in dat eewighe leuen. De vredentrijcke
Gheest Christi beware v allen, sampt heyl-
saem in der leere, vyerich in der liefde, on-
aenstootich in dat leuen, tot opbouwin-
ghe zijnder heylighen Ghemeynte/
ende tot prijs zijns heyligen
Naems, Anno.
1555.

Ondergheschreuen by my den
Cruypel, uwe broeder ende
dienaer, den 23. Nouembris.

Desen Brief is ghesonden van Menno
Simons/aen de Ghemeynte te Embden/
Datum als onder gheschreuen.

1, Corint.3.
Daer en mach gheen ander fondament
gheleyt worden, behaluen datter gheleyt is,
het welcke is Christus Jesus.

20d. Menno, *Letter to the Emden congregation* (1556) - UBA-DG

Een seer schoo-
ne/ende grontlijcke leringe
wt des Heeren woordt/allen menschen(die
haer na Christus name noemen laten)neer
stichlic vermanende tot die hemelsche Ghe
boorte eñ nieuwe Creatuer/sonder welcke
niemandt (die tot sijn verstandt ghecomen
is)een waerachtich Christen is/noch sijn en
can. Anno M.CCCCC.LVI. we-
derom met groter vlyte door
ghesien vermeerdt /
ende ghebe-
tert.

M. S.

Gal.vi.
In Christo Jesu gelt noch besnidenisse noch
onbesnidenisse/maer eē nieu
we Creatuer.

.i. Corinth.iij.
Daer mach geē ander Fondament ghelept
worden dā dat gelept is/ dat is
Jesus Christus.

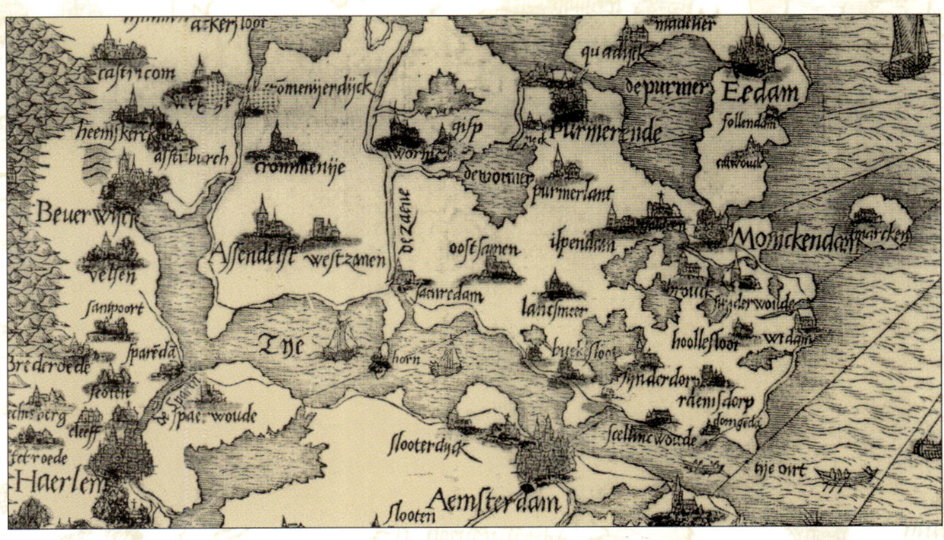

20e. Deventer, *Detail of North Holland, showing the Zaan and Waterland regions* (1558) - UBA

20b. Menno, *Three books printed by Jan Hendricksz van Schoonrewoerd at Franeker* (1556) - UBA-DG

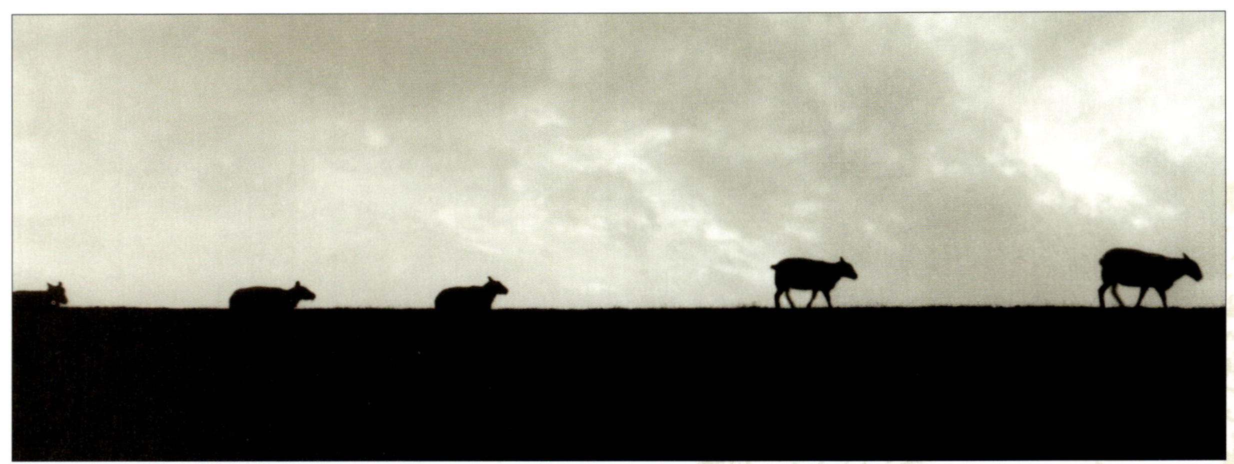

21a. *A divided flock on the sea dike near Harlingen* - EVW

DOKKUM FRANEKER HARLINGEN

21 ♦ 1557

If I find those of Harlingen of the same mind, then I will jump for joy upon my crutches. (Menno)

The movement is cracking on all sides. With the renewal of the imperial placards Menno's books remain forbidden. On February 20, 1557 even the mild countess Anna van Oldenburg issues a placard against the Anabaptists. On July 10 Gillis van Aken is beheaded in Antwerp. At home Menno has to bear the loss of his Geertruyd, who probably dies before September. In a letter he asks his brother-in-law Rein Edes for monetary support. In Friesland his arrival is urgently requested, for the dragged out conflict over the ban and shunning must be put out of its misery in Harlingen. Menno takes a ship to Dokkum and from there is accompanied by the teacher Nette Lupkes. In Leeuwarden a delegation joins them. They hold a first discussion in Franeker, at which Menno voices optimistically that the Franekers are 'still united ... in the understanding'. However, in Harlingen he is met with a rude awakening. Lenaert Bouwens plays a high stakes game and threatens the lame Menno with the ban: 'Menno has not yet risen above our head, since he cannot follow us, so we must do to him what is done to other teachers'. To the dismay of the Franekers, Menno yields to the rough sancture in order to preserve the beloved peace. He knows that this trip to Friesland – his last – has been a failure.

21b. Menno, *Harsh defence against Mikron*(1556) - UBA-DG

Een seer hardt-grontlijcke (doch sijerpe) sendebrief an Martinū Mikron seluen to een ghans nodelicke verantwoordinge sijn der onbeleefden loegenen/mishandelingen ende onuerdiende beschuldinghen/ van der Ouerheyt/Eedtsweerent/etc. Die hy thoe een so groten schande des heylighen Godtliken woords ende sijnder arme: Gemeenten/den ghansen werelt om tho leeren heeft voorgestelt. Oock mede tho een spiegel sijn der verdoolder sielen/om hem seluen leeren recht tho kennen/eñ dat hy/tsamen alle onser beyder leserswereten/hoe seer Godloselicken hi mit synen schriuen beyde teghenst God ende den menschen gehandelt heeft. Op dat hi hem beteren/boete doe/eñ saelich werde.

M. (∴) S.

Daer mach gheen ander grondt ghelecht worden dan die ghelecht is/ Jesus Christus. 1.Cor.3.

P

21e. M. Mikron, *Reply to Menno's accusations* (1558) - UBA-DG

EN APOLOgie of verandtwoordinghe, Martini Micron, op XX. verscheyden Artikelen die Menno Symons teghen het disputacy boecxken van het besprecck met hem ouer de leere ghehouden, in druck heeft wtghegeuen.

Waerin aldermeest van de heylighe menschwerdinge onses Heeren Jesu Christi/grondelick ende volcomelick/tot groot nut allen liefhebberen der godlicker waerheyt/in alle eenuoudicheyt eñ klaerheyt ghehandelt ende ghescreuen wert.

Item schoon Registers op't eynde toeghedaen, om alle stucken hier in ghehandelt, haestelick te vindē.

Joan. 7. g. 24.
Richtet niet na den aensien, maer richtet een oprecht gherichte.

An. 1558.
Nouemb, 12

21c. B&H III, *Harlingen* (ca. 1580) - UBA

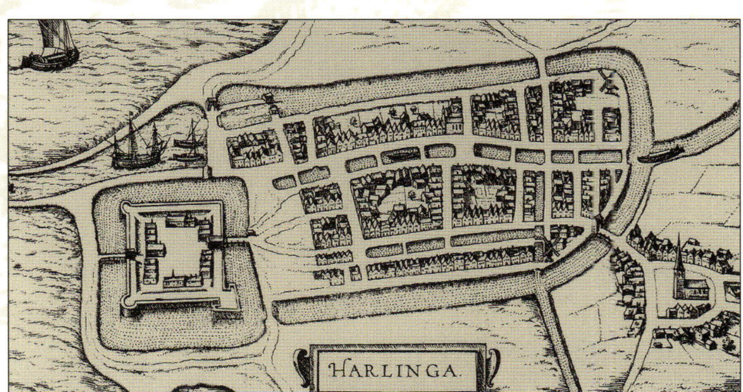

FRANICKER

FRANICHER Nobilissi hominum in Frisia Occidentali, ut plurimum sedes.

21f. B&H III, *Franeker* (ca. 1580) - UBA

Eene corte bekentenisse ende belydinghe vanden eenigen/almachtighen/leuendigen God/ Vader/ Soon/ eñ heylige Geest/ eñ van die scheppinghe/verlossinge/ eñ salichmakinge des menschen/ met een verclaringe des Christelicken eñ Apostolischen Dopes/daer in dat oock neder ghelept worden sommige argumenten/ die vandē tegensprekers der waerheyt opgeworpē of ingevoert worden. Ende ten laetsten van dat rechte gebruych des auōtmaels onses Heeren ende salichmaeckers Jhesu Christi.

1.Iohan.4.
Ghi alderliefste en geloof niet eenen yegelicken gheest/ maer proeft die geesten oft sy wt Godt sijn/ want het sijn vele valsche Propheten wt ghegaen/ in die Werelt.

D. P.

1. Tessa.5.
En blusschet den gheest niet wt/den prophetie verachtet niet/ proeuet al/dat goet is dat behout/midet alle bose schijn.

21d. Dirk Philips, *Confession of Faith* (1557) - UBA-DG

Een suyuerlijc Onderwijs eñ Leere/hoe alle vrome Ouders/haer kinderē (nae wtwijsen der Schrifturen) schuldich ende ghehouden zijn te regeren/ te castijden/ te onderrichten/ eñ in een vroom duechdelijc ende godsalich leuen op te voeden.

De wijse Man seght:
Een houdt niet op de Jongheren te castyden/ want al slaet ghy hem met roeden/ so en steruē sy daer af niet/maer ghy verlost daer by haer Sielen vander Hellen. Pro.23.b.

Castijende onderwijst uwen Sone/so sal hy v vermaken/ ende uwer Sielen saecht doen/ want de roede eñ straffinghe gheeft wijsheyt/ maer een kint hemseluen gelatē/ scheyndet zijn Moeder. Prouer.29.b.

Castijt uwen Sone ter wijlen datter hope aen is. Prouerbio.19.b.

Daer en mach gheen ander Fondament ghelept worden/ dan datter ghelept is: Twelck is Christus Jesus. 1.Corint.3.b.

21g. Menno, *The Nurture of Children, ca. 1557?* (1562) - UBA-DG

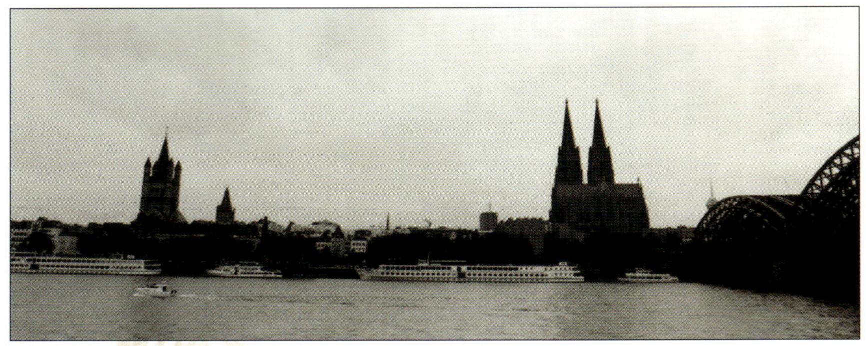

22a. *Cologne, on the bank of the Rhine* - EVW

COLOGNE OLDESLOE

22 ♦ 1558 - 1560

Here Menno bans Zylis and Lemmeke, and eats his own tongue, recanting at many points his own teaching. (V.P.)

Menno observes that his Harlingen prostration in fact has resulted in much bad blood, but for him there is no turning back. The mild Franekers or Waterlanders of Naeldeman and Scheedemaker – *Dreckwaghen* (Dung wagon) they are contemptuously named – are definitively banned. In some letters Menno endeavors to rationalize his inability to stay within his own boundaries. Above all the High German Mennonites feel themselves acquitted.Menno calls a meeting in Cologne, his earlier work terrain, in order to come to a compromise. It results in nothing, because hardly anyone shows up. *Van de excommunicatie* (*On Excommunication*), his third book on the ban, appears from the press of Jan Hendricksz in Franeker. In this he defends his volte-face and turns fiercely toward the High Germans. In the eyes of their elders, Zylis and Lemmeken, Menno is however a weather-vane. They revile him as a *ficfeyer* (imposter), 'an ignorant reed, April water, a flip-flop'. Menno has had enough, and he pronounces the ban over the High Germans. In January 1560 he attempts to justify this in writing with a bitter, but *Seer grontelijcke antwoort ... op Zylis ende Lemmekes* (*Very Basic Reply ... to Zylis and Lemmekes*). Also his relationship with Dirk Philips, to whom Menno had given a wide berth, has completely cooled under pressure of the discipline-lovers. Dirk had departed for Danzig in 1559 again. The always compromising leader has little remaining time. With a gnawing conscience he will realize that his roll has been nearly played out.

EENGANS
grontlijcke onderwijs oft bericht / van de Excommunicatie / Ban / Wtsluytinge/ofte Affonderinge der kercken Christi / wat sy inder cracht zy: Ouer wat luyden dat sy gaen moet/ende welcke hare principaelste oorsaecken ende eynden zijn/ &c. Daeromme si ons van des Heeren heylige Apostelen in zijn heylige woort beuolen/na ghelaten/ende gheleert is. Allen liefhebberen des eewighen waerheyts tot een dienste des heyligen Christelijcken vredes/sonder eenige vleysch oft partye/wt gront der heylighen Godtlijcken schrift in goede trouwe voorgestelt.

M. S.

Philip.2.
Zijt eenderley ghesinnet/en doet niet door twist ofte door ydel eere.

1.Corint.3.
Daer mach gheen ander Fundament ghelecht worden/behaluen dat gelecht is/ Christus Jesus.

22b. *Titlepage and conclusion of the third book on the ban* (1558) - UBA-DG

lasteraers geen roem en schaffe / noch oock den bloetgierigē geen oyre moet en geue. Maer dat wi ons in allen dingē also voorsien/dat wi onsen loop in Christo Jesu met volder vrucchden voleyndigen/ zijn heylige name groot maken/ons onder en ande ren in de vrede Christi verlustighen/onse crancke litmaten en ionge broederen stercken/den ongeordineerden bestraffen/ des Heeren waerheydt wtbreyden/ en ons tot een onbestraflijc Christelijc voorbeelt alle menschen setten moegen. Daer toe gunne ons al te samen de eewige God der crachten/de stercke geest zijnder ghenaden met volder ghehoorsaemheyt ende liefde in Christo Jesu onsen Heere. AMEN.

Och wtuercoorene kinderen / dat is aen v allen mijn Adieu: Kent Godt: Lieuet den broederen/en wachtet v van tweedracht.

Datum by my M. S. uwer al der dienaer ende broeder. Anno 1558. den 11. Junij.

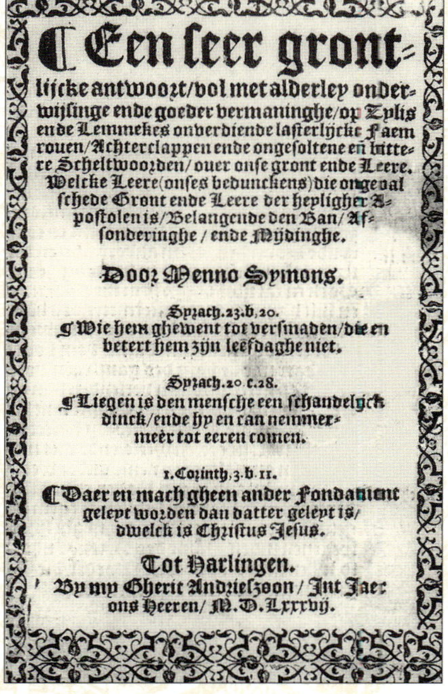
Een seer gront-
lijcke antwoort/vol met alderley onder-
wijsinge ende goeder vermaninghe/op Zylis
ende Lemmekes onverdiende lasterlijcke Faem
rouen/Achterclappen ende ongesoltene en bitte-
re Scheltwoorden/ ouer onse gront ende Leere.
Welcke Leere(onses beduncken)die ongevals
schede Gront ende Leere der heylighen A-
postolen is/Belangende den Ban/Af-
sonderinghe / ende Mydinghe.

Door Menno Symons.

Syrach.23.b.20.
Wie hem ghewent tot versmaden/die en
betert hem zijn leefdaghe niet.

Syrach.20 c.28.
Liegen is den mensche een schandelijck
dinck/ende hy en can nimmer-
meer tot eeren comen.

1.Corinth.3.b.11.
Daer en mach gheen ander Fondament
geleyt worden dan datter geleyt is/
dwelck is Christus Jesus.

Tot Harlingen.
By my Gherit Andrieszoon / Int Jaer
ons Heeren/ M.D.Lxxvij.

22c. Menno, *Reply to Zylis and Lemmeken* (1569) - UBA-DG

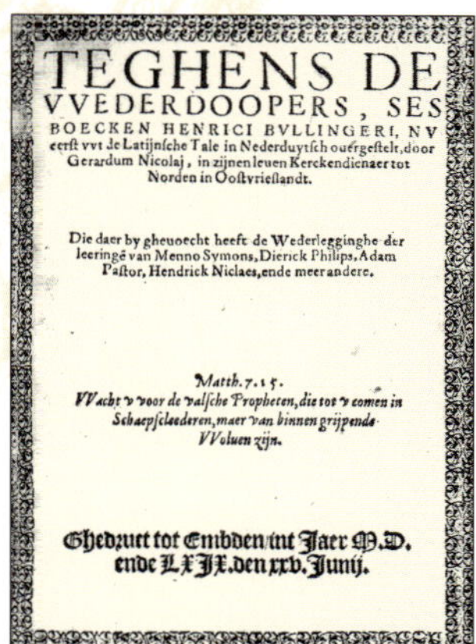
TEGHENS DE
VVEDERDOOPERS, SES
BOECKEN HENRICI BVLLINGERI, NV
eerst vvt de Latijnsche Tale in Nederduytsch ouergestelt, door
Gerardum Nicolaj, in zijnen leuen Kerckendienaer tot
Norden in Oostvrieslandt.

Die daer by gheuoecht heeft de Wederlegginghe der
leeringē van Menno Symons, Dierick Philips, Adam
Pastor, Hendrick Niclaes, ende meer andere.

Matth.7.15.
*VVacht v voor de valsche Propheten, die tot v comen in
Schaepscleederen, maer van binnen grijpende
VVoluen zijn.*

Ghedruct tot Embden int Jaer M.D.
ende LXIX. den xxv. Junij.

22e. Heinrich Bullinger, *Polemical writing against the Anabaptists, 1560* (1569) - UBA-DG

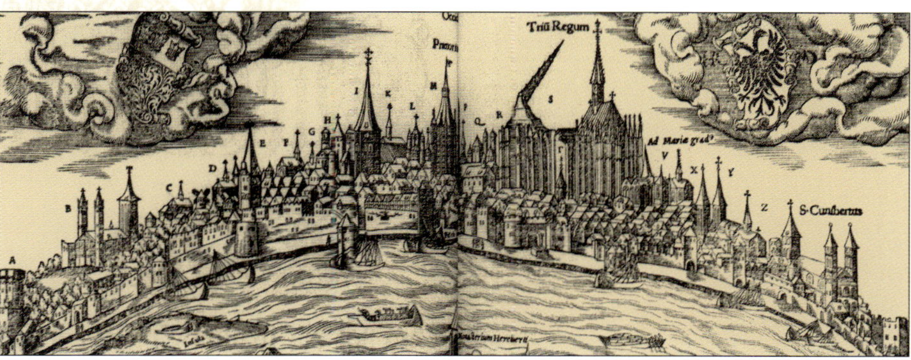

22d. Münster, *Cologne* (1550) - UBA

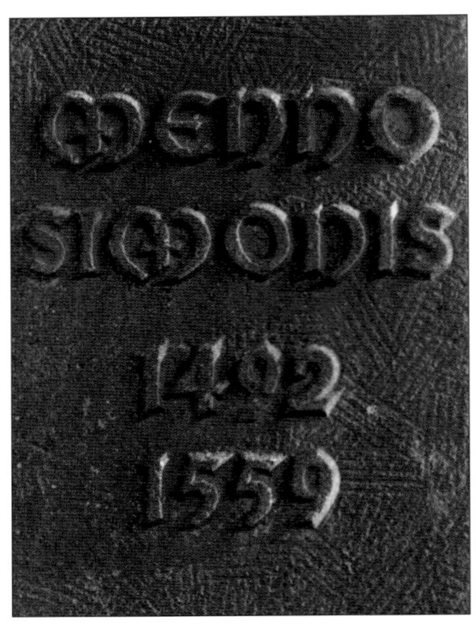

OLDESLOE

23 ♦ 13 January

So Alle Visscher had been with M. ... And when he was to depart from him, so he desired of M. something whereby he might remember him; then M. said to him: And be no servant of men like I have been. (Alenson)

In December of the previous year Menno had become very ill and is confined to his bed. Around the turn of the year he speaks from his sickbed a last admonition for a small crowd of the faithful. Certain acquaintances from the Netherlands call on him. His approaching death makes Menno milder and also makes him realize his weaknesses; 'How I am grieved that I have consented to the marriage-shunning', he confides to a female friend from Holland. To his old friend Alle Visscher, who visits him from the Frisian Bolsward, he confesses to having been too accommodating: 'be no servant of men'. He recovers the strength to stand up for another half week, but on the twelfth of January his weakened body can take no more. The priest who was always bathed in luxury and prestige has exhausted the last 25 years of his existence as a poor and hunted heretic upon whose head stands a price. With pain and difficulty he had earlier shown the peaceful way to a divided Anabaptism. He has given his followers their own voice, but the reward of his work is that his Mennonites had outgrown him. The following day, tormented and tired of fighting, Menno closes his eyes. A quarter century after his departure from the whore of Babylon he hopes only to meet with the Lord of his heavenly Jerusalem. The earthly remains of Menno rest in an unmarked grave in his kitchen garden.

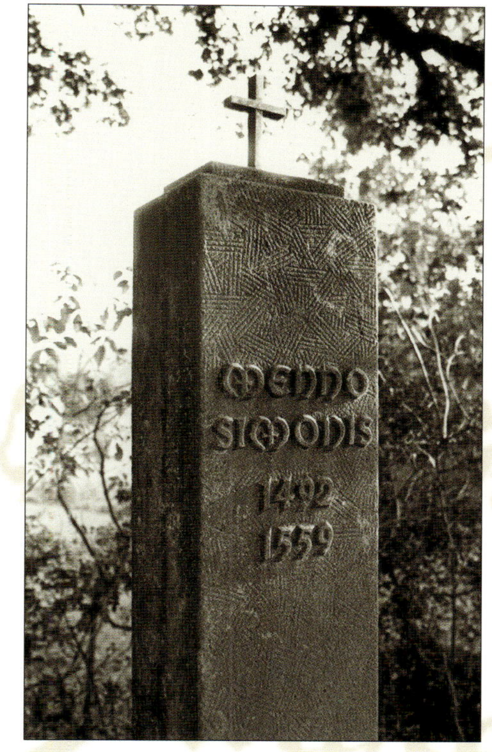

23b. *Memorial stone at Wüstenfelde, hidden under an oak tree(see p.10 for the dates)* - EVW

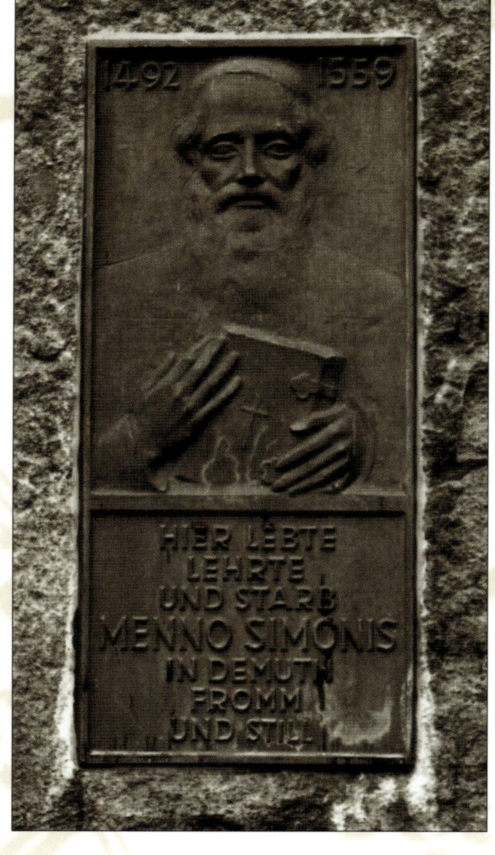

23a. *Memorial plaque in the back-garden of the Mennokate* - EVW

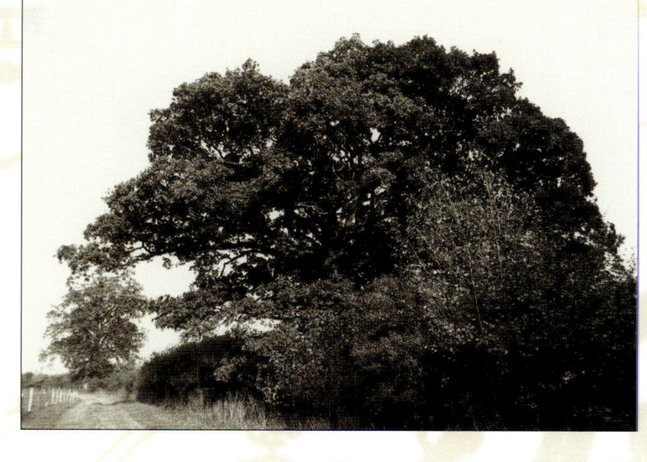

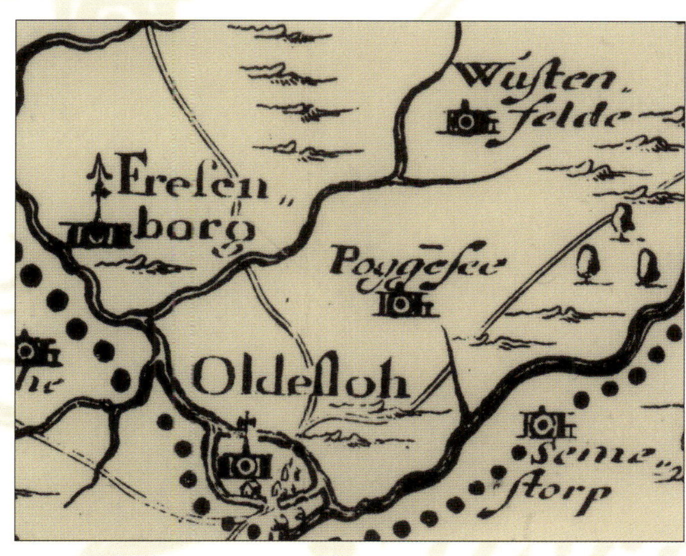

23c. J. Mejer, *Detail of the map of the Wagerland region* (1652) - UBA

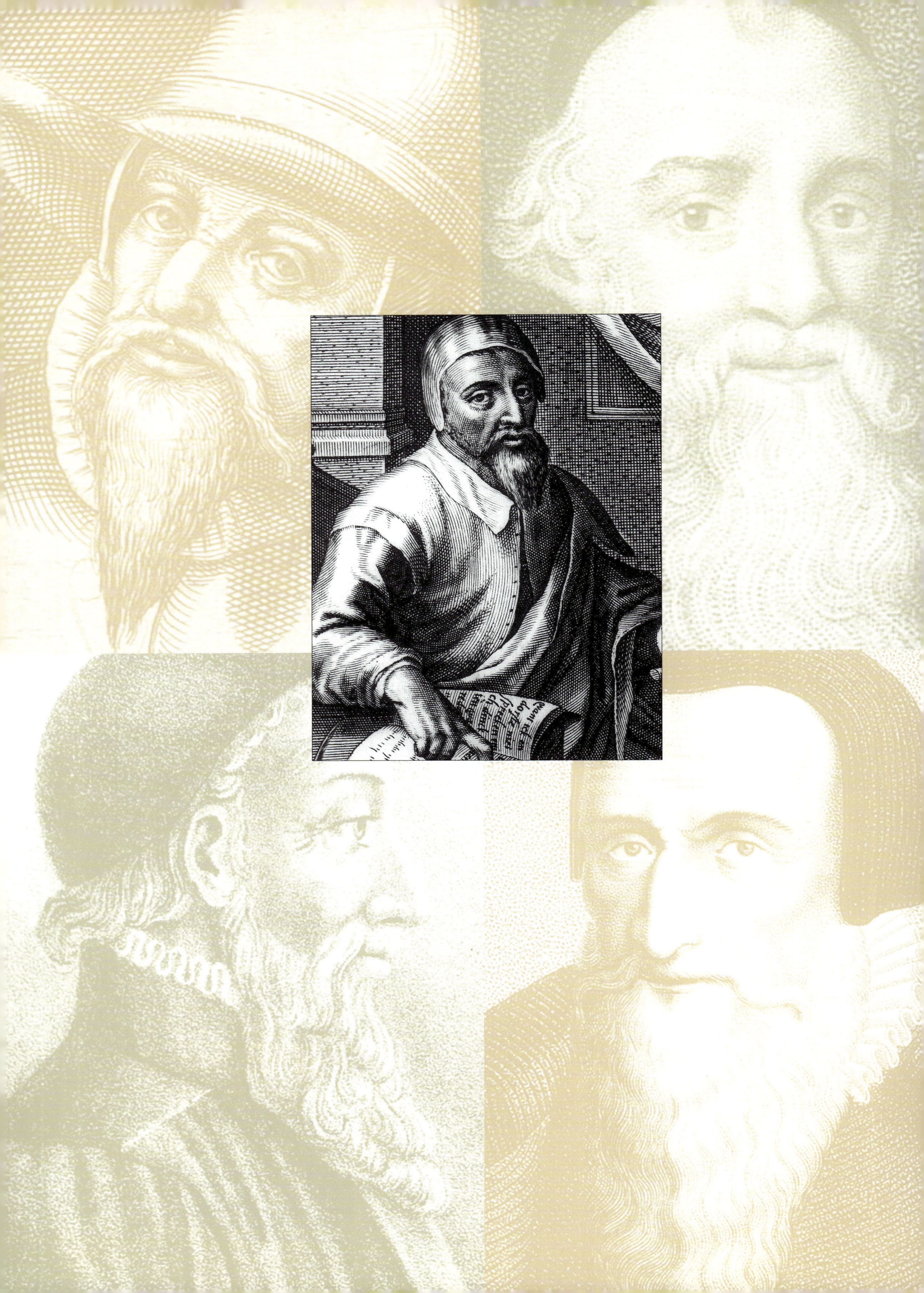

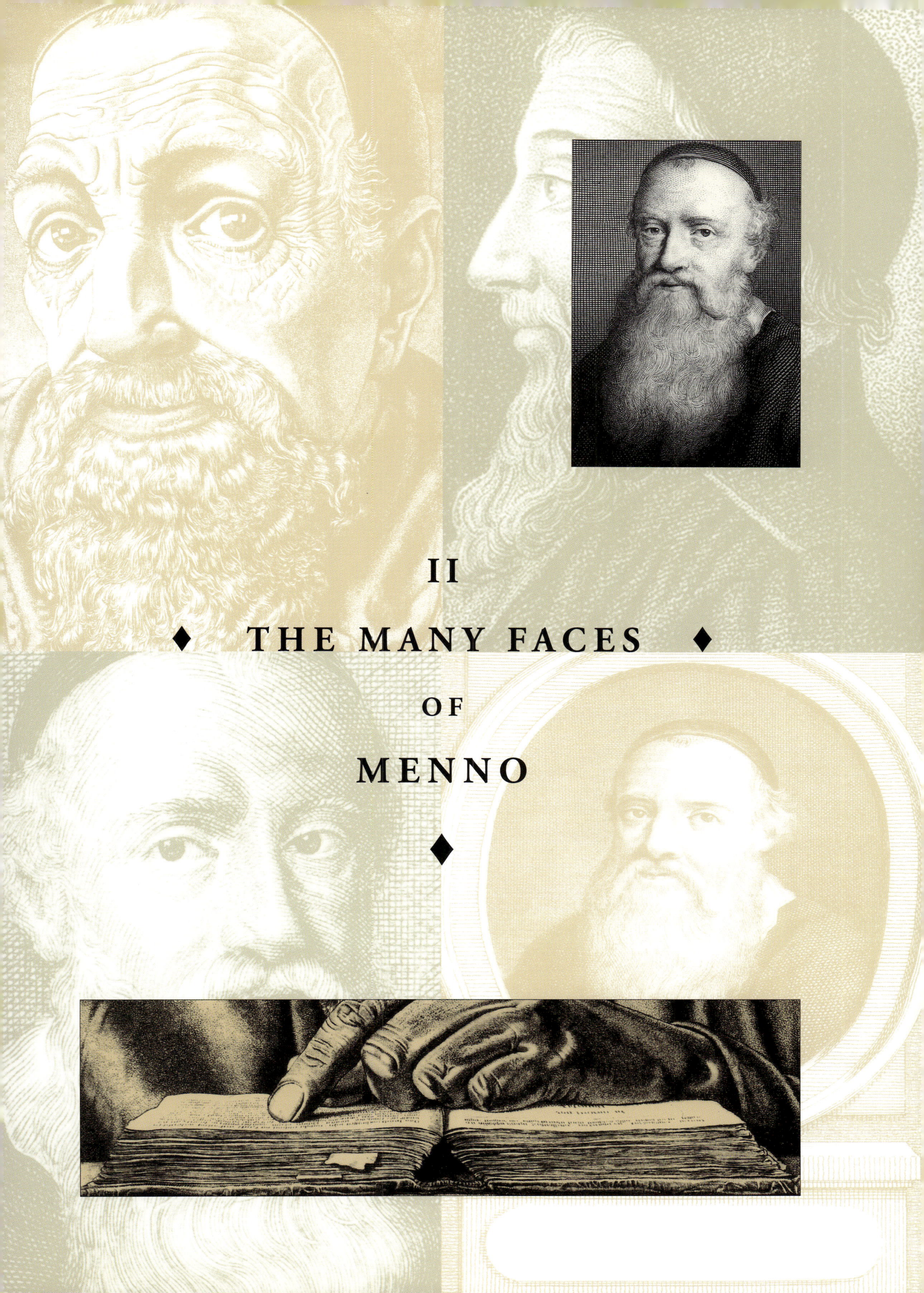

II

THE MANY FACES OF MENNO

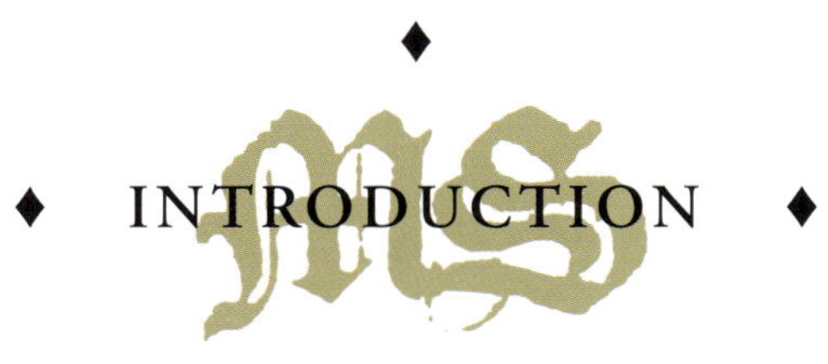

INTRODUCTION

In newspapers, books and on television we are flooded with the faces of prominent people recognizable in an instant. So too in the visual arts. The many self portraits made by Rembrandt from his youth on reveal the aging process of the painter. Even when he disguised himself as an Oriental or as the apostle Paul, we can recognize unerringly his striking head. Similarly, when we see a portrait of Menno Simons, we fortunately have a clear, previously formed image that makes recognition immediate. But what do we really see?

The earliest likeness, the engraving which Christoffel van Sichem I made of Menno (see 1), originated some 45 years after his death in 1561. It is therefore certainly not drawn 'from life'. How then, was the portrait conceived? The question is whether Van Sichem was aware of the description of Menno's appearance provided by Jan Neulen from Visschersweert in 1550: *A stout, fat, heavy man, broken or rough of face and a brown beard, could not walk well* (see part I, 14). A rough or broken face is not visible in this print. True, Menno is depicted with a crutch, but it was widely known that he walked with a limp. Yet this attribute becomes the focus for Van Sichem's characterization of Menno. Since we are looking at the portrait without foreknowledge, doubting its accuracy seems unreasonable. When placed next to Van Sichem's portrait of Adam Pastor (Holl 47), however, doubt does arise.

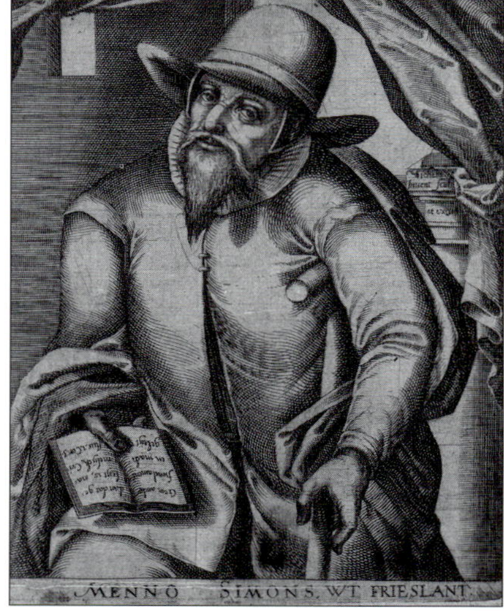

The artist apparently knew even less about Pastor's appearance. This we might conclude from a written description of both leaders in a letter of 19 June 1546 from Cleves: *and Menno seems to be a tall, corpulent man with a black shortly-trimmed beard, Adam Pastor is a tall man, having a pale face and short legs, both usually wearing Utrecht grey 'paltröcke' (small cloaks) and a rounded hat on their heads* (DB 55 (1918), p. 138). Van Sichem's portraits seem like two pictures of one and the same person: both men are of advanced age, furnished with beard and moustache and propped in simple habit with cloak and hat. Apart from their expressions the faces themselves are practically identical. What is absent from Pastor's portrait are the book and particularly the crutch: the only element distinct from Menno's portrait.

Both pictures belong to a series of portraits which were collected together in 1607 and 1608 under the title *Het tooneel der Hooft-Ketteren (The Stage of the Archheretics).* The series contains, along with the 'archheretic' Mohammed and the illustrious monk Broeder Cornelis, the most famous Anabaptist visages from the turbulent decade of the 1530's. What is remarkable is that Menno's portrait, dating from this same time, was *not* included therein. The accompanying texts provide explanations of their heresies, but the prints themselves are scarcely overdrawn. There are merely references, every now and then in background scenes, to the crimes of those portrayed; in the majority of cases the prints are presented nonjudgementally. Were the names and the explanations removed, we might interpret those portrayed as learned men of irreproachable conduct.

It is often supposed that the Catholic Van Sichem had intended his rendering of Menno as a satirical print (H 1). The crutch and the 'donkey ears' of the hat, or so the reasoning goes, formed the ingredients for the caricature of a foolish and spiritually crippled Menno. Such an interpretation cannot stand, however. As previously mentioned, the crutch was Van Sichem's only attribute to Menno's identity. At a time when medical science was less advanced, lameness appeared much more frequently. The nickname 'the lame' was not principally a name of derision, but served to distinguish him from 'Menno the blind', for ex-ample. Furthermore, was it not Menno himself who signed some of his writings with 'the lame'? In addition, the explanatory text speaks chiefly in positive terms about Menno, a 'very pious learned man'. The supposed 'donkey ears' on the hat are likely the unintentional result of this particular pose. Adam Pastor wears an identical hat, but the different angle of his head precludes misinterpretation. In other words, the fancied subtle derision is completely imagined. The argument is strengthened in that artists from this period had real donkey ears and fool's caps at their disposal by which to ridicule fools. It is illogical then, to deduce a caricatural interpretation within this series of heretics. A similar 'adaptation' would likely have been observed in heretics described in very negative fashion much earlier than Menno. But that, as we have said, has scarcely occurred. Most of the portraits are bound together by features such as gestures and the presence of books. Apparently the engraver intended these elements as a perfect means by which viewers would interpret the prints as self-styled character-portraits. In such a scenario the person portrayed is typified by means of traditional elements in the surroundings, by clothing and other attributes. Thankfully, the presence of books and particular gestures characterize those portrayed as 'interpreters of the scripture', or more generally as 'theologians' or 'scholars'. With certain men of the heretic series, such as with David Joris and Jan van Leyden, typifying was less important, because the features of the individual were well known.

The portrayal of someone whose appearance is not known has been a centuries-long problem for artists. From the end of the fifteenth century works which included portraits appeared intended for a public with a growing interest in history. The compilers did not hesitate in commencing their portrait series with pictures ranging from Adam and Eve to their contemporary princes (Haskell, pp. 26-79). The absence of sources therefore formed no insurmountable difficulty; inclusion was more important than accuracy. For such historical portrait series (for example of consecutive French kings, or popes) a stereotypical picture was frequently used, upon which were superimposed small variations. Problems became obvious only when similar series were compared with each other and disparities noted. Accuracy then indeed came into play, inducing a search for a solution. One such remedy created quite a stir in the last decade of the sixteenth century. Attempts were made to reveal character by comparing human features with those of animals (Haskell, pp. 61-64). This perspective, expounded by Pomponius Gauricus (1504), among others, returned to rather controversial physiognomic theories from classical antiquity. The Mennonite artist Karel van Mander (1604) was also familiar with this approach. Harking back to Aristotle these theorists believed, for example, that a large face pointed to ill-breeding, a fleshy face to love of ostentation, and a lean face to attributes including studiousness. Similar insights offered artists a workable method by which to create, on the basis of this theory, a supposedly reliable likeness of a deceased person.

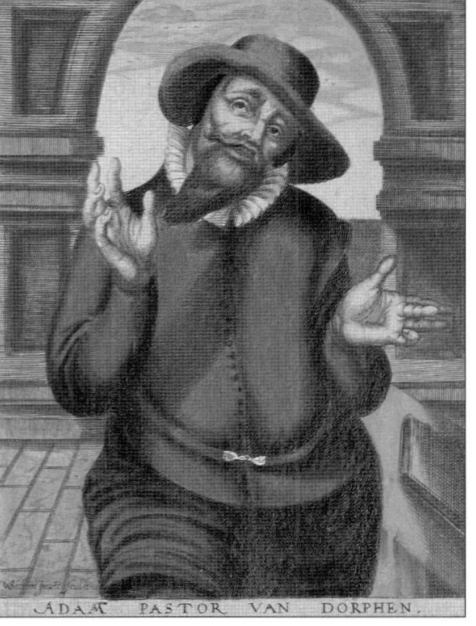

That such insights were applied literally in the specific case of the posthumous Menno portrait is naturally very questionable; although it is not impossible that they played a background role. If it is correct that Menno had a broken or rough countenance, then Van Sichem surely could, had he been aware of this framework, have taken pains to ensure that this distinguishing mark was not expressed too explicitly.

Accuracy came to the fore in the seventeenth century; however, this did not mean that no place remained for esthetic manipulation (Jongh 2, pp. 112-114). In the absence of factors limiting their control, the patron and the artist had the freedom to model a portrait according to their own insight, removing what appeared to them as unflattering elements. This explains why in Menno's later portraits his heretofore distinguishing mark, the crutch, has vanished. Menno was thus 'promoted' to the type-portrait of the learned which had come to flourish in the fifteenth century, with the portraits of Jerome and Erasmus acting as famous examples. These type-portraits frequently display the subject in profile or upper torso sitting or standing in the study where books and manuscripts demonstrate their erudition. The first full-length portrait of Menno in this setting appeared around 1662. The learned Menno is portrayed standing, every trace of lameness effaced, in an engraving attributed to Pieter Holsteyn (see 11.1). The portrait is, in respect to composition, entirely in accordance with Holsteyn's series of Erasmus, Luther, Melanchthon, Calvin and Arminius (Holl 33-37). This promotion to church reformer keeps pace with what was then a fairly general social elevatation of Mennonites in the Netherlands. The art of Luyken (nr. 24) and Burghart (nr. 31) further strengthened Menno's status as a gracious and respectable 'churchfather'.

Many temporally and contextually coded Mennos would of course continue to be recorded following this scheme. Where the crutch is missing, Menno the theologian can be typified by his beard, calotte and simple black habit. Through the iconological tradition, these specific details have filled in what was merely a sketchy outline, permitting the image to function as a unique and recognizable portrait through time. The accuracy of the picture is really no longer of any concern. As long as this general scheme remains fixed with these central distinguishing marks, small variations in the execution of the portrait will not diminish our powers of recognition. Thus the image of Menno's head is engraved in our memory and we can say every time, without hesitation, 'yes, this is Menno Simons'.

Daniel Horst

♦ ICONOGRAPHY OF MENNO PRINTS ♦

The history and elaboration of the portraits of Menno are rooted in the printed art - not in the painted arts. Therefore only portraits are described, transmitted via a graphic arts technique. What has been produced in painting or other forms of visual image (see the appendix) is rooted in large measure in this print tradition. A second demarcation concerns the charting of only 'serious' portraits. The last decade has seen the production of a number of Menno-gags, for example on badges and t-shirts, such as a Menno-Lisa or a cartoon-Menno. Obviously for practical reasons many of these frequently incidental and adapted portraits are not included. Some are depicted here in the appendix.

The classification is typological: each portrait that exists as a more or less independent model for a further development, is designated a main type. Those portraits which are successive variants and/or are derived from the main type (indicated by subnumbering) are described in chronological order. Gerrit Jacob Boekenoogen has laid the basis for this classification in his overview of Menno portraits in the *Doopsgezinde Bijdragen* of 1916. His still indispensible study is here posthumously honored.

The descriptions are kept as concise as possible. Later reproductions (in autotype and photos) mostly go unrecorded. The names of the designers (inv., del. or pinx.), makers (fec., sculp., ill. or lith.) and publishers (exc. or impr.) are standardized according to the commonly used rules of the art history literature. Their years of activty, as far as they are known, are given only if an exact dating is absent. The measurements (height x width) are provided in millimeters; with copper engravings the picture is measured along with the plate impression. For a complete listing of the literary references placed between brackets and the abbreviations of locations, see the end of the book.

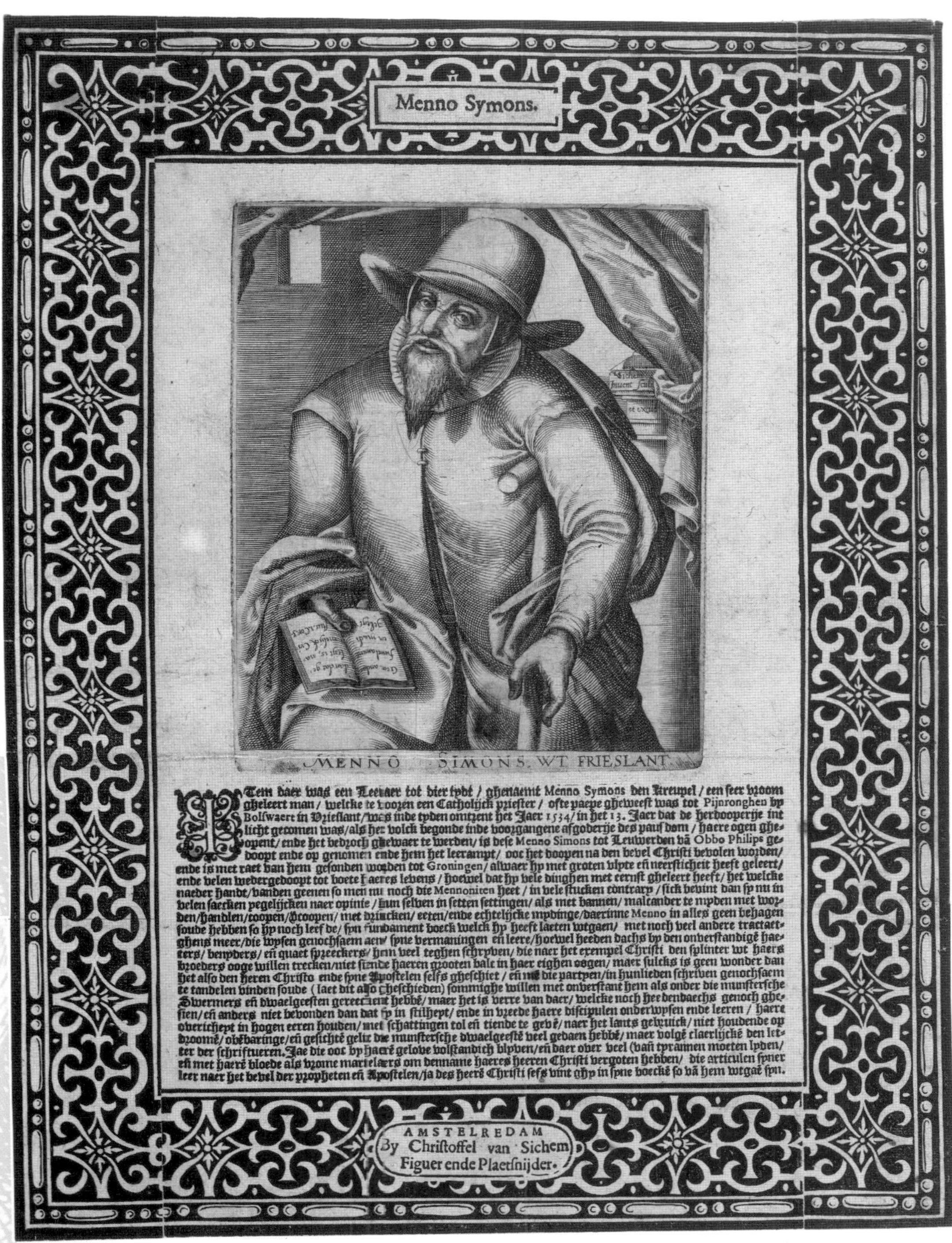

1a. ca. 1607

CHRISTOFFEL VAN SICHEM [I] inv., sculp , exc.

Engraving 151 x 127 / 160 x 129. *MENNO SIMONS. WT FRIESLANT.* Inside the printed ornamental frame with heading 'Menno Symons' and impressum of Van Sichem: 24-line typographical inscription: 'ITem daer ... syn.' (B 3a; Holl 37) - RPA; RPL; UBA-DG.

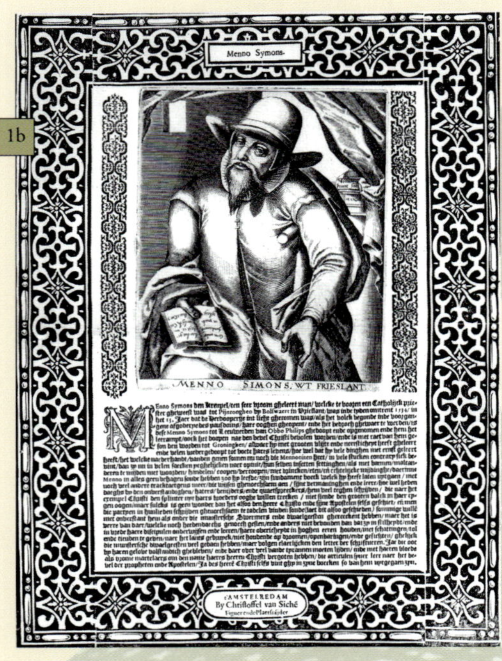
1b

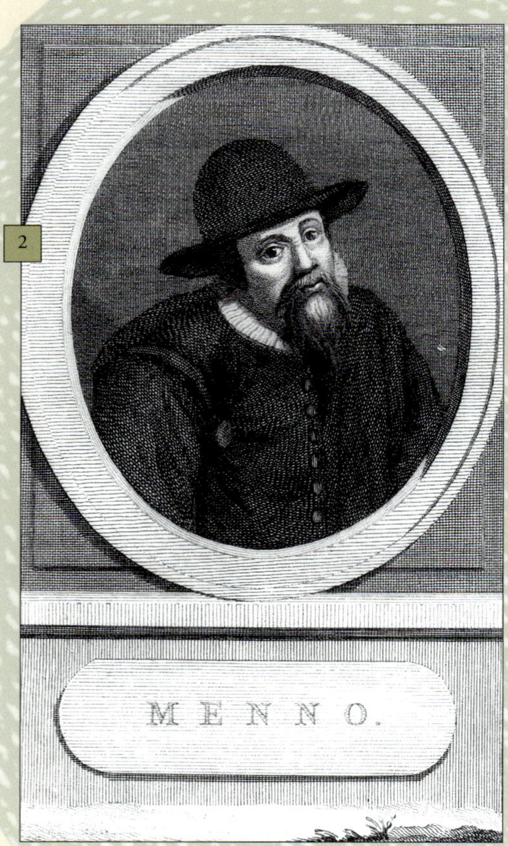
2

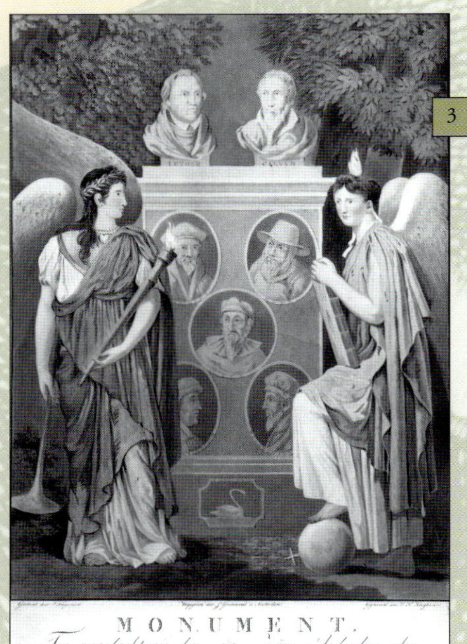
3

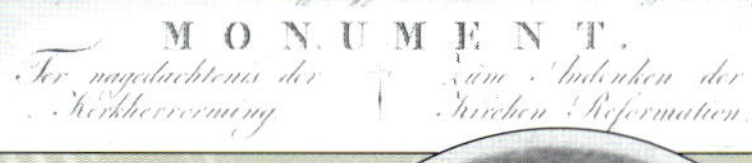

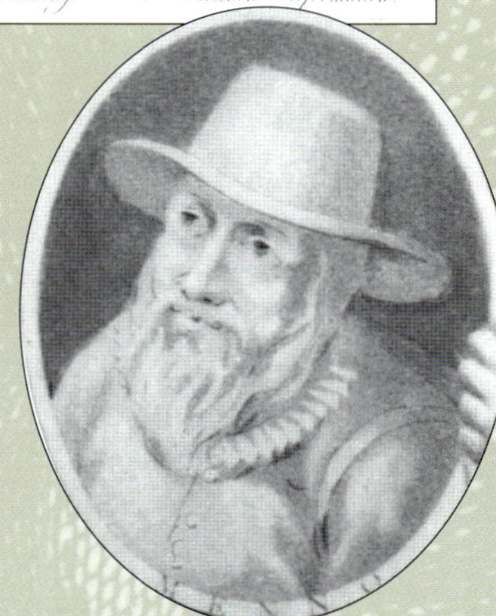

1b. As 1a, ca. 1608: 25-line with respect to a. corrected text: 'MEnno Symons ... zyn.' (Holl 37) - UBA-DG.

1c. As 1a, 1677: only the print in the same state in C. van Sichem, *Het Tooneel Der Hooft-Ketteren* (Middelburg 1677) (B 3b; H 1; M 3563; Holl 37 & 51) - UBA-DG; CCU.

2. end 18th century
ANONYMOUS
Engraving 148 x 87 / 242 x 184.
MENNO. (B 4b; H 2; M 3564) - UBA-DG; FML.

3. 1817
J. FRAGONARD del.; W. HOOGKAMER sculp.; J. GROENEWOUD [Amsterdam], exc.
Coloured engraving 520 x 350.
MONUMENT. // Ter nagedachtenis der Kerkhervorming / Zum Andenken der Kirchen-Reformation.
Images of the busts of Luther and Calvin on a tombstone with medallions of five reformers, among them Menno (M-his 6120) - AVS.

4.1 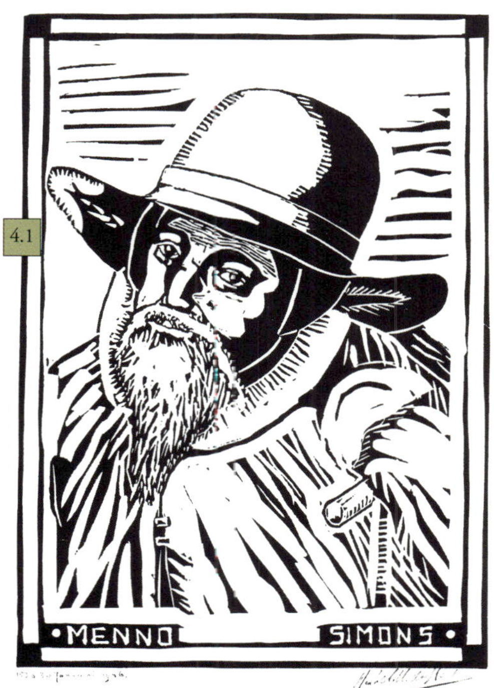

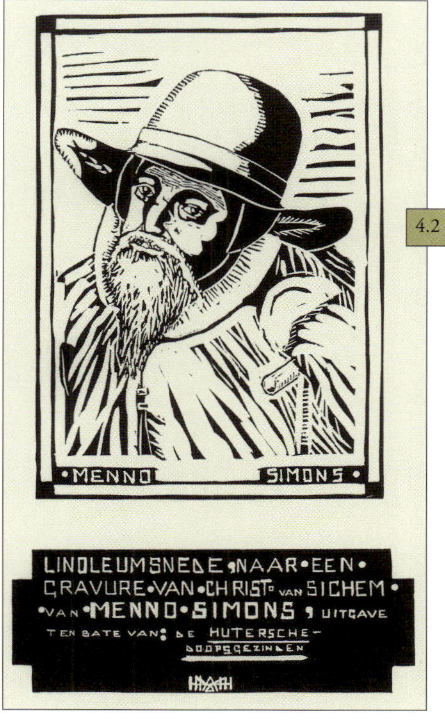 4.2

5 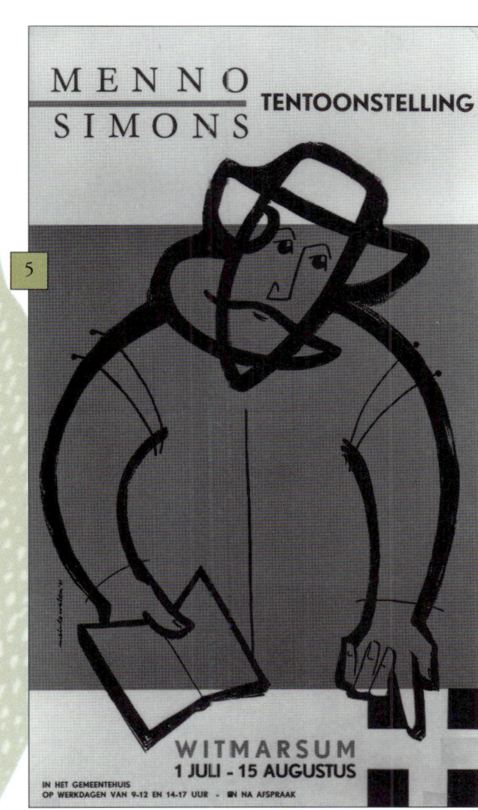

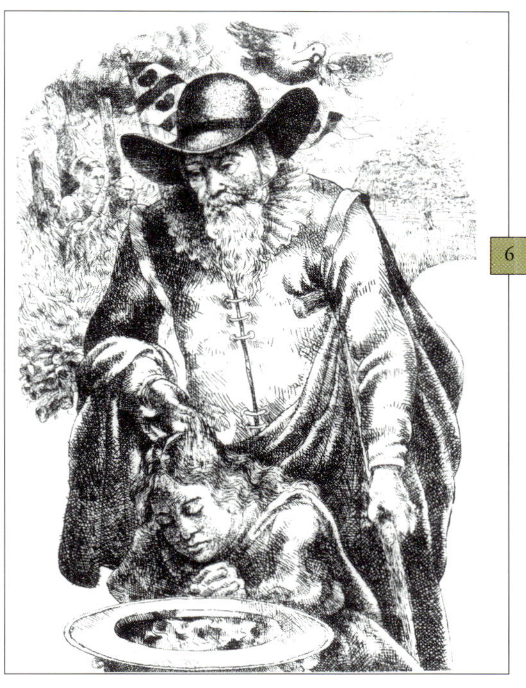 6

4.1 1936
HENDRIK ARNOLDUS
MARTINUS DEN HERDER
Linocut 150 x 106. Dated and signed in pencil: '1536 30 januari 1936 Henk A.M. den Herder' - UBA-DG.

4.2 1936
As 3.1: 209 x 124. *MENNO SIMONS,* with 5-line inscription: *Lioleumsnede. naar. ... doopsgezinden,* provided with Den Herder's monogram. Produced for the support of the Hutterites in Liechtenstein (*Zondagsbode* 49 (1936) nr. 14, p. 54; cf. H 3) - UBA-DG.

5. 1961
MEINTE WALTA
Three colored print 596 x 352. *MENNO SIMONS TENTOONSTELLING,* with 4-line text: *Witmarsum ... na afspraak.* Poster for the exhibition in Witmarsum (Friesland) in 1961 to commemrate the 400th anniversary of Menno's death (H 4) - UBA-DG.

6.1996
ENRIC ADSERÀRIBA
Etching 156 x 110. Made in commission by C. Knijnenberg for P. Visser, *Indruk van Menno Simons in druk* (Krommenie, Knijnenberg bv, 1996) - UBA-DG.

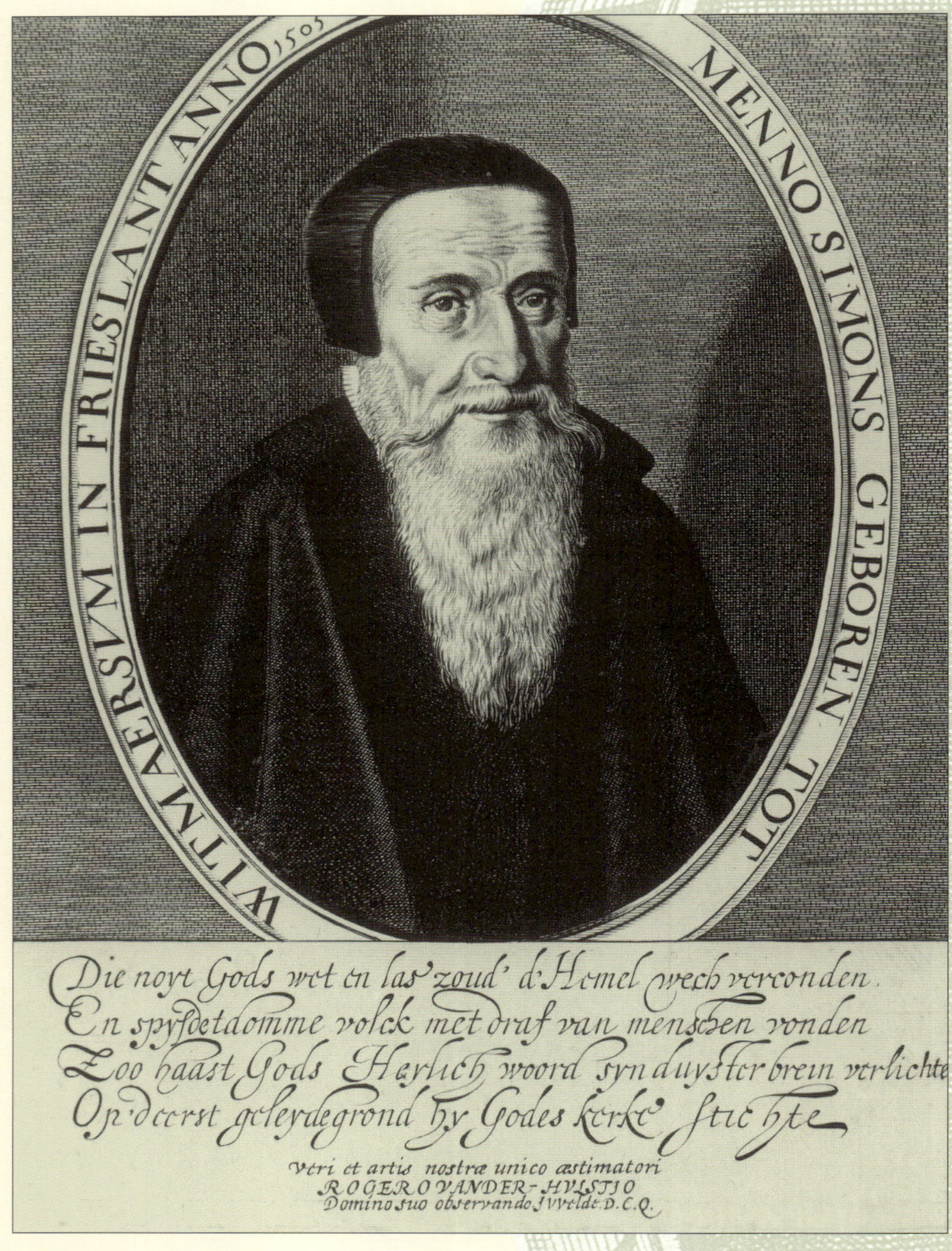

7.1 ca. 1625
JAN VAN DE VELDE [II] [1593-1641; inv.]
Engraving: 162 x 162 / 216 x 170. Legend *MENNO SIMONS GEBOREN TOT WITMARSVM IN FRIESLANT ANNO 1505,* 4-line inscription in rhyme *Die noyt ... stichte* and 3-line dedication *veri et ... D.C.Q.* by Van de Velde to Rogier van der Hulst (1566-1536) (B 7a; H 6; Holl 409[I]) - GAH.

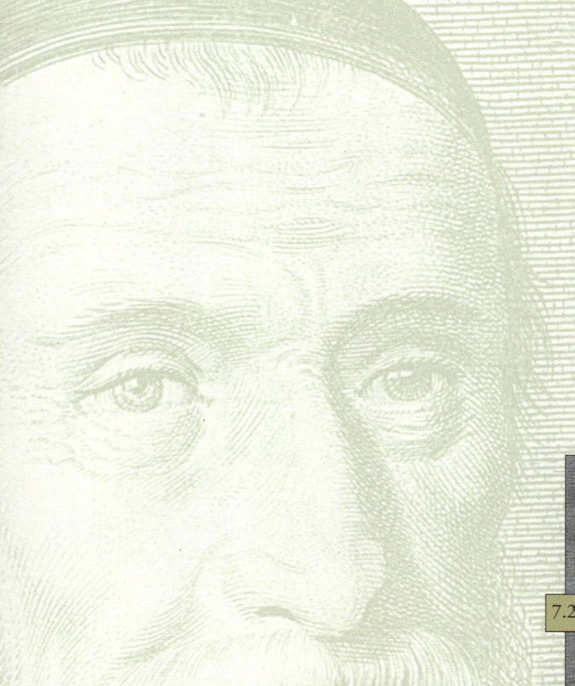

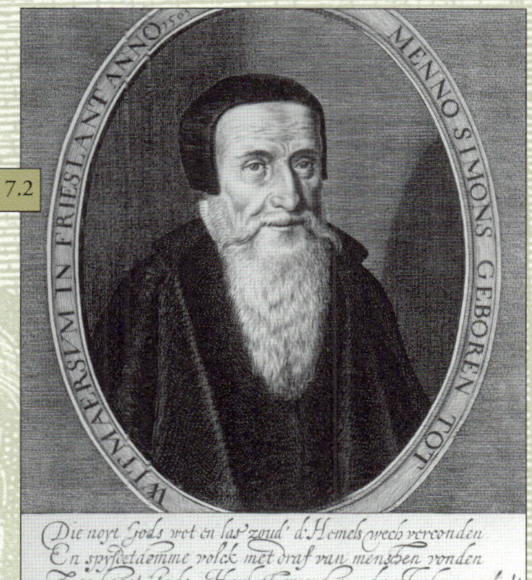

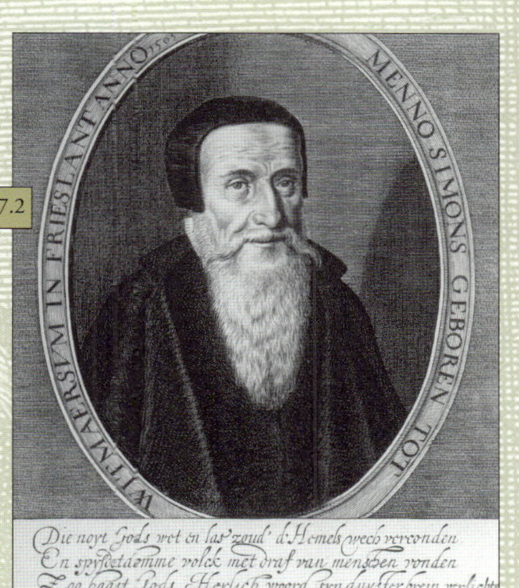

7.2

7.3

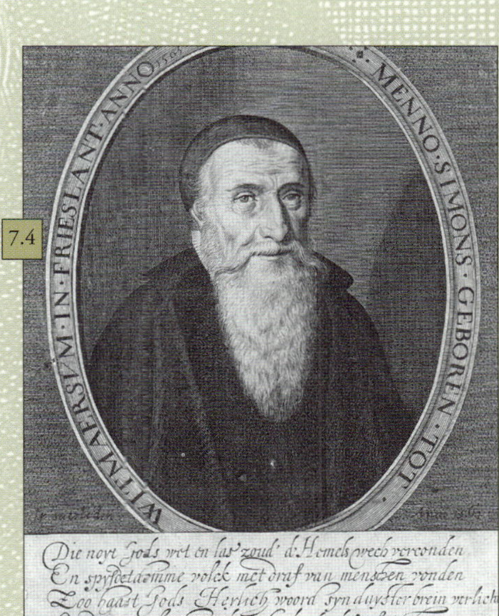

7.4

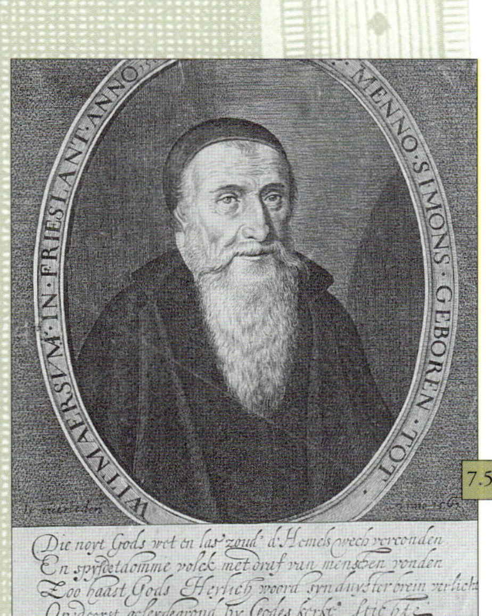

7.5

7.2 ca. 1640
As 7.1.: CORNELIS KONING [fec., Haarlem, ca. 1610-1671], exc.
Medallion legend with shading; extra shading on other parts. (B 7b; W 322; Holl 409^{II}) - RPA.

7.3 ca. 1650
As 7.2: the headgear is changed, so that the right ear and a small tuft of hair is made visible (B 7c) - UBA-DG.

7.4 < 1696
As 7.3: under which is added *Is overleden Anno 1561;* the 3-line dedication is missing (B 7d; H 7; Holl 409^{III}) - FML.

7.5 ca. 1700
As 7.4: added CORNELIS DANCKERTSZ [II; Amsterdam, ca. 1696-1717] exc. (B 7e; Holl 409^{IV}) - FML; RPA.

8.1

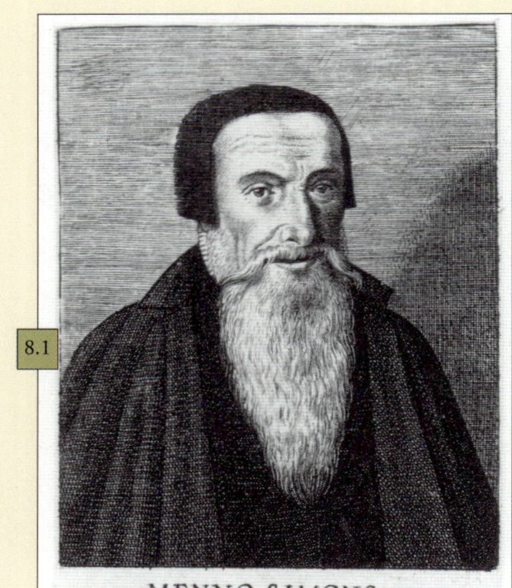

9b

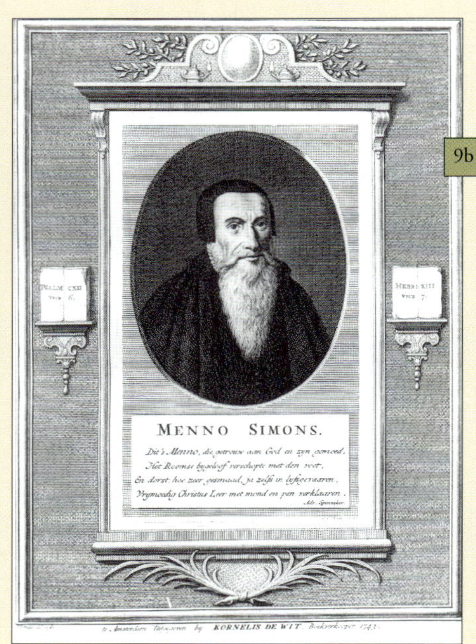

9a

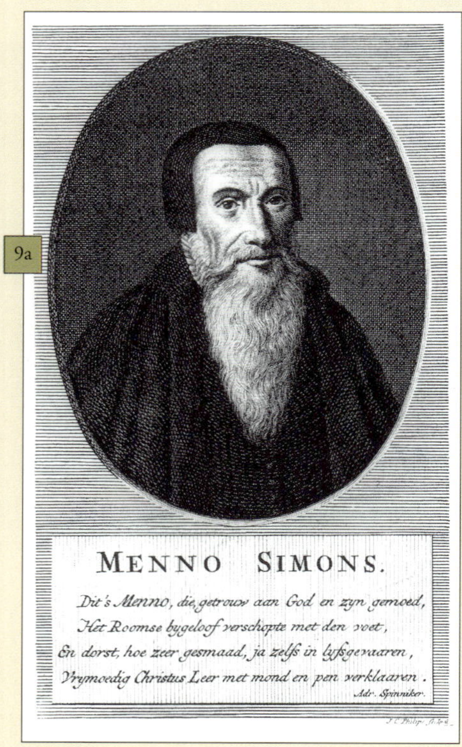

10

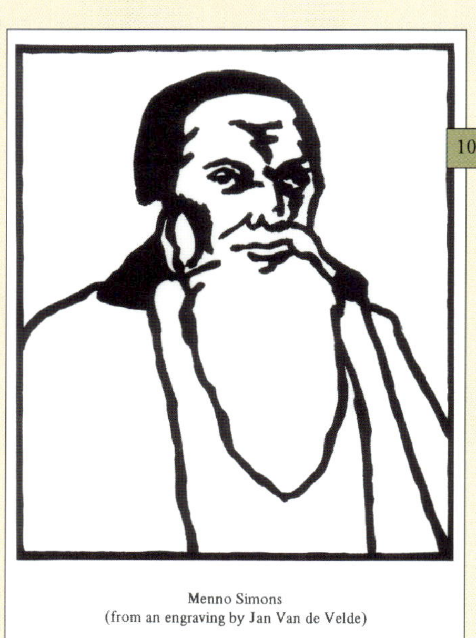

Menno Simons
(from an engraving by Jan Van de Velde)

8.1 ca. 1635

JAN VAN DE VELDE [II] [inv.] fec. / HANS PASSCHIERS VAN WESBUSCH [Haarlem, 1623-1648] exc.

Engraving: 82 x 65 / 114 x 68. *MENNO SIMONS.*, with 4-line inscription in rhyme: *Die noyt ... stichte* (B 6a; H 5; Holl 410[I]; vS 3590a) - RPA; UBA-DG; FML.

8.2 ca. 1650

As 8.1: new publisher PIETER ZACHARIASZ HARTEVELT [Hoorn, 1639-1661] exc. (B 6b; Holl 410[II]; vS 3590b) - SMK.

9a. 1743

JAN CASPAR PHILIPS sculp. / [KORNELIS DE WIT, Amsterdam, exc.]

Engraving 133 x 79 / 137 x 83. *MENNO SIMONS*, with 4-line rhymed inscription *Dit's Menno ... verklaaren* by Adriaan Spinniker. Illustration in Schyn/Maatschoen, *Uitvoeriger Verhandeling Van De Geschiedenisse Der Mennoniten* [II] (Amsterdam 1744), opposite p. 214. The same state is found in *Verzaameling van ... Doopsgezinde Leeraaren* (Amsterdam, Jan Morterre, 1780), nr. I (B 9, 9c en 9d; H 8) - UBA-DG; FML.

9b. As 9a, furnished with a separately engraved framing (211 x 157) with the name of Philips and De Wit, 1743, in *Verzaameling Van ... Veele Voorname Mannen en Leeraren* (Amsterdam 1743), nr. 1 (B 9b; M 3561) - UBA-DG; UBA; FML.

10. 1976

MARCIA S. STAYER

Pen drawing in off-set 116 x 98. Below in print 'Menno Simons (from an engraving by Jan Van de Velde)'; illustration in J.M. Stayer, *Anabaptists and the sword - New Edition* (Lawrence, KS, 1976), p. 307 - UBA-DG.

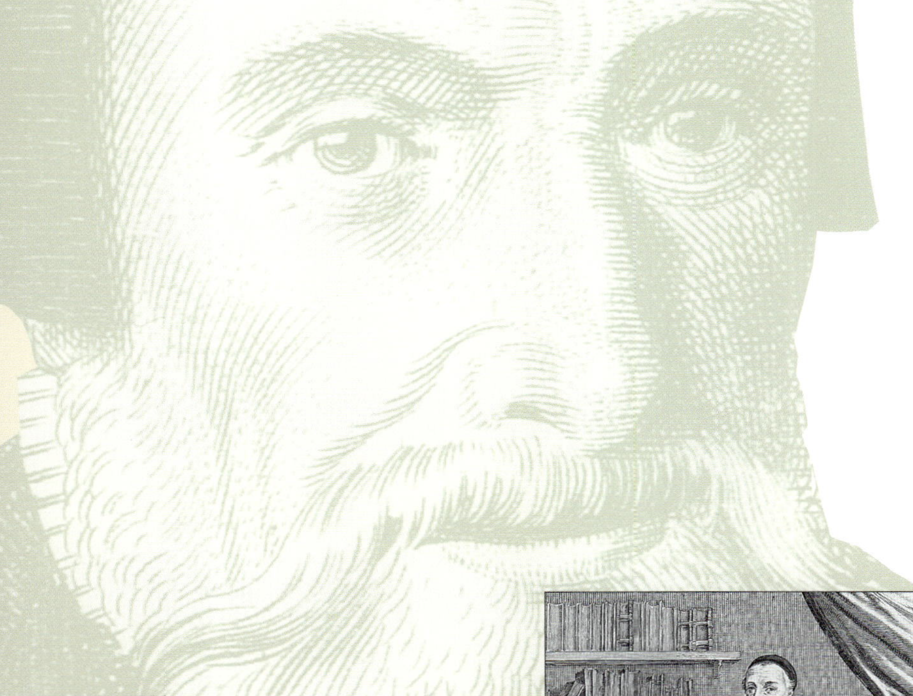

VAN DE VELDE/(HOLSTEYN) TYPE

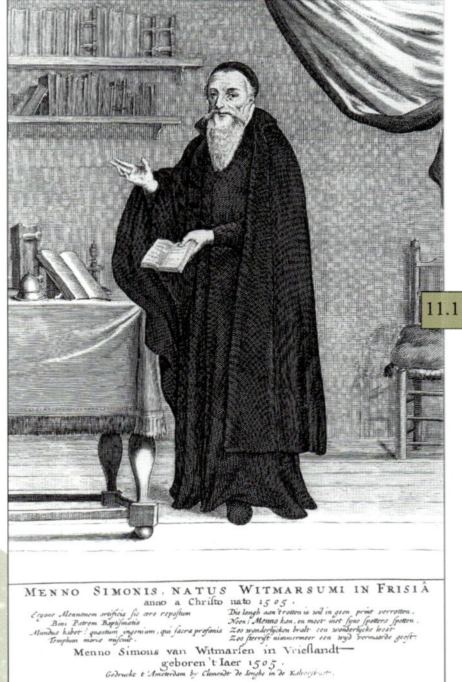

11.1

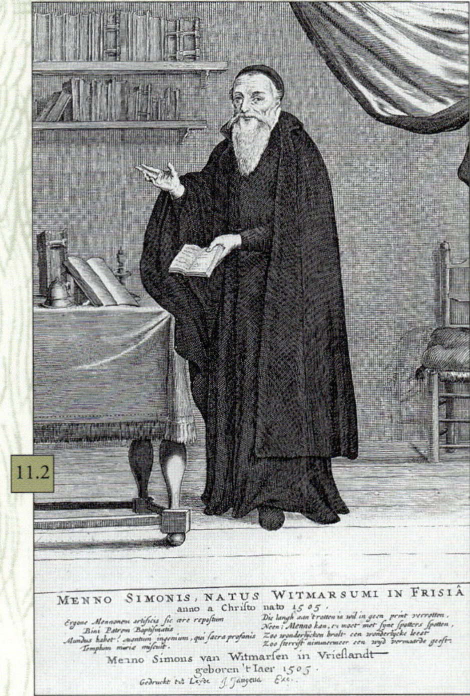

11.2

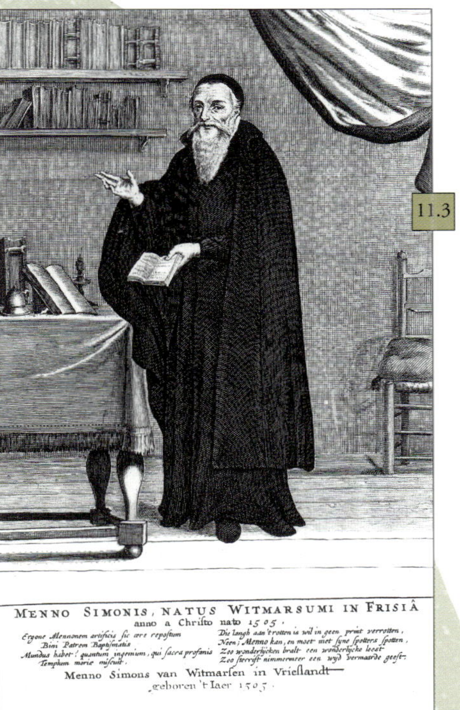

11.3

11.1 ca. 1662
CLEMENT DE JONGHE [Amsterdam, Kalverstraat 1662-1677] exc.
Engraving [by Pieter Holsteyn?] 267 x 200 / 316 x 210. *MENNO SIMONIS, NATUS WITMARSUMI IN FRISIÂ // anno a Christo nato 1505.*, plus 2x 4-line rhyme: *Ergone Mennonem ... geest* and the Dutch version of the inscription in 2 lines (B 10a; M 3549; cf. Holl 33-37) - FML.

11.2 ca. 1687
As 11.1: new publisher JOHANNES TANGENA [Leiden, 1683-1691] exc. (B 10b; M 3548) - FML.

11.3 ca. 1700
As 11.2: without printer's name. The underside of the *g* of 'geboren' and *5* of '1505' are cut off (B 10c; M 3550) - UBA-DG; FML.

12.1 < 1663
JAN CRALINGE [Amsterdam, 1655-1663] exc.
Engraving 260 x 202 / 315 x 212. *MENNO SIMONIS, NATUS WITMARSUMI IN FRISIÂ anno a Christo nato 1505,* plus 2x 4-line rhyme: *Ergone Mennonem ... geest* and the Dutch version of the inscription in 2 lines. The collar is omitted; small text variants (B 13a; M 3548) - L.U.

12.2 ca. 1700
As 12.1: new publisher EVERT VAN SWEYNEN [Amsterdam, ca. 1686-1710] exc. (B 13b; W 685) - L.U.

13
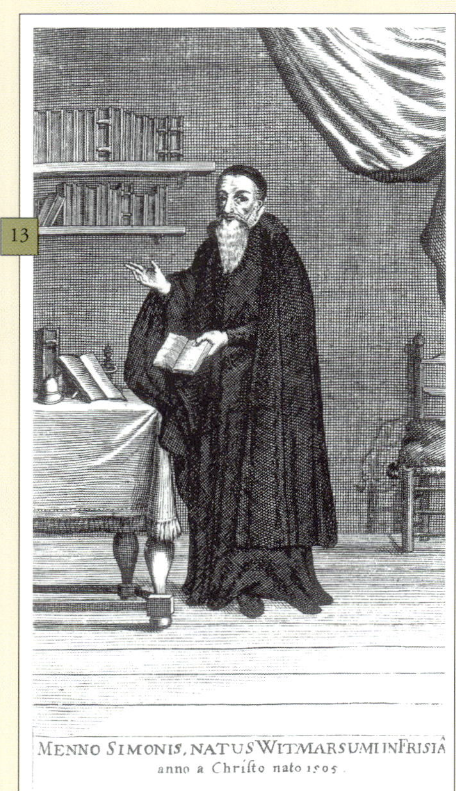

14
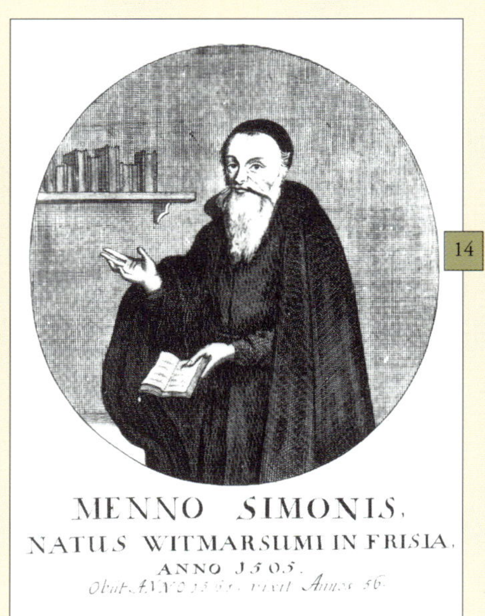

15
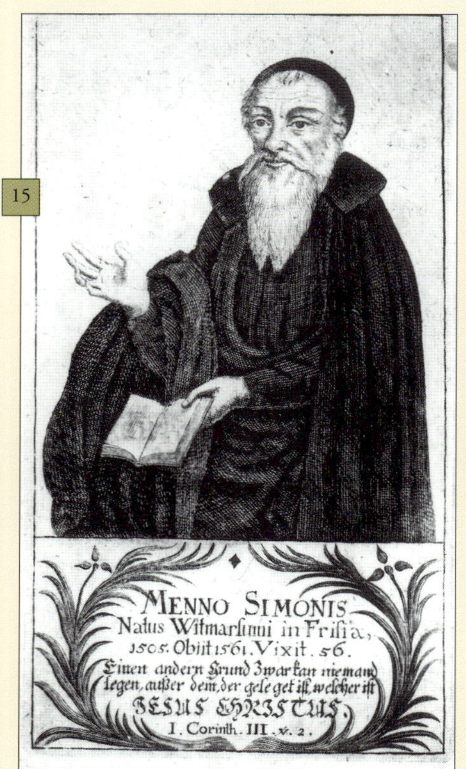

16
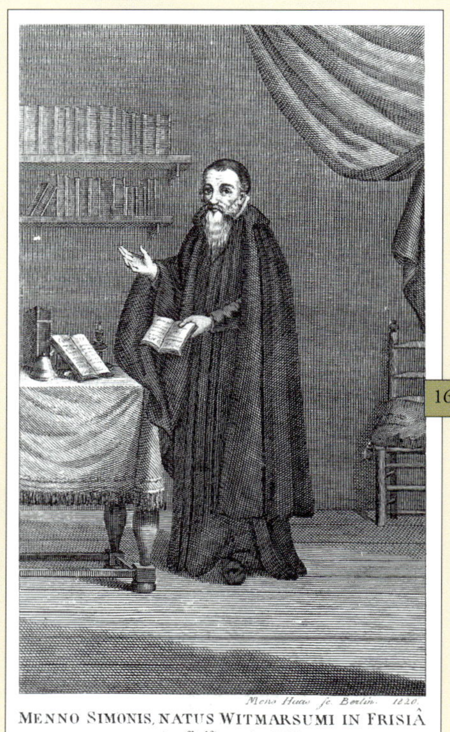

13. 1698
ANONYMOUS
Engraving 140 x 80 / 156 x >99. *MENNO SIMONIS, NATUS WITMARSUMI IN FRISIA // anno a Christo nato 1505.* Illustration in H.L. Benthem, *Holländischer Kirch- und Schulen-Staat* (Frankfurt & Leipzig, Nicolaus Föster / Hannover, Merseburg, Christian Gottschick, 1698), opposite p. 825 (B 11) - UBA-DG; UBA.

14. 1702
ANONYMOUS
Engraving 150 x 139 / 195 x 162. *MENNO SIMONIS, // NATUS WITMARSUMI IN FRISIA, // ANNO 1505. // Obiit ANNO 1561. vixit Annos 56.* Illustration in *Alte und Neue Schwarm-Geister-Bruth* ([Frankfurt am Main], n.p., 1702), opposite p. 362 (B 14; H 9; vS 3588) - UBA-DG.

15. ca. 1705
ANONYMOUS
Engraving 101 x 78 / 144 x 81. *MENNO SIMONIS*, plus 6-line inscription in palm cartouche *Natus Witmarsumi ... 1. Corinth. III.v.2.*[= 11]; bookshelve is omitted. Frontispiece of Menno Simons, *Der Ausgang oder Bekehrung* (Frankfurt & Leipzig, Abraham Jerischen, n.y.) (B 15; Bircher B 4891) -UBA-DG.

16. 1820
MENO HAAS [Berlin] sculp.
Engraving 139 x 83 / 172 x >110. *MENNO SIMONIS, NATUS WITMARSUMI IN FRISIÂ // anno a Christo nato 1505.* Frontispiece of G.L. von Reiswitz & F. Wadzeck, *Beiträge zur Kenntniß der Mennoniten-Gemeinden in Europa und America* (Berlin 1821) (B 12) - UBA-DG.

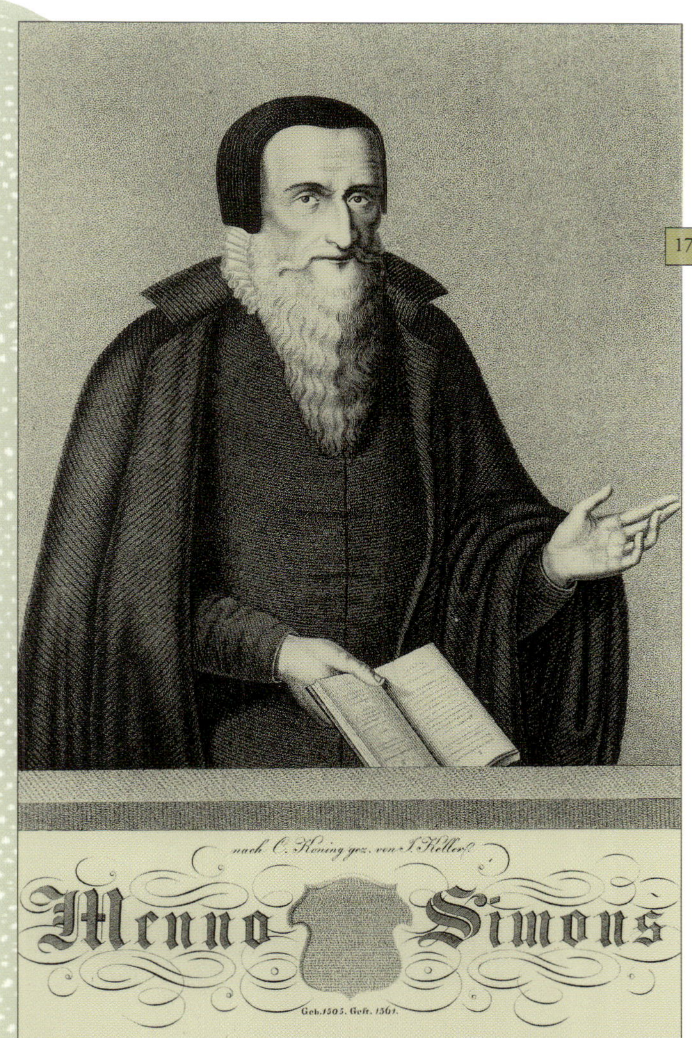

17

17. ca. 1830
JOSEF KELLER fec. / C. SCHULGEN-BETTENDORFF [copper printshop, Bonn] exc.
Engraving 202 x 166 / 298 x 223. *Menno / Simons,* below which *Geb. 1505. Gest. 1561.* The portrait is based on nr. 7.2 [*nach C. Koning*] and 12 (B 16; H 10; M 3559; vS 3589) - UBA-DG; FML.

18. ca. 1835
J.M. BILLROTH [art dealer, Groningen, 1829->1850]
Litho 200 x 165. *Menno / Simons* (B 17) - L.U.

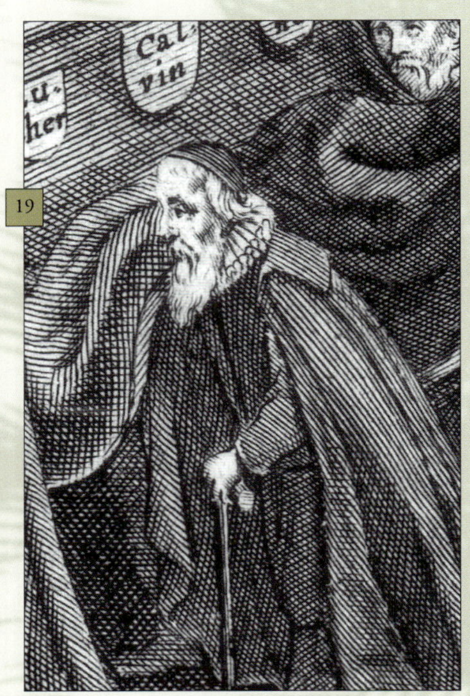

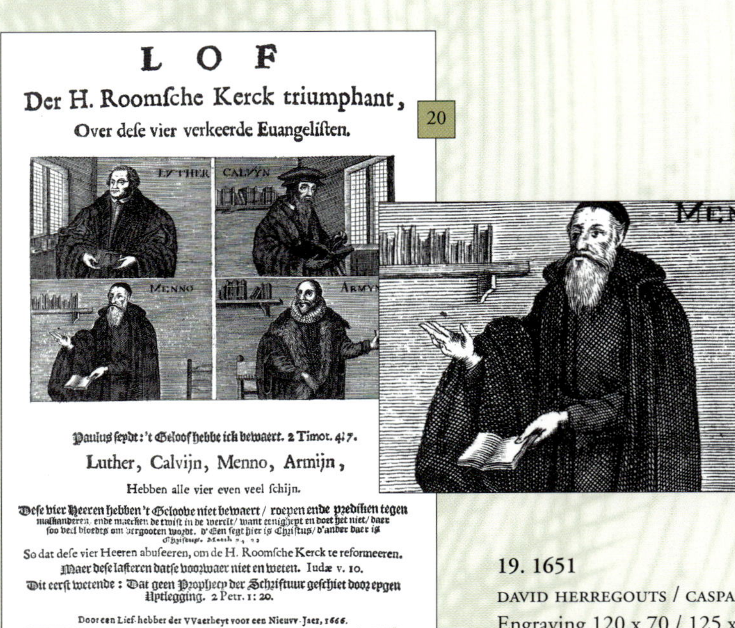

LOF
Der H. Roomſche Kerck triumphant,
Over deſe vier verkeerde Euangeliſten.

Paulus ſeydt: 't Geloof hebbe ick bewaert. 2 Timot. 4:7.

Luther, Calvijn, Menno, Armijn,

Hebben alle vier even veel ſchijn.

Deſe vier Heeren hebben 't Geloove niet bewaert / roepen ende predicken tegen malkanderen, ende maecken de twiſt in de wereldt / want eenigheyt en doet het niet / daer soo veel bloedts om vergooten wordt. d'Een segt hier is Christus / d'ander daer is Christus. Matth. 24, 23

So dat deſe vier Heeren abuſeeren, om de H. Roomſche Kerck te reformeeren.

Maer deſe laſteren datſe voorwaer niet en weten. Iudæ v. 10.

Dit eerſt wetende: Dat geen Prophecy der Schriftuur geschiet door eygen Uytlegging. 2 Petr. 1: 20.

Door een Lief-hebber der VVaerheyt voor een Nieuvv-Jaer, 1666.

Te Roermunde, by NICOLAES PETTER, 1667.

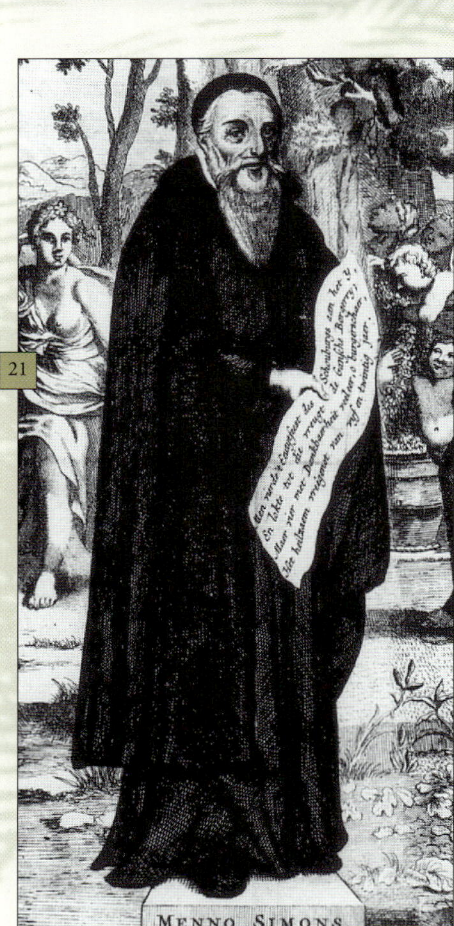

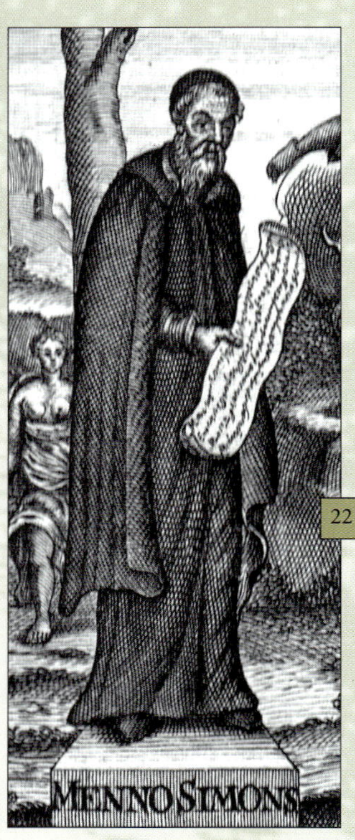

19. 1651
DAVID HERREGOUTS / CASPAR DU PREE impr.
Engraving 120 x 70 / 125 x 75, in which Menno walks with four others, bearing a coffin. Part of the frontispiece of *Uitvaert Van alle Oncatholijcke Religien* (Roermond 1651) (see p. 117) - UBA.

20. 1666/67
ANONYMOUS
Engraving 70 x 105 / 73 x 110. Picture of Luther, Calvin, Arminius and Menno (bottom left; 35 x 53) on the titlepage of *Lof der H. Roomsche Kerck triumphant, over dese vier verkeede Euangelisten ... voor een Nieuw-Jaer 1666* (Roermond, Nicolaes Petter, 1667) (B 18) - UBA.

21. 1738
ANONYMOUS
Engraving 500 x 585 / 509 x 619. *Jubel Feest des Amsteldamschen Schouburgs 1738,* in which Menno is flanked by Luther and Calvin. The text in Menno's hand says: *Men vierde 't Eeutytfeest des Schouburgs aan het Y, // En lokte tot die vreugt de Gansche Borgery; // Maer vier met Dankbaerheit veel eer, o burgerschaer, // Het heilzaem vreêgenot van vyf en twintig jaer.* (One celebrated the centenary of the Theatre on the River IJ, And persuaded the entire citizenry to be joyful; But celebrate with gratitude instead, o citizens, The beneficial peace treaty these five and twenty years) (see p. 115) (M-his 3763) - UBA-DG; RPA.

22. 1738
ANONYMOUS
As 21: Engraving 148 x 168 / 157 x 176. Reduced copy of nr. 21 (see M-his 3763) - UBA.

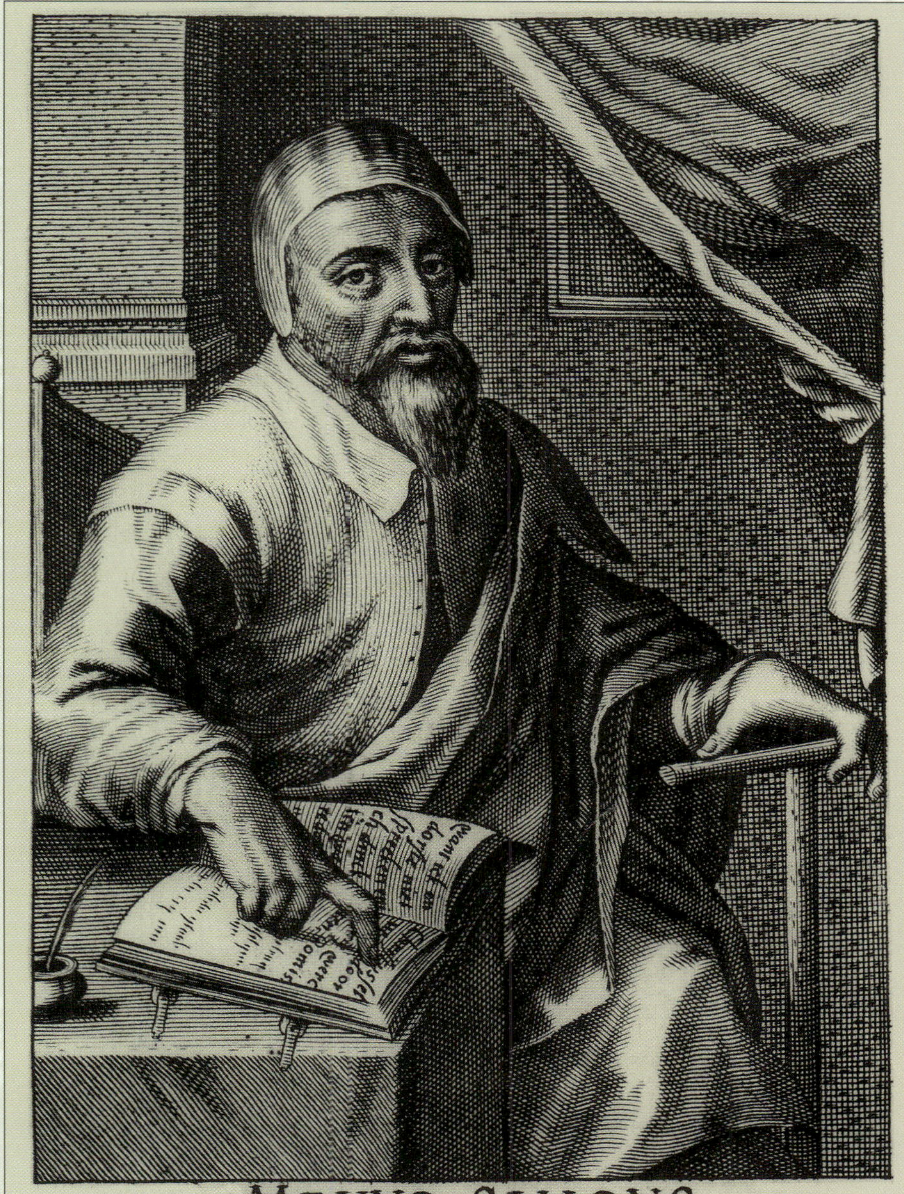

23. ca. 1650
ABRAHAM DE COOGE fec.
Engraving 128 x 93 / 149 x 98. *MENNO SIMONS*, with 2-line inscription: *Daer en mach ... i Corr : 3.*[:11] (B 5; Holl 2) - UBA-DG; RPA.

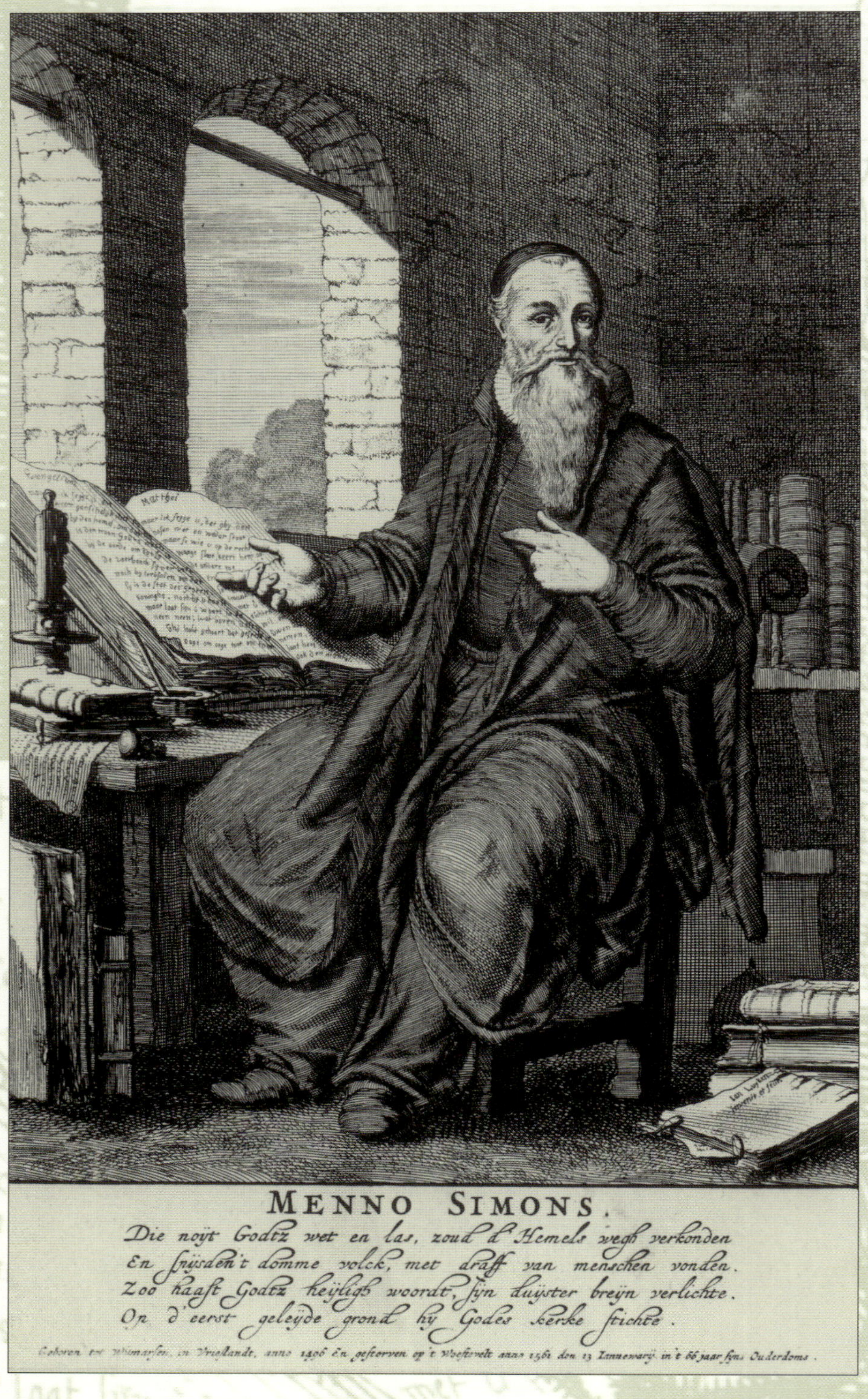

24. 1681

JAN LUYKEN inv., fec.

Engraving 235 x 169 / 275 x 175. *MENNO SIMONS,* with 4-line inscription in rhyme: *Die noijt ... stichte;* final line *Geboren te Witmarsen ... Ouderdoms.* In Menno Simons, *Opera Omnia Theologica* (Amsterdam 1681), opposite p. **4^{v}. The copperplate is located in UBA-DG (B 19; H 11; M 3556k; vE&vdK 46 [370]) - UBA-DG; UBA; RPA; RPL; AHM; CCU.

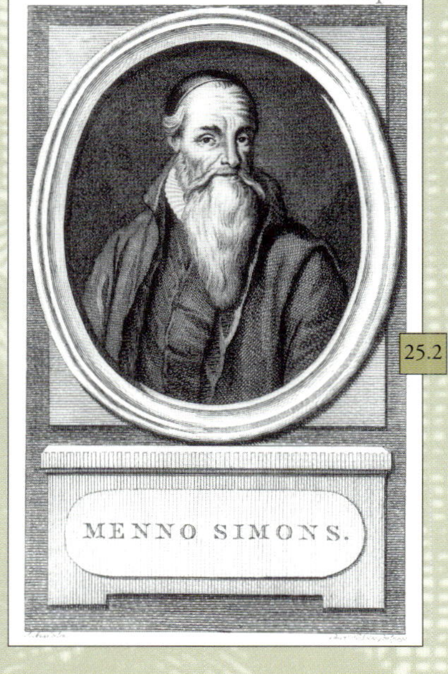

25.2

25.1 1792
JACOB BUYS del. / REINIER VINKELES sculp.
Engraving 148 x 89 / 238 x 159. Without inscription (B 20a; M 3558) - FML.

25.2 1792
As 25.1: *MENNO SIMONS;* above right: *XXVII.Dl.pl.II.* Illustration in J. Kok, *Vaderlandsch Woordenboek* (Amsterdam, Johannes Allard, 1792) vol. 27, opposite p. 96 (B 20b; H 12; M 3557) - UBA-DG; UBA; FML.

26. 1876
ACME.CO (?) [Chicago]
Woodcut 164 x 116. In print 'Menno Simons.', with 2-line inscription 'Geboren zu ... Alters.' Titleprint of Menno Simons, *Die vollständigen Werke* (Elkart, Indiana, Mennonitische Verlags-Handlung, 1876) (B 24) - UBA-DG.

27. 1893
ANONYMOUS
Litho (diameter 52). Illustration of the commemorative medal for the occasion of the 150th anniversary of the *FRIESCHE DOOPSGEZINDE SOCIETEIT* in 1845, commissioned by T.A. Keikes, in J. Dirks, *Atlas ... der Nederlandse ... Penningen* (Haarlem, Erven Bohn, 1893) IVth piece, plate LXXVII nr. 638 (B 23) - MMR.

28. (1936) 1986
[JOHAN MEKKINK]
Photo 93 x 116 of a stained glass window in the House Mooi-Land at Doorwerth (1936). At the top: *MATTH V vs XXXIV-XLVIII* and below *MENNO SIMONS.* Illustration in H.J. Leloux, *Kroniek Van Mooi-Land Doopsgezind Tehuis 1936-1986* (Zutphen, De Walburg Pers, 1986), p. 8. - UBA-DG.

29. 1986
E. KIESTRA
Pen drawing 80 x 40. Illustration on the back jacket cover of H.J. Leloux, *Kroniek* (see 28) - UBA-DG.

25.1
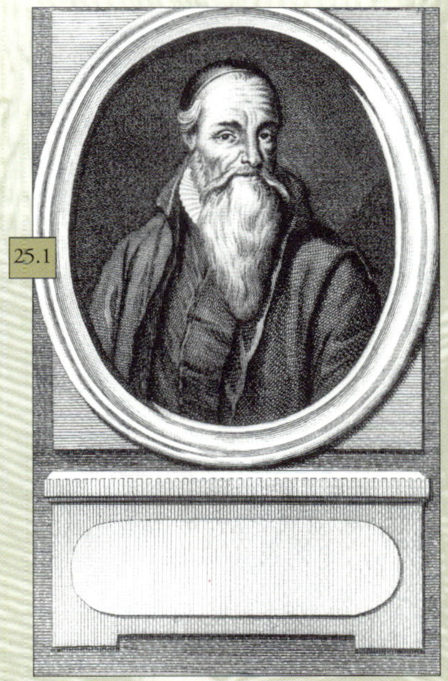

26
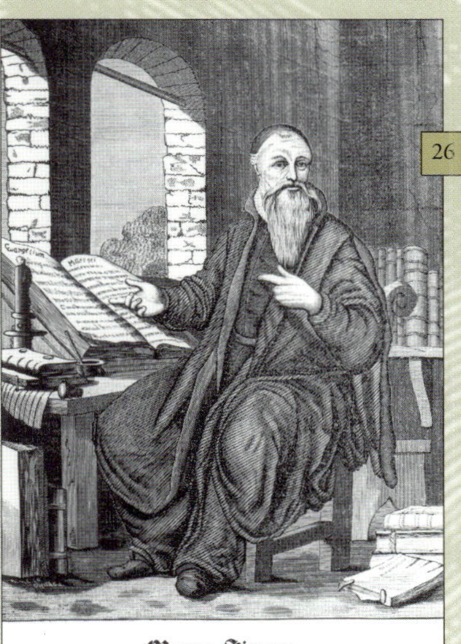

27
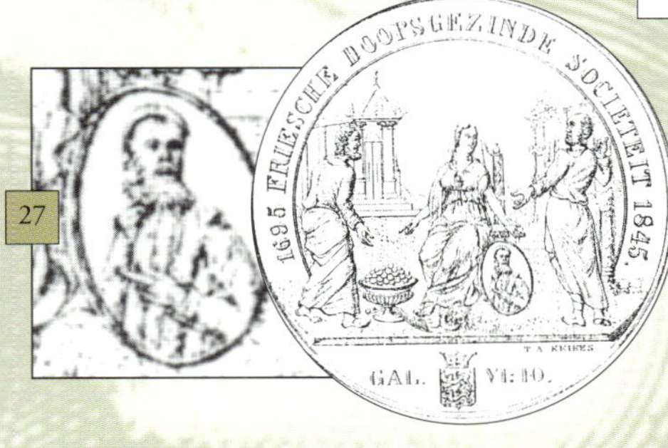

28
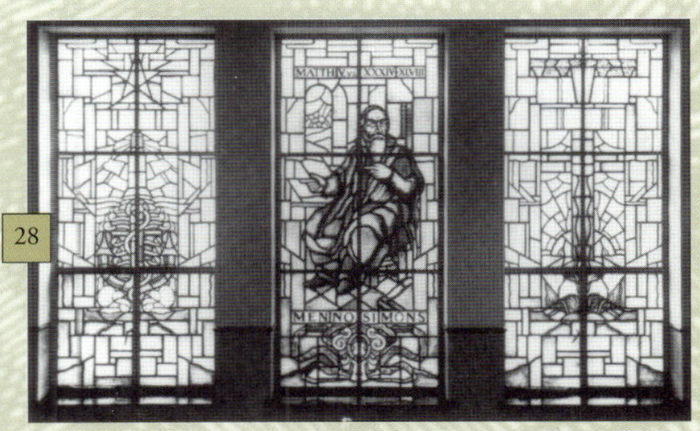

29
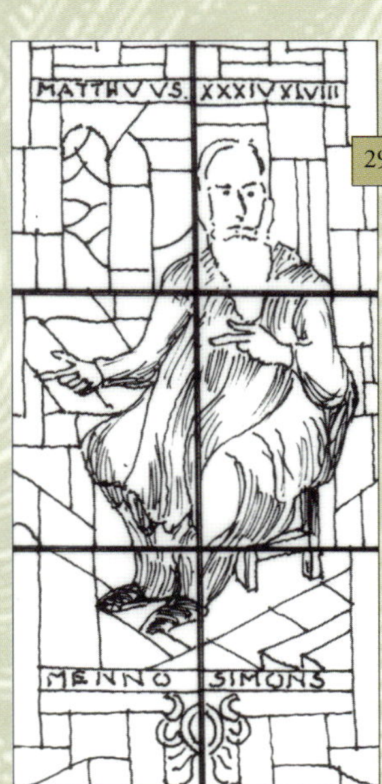

LUYKEN TYPE IN A LARGER COMPOSITION

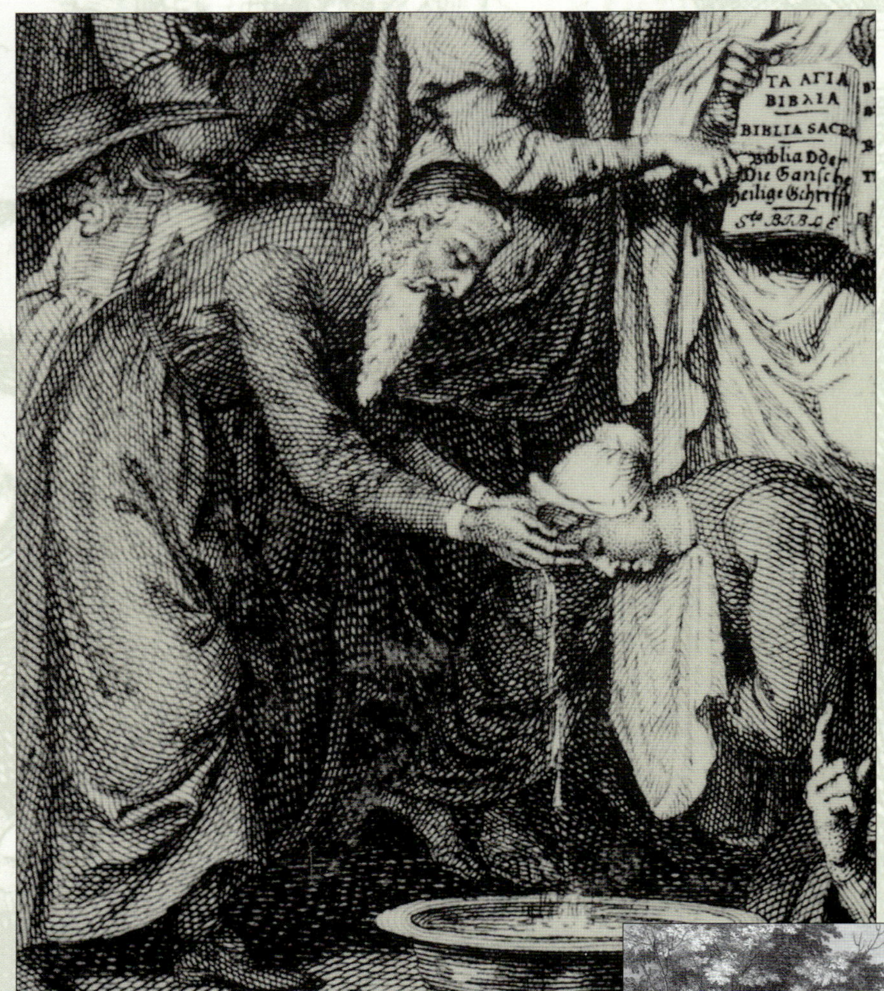

30.1 ca. 1727
Engraving [by Bernard Picart] 325 x 209 / >355 x 223. Without inscription. Polyscenic image with representatives of different religions, on the left of which is Menno 'who is fervently occupied // With joining an aged maiden through Baptism.' (following the explanatory text of 30.3) - RPA.

30.2 1727

BERNARD PICART inv., fec.

As 30.1: 330 x 214 / 373 x 223. Image furnished with a double frame and the Arab's plate with a French text. *TABLEAU DES PRINCIPALES RELIGIONS DU MONDE.* At the bottom a 9-line explication: *En premier ... Lapons. &c.* and 3 columns of 6 lines of explanatory notes. Under nr. 6*: ... a coté Menno Simons bâtisant un Adulte, c'est Le chef des Ménnonites qu'on nomme par abus Anabatistes* - RPA.

30.3 1727

As 30.2.: id. / 343 x 223. *TAFEREEL VAN DE VOORNAAMSTE GODSDIENSTEN DER WAERELDT.* French text replaced by Dutch and partly touched up. The bottom part with text is cut off; the explication in bookprint is on a separate page. Frontispiece of *Naukeurige Beschryving Der Uitwendige Godtsdienst-plichten ... Geteekent door Bernard Picard ... overgezet Door Abraham Moubach* ('s-Gravenhage 1727) vol. I - UBA.

30.4 (1727) 1733

As 30.2: id. / 337 x 223. *TABLEAU DES PRINCIPALES RELIGIONS DU MONDE.* Dutch text replaced again by French. Under the explication (as in 30.2) on a new plate (38 x 221). Frontispiece of *Ceremonies Et Coutumes Religieuses De Tous Les Peuples ... Dessinées ... de Bernard Picard* (Amsterdam 1733), vol. I - P.C.4.

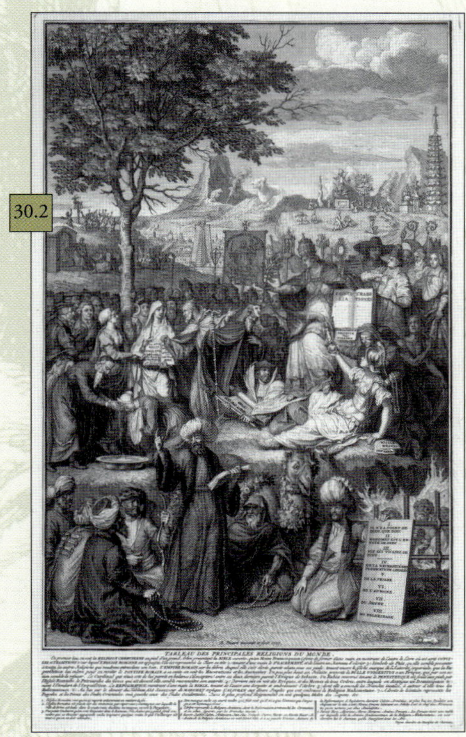

30.2

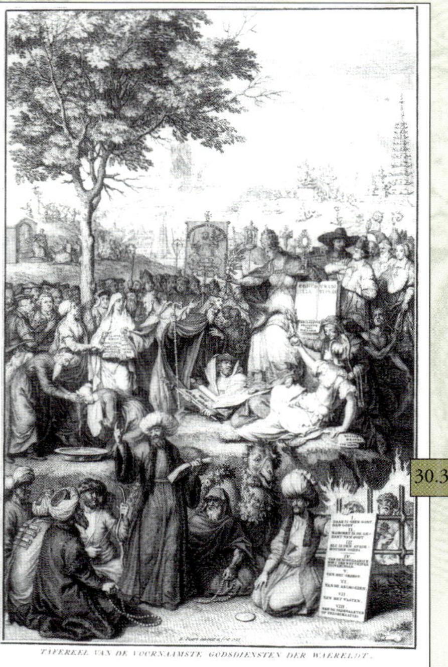

30.3

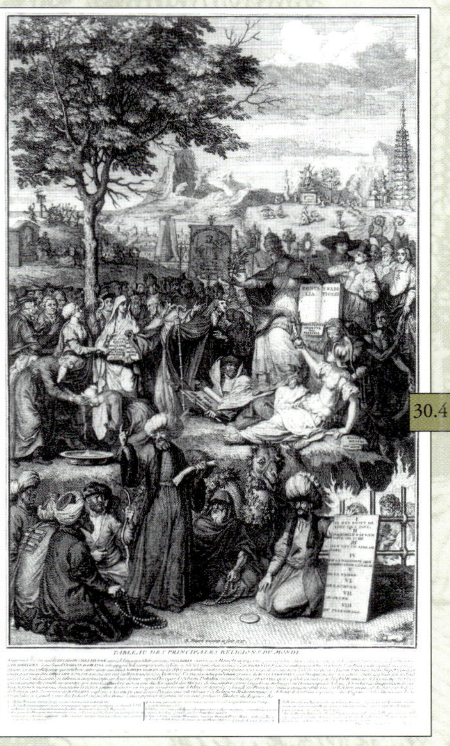

30.4

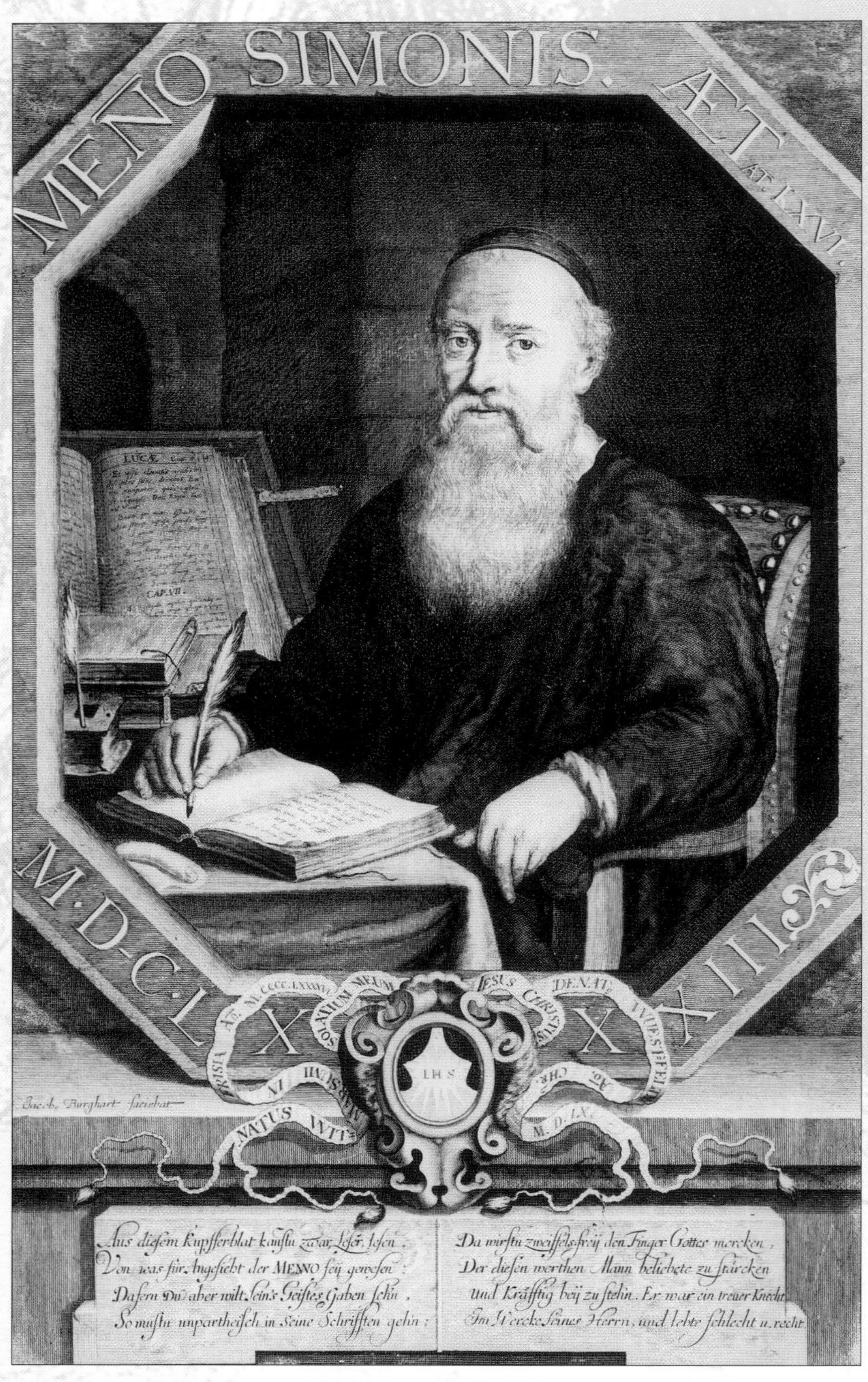

31.1 1683

JACOBUS BURGHART fec.

Engraving 478 x 304 / 490 x 308. In framing *ME*[N]*NO SIMONS. AETAT. LXVI* en *M.D-C.L X X X III;* in medallion cartouche a cross and *IHS,* surrounded by: *SOLATIUM MEUM IESUS CHRISTUS, NATUS WITMARSUMI IN FRISIA A*[nn]*0. M. CCCC. LXXXXVI, DENATUS WUESTEFELDI A*[nn]*O CHR. M. D. LX.;* on the pedastal a 2 x 4-line rhyme: *Aus diesem ... recht.* (B 25; W 224) - UBA-DG.

31.2 1683
As 31.1: added PETRUS GROOTE[N] [Hamburg] exc. (B 25b; H 13; M 3547; Holl 52) - UBA-DG; RPL.

31.3 1889
HERMANN BRAAMS [Norden & Norderney] exc.
As 31.2: lower middle *Diese Platte ist Eygenthum der Mennoniten-Gemeinde in Hamburg-Altona.* Partly touched up, esp. at Menno's hair; birth and death years changed: *M. CCCC. LXXXXIII* and *M. D. LIX* (B 25c; Holl 52) - UBA-DG.

31.4 1889
J.H. OR H.J. / HERMANN BRAAMS exc.
Zinc etching: 179 x 113. Reproduction in black on green paper (likewise in red) on the prospectus of the Kunstverlag Braams. Lower right monogram *JH* or *HJ* (MB 1890, p. 143; at B 25c) - FML; UBA-DG.

31.5 1892
ANONYMOUS/[HERMANN BRAAMS exc.]
As 31.4: 135 x 85. *Menno Simons.* Reproduction in phototype of only the portrait; the sides are shortened, whereby the inkstand and the opened page of the bible are missing. Pasted onto the title of C.P. van Eeghen Jr. (ed.), *Menno Simons, Tractaten over Den Doop, Het Avondmaal, Enz.* (Amsterdam 1892[2]) (at B 25c) - UBA-DG.

31.2

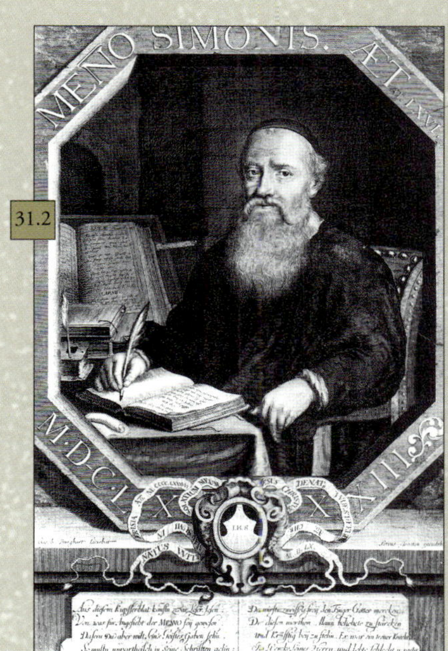

31.3

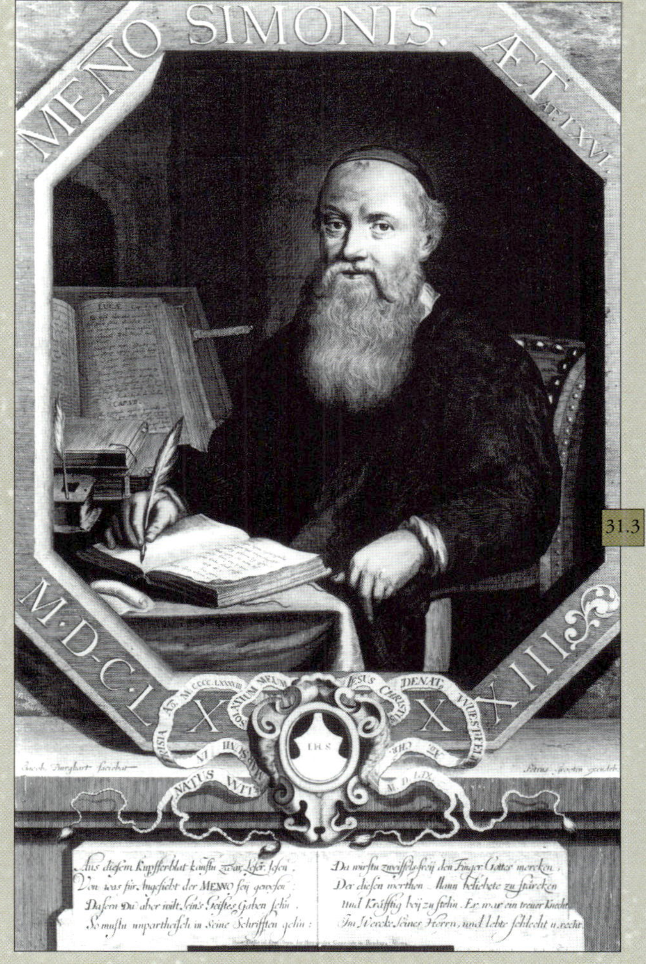

31.4

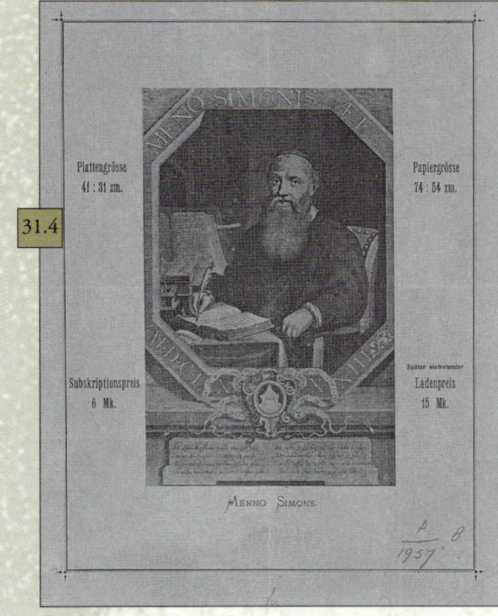

31.5

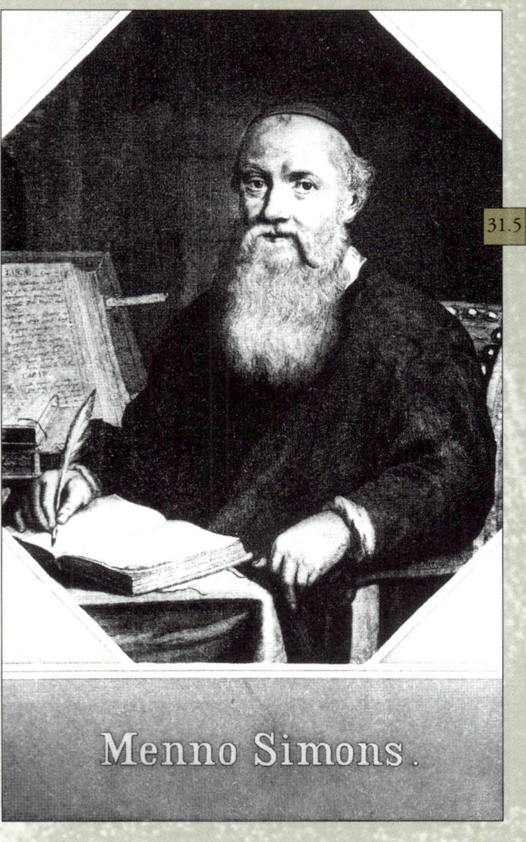

32 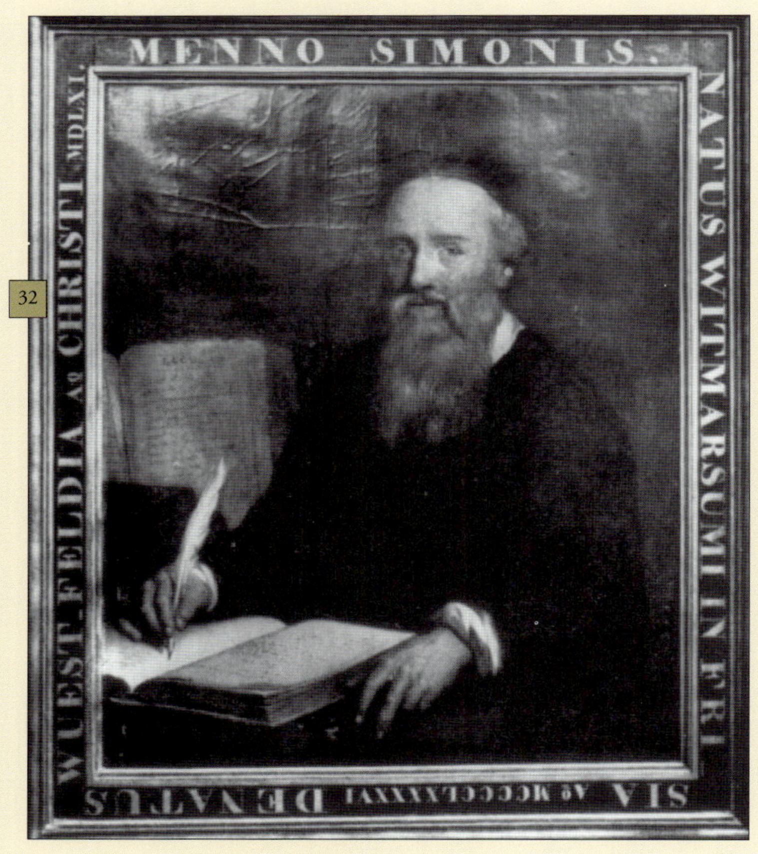

33 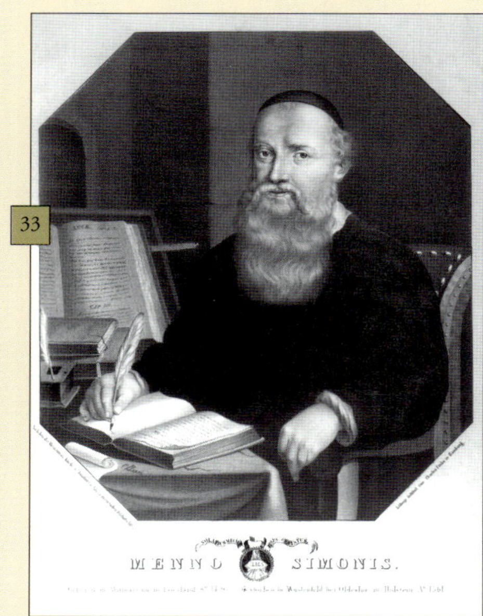

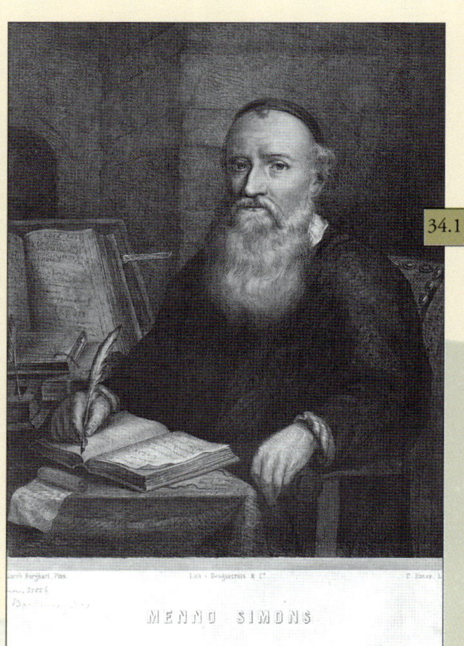 34.1

32. (1824) 1950
[WILLEM BARTEL VAN DER KOOI, pinx.]
Photoreproduction 115 x 100 of the canvas painting (1120 x 780) of the Mennonite Congregation Witmarsum (Friesland), with legend on the frame: *MENNO SIMONS ... MDLXI.* Illustration in John Horsch, *Mennonite History. Volume I: Mennonites in Europe* (Scottdale, PA, 1950[2]), between p. 140 en 141 (see A20) (cf. B 27) - UBA-DG.

33. ca. 1848
C. BEER/CHARLES FUCHS [lithographic printshop, Hamburg]
Litho 301 x 266. *MENNO / SIMONIS.;* medallion with *IHS;* above: *SOLATIUM MEUM / JESUS CHRISTUS,* below: *Geboren in ... 1561;* below left: *Nach dem ... lith* (B 30) - RPA.

34.1 < 1860
JACOB BURGHART pinx. / C. HOTZE [1835-1860] lith. / DESGUERROIS & CO. [lithopgraph printshop, Amsterdam] / WILHELM GILBERS [Amsterdam, 1856-1862].
Litho 319 x 265 on chine collé: *MENNO SIMONS;* text of 1 Cor. 3:11 on rolled out paper (B 32b) - FML.

34.2 > 1860
As 34.1: new publisher J. LEENDERTZ [Amsterdam, 1856-1885] exc.
(B 32a; H 18; vS 3585b) - UBA-DG.

35. ca. 1870
JACOB BURGHART pinx. / C. HOTZE del. / B.C. ALBEK [lithographic printshop, Amsterdam] / J. LEENDERTZ [Amsterdam, 1856-1885] exc.
Litho 304 x 261 on chine collé: *MENNO SIMONS;* text on the rolled out paper is incorrect (B 31; vS 3585a) - L.U.

36. ca. 1875
FR. WENTZEL [lithographic printshop, Weissenburg]
Litho 300 x 254. Between banners with *SOLATIUM MEUM / JESUS CHRISTUS* and medallion with *IHS: MENNO SIMONIS. Geboren in ... 1561.* Below left: *Nach dem ... Lith.* (MB 1889, p. 132; B 33) - UBA-DG.

37. 1936
ALEXANDER HARDER
Colour print after an oil painting 618 x 465. The bottom half of the face exhibits similarities with 24 (Luyken). A black and white reprint in MB 83 (1936) nr. 5, p. 36 (H 21) - MSHL/EMU.

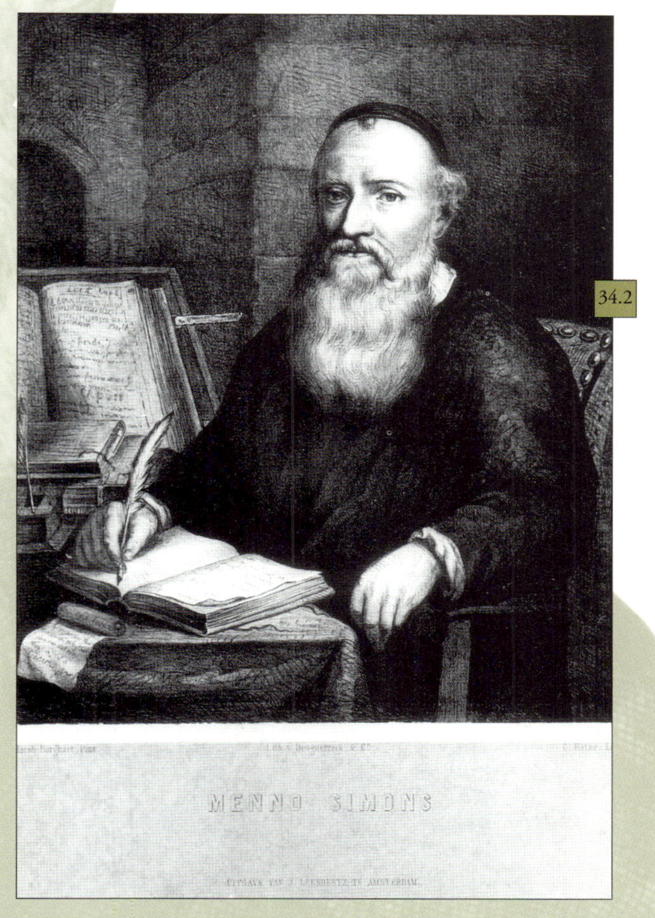
MENNO SIMONS

34.2

36

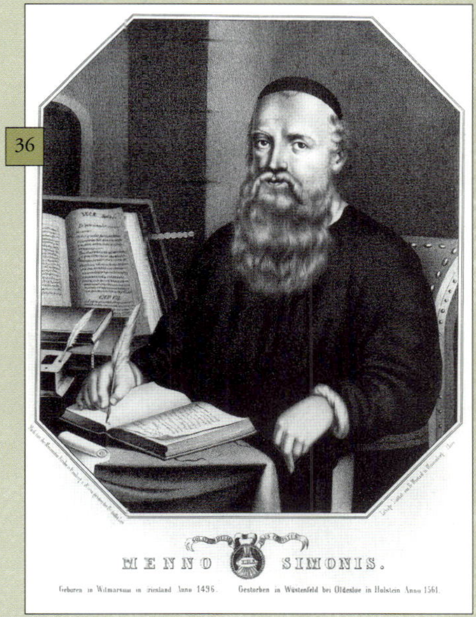
MENNO SIMONIS.
Geboren in Witmarsum in Friesland Anno 1496. Gestorben in Wüstenfeld bei Oldesloe in Holstein Anno 1561.

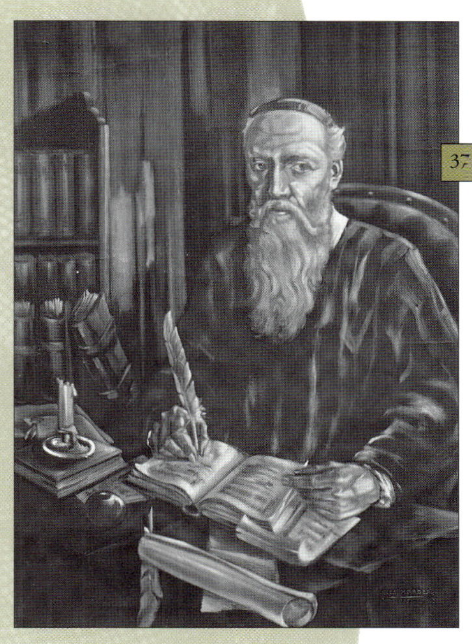

37

BURGHART TYPE B: BUST WITH CHAIRBACK

38.1

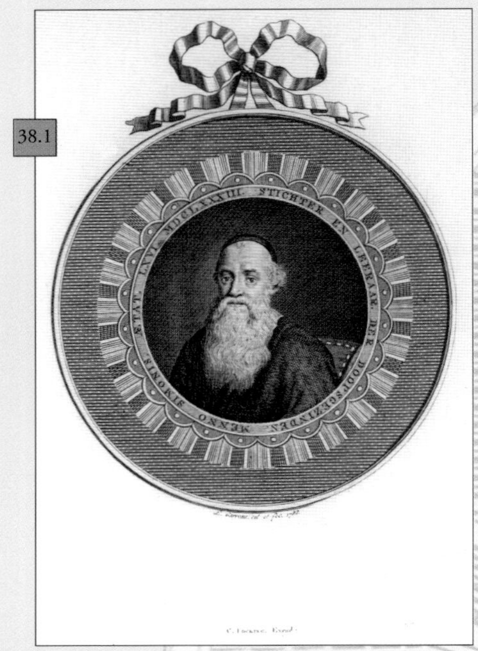

38.2b

Verdraagzaamheid, Ge-
-duld, oprechte nedrigheid,
En Deugd, die tegen Wraak en 't
bloedig Oorlog pleit,
Gepaard met Godvrucht, ſtraalt uit dit
Eerwaardig Weezen
Van MENNO, als een ſtar aan Frieſlands
kuſt verreezen;
Vervolgzucht zogt vergeefsch de taa-
-ning van dat Licht,
't Welk Eeuwen heeft geduurt en
voor geen Kerkdwang zwicht.
1788. M. NIEUWENHUYZEN.

38.2a

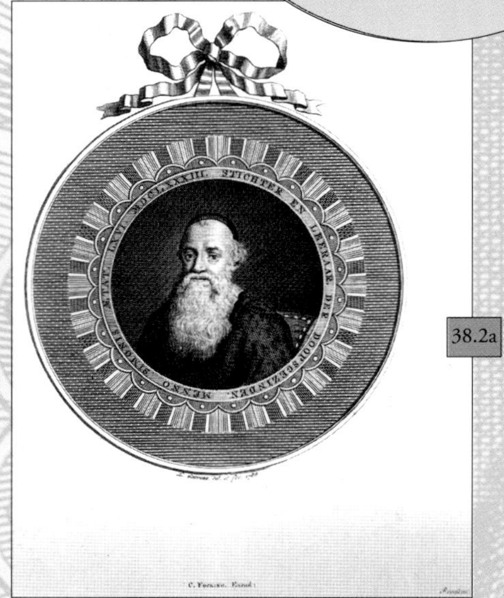

39

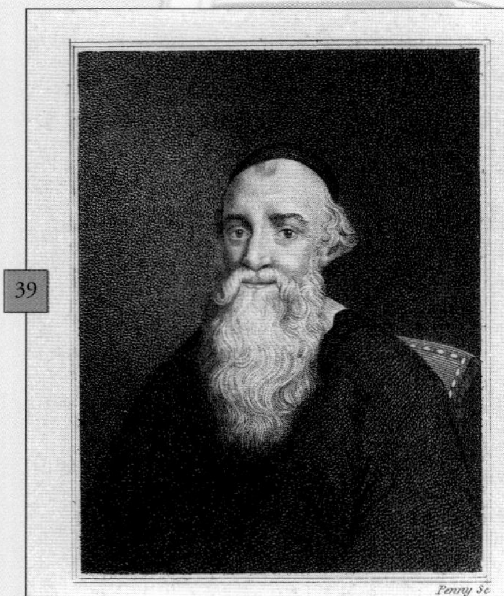

Penny Sc.

Menno Simon.
Aged 63, 1561,
Founder and Teacher
of
the Dutch Baptists.
From a scarce Dutch Engraving.
Published by Button & Son, Pater Noster Row, Oct.r 1818.

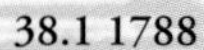

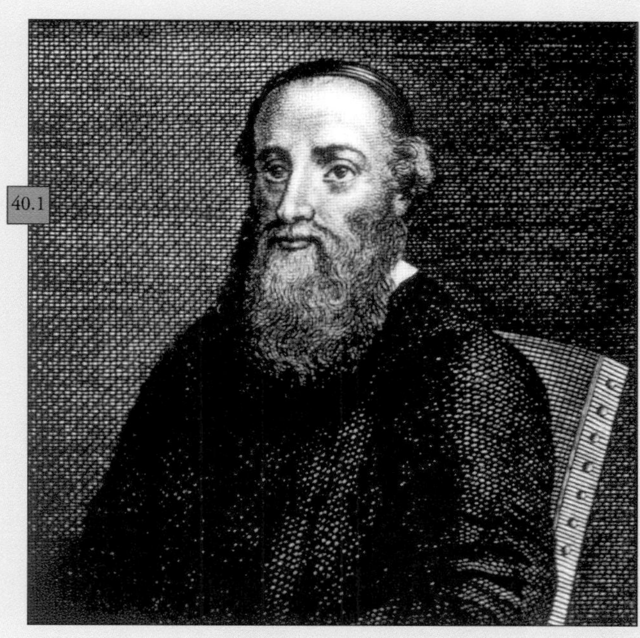

40.1

38.1 1788
L.E.F. GARREAU del., fec. / CORNELIS FOCKING [Amsterdam] exc.
Engraving (diameter 58) / 158 x 129. Legend *MENNO SIMONIS. AETAT. LXVI. MDCLXXXIII STICHTER EN LEERAAR DER DOOPSGEZINDEN.* Before the addition of *Proefdruk*. The year MDCLXXXIII refers to 31 (Burghart) - FML; CCU.

38.2a 1788
As 38.1: lower right *Proefdruk* (B 34a; H 14) - UBA-DG.

38.2b As 38.2a: on the back, concentric with the front, an engraving (diameter 58) / 158 x 129 with 12-line text: *Verdraagzaamheid ... zwicht,* signed: *1788. M. NIEUWENHUYZEN.* (B 34b; M 3555) - UBA-DG; RPA; RPL.

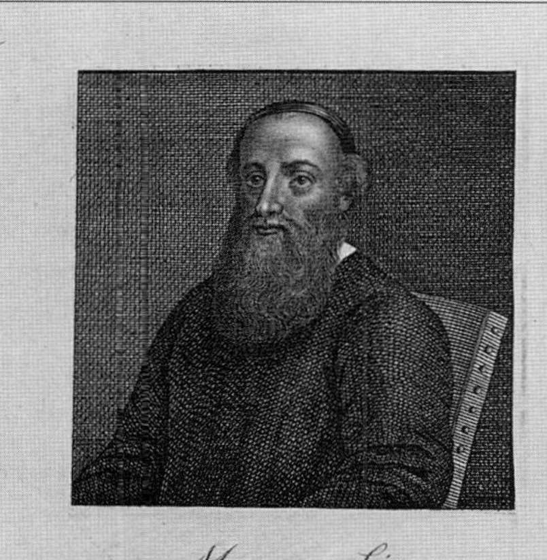

40.2

39. 1818
PENNY sculp. / BUTTON & SON [London, exc.]
Engraving 84 x 64 / 175 x 110. *Menno Simon.,* with 5-line inscription *Aged 65. ... Engraving* (B 35) - RPA.

40.1 ca. 1838
H. THEPASS del. / DIRK JURIAEN SLUYTER sculp. / M. STOFFELS [Zaandam, 1829-1847] exc.
Engraving 69 x 70. In a separate framework part of a large print (349 x 457): *AFBEELDING // van het MENNO SIMONS KERKJE* (see 62) (B 28) - UBA-DG; CCU.

40.2 > ca. 1838
As 40.1.: unsigned. 69 x 70 / 175 x 119. Cut out of the copper plate of 40.1, whereby the rest of the image and text is missing; 4-line inscription on a separate plate (172 x 123): *Menno Simons ... Ao. 1561.* (B 29) - UBA-DG; FML.

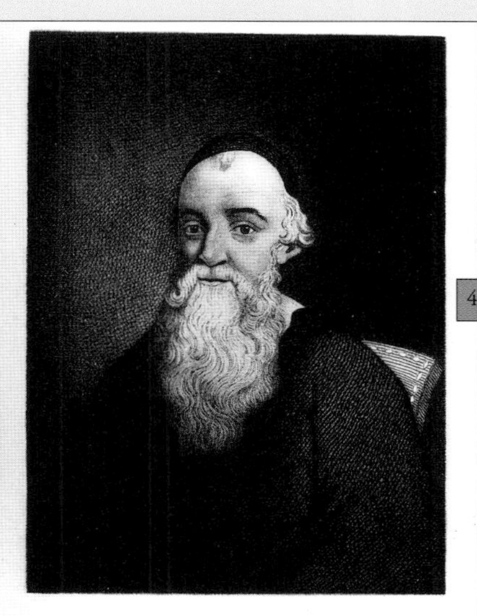

41

41. 1853
J.D. GROSS
Engraving 85 x 63. *MENNO SIMON.,* with 2-line inscription: *FOUNDER AND ... Aged 65. 1561.* Titleprint of J. Newton Brown, *The Life And Times Of Menno, The Celebrated Dutch Reformer* (Philadelphia [1853]) (B 36) - UBA-DG.

42

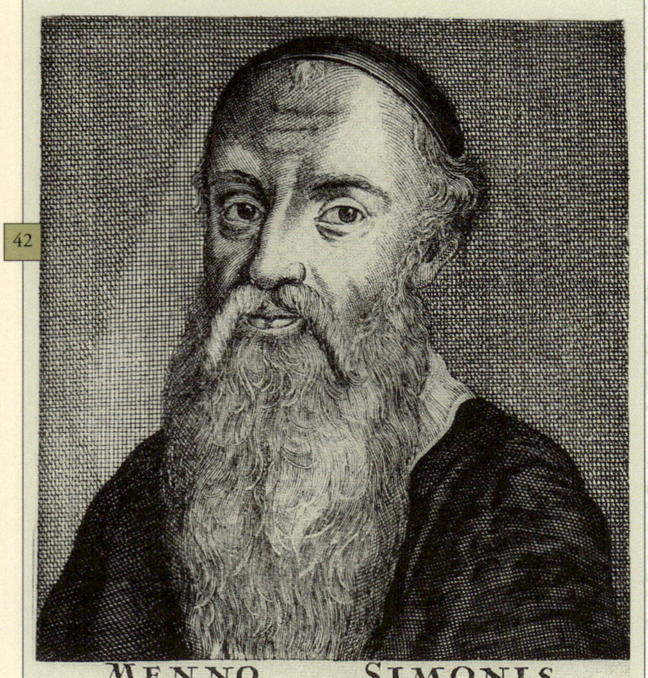

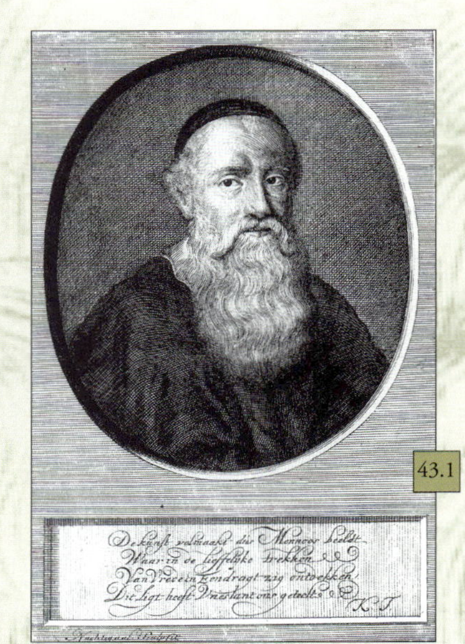

43.1

43.2

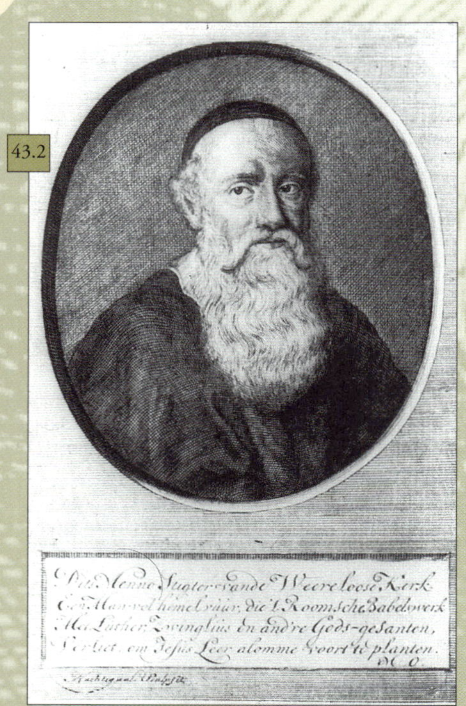

43.3

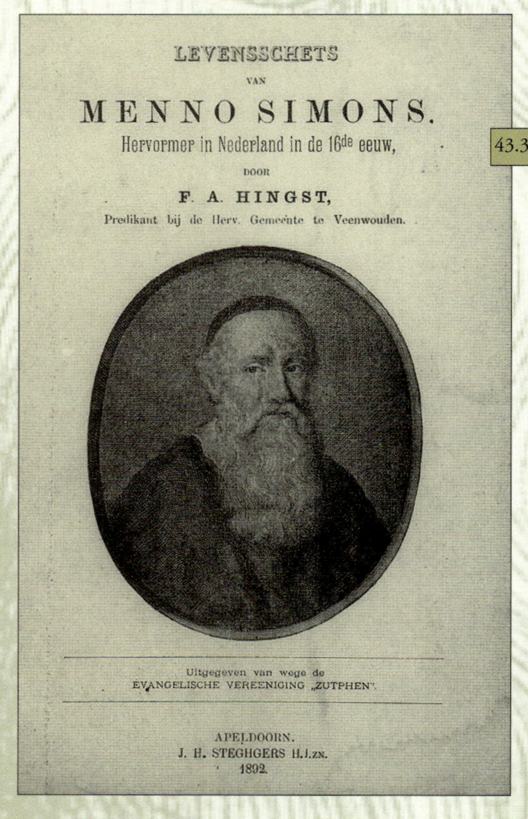

LEVENSSCHETS

VAN

MENNO SIMONS,

Hervormer in Nederland in de 16de eeuw,

DOOR

F. A. HINGST,

Predikant bij de Herv. Gemeente te Veenwouden.

Uitgegeven van wege de
EVANGELISCHE VEREENIGING „ZUTPHEN".

APELDOORN.
J. H. STEGHGERS H.1.ZN.
1892

42. 1682?
ANONYMOUS (German?)
Engraving 110 x 100 / 135 x 104. *MENNO SIMONIS. // Witmarsumia-Friso.*, with 4-line Latin inscription: *Deserta Pontif. ... Den. 1561.* See B 37 for dating as a possible link between 24 (Luyken) and 31 (Burghart) (B 37, after which it is reproduced, p. 87) - L.U.

43.1 ca. 1729
CLEMENT NACHTEGAAL
[1685->1729] sculp.
Engraving 140 x 78 / 149 x 93. 4-line rhymed inscription: *De kunst ... geteelt* by *K.T.* Also in G. Brandt, *Kort Verhaal van de Reformatie* (Utrecht 1730), 4th ed., opposite p. 4 (B 38; cf. H 15) - UBA-DG; RPA.

43.2 > 1730
As 43.1: with another 4-line rhymed inscription: *Dits Menno ... planten* by *M.O.* (H 15, after which it is reproduced) - L.U.

43.3 1892
As 43.1: reproduction in autotype 94 x 79 of only the portrait, on the cover of F.A. Hingst, *Levensschets van Menno Simons* (Apeldoorn 1892) (at B 38) - UBA-DG.

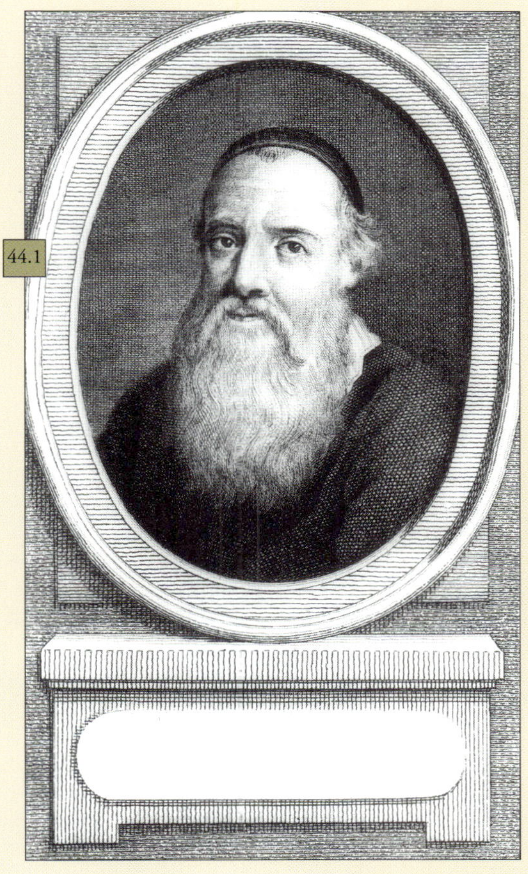
44.1

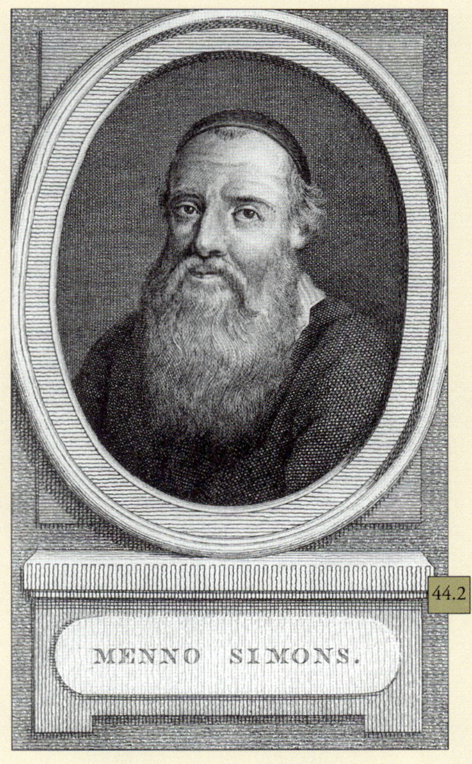

44.2

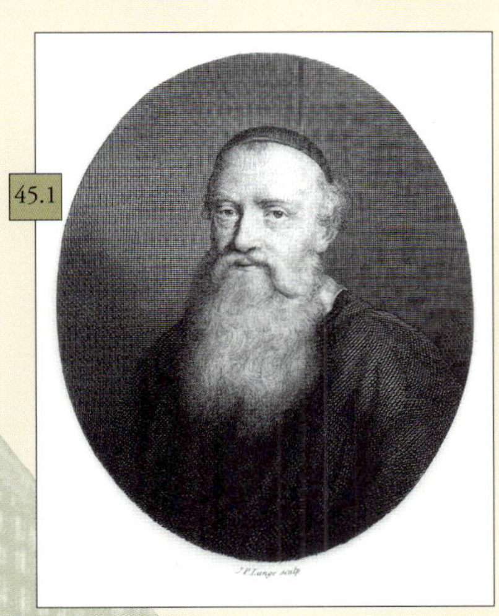

45.1

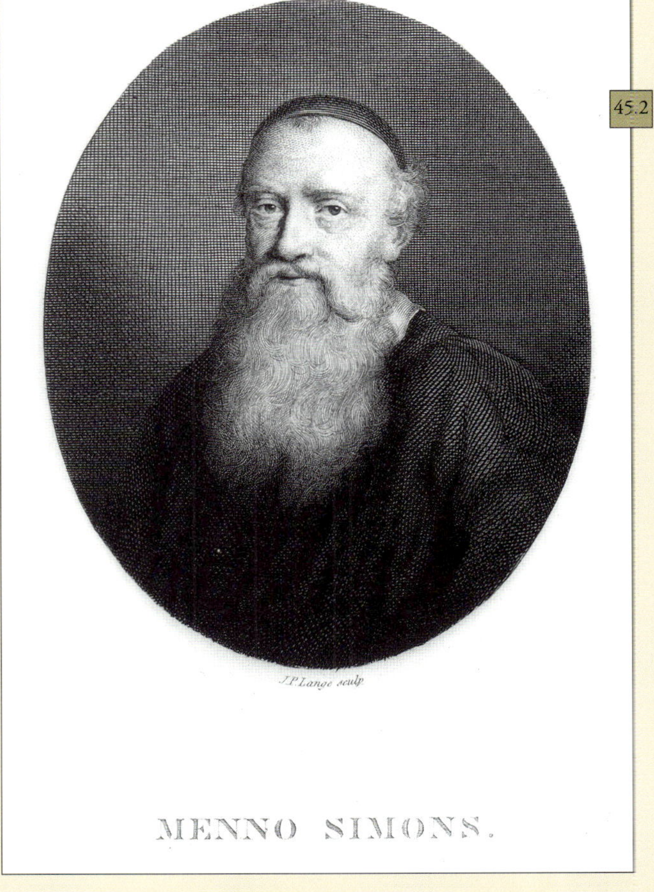

45.2

44.1 ca. 1800
JACOB BURGHART pinx. / REINIER VINKELES [1741-1816] fec. Engraving 152 x 87 / 233 x 153. Without inscription (B 41a; H 16) - UBA-DG; RPL; CCU.

44.2 ca. 1800
As 44.1: on pedestal *MENNO SIMONS* (B 41b) - RPL.

45.1 1837
Engraving [by J. Ph. Lange] 106 x 87 / 240 x 152. Without inscription, on chine collé (B 42a; M 3553) - RPA

45.2 1837
JOHANNES PHILIPPUS LANGE sculp. As 45.1: *MENNO SIMONS;* on common paper as titleprint of A.M. Cramer, *Het Leven En De Verrigtingen Van Menno Simons* (Amsterdam 1837) (B 42b & c; H 17; M 3552, 3551; vS 3591) - UBA-DG; RPL

46 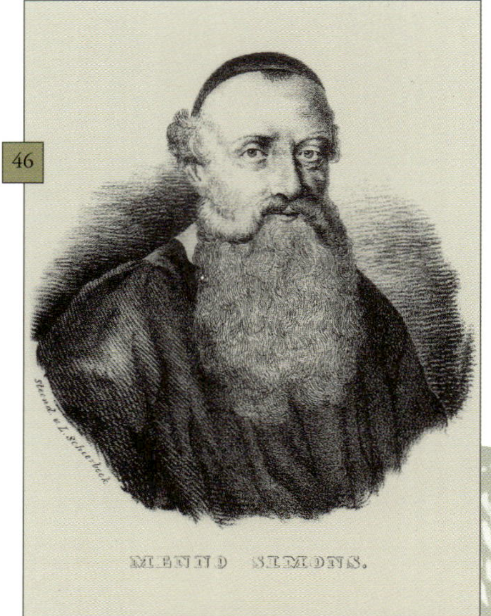

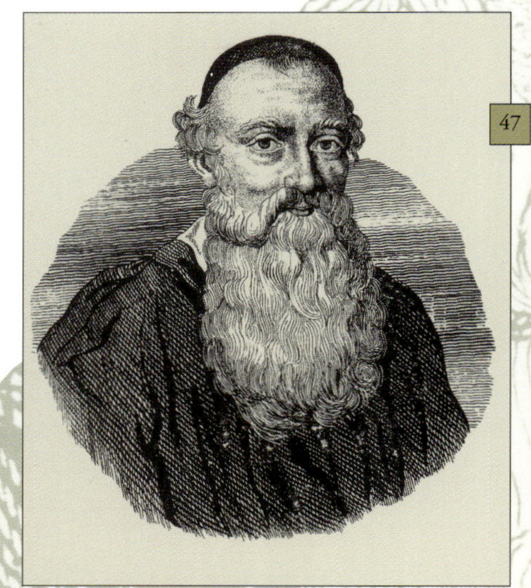 47

48 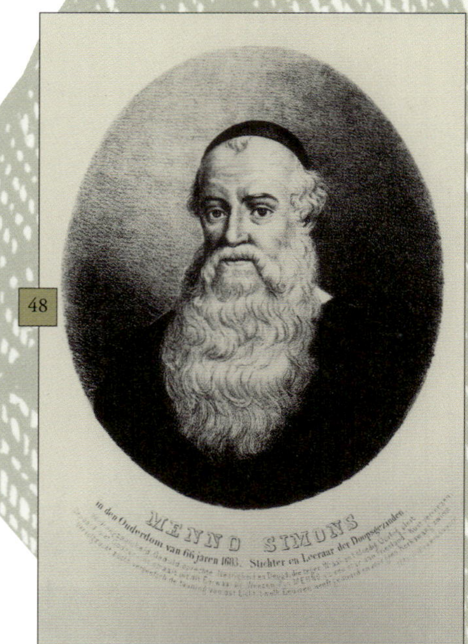

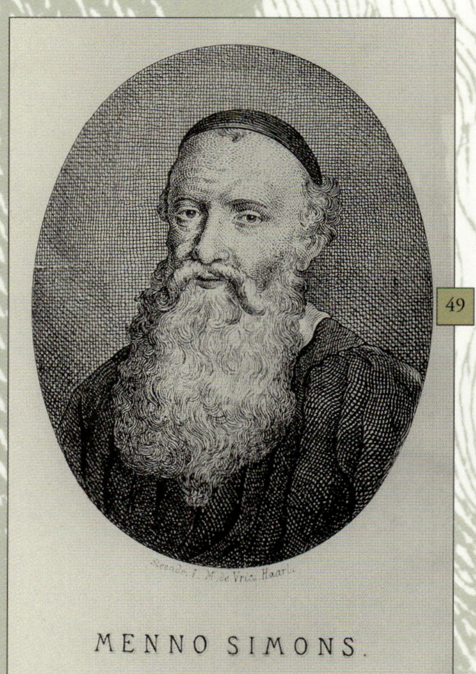 49

46. 1838
LAMBERTUS SCHIERBEEK [exc.]
Litho 86 x 81. *MENNO SIMONS.* Both separately and as an illustration in the *Friesche Volks-Almanak voor het Jaar 1839* (Leeuwarden [1838]) (B 43) - UBA-DG; RPL; FML.

47. 1840
ANONYMOUS
Litho 86 x 78. Illustration in *Hollandsch Penning-Magazijn Voor De Jeugd* (Zaltbommel, Joh. Noman en Zoon, 1840, 6th annual), p. 100 (B 44) - UBA.

48. ca. 1870
H. DILCHER [Amsterdam: 1853-1885] del.
Litho 196 x 159. *MENNO SIMONS // in den Ouderdom van 66 jaren 1683,* [sic] ... *Doopsgezinden.*, with 3-line text of M. Nieuwenhuyzen: *Verdraagzaamheid ... zwicht,* dated 1783 [= 1788]. *Naar eene schilderij v. 1783* [= 1683] (B 46) - UBA-DG.

49. 1877
I.M. DE VRIES [lithographer]
Litho 88 x 69. *MENNO SIMONS.* Titleprint of J. Newton Brown, *Het Leven En De Arbeid Van Menno Simons* (Haarlem [1877]) (B 47) - UBA-DG.

50. 1891
ANONYMOUS
Wood engraving 80 x 65. *Menno Simons, geb. anno 1492, gest. 13. Januar 1559.* Titleprint in H.G. Mannhardt, *Festschrift zu Menno Simons' 400-jähriger Geburtstagsfeier* (Danzig 1892); also in *Christlicher Gemeinde-Kalender auf das Jahr 1892* (Frankfurt am Main 1891) (B 48) - UBA-DG.

50

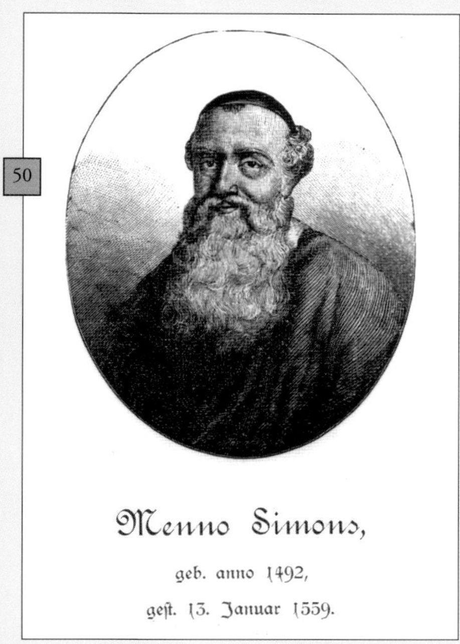

52.1

DOOPSGEZIND MAANDBLAD VOOR UIT- EN INWENDIGE ZENDING.

MENNO SIMONS 1492

NIEMAND KAN EEN ANDER FONDAMENT LEGGEN DAN HETGEEN GELEGD IS, HETWELK IS JESUS CHRISTUS. I. CORINTHE 3:11.

Met bijdragen van C. P. van Eeghen Jr., Amsterdam; G. Hofstede, Blokzijl; Jh. Loosjes, Hollum; K. W. Rössing, Ouddorp; J. W. van Stuyvenberg, Westzaan(Zuid); P. A. Jansz, N. Thiessen; Dr. H. Bervoets, Margôredjô; J. Hübert, Kedoeng-Pendjalin; Joh. Klaassen, te Kajoe-apoe; H. Siemens te Pati op Java; J. Thiessen; D. Dirks, Pakanten op Sumatra, en anderen.

52.2

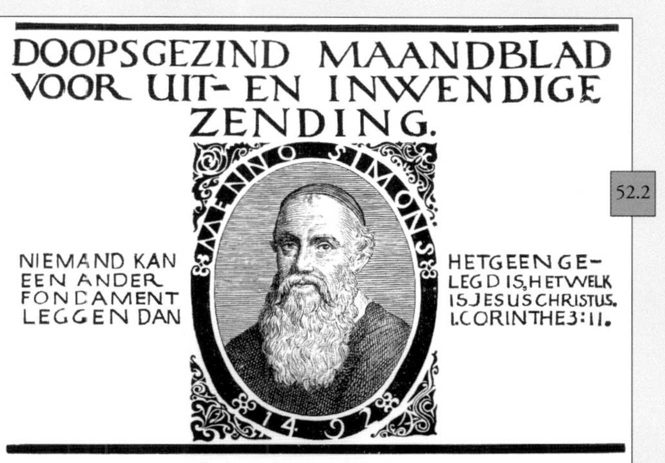

53

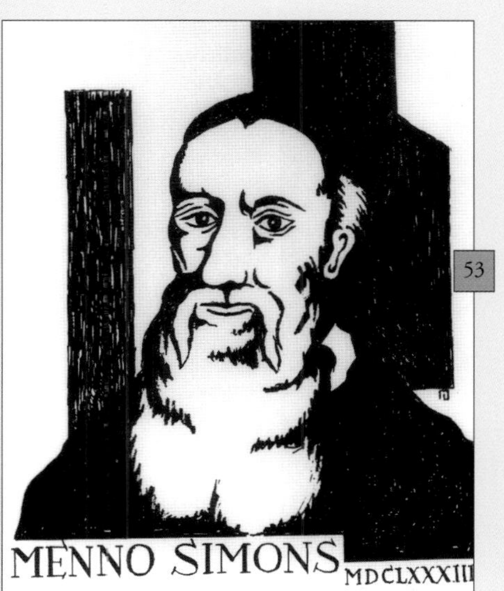

51. 1899

FADDEGON & CO.

Chromolithograph 90 x 68. *MENNO SIMONSZ 1492-1559.* On the shield of the *Mennokalender* for 1900 (A.J. Bronswijk, Oostburg [1899]) (B 49) - L.U.

52.1 1910

CAREL ADOLF LION CACHET

Woodcut in letterpress-cliché 100 x 145. Engraving *MENNO SIMONS // 1492.* Part of the head of the *Doopsgezind Maandblad Voor Uit- En Inwendige Zending* (from vol. 13 (1911) nr. 1); left and right 2x 4 lines: *NIEMAND KAN ... I.CORINTHE 3:11.* (cf. B 50b) - UBA-DG.

52.2 1915

As 52.1: In july 1915 (nr. 7) is the cliché repaired, whereby on the right side the last *E* of *INWENDIGE* has received a waving baseline. Also in unbacked sheet (cf. B 50a) - UBA-DG.

53. 1969

DANIEL DUBOIS

Reproduction of pen drawing: 92 x 75. *MENNO SIMONS MDCLXXXIII* [sic]. Illustration in Ch. et Cl. Ummel, *L'Église Mennonite Ou Anabaptiste En Pays Neuchâtelois* (La Chaux-de Fonds, Suisse, 1969), p. 9 - UBA-DG.

BURGHART TYPE D: BUST ON MEDALS AND COMMEMORATIVE PLAQUES

54

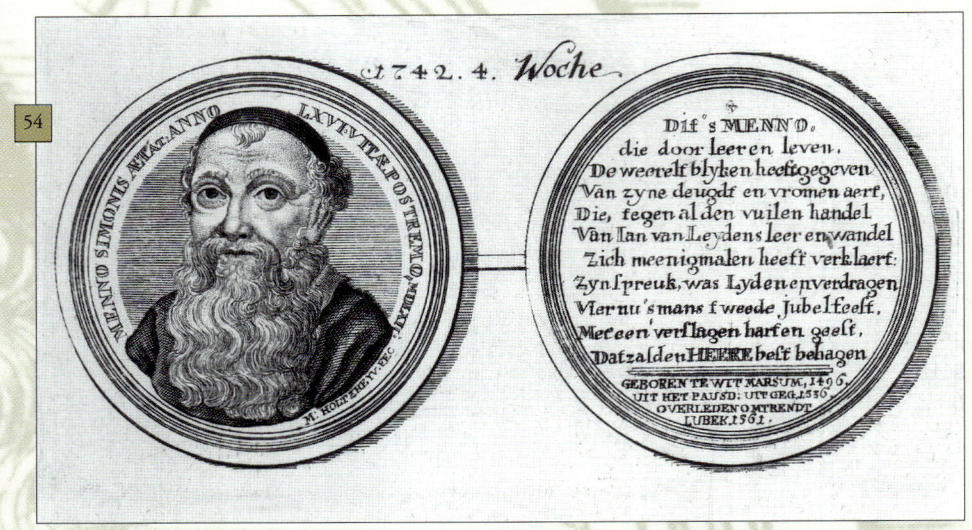

55

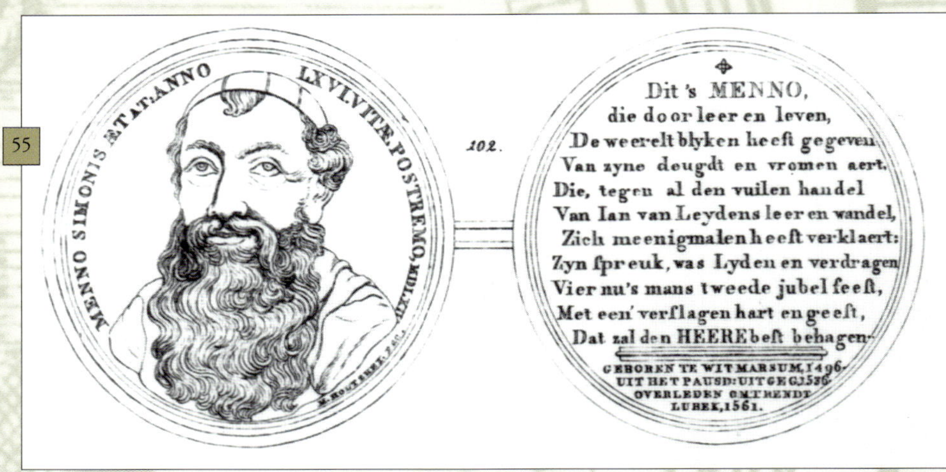

56

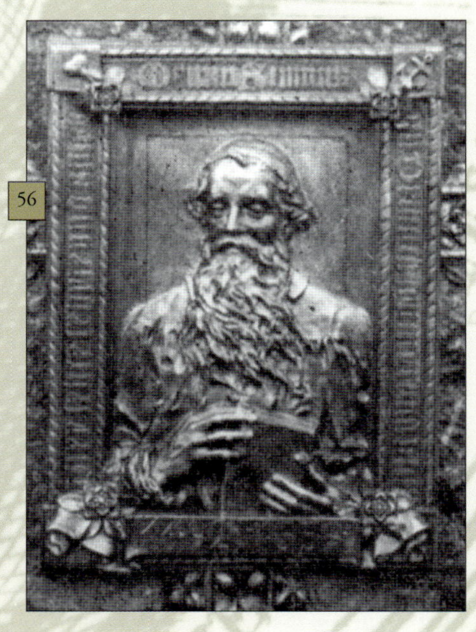

54. (1736) 1742

A. NUNZER

Engraving 68 x 132, of the medal (diameter 58) from 1736 by Martinus Holtzhey (see A5), above which is *1742. 4. Woche.* Illustration in J.H. Lochner, *Samlung Merkwürdiger Medaillen. Sechstes Jahr 1742,* 27 Jan. (Nürnberg), p. 25 (B 53) - IBH.

55. (1736) 1824

JOHANNES PHILIPPUS LANGE, fec.

Engraving (with seven other medals on one plate) 340 x 200 of the medal from 1736 (diameter 54; see A5). Illustration in *Beschrijving van Nederlandsche historie-penningen ten vervolge op het werk van Mr. Gerard van Loon,* 2nd part (Amsterdam 1824), plate X, nr. 102 (B 54) - UBA; FML.

56. (1905) 1906

[P. DÜYFFCKE]

Autotype of photo of the bronze commemorative plaque of granite block on the so-called Mennoberg at Wüstenfelde. Legend: *Hier lebte, lehrte und starb // Menno Simons, // in Demut, fromm und still,* below it *1492-1559.* Illustration in: MB 53 (1906) nr. 8, August, p. 69 (at B 58) - UBA-DG.

57. 1947

ANONYMOUS

Cliché (diameter 45): *MENNO SIMONSZ;* legend *EEN HEER, EEN GELOOVE, EEN DOOP.* On the cover of N. van der Zijpp, *Menno Simonsz* (Amsterdam, J.H. de Bussy [1947]) and later publications in the series 'Van Wege De Algemene Doopsgezinde Sociëteit' - UBA-DG.

58. (1958) ca. 1980

ANONYMOUS

Photo 105 x 66 of the bronze commemorative plaque in the garden of the Menno Kate at Bad Oldesloe. *1492 / 1559;* inscription: *HIER LEBTE LEHRTE UND STARB MENNO SIMONIS IN DEMUTH FROMM UND STILL.* Illustration in: W. Schroeder & A.D. Schroeder, *Was sollen diese Steine bedeuten?* (Winnipeg, Man., n.d.), p. [8] - UBA-DG.

57

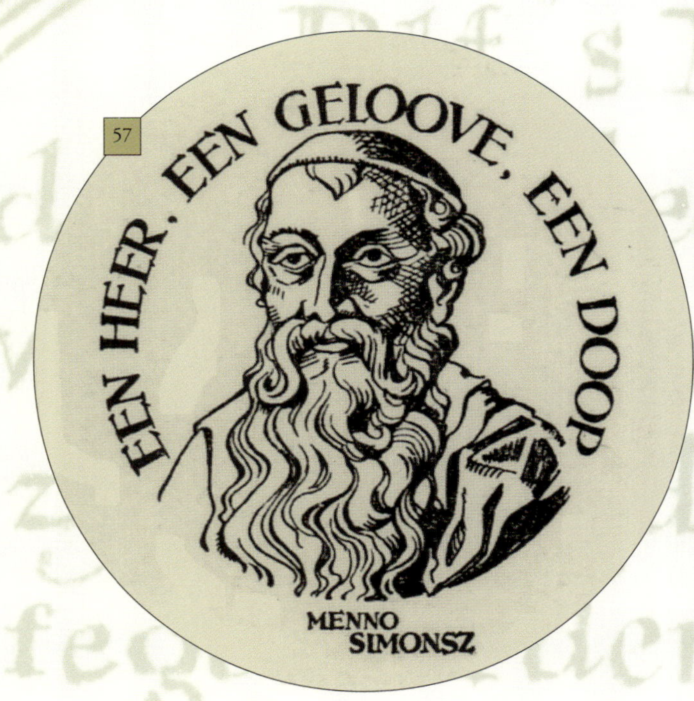

58

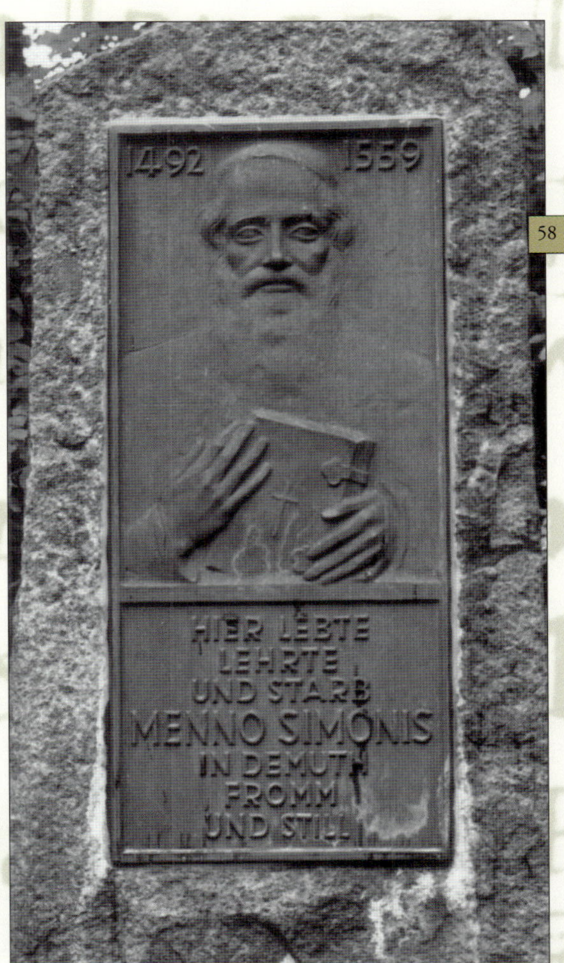

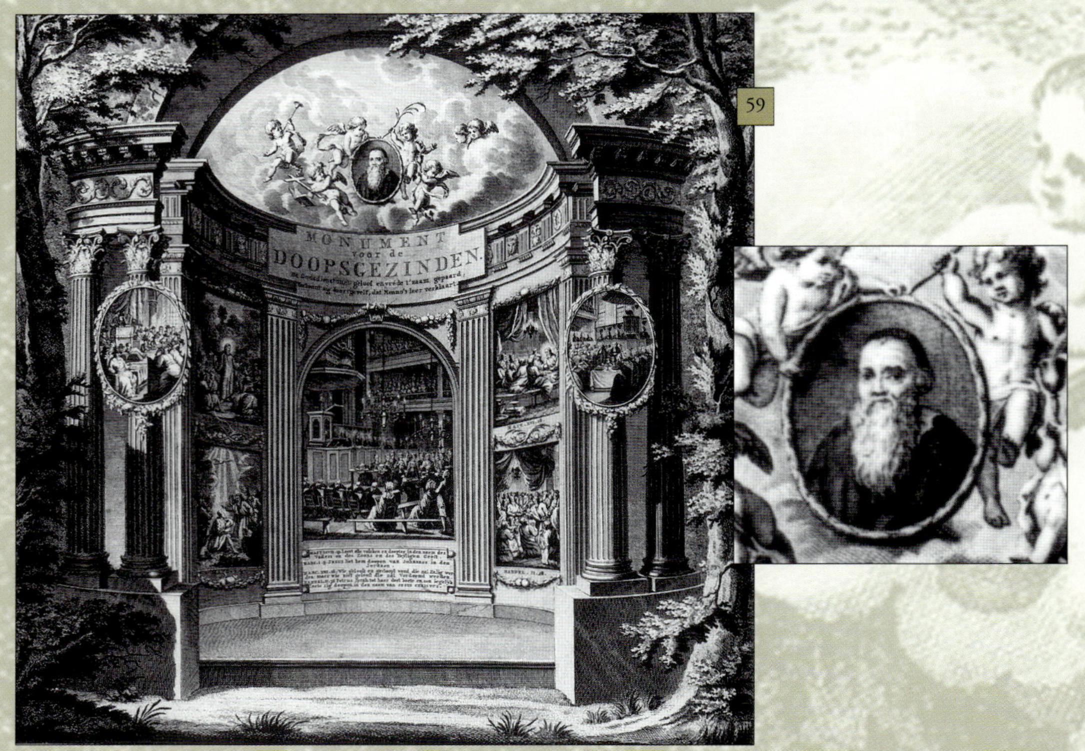

59

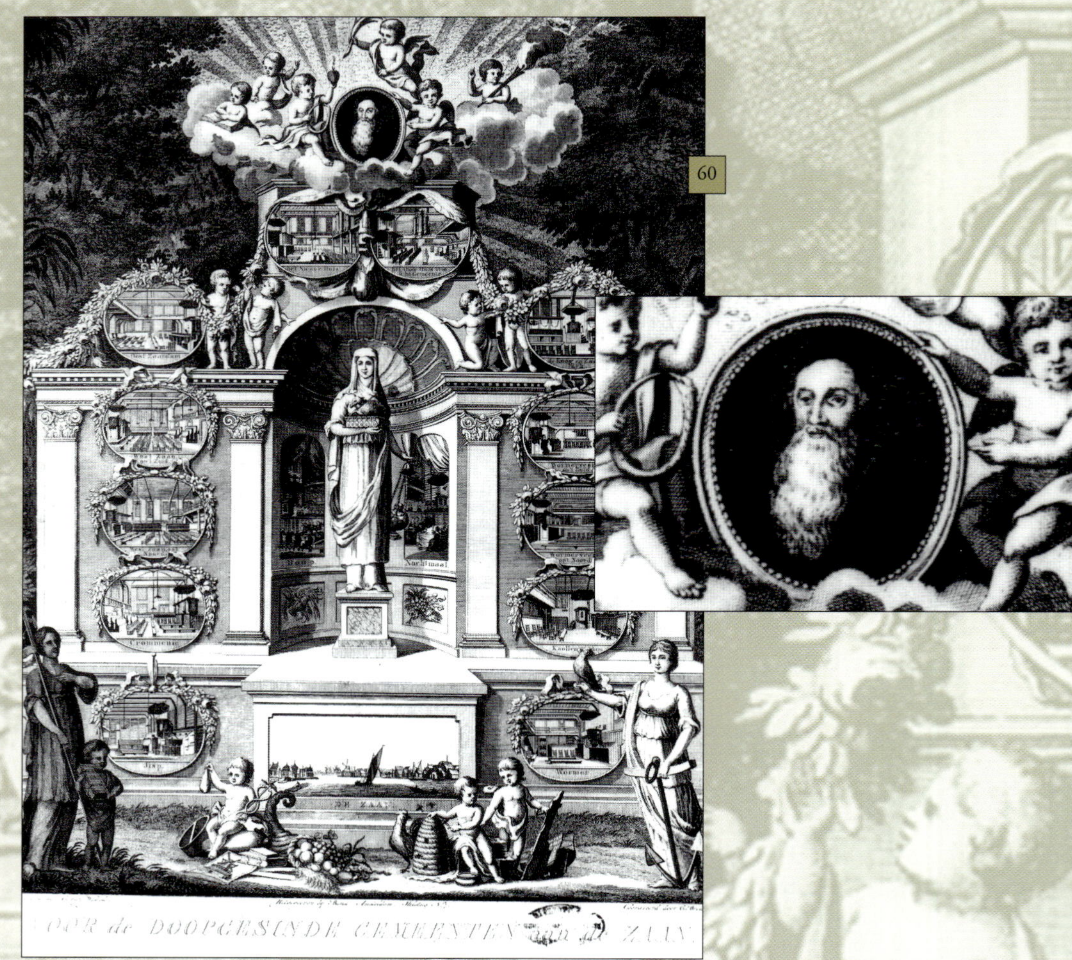

60

59. 1792
D. KERKHOFF del. / CORNELIS BROUWER sculp. / DIRK MELAND LANGEVELD [Amsterdam] exc. Engraving 413 x 421 / ca. 465 x 450. *MONUMENT voor de DOOPSGEZINDEN,* with 2-line rhyme: *De Godsdienst ... verklaart;* below right *Proefdruk.* Menno in oval wreath above a temple archway; in the interior of the Singelkerk at Amsterdam: a baptismal ceremony, flanked by four biblical scenes (Matt. 27:19; Mark 1:9; Mark. 16:16; Acts 2:38), a sermon and Lord's Supper scene (B 39) - UBA-DG.

60. ca. 1800
C. VAN WAARD [act. 1793-1814] dr. / CORNELIS BROUWER [act. 1775-1803] sculp. / H.A. BANSE [art dealer Amsterdam, 1790-1807] exc. Engraving 535 x 403 / 557 x 440. *VOOR de DOOPSGESINDE GEMEENTEN aan de ZAAN;* below right *Proefdruk.* Menno at the top; more scenes of baptism, Lord's Supper, and allegorical attributes of business and industry; below in two rows 12 medallions with interiors of the meeting-houses of the Zaan region (B 40) - UBA-DG.

61. 1817
ANONYMOUS
Dotted engraving 394 x 283 / 356 x 259. *MONUMENT. VOOR HET DERDE EEUW-FEEST DER KERKHERVORMING.* Ten reformers in medallion, among them Menno, on pillars of gothic architecture; above in the middle Luther and Calvin; below left: *Proefdruk* (M-his 6117) - AVS; RPA.

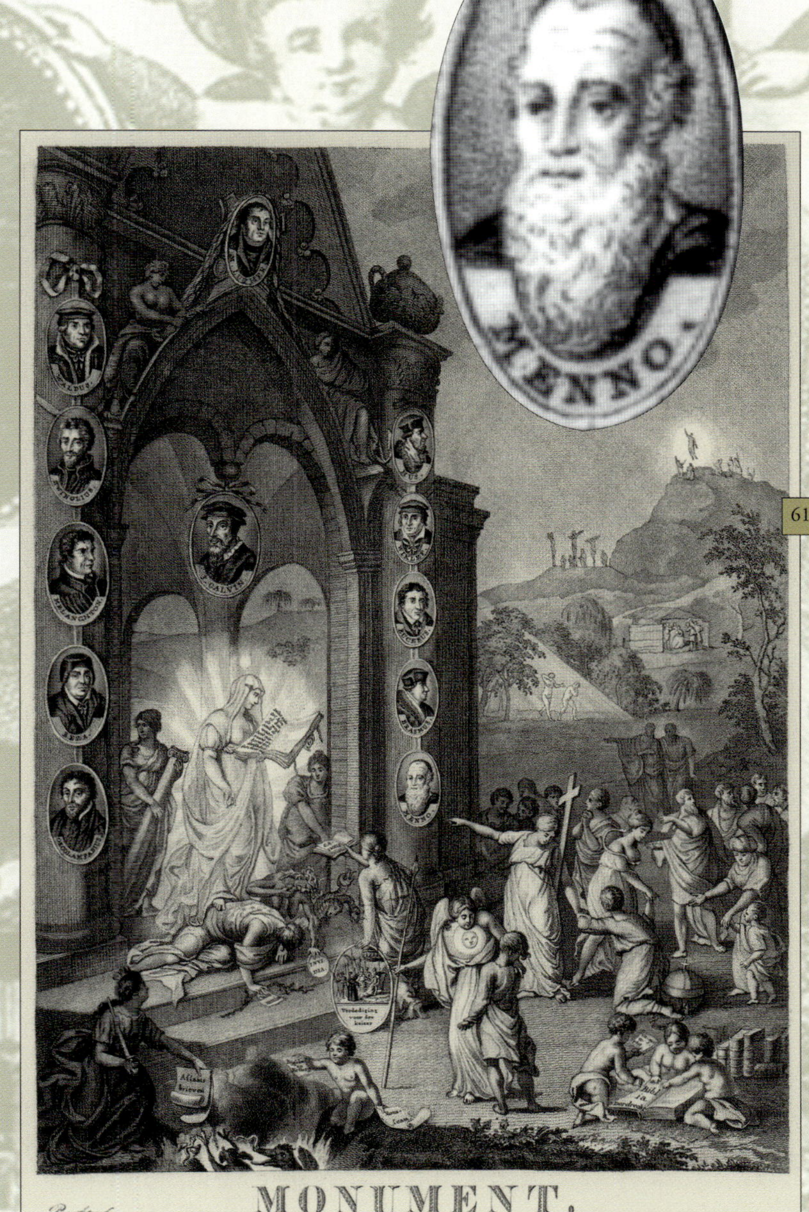

61

62

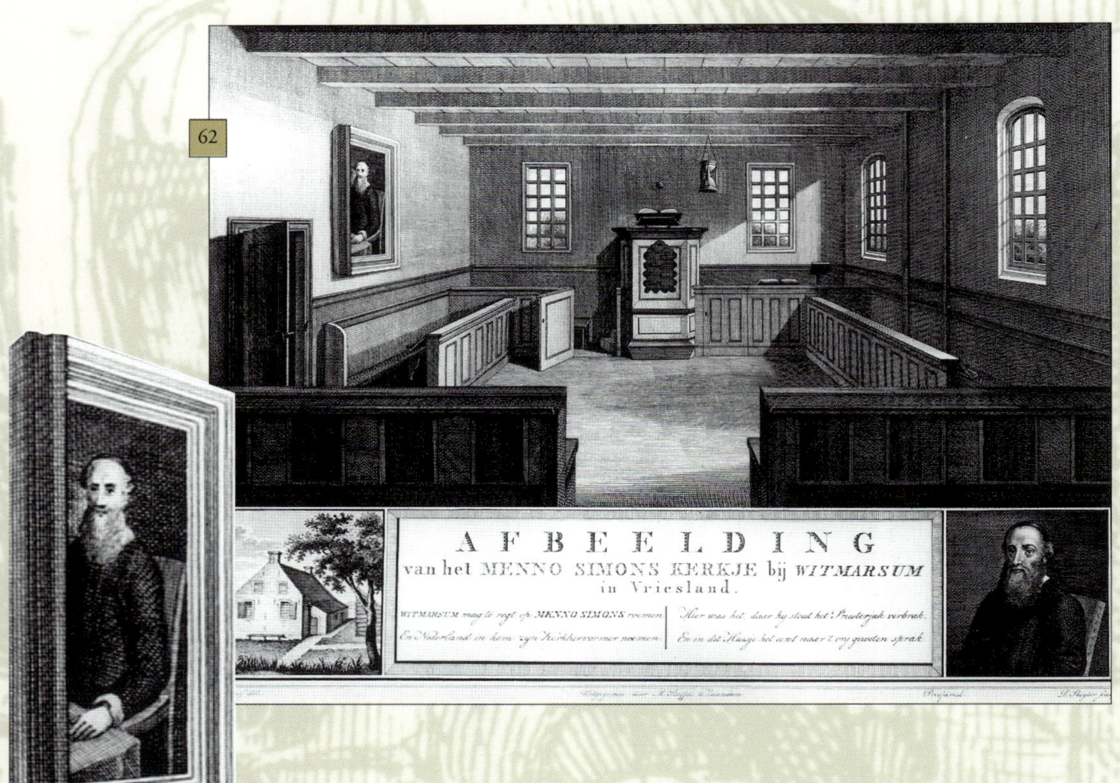
AFBEELDING
van het MENNO SIMONS KERKJE bij WITMARSUM
in Vriesland.
WITMARSUM mag te regt op MENNO SIMONS roemen
En Nederland in hem zyn Kerkhervormer noemen
Hier was het, daar hy stout het Priesterjuk verbrak,
En in dit Huisje het eerst naar 't vry geweten sprak

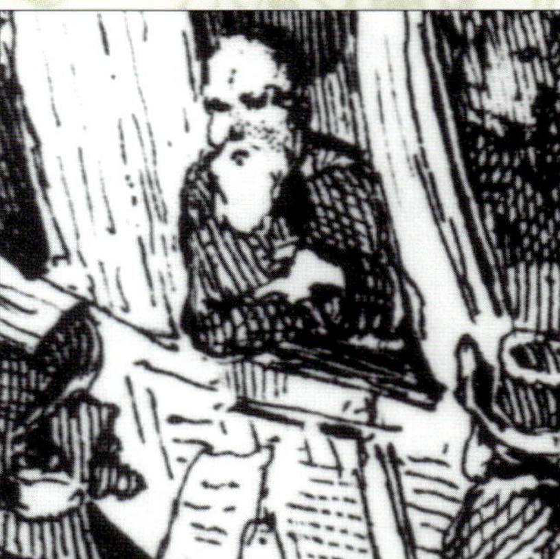

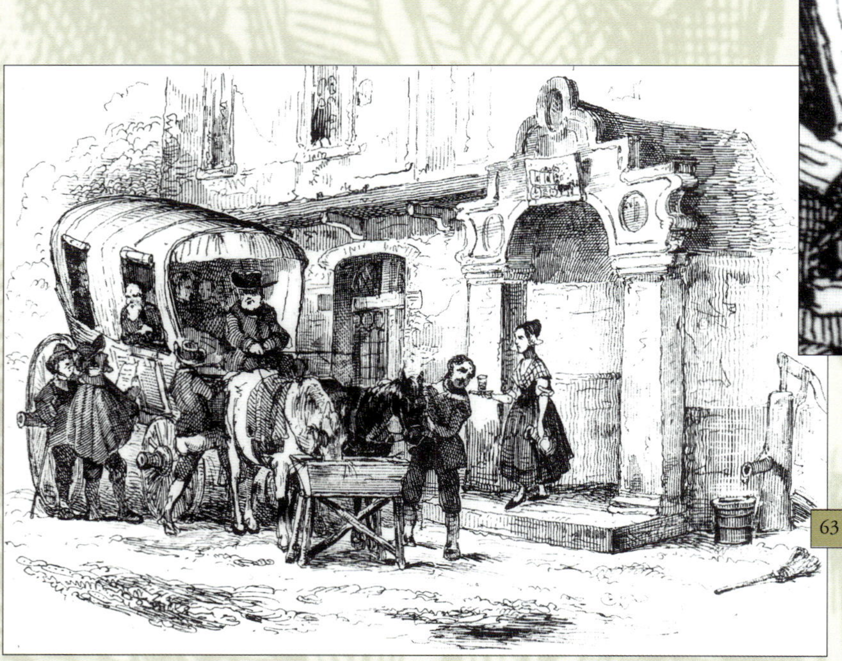

63

62. ca. 1838
H. THEPASS del. / DIRK JURIAEN SLUYTER sculp. / M. STOFFELS [Zaandam, 1829-1847] exc. Engraving 284 x 392 / 349 x 457. *AFBEELDING // van het MENNO SIMONS KERKJE bij WITMARSUM // in Vriesland.*, followed by 2 x 2 rhymed lines *WITMARSUM mag ... sprak.* On the left wall the painting by van der Kooi (nr. 32); below right portrait 40.1 (B 28; H 20; vR 250) - UBA-DG; CCU.

63. 1840
ANONYMOUS
Litho 90 x 122. Leaning out of a window of a coach, illustrating the mailcoach legend in *Hollandsch Penning-Magazijn Voor De Jeugd* (Zaltbommel, Joh. Noman en Zoon, 1840, 6th annual), p. 97 (fol. 47) (at B 44) - UBA.

64. 1856
VALENTIN BING inv., del. / W. STEELINK sculp.
Steel engraving 150 x 220 / 194 x 282. Menno in medallion cartouche with five others around a religious debate between Luther and Zwingli at Marburg (1529). Titleprint of P. Hofstede de Groot et al. (eds.), *Geschiedenis Der Christelijke Kerk in tafereelen* (Amsterdam 1856) vol. IV (B 45) - UBA.

65. 1914
ANONYMOUS
Zinc etching 170 x 120. *FEESTMAALTIJD ter gelegenheid van het eeuwfeest van E.T.E.B.O.N.* Front page of the program of the student union *E*igen *T*abak *E*n *B*ollen *O*m *N*iet (Your own tobacco and rolls free), June 9, 1914 (B 51) - UBA-DG.

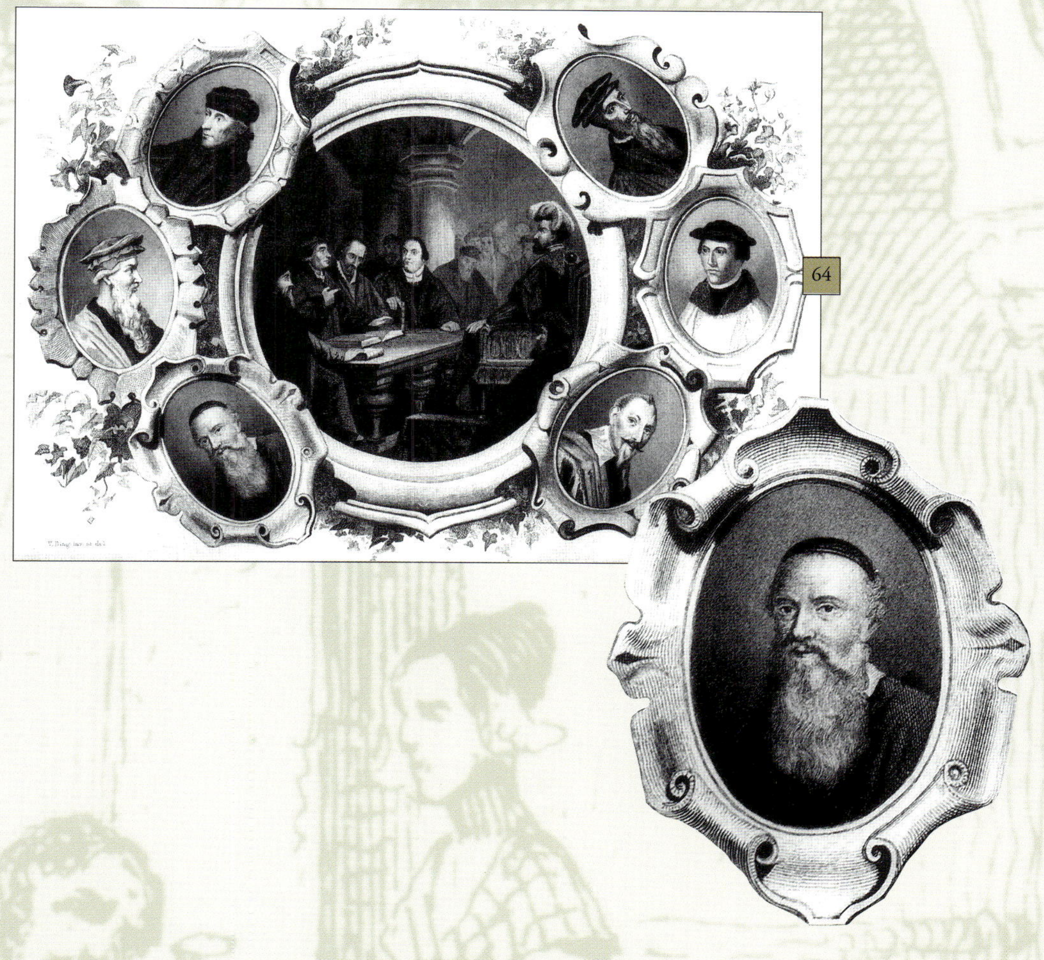

64

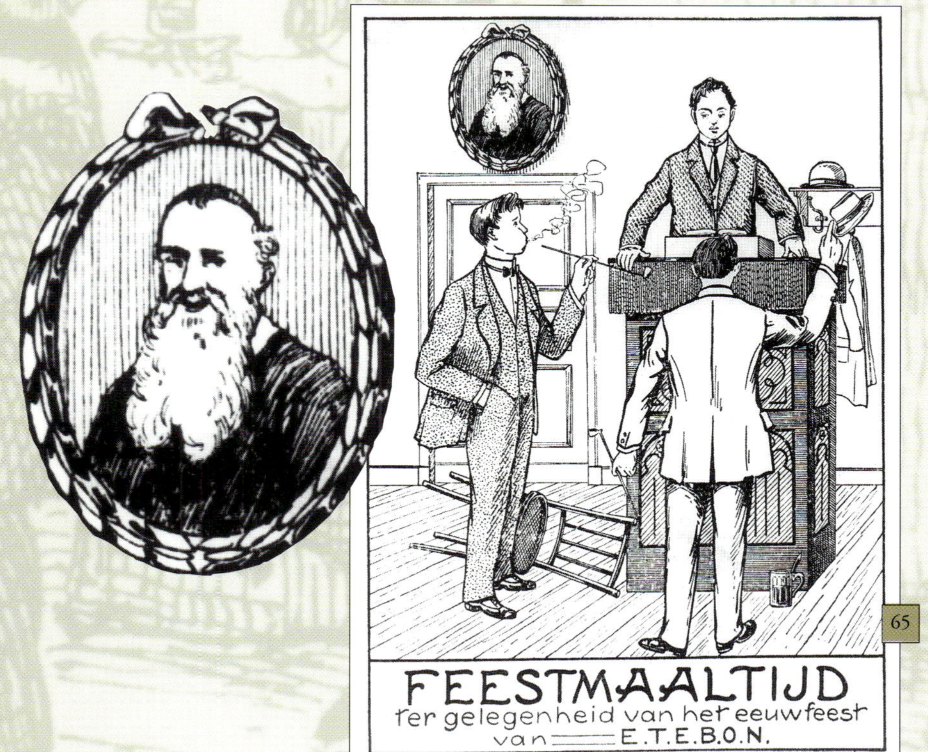

65

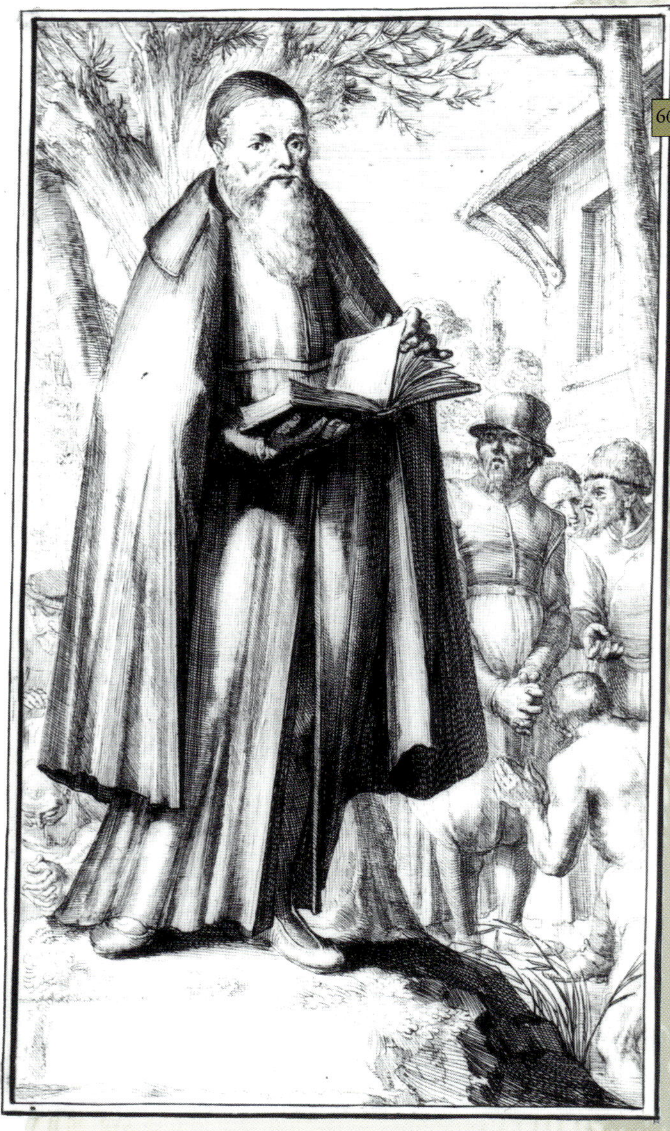

66.1 ca. 1701
Etching [by Romeyn de Hooghe] 259 x 152 / 263 x 157. Without inscription; inspired by 11 (van de Velde) (B 59a) - UBA-DG.

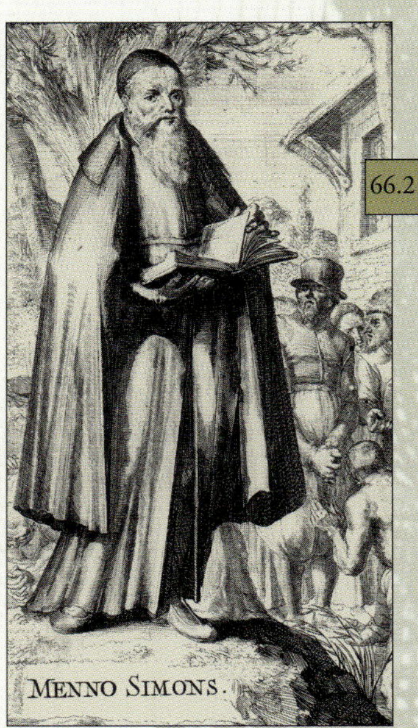

66.2 1701
ROMEYN DE HOOGHE
As 66.1: *MENNO SIMONS.*, above left *2 Deel*, above right *Pag. 533*. Illustration in G. Arnold, *Historie Der Kerken En Ketteren ... Vercierd ... Door ... Romeyn De Hooghe* (Amsterdam 1701) vol. II, opposite p. 533 (B 59b; H 19; M 3562; L 93) - UBA-DG.

CHODOWIECKI TYPE

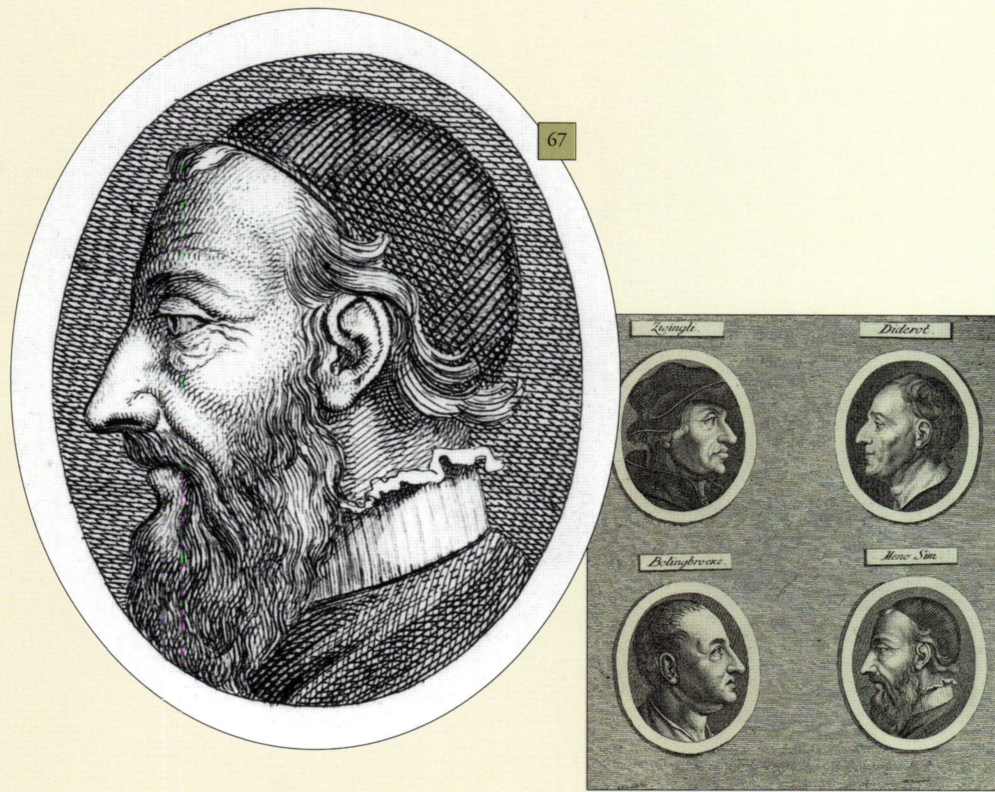

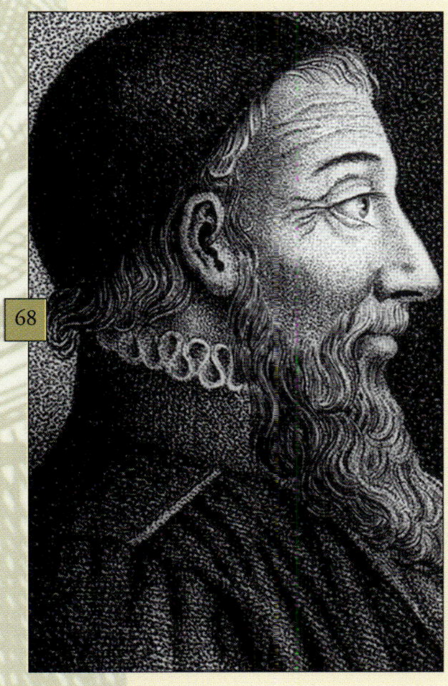

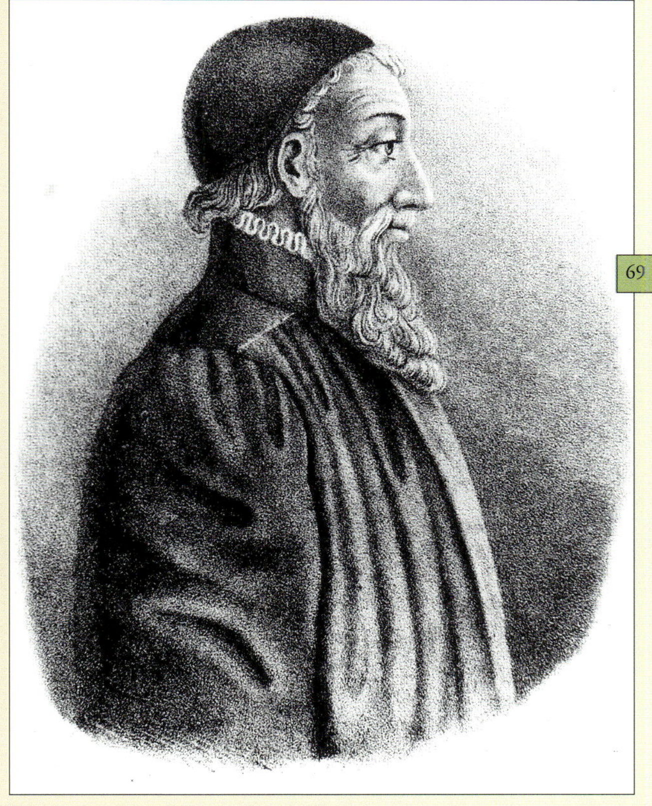

67. 1777
DANIEL CHODOWIECKI del. / JOH. H. LIPS fec.
Engraving 192 x 169 / 200 x 178 (Menno 50 x 38). *Meno Sim.* above portrait below right, on a page with three others. Illustration in J.K. Lavater, *Physiognomische Fragmente zur Beförderung der Menschenkenntnis* (Leipzig-Winterthur 1775-1778) III, opposite p. 276. Inspired by 31 (Burghart) (B 60) - KBH.

68. 1812
L. SCHLEMMER, fec.
Dotted engraving 75 x 59 / 110 x 73. *MENNO SIMONIS // gebohren Ao. 1505 // gestorben Ao. 1561.* Title illustration in J.H. Jung Stilling, *Taschenbuch für Freunde des Christenthums ... 1813* (Nürnberg [1812]) (B 61) - UBA-DG; MFW.

69. ca. 1848
WAGNER & MCGUIGAN
[Philadelphia, VS] lith.
Litho 153 x 121. *MENNO SIMON.* Illustration in I.D. Rupp (ed.), *History of All the Religious Denominations in the United States.* 2nd Impr. Ed. (Harrisburg, PA, 1848), between pp. 406-407 - MHSL/EMU.

71

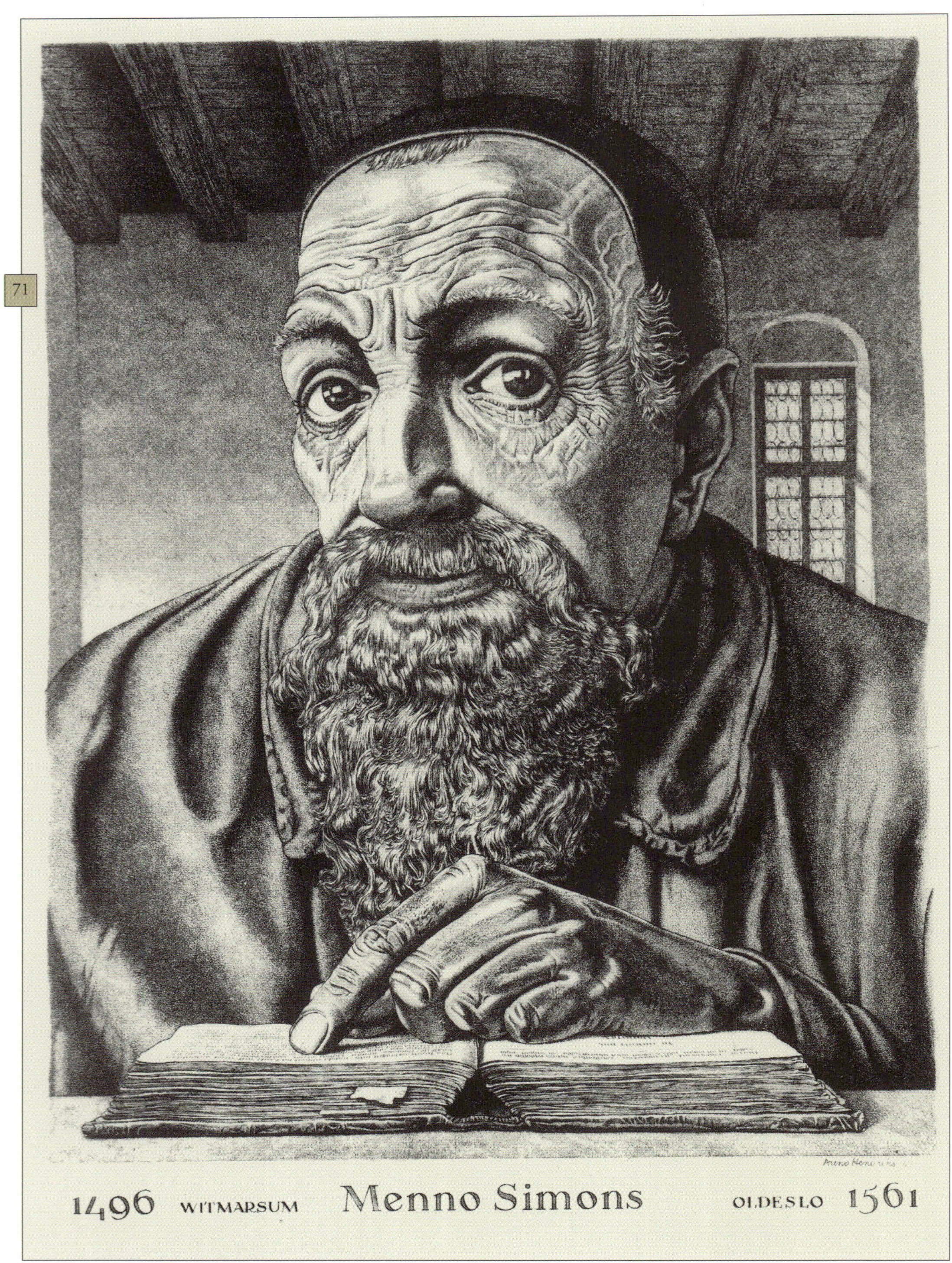

71. 1948

AREND HENDRIKS

Etching 263 x 210 / 285 x 210. *1496-WITMARSUM Menno Simons OLDESLO-1561.* Commissioned by the Publicity Committee of the Dutch Mennonite Conference; printed on hand-made and common paper. The copperplate is located in UBA-DG (H 22) - MHL/GC; UBA-DG; RPA; MSHL/EMU.

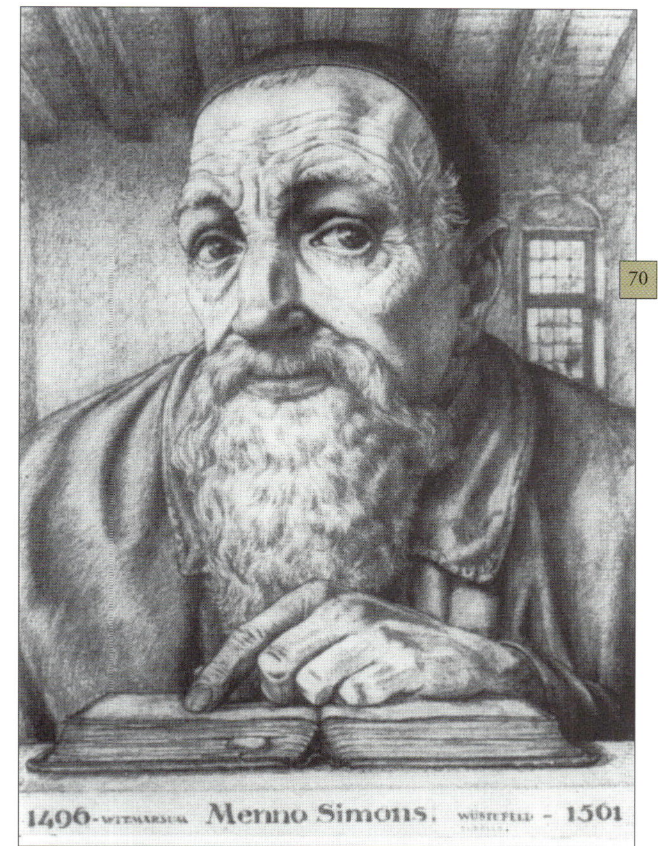

70

70. (1947) 1948

AREND HENDRIKS

Photo of pencil drawing 136 x 101. *1496-WIT-MARSUM Menno Simons. WÜSTEFELDE-1561* (1947), design for nr. 71. Illustration in *Mennonite Life,* July 1948, p. 19. Location of the original unknown - UBA-DG.

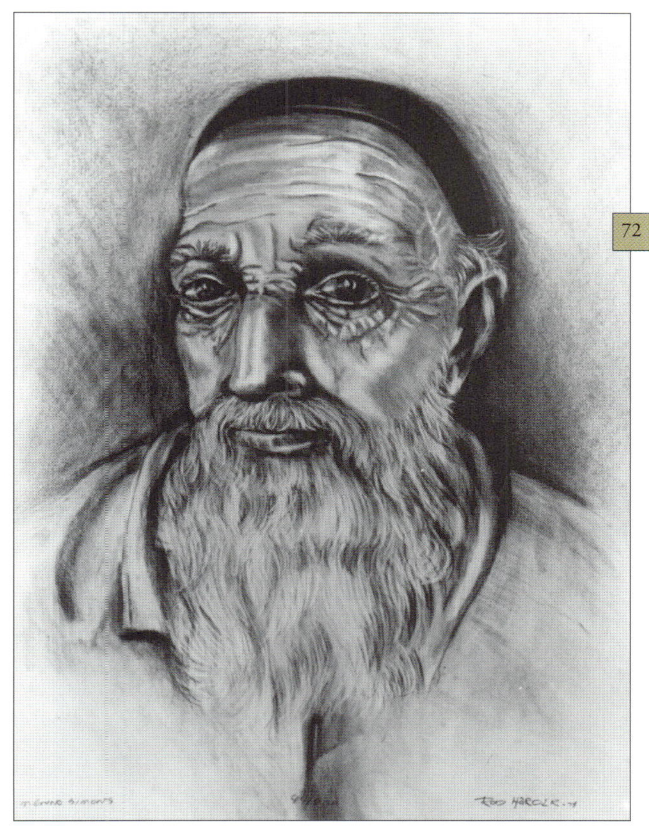

72

72. 1978

RON HARDER

Photolithographic reproduction of a pen drawing 393 x 304. *Menno Simons.* Published by the California Mennonite Historical Society - UBA-DG.

DIVERSE PORTRAITS

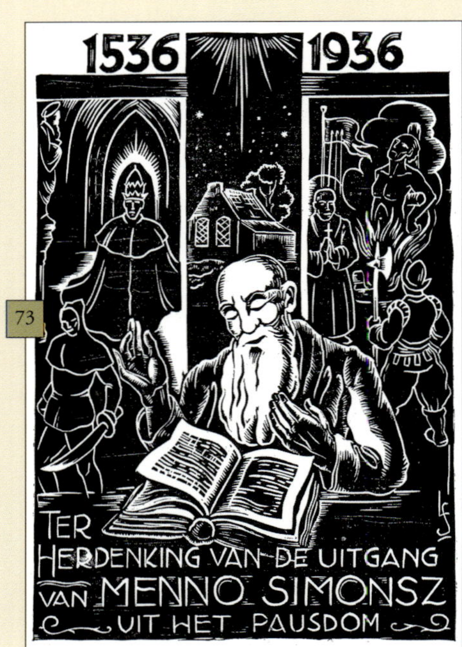

73

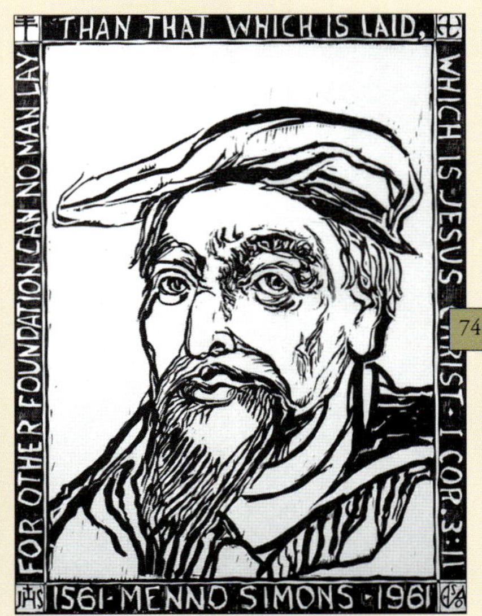

74

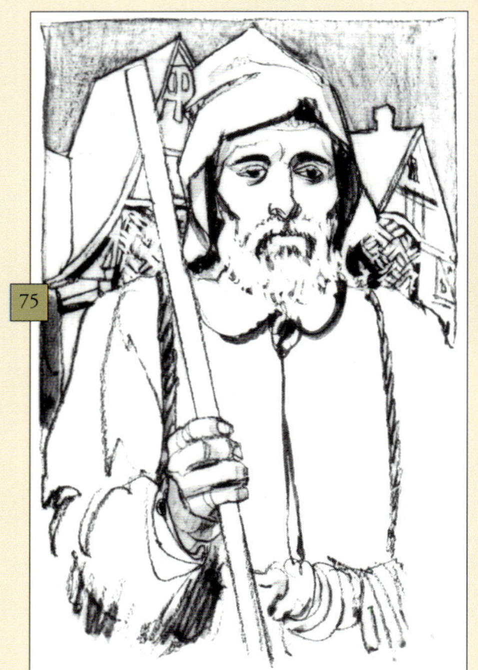
75

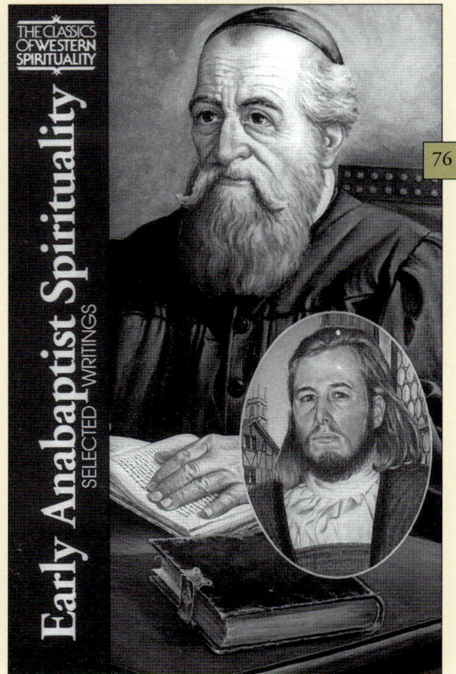

76

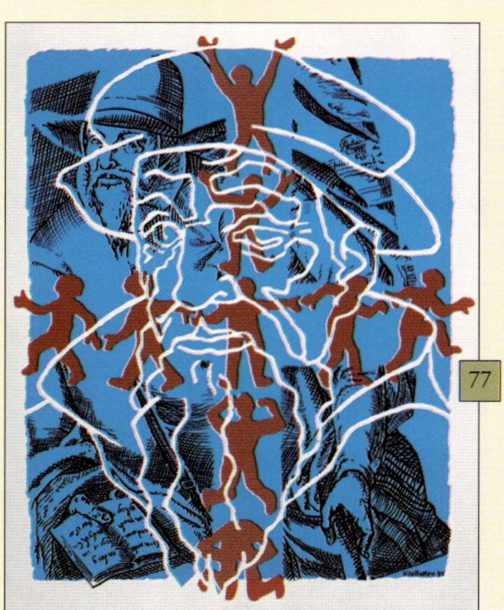
77

73. 1935
LOUIS SCHRIKKEL
Woodcut in reddish-brown ink 209 x 144. *TER HERDENKING VAN DE UITGANG VAN MENNO SIMONSZ UIT HET PAUSDOM.* (*Zondagsbode* 49 (1935) nr. 6, 8 December, p. 23) - UBA-DG.

74. 1961
WARREN ROHRER
Woodcut 545 x 415. *1561 - MENNO SIMONS - 1961*, with legend in black background *FOR OTHER ... I COR. 3:11.* Commissioned by Eastern Mennonite University, Harrisonburg, VA, where the woodblock is also located (H 23) - MSHL/EMU.

75. 1973
RICHARD LOEHLE
Reproduction of a pencil drawing 105 x 68. In C.J. Dyck, *Twelve Becoming: Biographies of Mennonite Disciples from the Sixteenth to the Twentieth Century* (Newton, KS, 1973), p. 16 - UBA-DG.

76. (1975) 1994
[TOM (OLIVER WENDELL) SCHENK]
Reproduction in 4-colour-printing 227 x 112 of the painting by Schenk (see A4), with insert in medallion of Felix Mantz. Illustration on the cover of D. Liechty, *Early Anabaptist Spirituality: Selected Writings* (Mahwah, NJ, 1994) (H 24) - UBA-DG.

77. 1995
AIZO BETTEN
Serigraph in three colours 463 x 383. Commisioned by the Menno-500 Committee of the Dutch Mennonite Conference for the commemoration of the 500th birthday of Menno in 1996. Based on 1 (van Sichem) and 74 (Rohrer) (see A21) - UBA-DG.

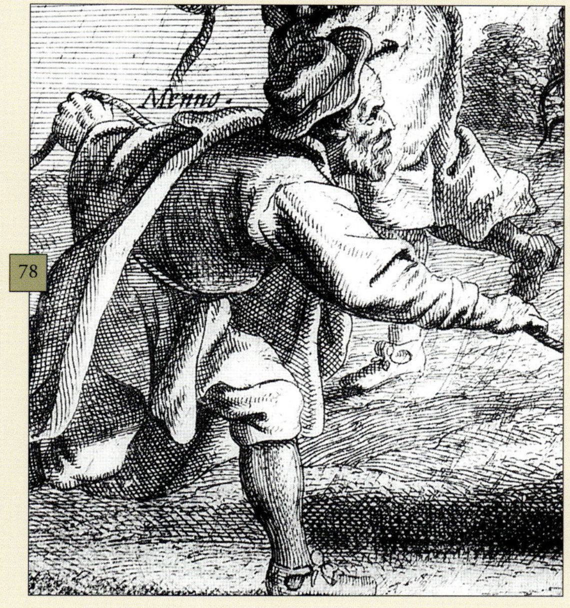

78

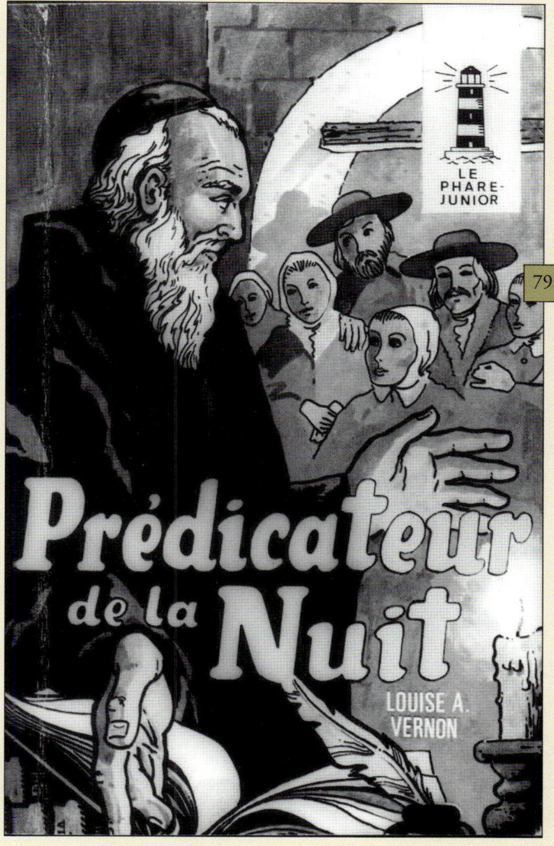

79

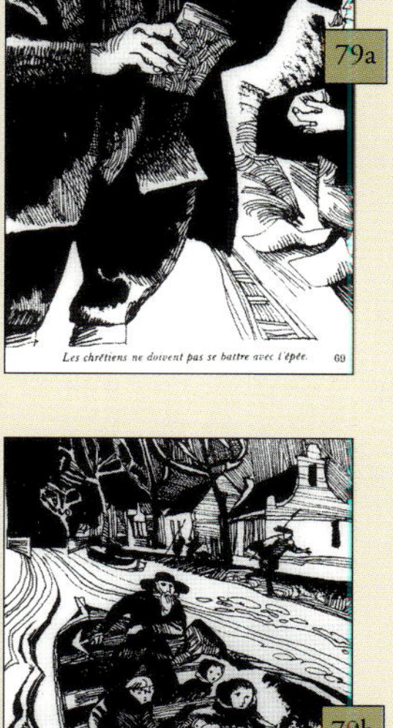

79a

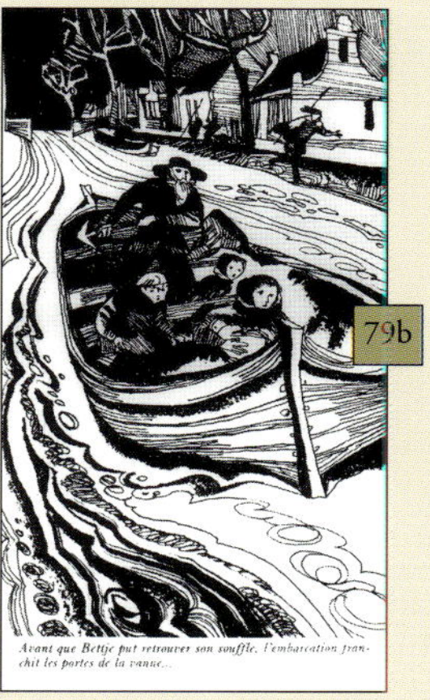

79b

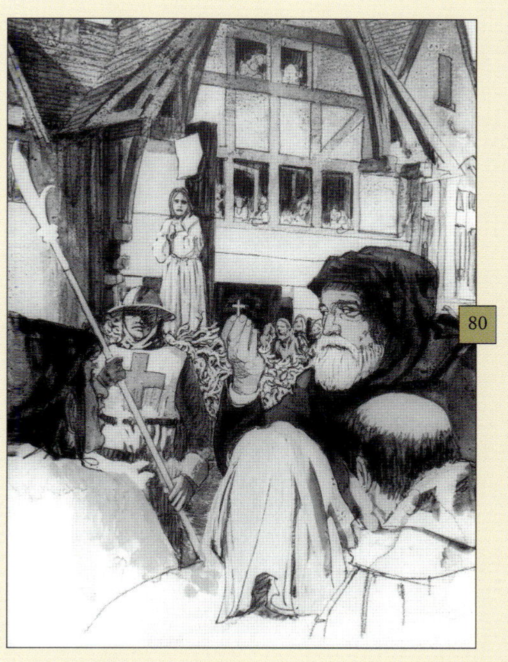
80

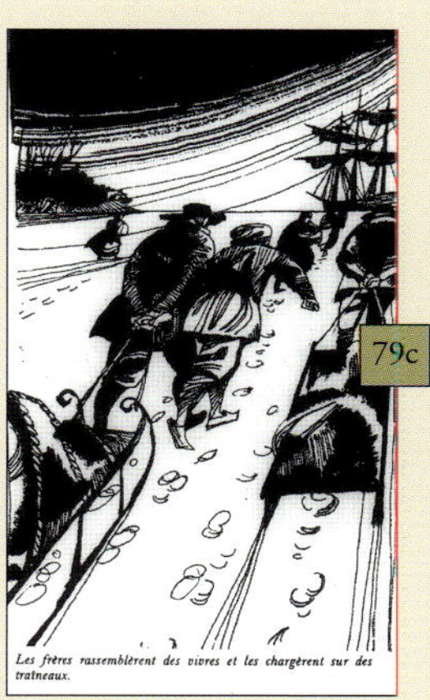

79c

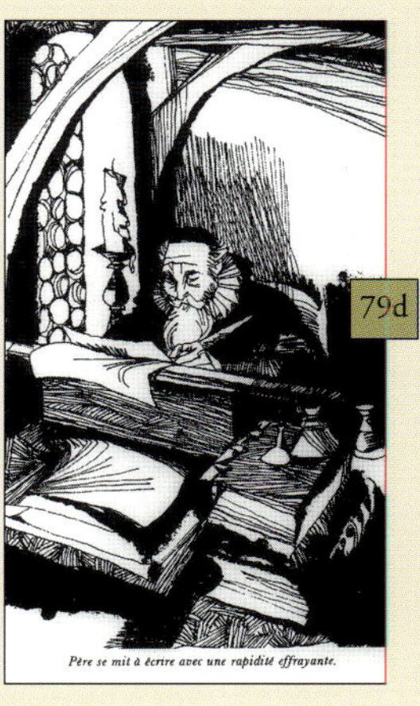

79d

78. 1656
ANONYMOUS
Engraving 110 x 164 / 117 x 170. Menno, Luther and Calvin are pulling at John the Baptist. Lower part of an illustration in Aernout van Geluwe, *Eerste Deel Over De Ontledinghe Van dry verscheyden Nieuw-Ghereformeerde Martelaers Boecken* (Antwerpen, Widow and heirs of Jan Cnobbaert, 1656), p. 26 (see p. 117) - UBA-DG.

79. 1972
ANONYMOUS
Colour illustration 177 x 115. On the cover of L.A. Vernon, *Predicateur de la Nuit* (Flavion (B) [1972]), also containing four illustrations with a 'divergent' Menno on pp. 69, 87, 122 en 138 - UBA-DG.

80. 1973
RICHARD LOEHLE, ill.
Reproduction of a pencil drawing 260 x 200. In C.J. Dyck, *Twelve Becoming* (see 75), opposite p. 13 - UBA-DG.

APPENDIX: A SELECTION OF ALTERNATIVE PICTURES

The appendix is intended to illustrate the broader application of the Menno-portrait. This diverges from serious paintings and drawings to cartoons and teaspoons - from devotion to commerce. This part is in no way complete, but demonstrates at best the diversity of a modest 'Menno-mania'.

A1

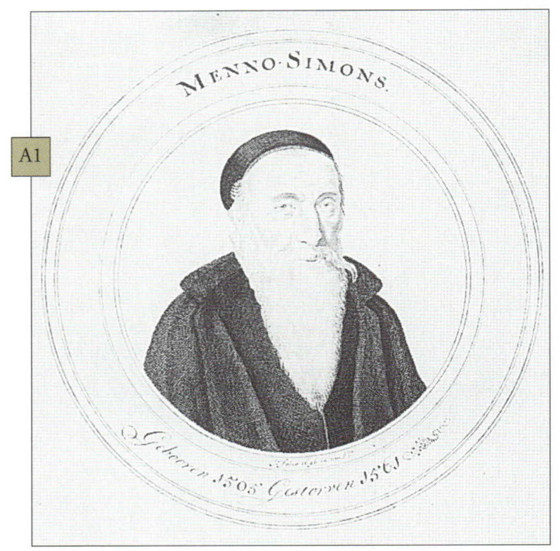

A2

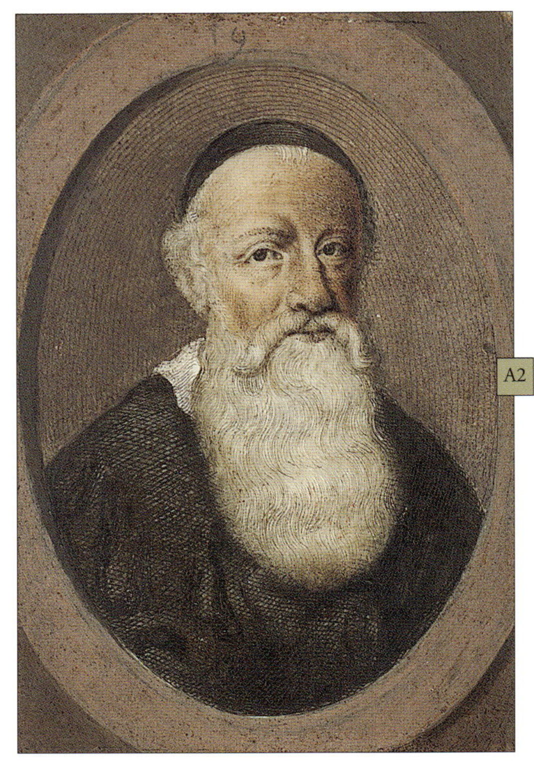

A3

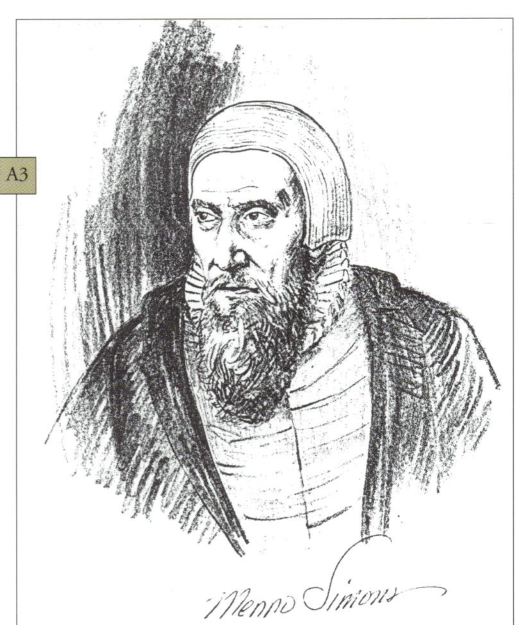

A4

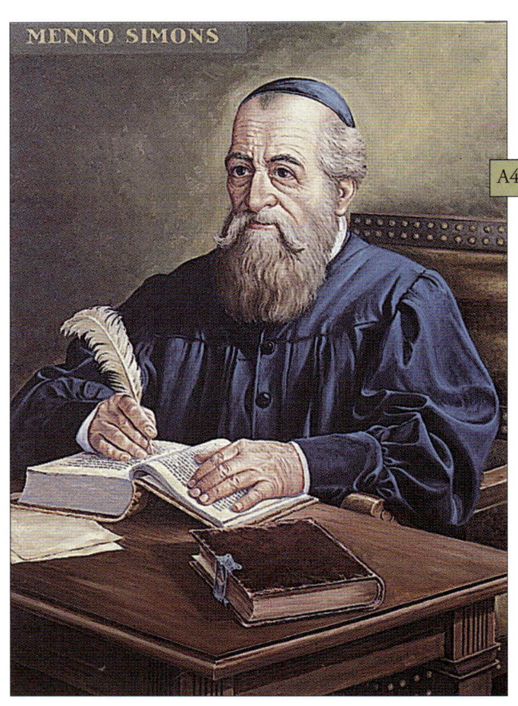

Paintings & Drawings

A1. 1696
JOHAN FABER, Amsterdam
Pen drawing on parchment (diameter 123). *Menno Simons,* below it *Gebooren 1505 Gestorven 1561.* Drawn after 7.4 (van de Velde) (B) - FML.

A2. > ca. 1729
CLEMENT NACHTEGAAL sculp.
Painted engraving on ivory 100 x 69; after 43.1 - P.C.I.

A3. 1970
EDWIN B. WALLACE
Drawing 162 x 138. *Menno Simons.* Designed for a book by Myron S. Augsburger, that was never published - P.C.3.

A4. 1975
TOM (OLIVER WENDELL) SCHENK
Oil painting on canvas. *MENNO SIMONS.* Inspired by Burghart (31). Commissioned by Myron S. Augsburger for Eastern Mennonite Seminary (see 76) (H 24) - EMS.

Medals

A5. 1736
MARTINUS HOLTZHEY fec.
Silver commemorative medal (diameter 54) for the occasion of the second centenary celebration of Menno's renunciation of Rome. Front: *MENNO SIMONIS AETAT ANNO LXVI VITAE POSTREMO, MDLXII.* Obverse 11-line rhyme *Dit's MENNO ... behagen,* underneath: *GEBOREN TE ... LUBEK, 1561.* (B 52) - UBA-DG.

A6. 1909

JOHANNES VON LANGA

Commemorative medal in silver and in bronze (diameter 50) for the occasion of the 350th anniversary of his death. Front: *MENNO SIMONS* and *1. CORINTHER 3 Vs. 11.*, around the edge: *GEB. ZU ... JAN. 1559;* obverse: impress of the Hamburg-Altona Congregation with motto *IDEM NOS UNIT,* around the edge: *MENNONITEN-GEMEINDE ZU HAMBURG UND ALTONA;* stamped at the bottom in cartouche: *13. JAN. 1909.* (MB 56 (1909) nr. 4, April, p. 33; B 55) - UBA-DG.

A7. 1911

JOHANNES VON LANGA

Commemorative medal in silver and in bronze (diameter 50) for the 25-year union of the German congregations. Front: *MENNO SIMONS,* around the edge: *ZUR ERINNERUNG ... GEMEINDEN i. D.R. 1911;* obverse: *GEGRÜNDET ... DEM GEMEINDEN:* with enumeration of the churches in 12 lines and *JETZIGER VORSTAND:* with the names in 4 lines (B 56) - UBA-DG.

A8. 1912

JOHANNES VON LANGA

Commemorative medal in silver and in bronze (diameter 50) for the occasion of the 25-year existence of the Mennonite Congregation Berlin (Germ.). Front as A7: legend below: *MENNO SIMONS,* above along the edge: *GOTT DIE EHRE FREI DIE LEHRE;* obverse: *ZUR // ERINNERUNG ... GEMEINDE // 1912* (B 57) - UBA-DG.

Sculptures

A9. 1849

E.F. GEORGES

Plaster bust (height 310), *MENNO SIMONS* in the socle. Modelled after the so-called Utrecht portrait of Menno, which actually represents Viglius van Aytta (1507-1577) (cf. B 1) - DGS.

A10. 1987

ESTHER K. AUGSBURGER

Bonded copper (height 290) - MSHL/EMU.

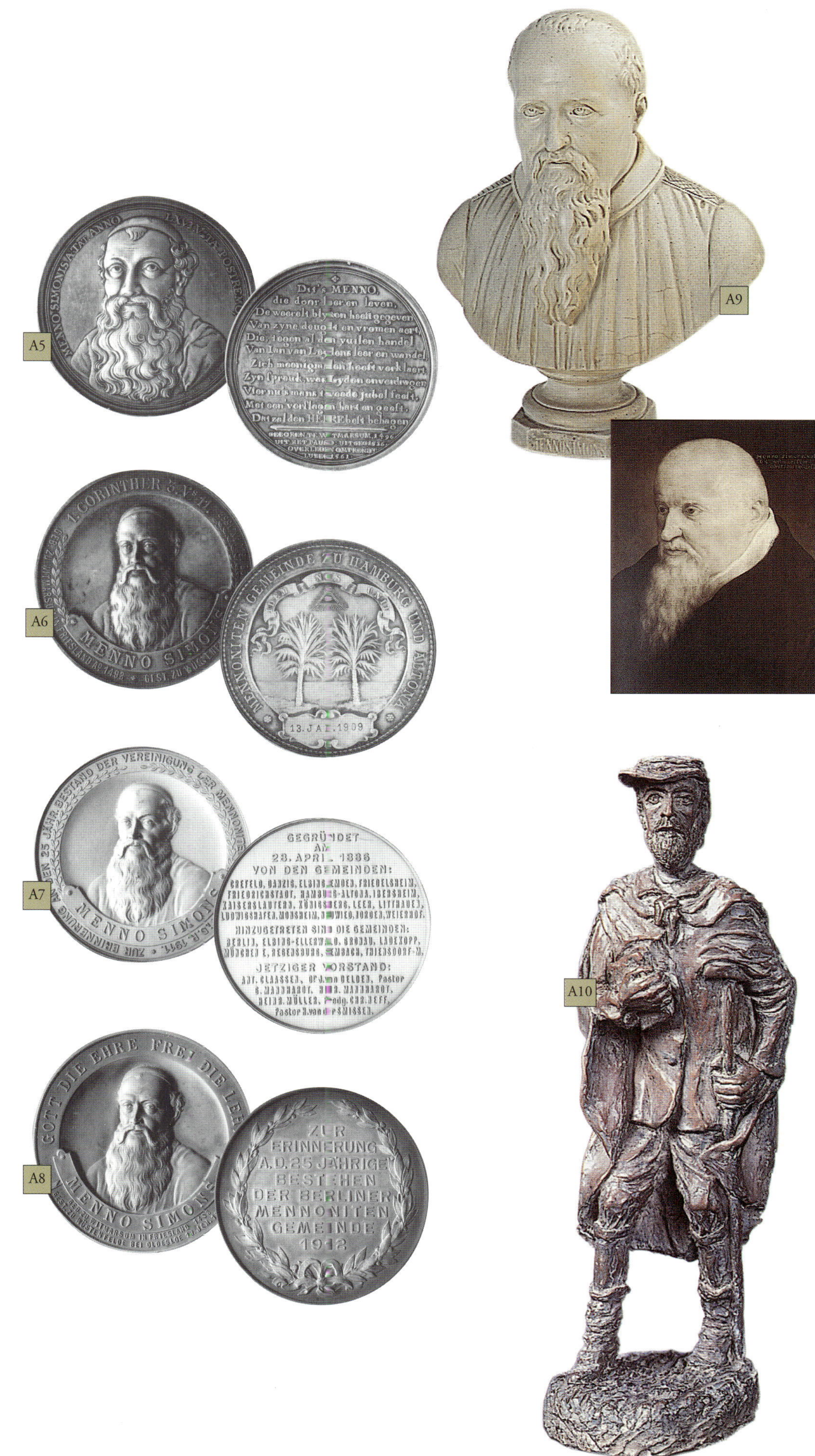

A11

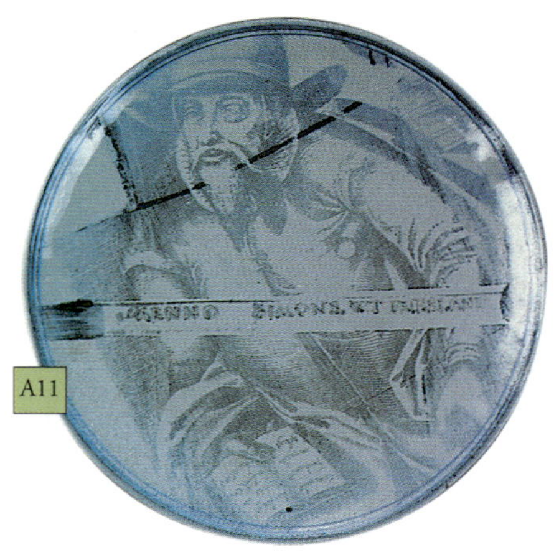

A12

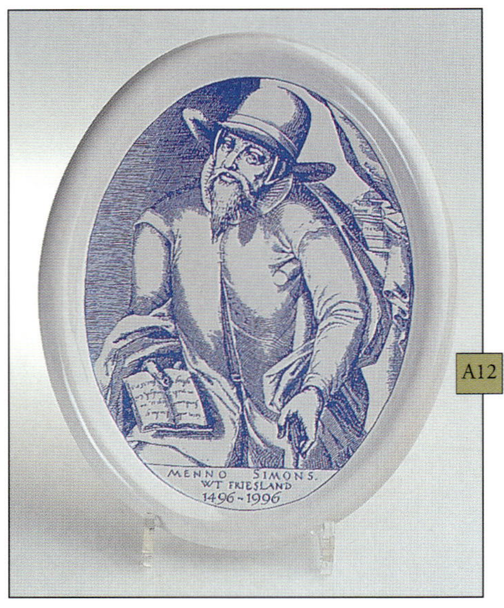

A13

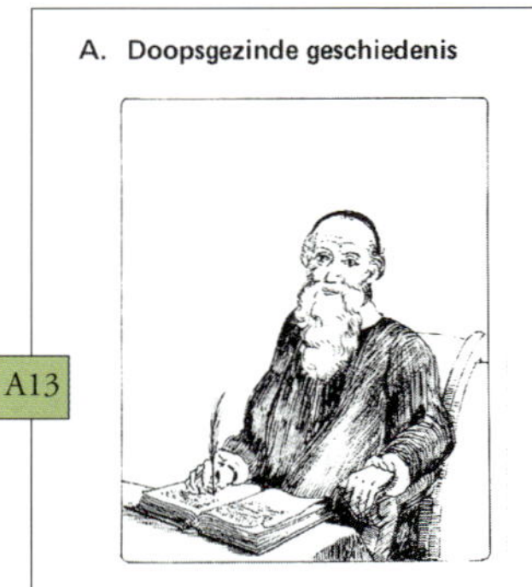

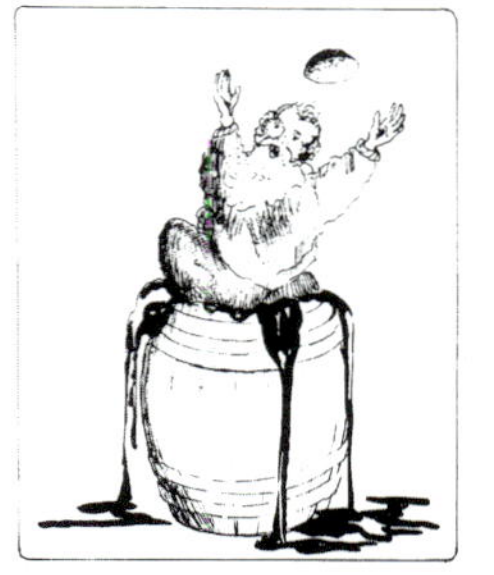

A15

Was Menno Simons gay?
See page seven.

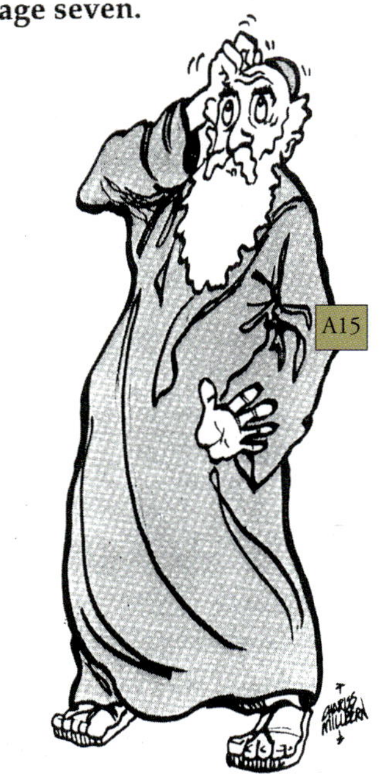

A14

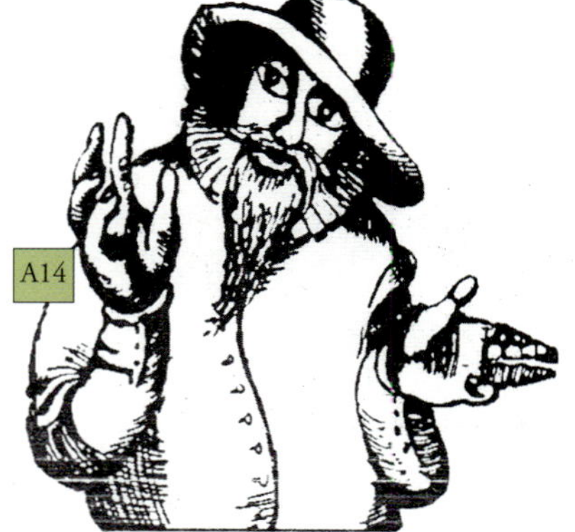

'Hi fellows, let's call it a day!'

A16

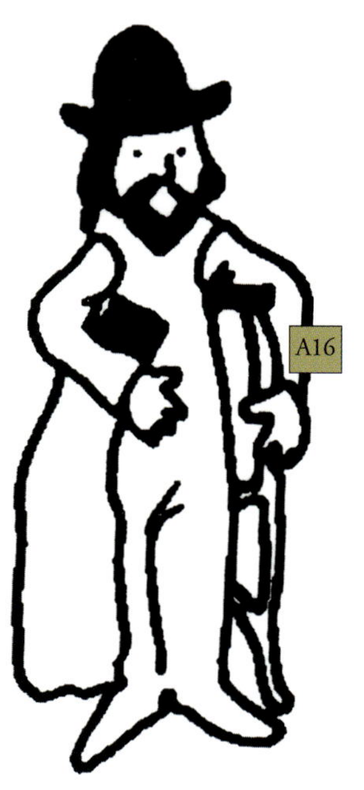

Ceramics

A11. ca. 1985
MARVIN BARTEL
Plate (diameter 385). On reverse: 'Image after engraving by Christoffel van Sichem 1546-1624. Image engraving ca. 1608'- MSHL/EMU.

A12. 1996
ROYAL TICHELAAR, Makkum
Oval plaque (also in purple) 290 x 235. On reverse: 'After an engraving by Christoffel van Sichem' - UBA-DG.

Cartoons

A13. ca. 1980
T. SCHAAP-STUURMAN dr. / FIRMA J. ROGGEBAND printer.
Pendrawing on two playing cards 63 x 50 of the *Doopsgezind Kwartetspel;* inspired by Burghart (31) - UBA-DG.

A14. 1990
JOANNA HORST
Cliché of pen drawing: 51 x 65. Menno as commentator in the ADW, from 45 (1990) nr. 1; de facto representing Adam Pastor, by van Sichem (see p. 63) - UBA-DG.

A15. ca. 1990
CHARLES MILLBERN
Drawing 159 x 55. 'Was Menno Simons gay?'. On the cover of *The Mennonite Distorter* [ca. 1990] - UBA-DG.

A16. 1993
CHERYL BENNER
Computer drawing 33 x 6. On the titlepage of G. Haas & S. Nolt, *The Mennonite Starter Kit* (Intercourse, PA, 1993); also on pp. 18-19: 'Where's Menno at the Relief Sale?'- UBA-DG.

Diverse

A17. ca. 1800?
ANONYMOUS
Bent relief in brass 43 x 39, fixed on an oval shield (58 x 84) with chain; cast of A5 (cf. B 52) - P.C.1.

A17

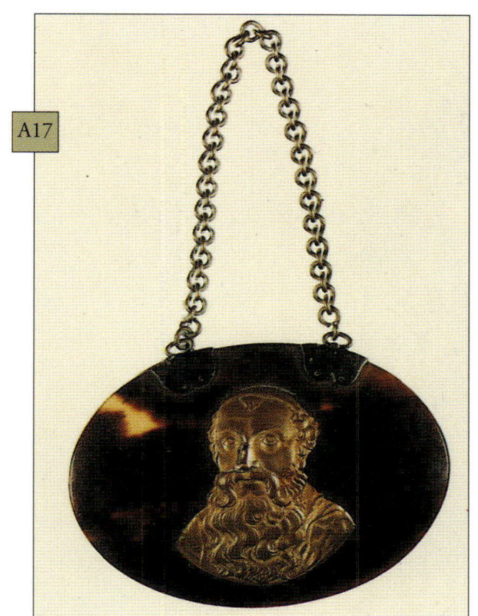

A18. 1960
J.M. THUNACK [Brummen]
Stained glass window 800 x 490 / 451 x 326. *MENNO SIMONS.* Loosely after 31 (Burghart) and 66 (de Hooghe). Commissioned by W.G. Rijks-Vaags at Doetinchem (ADW 41 (1961) nr. 41, p. 5) -DGS.

A18

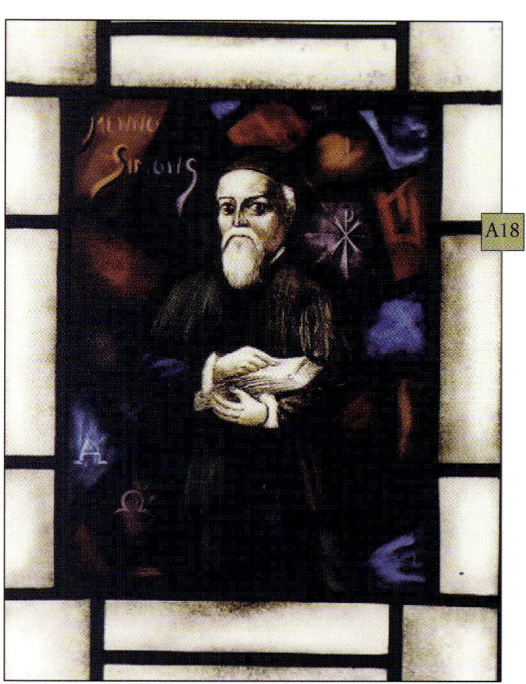

A18.1 ca. 1965
W.G. RIJKS-VAAGS
Glazed wall tile 150 x 150 (Mosa). Handpainted copy after A18 - UBA-DG.

A18.1

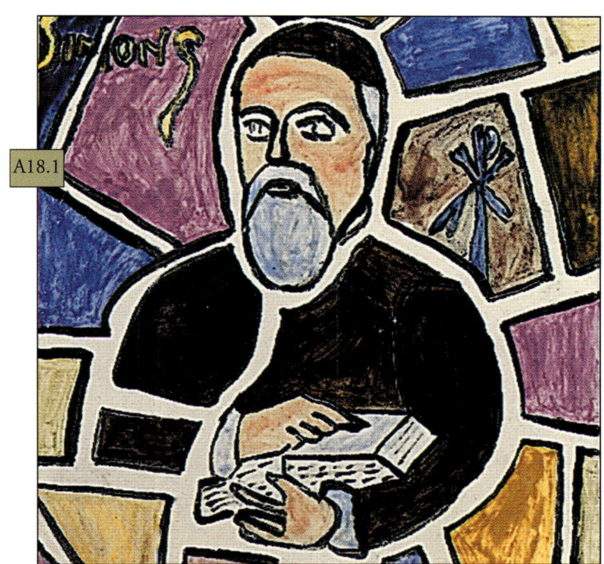

A19. 1961
Silver and gilded teaspoon (length 124) after van Sichem (1). Made for the occassion of Menno's 400th anniversary of his death and the 150-year existence of the Dutch Mennonite Conference in 1961 (ADW 16 (1961), nr. 10, p. 7) - P.C.2.

A19

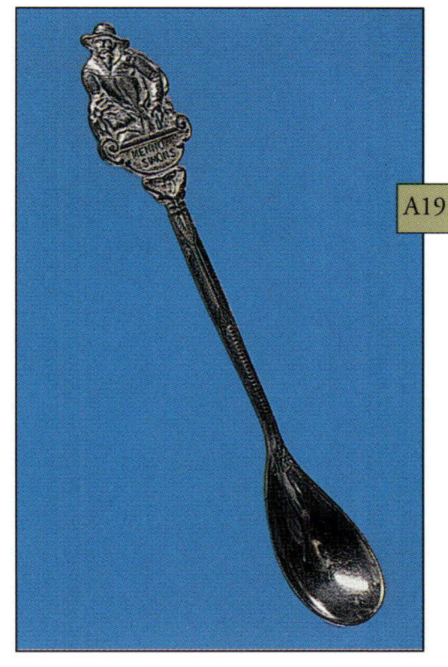

A20. 1996
LANSA, Kollum
Sheet 100 x 150 with 10 postage stamps of the Regional Mail Company North-East Friesland, value of 50 cents; reproduction of the painting by van der Kooi from 1824 (see 32) - UBA-DG.

A20

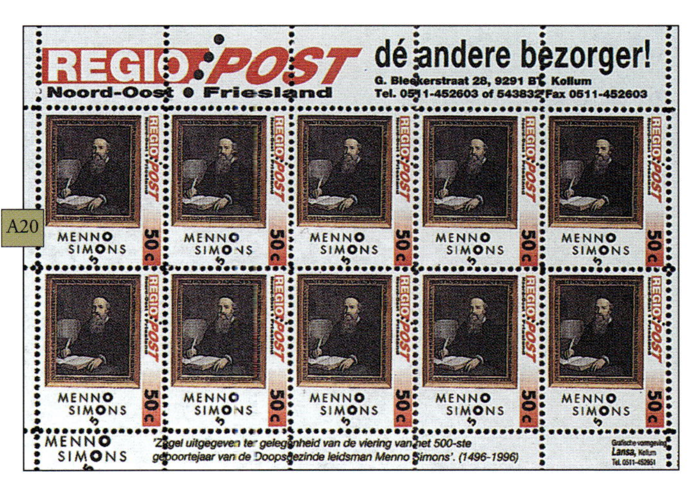

A21. 1996
[AIZO BETTEN]
Sticker 100 x 70. *MENNO SIMONS 500.* Reproduction after nr. 77 - UBA-DG.

A21

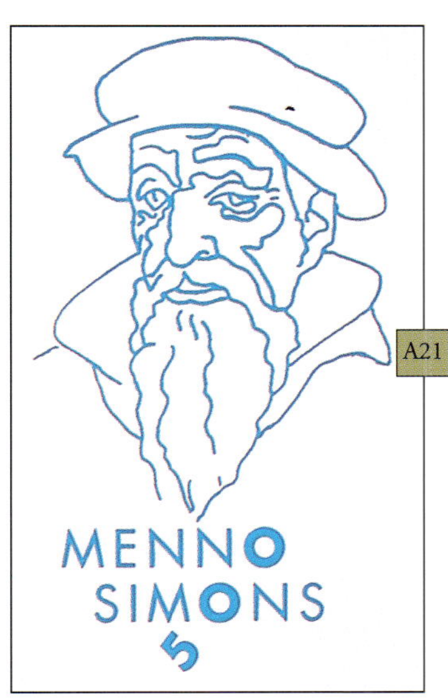

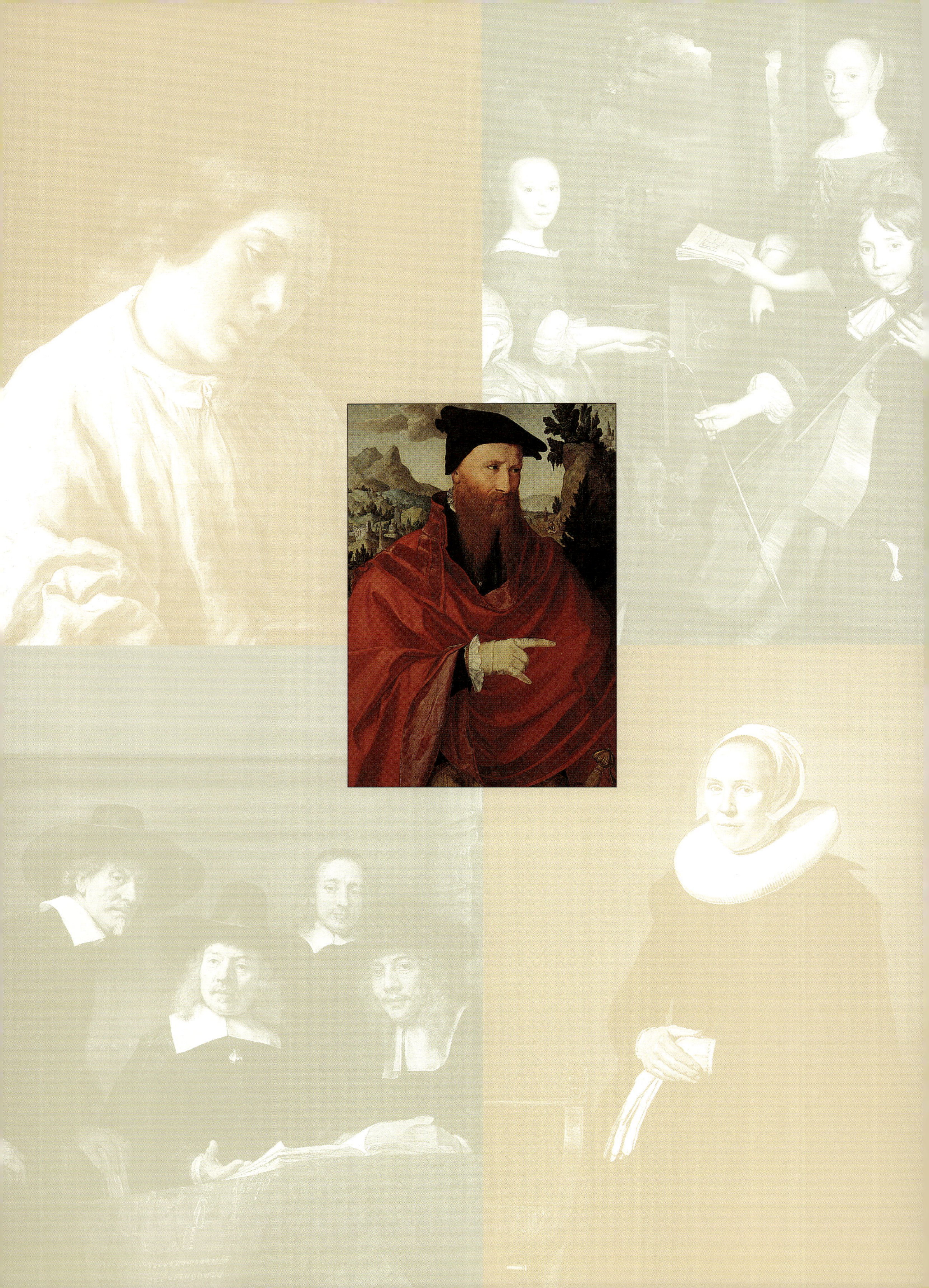

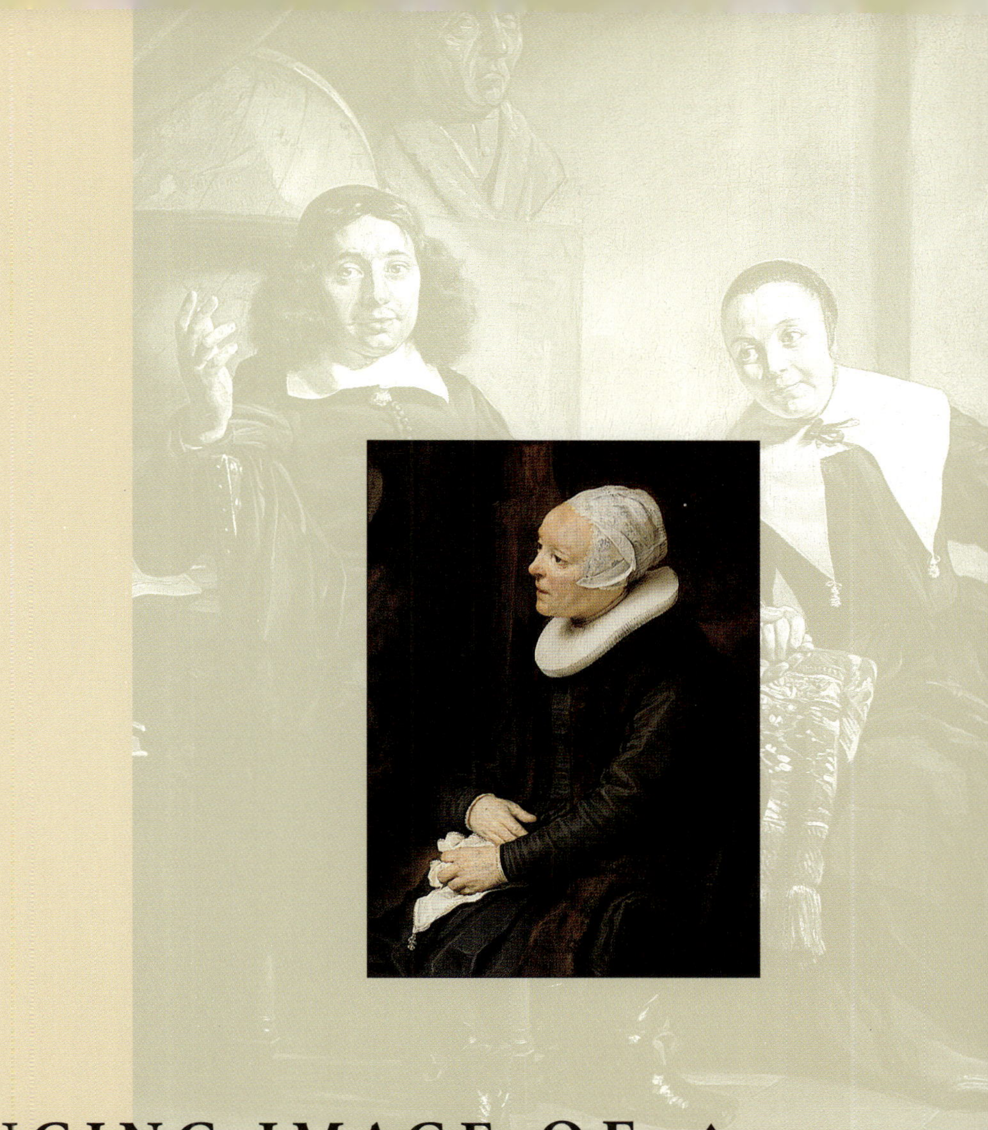

♦ THE CHANGING IMAGE OF ♦

MENNO AND THE MENNONITES

IN DUTCH ART

(CA. 1535 - 1740)

♦

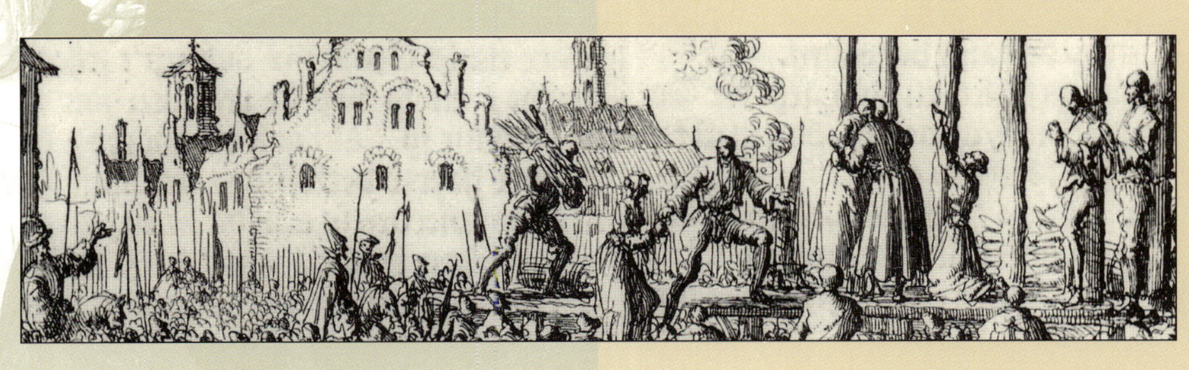

♦

MENNO EN MÜNSTER:
♦ THE HAUNTED MINORITY ♦

No other reformation movement in the Netherlands has precipitated so much action and reaction as Anabaptism. This was the case from the beginning and became much more acute with the advent of Münsterite Anabaptism. What looked at first like a successful movement, inspired by Melchior Hoffman, was mercilessly crushed in the end. Church and Emperor reacted harshly to the unprecedented enthusiasm of Hoffman's followers and meted out fatal punishment. Menno's calling was with the peaceful – but nevertheless outlawed – Anabaptists who continued in their clandestine faith even in the aftermath of Münster. A grim hunt for heretics characterized this period until 1574 in the Northern and 1597 in the Southern Netherlands. In spite of it all, thousands of followers, depicted by their persecutors as the basest people imaginable, remained steadfast in their newly acquired faith to the death upon scaffold and stake. For the spectators, these events provided enough material not only to talk and write about, but also to record in image. The first has occurred in many forms, for the number of extant documents, both manuscript and printed, enlightens us about the unequal battle between ruthless persecution and passive suffering. Only occasionally, however, have these oppressive episodes been documented in drawings or paintings.

Unlike journalists today, who seek out the sensational, sixteenth-century reporters had a different purpose in mind. The Anabaptist minority was regarded as newsworthy not out of some religious-anthropological curiosity, as our newscasts might portray the sect, but as an example of disorder and heresy. Only when the Anabaptist revolt could be used as an objectionable example in the propaganda of the ruling morality and power were images considered useful. The burgomasters in the old City Hall of Amsterdam took daily warning from the painted scenes (destroyed by fire in 1652) of the shocking events which occurred in their city in the days of May 1535. The lesson was that Anabaptists posed a grave danger to order and authority; hence their lot was the eternal fire of hell – like the sea of flames of the Davidians at Waco, Texas. The harsh reality of daily life, with its public executions of these foolish Anabaptists, who called their victims 'martyrs', furnished a more frightening image than any artist could record with pen or brush.

We know very little about what daily life was like for the average Anabaptist or how they practised faith. It was too dangerous for those involved to record their activities on paper. And for a painter or engraver, documenting the ordinary was neither a completely honorable nor profitable subject. Not until the seventeenth century could artists let their imaginations loose. Even then, most continued to work within the framework of the ruling political and ecclesiastical propaganda. Only a few artists, who saw in the Anabaptist martyr history a New Testament dimension, used their talent out of empathy for the victims and their spiritual descendents. Jan Luyken was one such artist who, although paid to do so, illustrated the martyr stories with an innovative depth of understanding, more than one hundred years after the gruesome events took place.

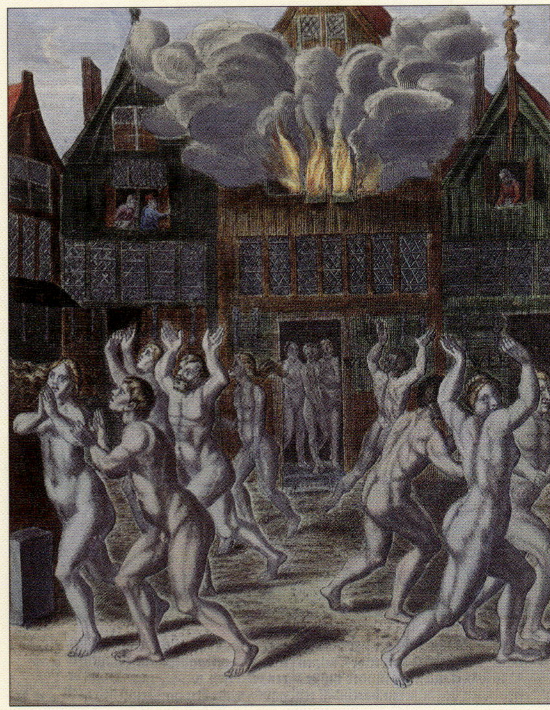

1. Anonymous, engraving in Hortensius, colored by Dirck Jansz van Santen - UBA

2. Anonymous, engraving in Hortensius, colored by Dirck Jansz van Santen - UBA

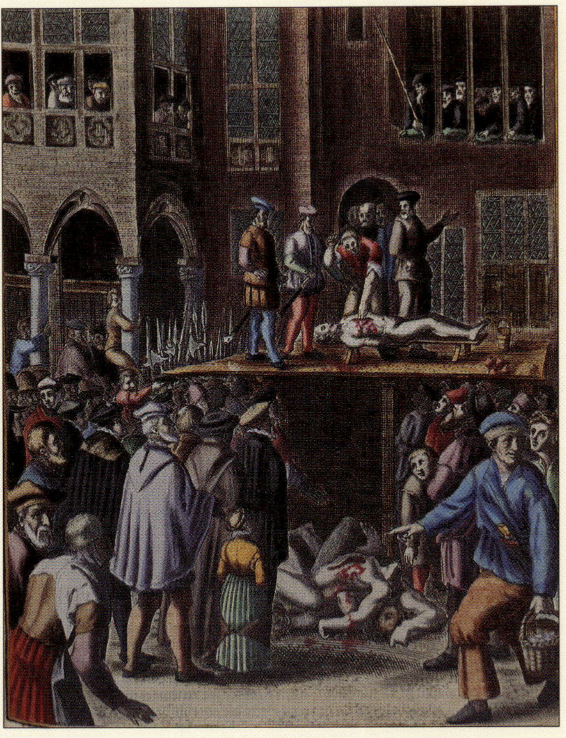

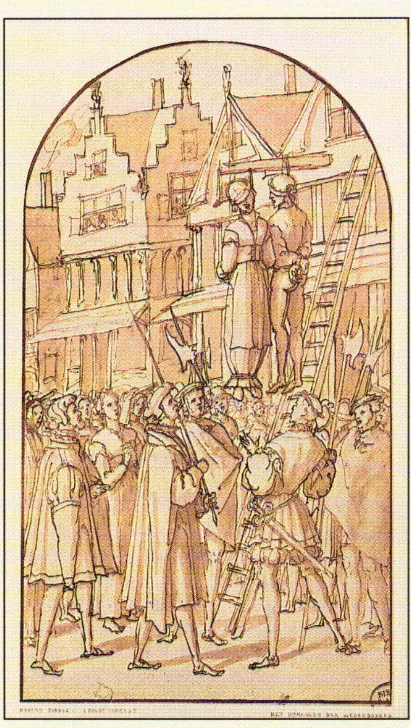

3a&b. Barent Dircksz, drawing (ca. 1535) - AHM

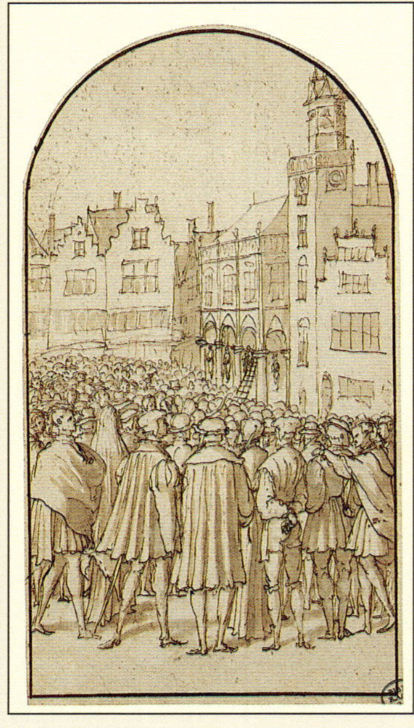

1.
On the 10th and 11th of February, 1535, several men and women ran naked through the streets of Amsterdam. The prophet Henrick Henricksz Snyder had first taken off the 'old Adam'; as the born again they proclaimed the naked truth. Crying 'Woe! Woe! The wrath of God! The wrath of God!', these Anabaptists warned their fellow townspeople of the approaching Final Judgement. In so doing these *naaktlopers* (naked-runners) signed their own death sentences (Mellink pp. 122-125).

2&3.
In the night of May 10, 1535, about forty Anabaptists under the leadership of Jan van Geelen occupied the City Hall of Amsterdam in order to establish a second Münster there. The rebels and their following were locked in by the militia, who succeeded in putting down the revolt at the cost of 36 lives. Already on May 14, eleven culprits were beheaded after first having their hearts cut out of their bodies and flung into their faces. The following days witnessed dozens more executions, including those of female participants (Mellink pp. 135-149).

4.
On May 23, 1641, Pieter Codde's play, *Herdoopers Anslagh op Amsterdam* (*The Anabaptists' Attack on Amsterdam*), had its premier in the Amsterdam Theater. It dealt with the revolt of 1535 as an example of the city government's courage and spirit of liberty. The play enjoyed success for years to come. (Worp I, p. 296).

5.
Around 1560, the Mennonites began recording their own martyr history in the *Offer des Heeren (Lord's Sacrifice)*. In this story there was no place for radical Anabaptism: for centuries, Mennonites denied completely any connection with Münster. After eleven reprintings of the *Offer*, at the initiative of Hans de Ries (see 25), the voluminous *Historie der Martelaren (History of the Martyrs)* (1615) appeared. The fourth edition of 1631 formed the basis for Tieleman van Braght's *Bloedig Tooneel (Bloody Theater or Martyrs' Mirror)* (1660; 1685). The cartouches show various martyr and execution methods. Beneath them the pope and the authorities sign the death pact, while above, in the heavenly counterpart from the apocryphal book 4 Ezra 2:43, God's Son crowns the immortal ones (ME III, pp. 518-519).

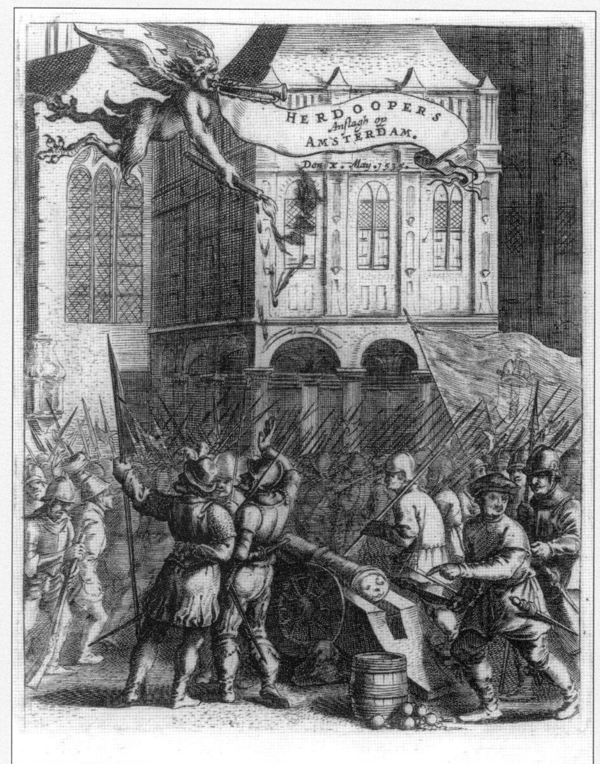

4. Anonymous, engraved frontispiece of P. Codde, *Herdoopers Anslagh* (Amsterdam 1641) - UBA

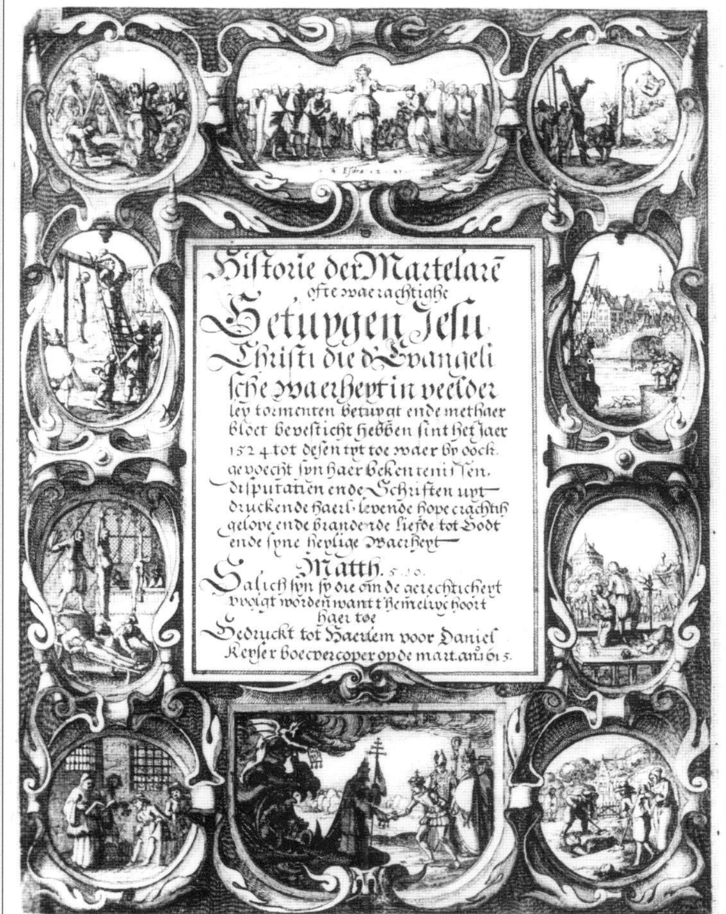
Historie der Martelaren
ofte waerachtighe
Getuygen Jesu
Christi die d'Evangeli
sche waerheyt in veelder
ley tormenten betuygt ende met haer
bloet bevesticht hebben sint het jaer
1524 tot desen tyt toe waer by oock
ghevoecht syn haer bekentenissen,
disputatien ende Schriften uyt
druckende haer levende hope crachtich
gelove ende brandende liefde tot Godt
ende syne heylige Waerheyt
Matth. 5.10.
Salich syn sy die om de gerechticheyt
vervolgt worden want t'hemelryc hoort
haer toe
Gedruckt tot Haerlem voor Daniel
Keyser boecvercoper op de mart. an̄o 1615.

5. Anonymous, engraved titelpage of De Ries et al., *Historie der Martelaren* (Haarlem 1615) - UBA-DG

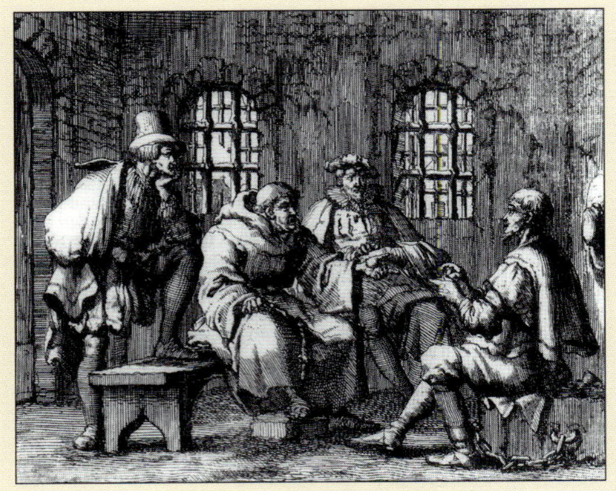

6. Jan Luyken, engraving in Braght II, p. 425 (MM, p. 775) - UBA-DG

7a. Jan Luyken, washed pen drawing; design for the engraving in Braght - AHM

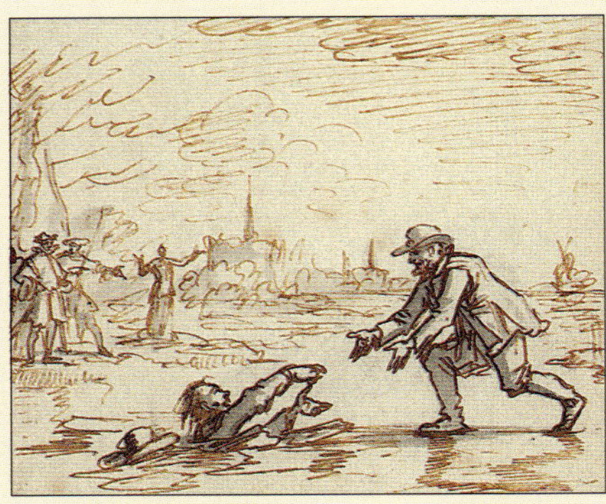

7b. Idem, engraving in Braght II, p. 387 (MM, p. 741) - UBA-DG

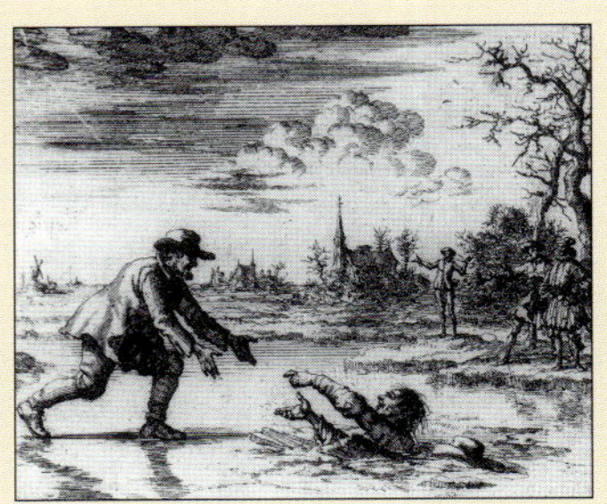

6.
The Flemish leader Jacob de Keersgieter, or De Rore, was arrested in April 1569 in Bruges, together with Herman van Vlekwijk. Between cruel tortures the prisoners underwent lengthy hearings. Before his death at the stake, Jacob conducted fierce debates with the notorious Franciscan monk Broeder Cornelis (ME III, pp. 62-63; vE&vdK 737).

7.
In the winter of 1569, Dirck Willemsz managed to escape from prison in Asperen, making his way over some ice. When the thiefcatcher, close on the fugitive's heels, fell through the ice, Dirck cut short his escape to save the man from drowning. Despite Dirck's heroic deed, the burgomaster issued no pardon, and on May 16, Dirck was burned outside of Asperen (ME II, pp. 66-67; vE&vdK 736 and p. 786).

8. Jan Luyken, engraving in Braght II, p. 553 (MM, p. 886) - UBA-DG

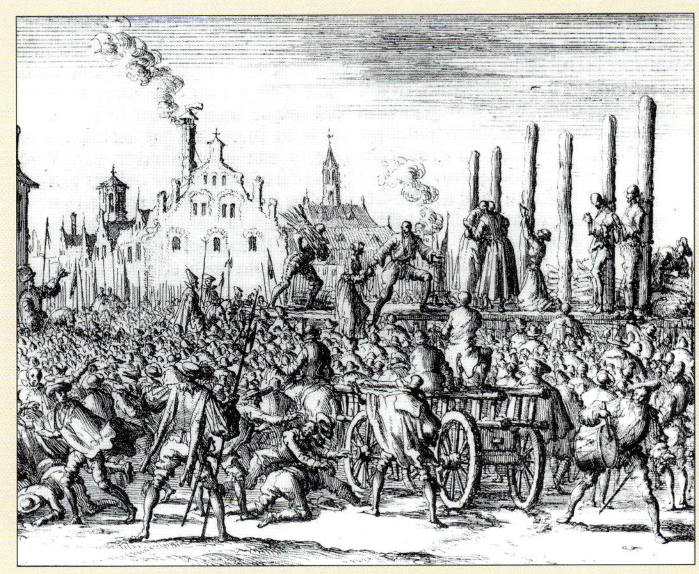

8.
Returning from a tournament during the night of March 11, 1571, some Spanish soldiers delivered six men and seven women into the hands of the Deventer law authorities. On May 24, six of the Anabaptists were killed by burning on the Brink Square; baskets filled with their heretical books also went up in flames. The other six - one young woman had repented - endured the same lot on June 16 (Rademaker 1, pp. 48-50; vE&vdK 743).

9.
'Geleyn de Schoenmaker was totured most cruelly of all. They stripped him naked, and suspended him by his right thumb, with a weight attached to his left foot, and while thus suspended he was burned under his arms with candles and fire, and scourged until the two commissaries of the Duke of Alva ... themselves became tired, and went away and set down to play cards'. Geleyn was arrested on August 5, 1572 near Breda, along with six other heretics (ME II, p. 451; MM, p. 931; vE&vdK 746).

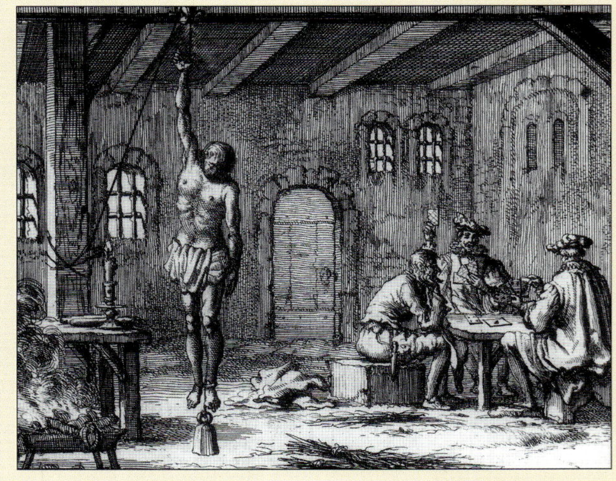

9. Jan Luyken, engraving in Braght II p. 605 (MM, p. 930) - UBA-DG

♦

MENNONITERY:
♦ CARICATURES OF MENNONITE MORALITY ♦

The signing of the Union of Utrecht in 1579 by the Northern provinces of the Low Countries formalized the separation from the Spanish Catholic South. While this Union acknowledged freedom of worship and ended religious persecution, there was still no talk of unconditional tolerance. It was the Reformed Church that received a privileged status. Like the Catholics who had been expelled from their parish churches, the Mennonites had to worship in hidden (although not secret) churches. For the most part, governmental offices were closed to Mennonites, and, for reasons of principle, they did not want them anyway. Nevertheless, they clearly enjoyed more societal freedoms than they had under Spanish rule. The once persecuted Anabaptists availed themselves of the doors that were open to them and quietly but steadily applied their talents to the economic sphere.

Mennonite Netherlanders gained respect and became known as a reliable, hard-working community with high moral standards. Indeed, they were called the 'worker bees of the state.' This positive image was, however, still undermined by the spector of Münster and by their divisiveness. The 'Anabaptist Babel' was a favorite subject of ridicule, especially from Reformed critics. The chuckling outsiders also derived perverse enjoyment when they quickly realized that the pious Mennonites 'without spot and wrinkle' did not hold themselves completely aloof from all earthly pleasures. Mennonites thus obtained a reputation for being hypocritical. Under the sober clothes hid secret stores of sweets: expressions such as 'Mennonite beer' (sweet beer), 'Mennonite collar' (an extremely full glass of wine or beer), or 'Mennonite cake' became part of the Dutch language. The 'Mennonite sister', the sanctimoniously pious Bible-quoting young woman who, despite her high principles, succumbs to temptations of the flesh, became the figurehead of Mennonite hypocrisy. She would inspire a number of artists.

The battle against dissent, conducted primarily by the Southern Netherlands that remained Catholic, was always directed against the Protestants in general. From the Catholic perspective, Mennonites had long been emancipated, and Menno, in his roll as Dutch Reformation leader, was lumped together with Luther and Calvin as the Protestant enemies of Rome.

Although the Mennonites themselves would not lack for artistic talent, they did not, with one exception, produce satirical prints from within their own ranks. They lectured each other – and not always gently or with much tact – orally and in a great quantity of polemical writings. One of the many conflicts concerned the question of the 'written or unwritten Word' among the Waterlanders between 1622 and 1627. This was conducted by the most prominent opponents: Hans de Ries (see 25) and Nittert Obbesz. The latter a preacher in Amsterdam, was accused of Socinianism, or *letterknechterij* (literalism) in the jargon of that time, while De Ries and his supporters were accused of *geestdrijverij* (spiritualism or enthusiasm), or subordinating the importance of Scripture to the Spirit. This was graphically portrayed in an image from a pamphlet of 1627 by Nittert's supporter Jan Theunisz. He shows De Ries kneeling on an unprinted bible.

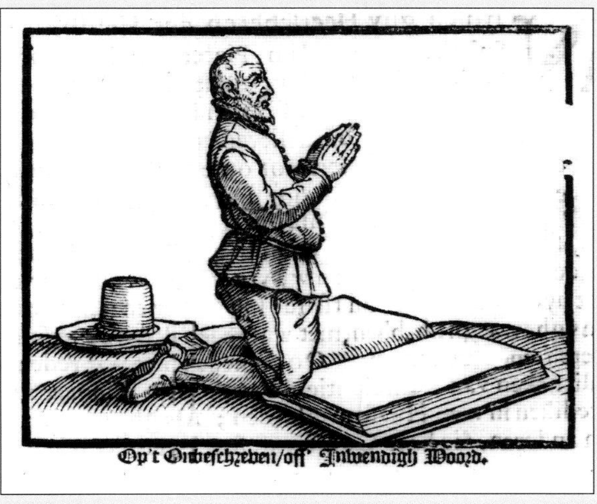

Anonymous, woodcut 'Upon the Unwritten, or the Inward Word'; titleprint of Jan Theunisz, *Een Vraghe Van Nitter Obbesz* (Amsterdam 1627) - UBA-DG

11. Anonymous, canvas: *Peace admonishes the churches to toleration* (ca. 1625) - CCU

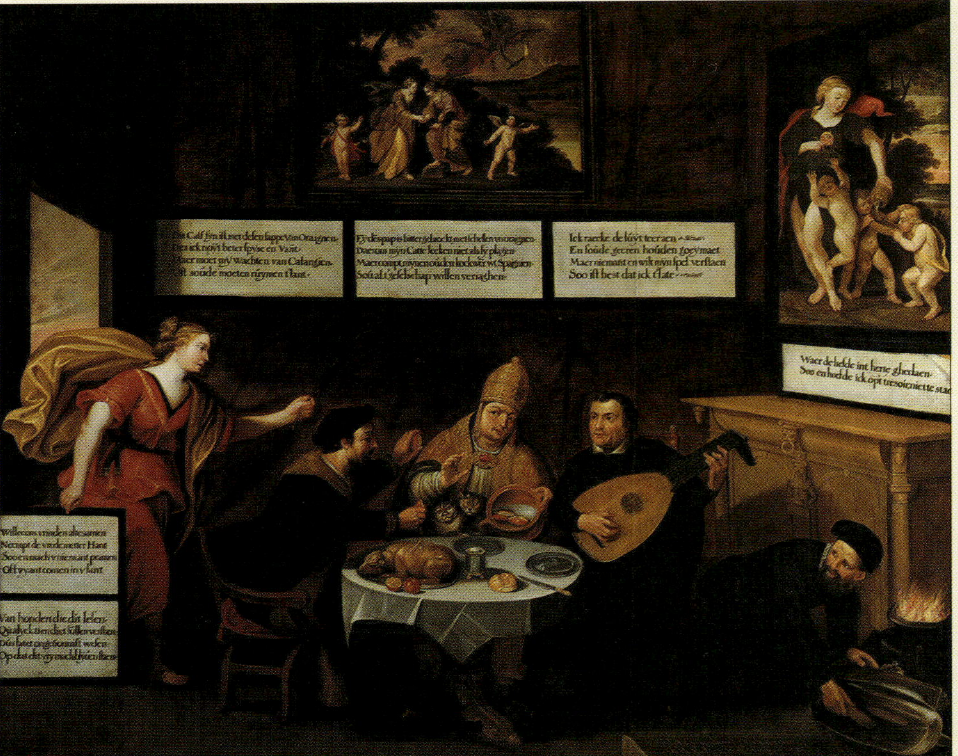

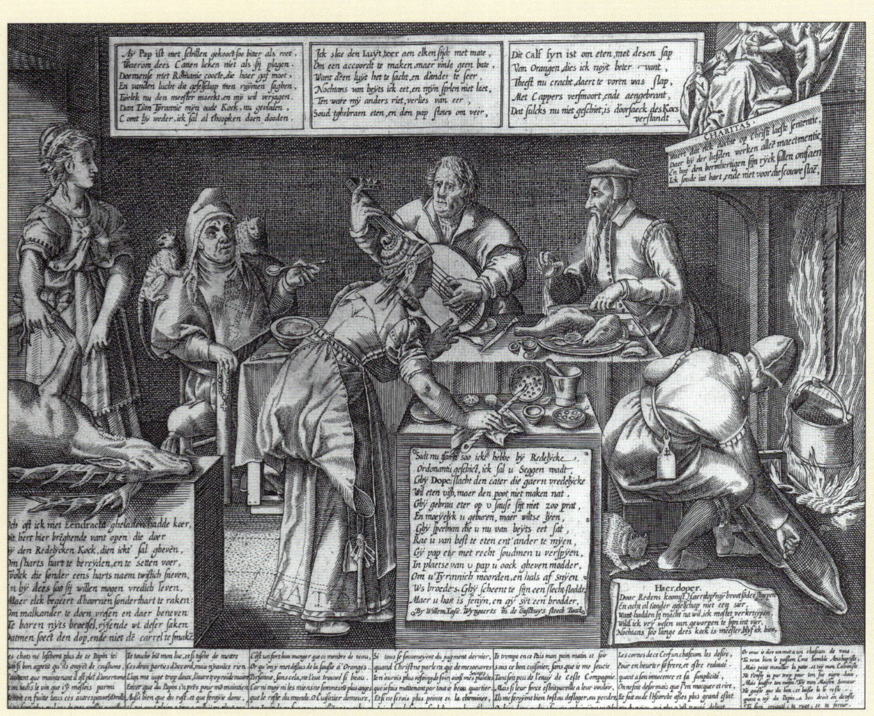

10. Anonymous, engraving, printed by Willem Jansz. Wijngaerts (Amsterdam 1625-1632) - AVS

10&11.

In this allegorical print about goods baked in the kitchen of religious disputes, *Unitas* (*Unity*) brings inside the red deer (peace), whose heart she will grant to everyone. The guests are, however, very divided by hate and envy and do not trouble themselves over the crux of the matter, love of neighbor, *Charitas (Charity).* She is forced to stand over the fire-place, where no one pays attention to her. From her vantage point she observes the scene with sorrowful eyes. *Ratio,* cool *Reason,* shows each person to his place: the *cat*holic, who eats porridge (in Dutch: *pa[a]p*, which also is a nickname for a Roman Catholic); Luther, who strikes the *lute*, and Calvin, who sprinkles the *calf fine* with *Orange* juice. Sit-ting aloof near the (heretic-) fire is the *Haerd-doper* (meaning both Anabaptist and 'baptizer near the fire-place'), who, without getting his feet wet, is carefully baptizing the bread in water. He says:

> Due to Reason's support I, Anabaptist,
> dunk my bread without stealing
> And regard all the other company not
> a whit,
> For if they had the power they desire,
> I would have to creep away,
> I would quickly be cast into the fire,
> Nevertheless, as long as this cook is
> master, I will stay here.

The painting is a variant of this print, in which the Anabaptist appears to have been given the face of Menno Simons (Rademaker 2, pp. 89-91, nrs. 111 & 112).

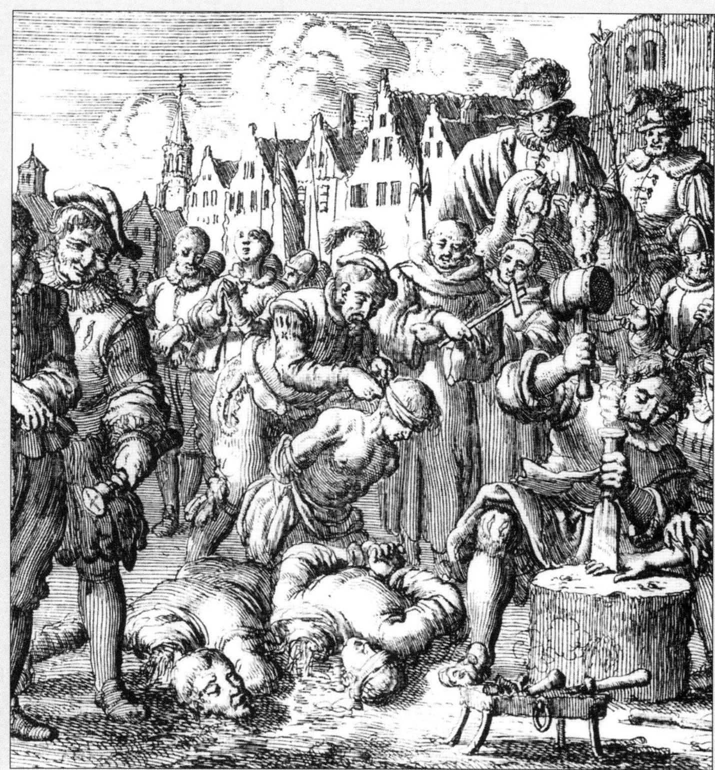

12. Anonymous, panel: *The Poetic Servants of Rhetorica* (1659) - FHM

12.
In a Haarlem chamber of rhetoric (a society of poets), all of the religious currents from the middle of the seventeenth century are represented. Right behind the table, Calvin disputes with Arminius; next to them sit Luther and Menno. Also present are Socinus, a libertine, a Jew, an atheist, a Turk, a Collegiant, a sophist and, at the corner of the table, a priest, whose rosary points to the Council of Trent. *Charitas (Charity)* has again taken her place above the fire-place. The satire touches not only on religious divisiveness, but also on the tendency of the rhetoricians to meddle in theological hair-splitting in their plays and poems (Koster, pp. 87-91).

13.
This print, which was produced for the centenary anniversary of the Amsterdam *Schouwburg* (Theater) on January 3, 1738, sets up Luther, Menno and Calvin not only as critics of secular drama, but also as opponents of one another. The church leaders hold scrolls with texts hostile to drama. Menno's complaint, however, is strikingly neutral, although he would prefer to have commemorated the twenty-fifth anniversary of the 'salutary peace' that marked an end to the War of Spanish Succession in 1713 (see part II, 21). That Menno's judgment is so mild regarding drama is probably due to the involvement of a fair number of Mennonites in Amsterdam's theatrical circle (Wybrands 1, pp. 183-184; M-his 3736).

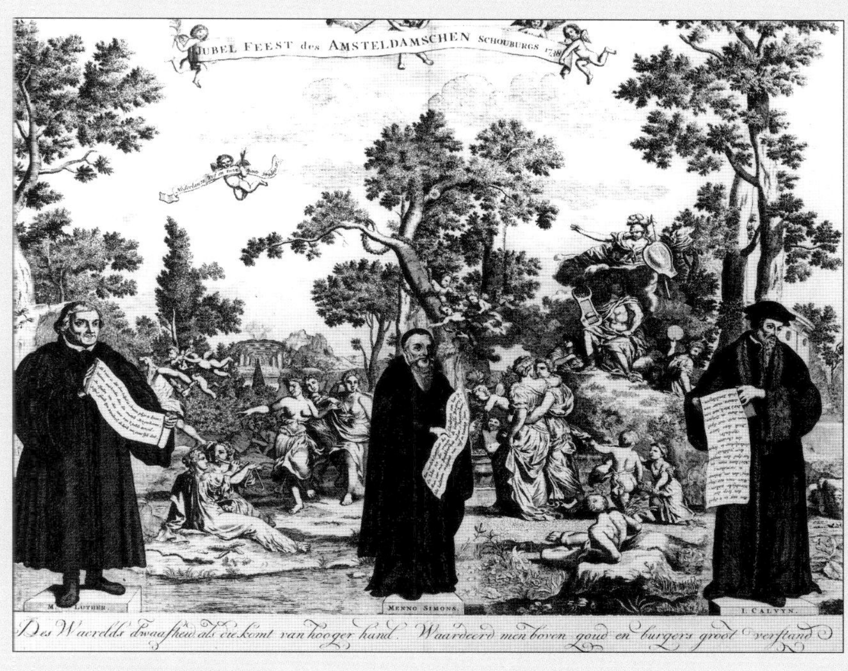

13. Anonymous, engraving: *Jubilee Festival of the Amsterdam Theater 1738* - UBA-DG

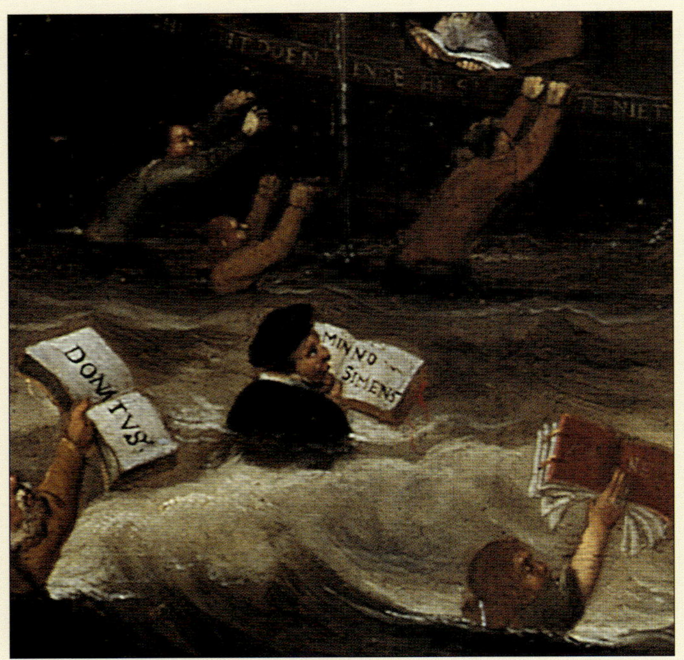

14.

Here the Catholic Church is portrayed as a ship, flying a pirate flag to intimidate the high seas near and far. Peter successfully steers the ship past the reef of pride, only to be attacked by the sworn enemies of Rome: Mohammed, Nestorius, Calvin, Luther, Donatus, Jan Hus, Arius, Simon Magus and in the middle, the unarmed Menno Simons. On board the crew attempts to maintain the course and defeat the enemy with the help of *Vrijwille* (Free Will), *Iustitia* (Justice), *Penitensi* (Penitence), *Verkiesinge* (Election) and *Dei Gratia* (Grace of God). The text on the wreckage in the foreground reads: 'You have strengthed the sea by your strength. You have smashed together the heads of the dragon in the waters. Psalm 73[74:13]' (Rademaker 2, p. 88, nr. 108).

14. Jacob Gerritsz Loef, canvas: *The ship of the church* (ca. 1640) - CCU

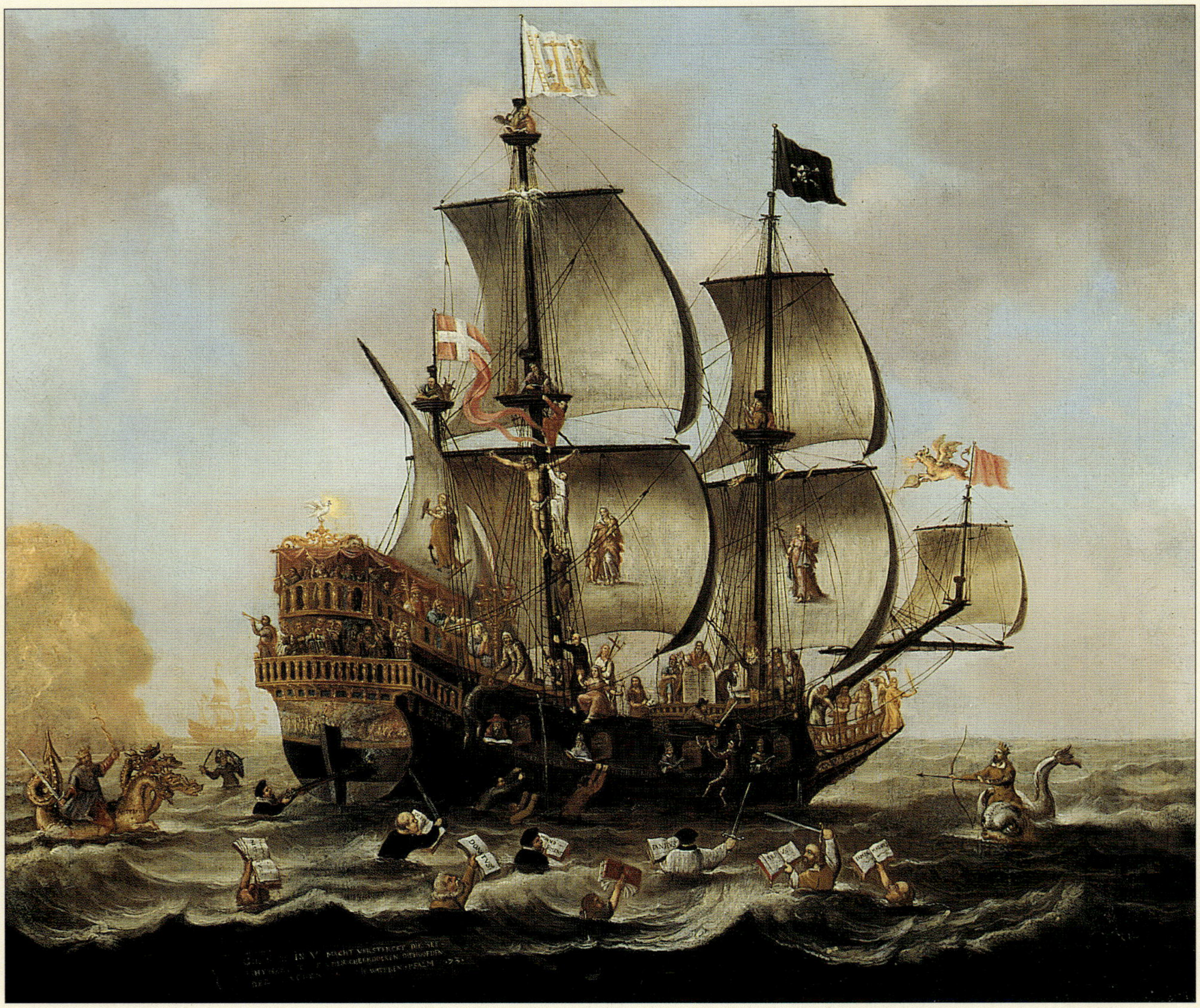

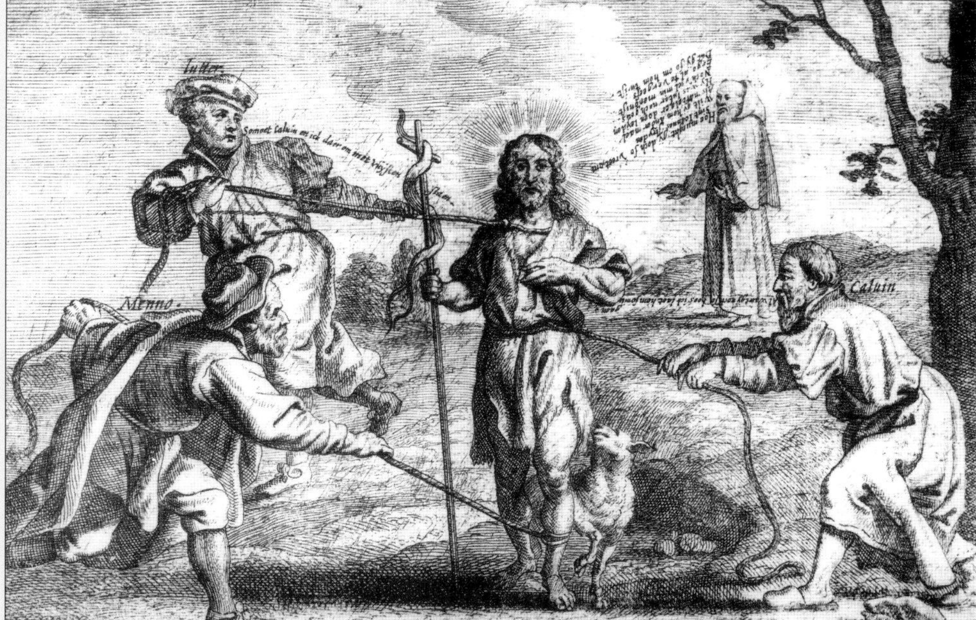

16. Anonymous, engraving in Van Geluwe, *Ontledinghe* (Antwerpen 1656), p. 26 - UBA-DG

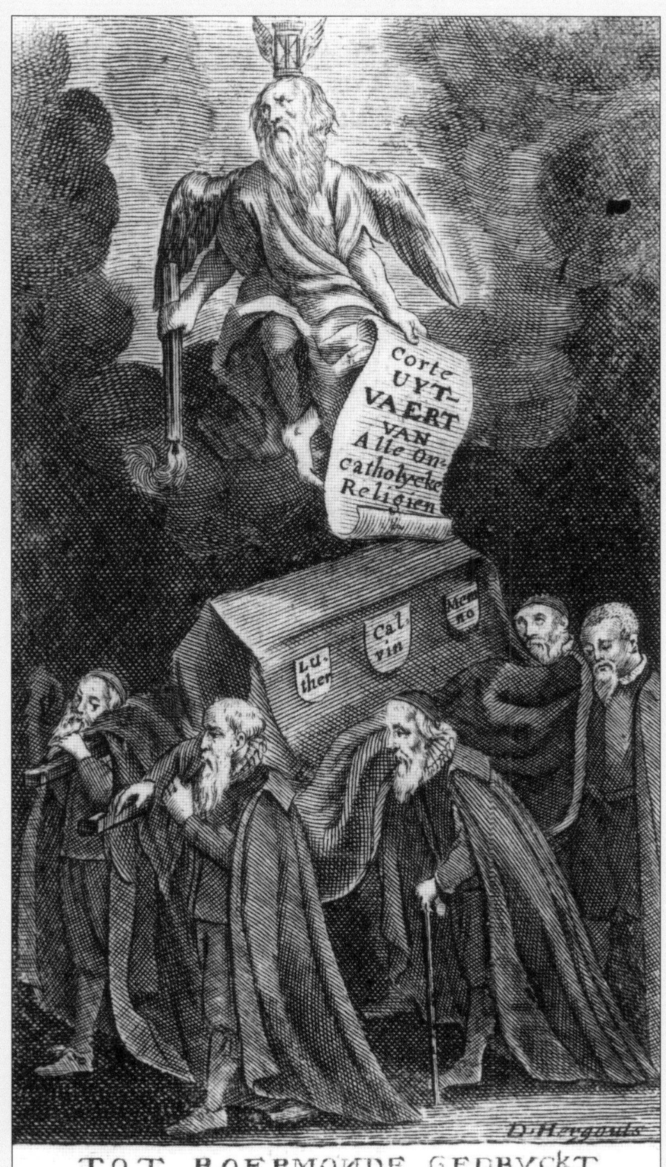

15. David Herregouts, engraved frontispiece of *Corte Uytvaert* (Roermond 1651) - UBA

15.
The frontpiece of the anonymous booklet, printed by Caspar du Pree in 1651 at Roermond, *Van alle Oncatholijcke Religien ... Toe-ge-eygent aen alle de Catholijcken, die aen oncatholijcken getrouwt syn (On Non-Catholic Religions ... Dedicated to all Catholics who married non-catholics),* shows Menno (with crutch) and the other reformers, who can scarcely be distinguished from each other, carrying their faith to the grave. The coffin bears the names of *Luther, Calvin and Memno* [sic] (see part II, 19).

16.
Aernout van Geluwe, nicknamed the 'unstudied Flemish peasant', in the *Eerste Deel Over De Ontledinghe Van dry verscheyden Nieuw-Ghereformeerde Martelaers Boecken (Part One of the Analysis of three different Newly Reformed Martyr-ologies)* (Antwerp, widow of Jan Cnobbaert, 1656) challenges Protestant claims upon the martyrs of his Holy Church. The print ridicules the disputing Reformers who are playing a tug-of-war over John the Baptist. Luther says: 'So Calvin and I must have fistidcuffs over him'; Calvin: 'No matter how angry you become I will not let him go.' As the wisest, Menno is silent. In the background the Capucian monk comments on the senseless fight as follows:

> How greedy you must be, to fight over St. John
> You will lead him a second time into martyrdom
> He was neither Lutheran nor Reformed
> Nor much less Mennonite
> Therefore it is all in vain that you fight over him so

(See part II, 76; Nissen, pp. 226-235).

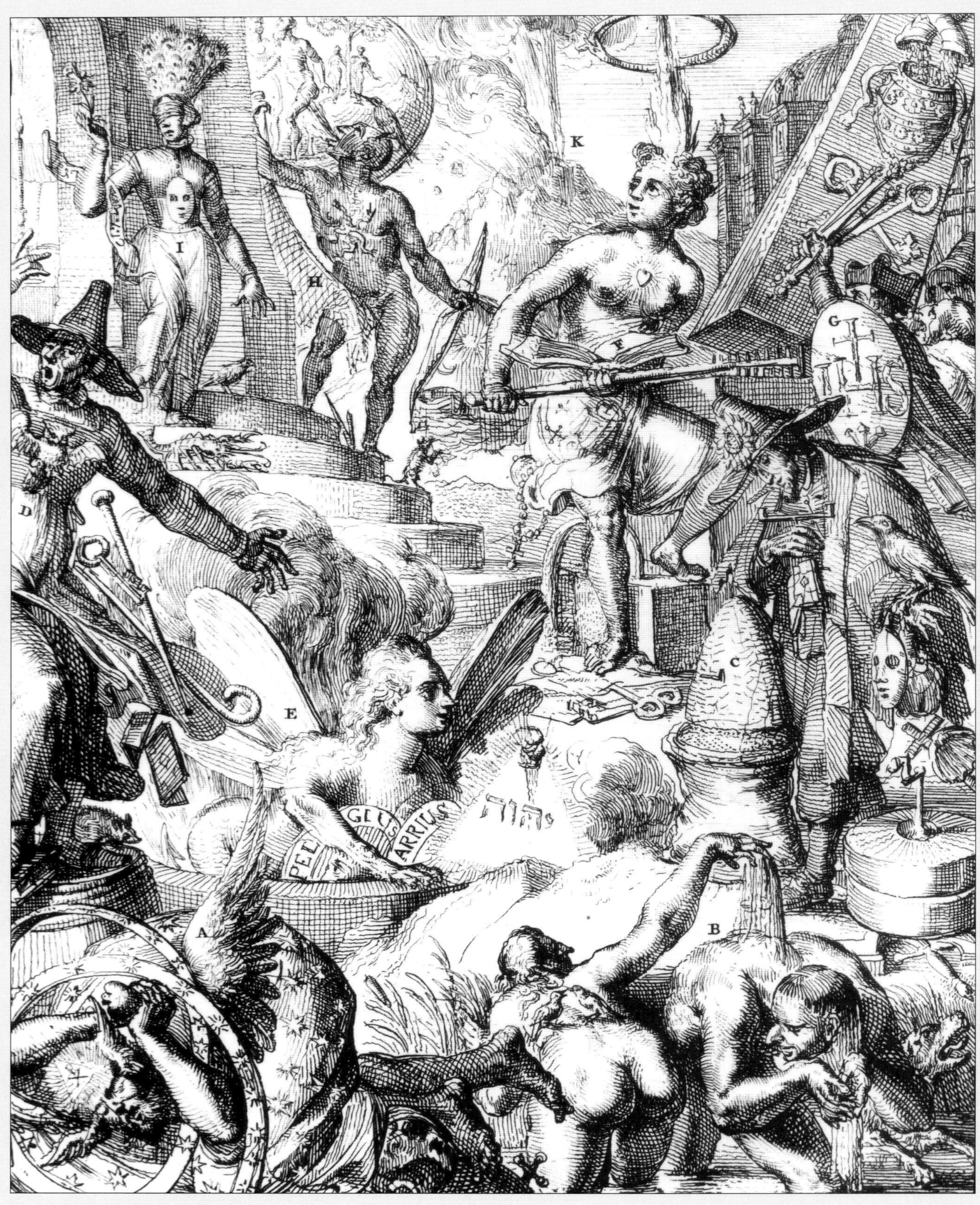

17. Romeyn de Hooghe, engraving in *Hieroglyphica of Merkbeelden der oude Volkeren* (Amsterdam 1735), opposite p. 427 - UBA

17.
In 1735 a manuscript with a series of prints by the illustrious engraver Romeyn de Hooghe (1645-1708) was published posthumously, in which he satirized all religions. The Mennonites get their turn in chapter 60, in the print introduced under the letter C, together with the so-called *dompelaars* (Immersers) or Collegiants (B), Quakers (D), Socinians (E), Jansenists (F) and Jesuits (G). The explanation goes as follows:

> The *Reasonable Zealots of the Innocence-baptism are the 'Doopsgezinden'* (Mennonites), associates of *Menno Simons of Witmarsum,* unesteemed and bedecked in lowly clothed, with a large, tattered Hat of Freedom with the Sunflower in front, the trade mark of Religious Ecstacy. His head hangs like a Quillwort, with cast down eyes, scarcely wearing any linen around his Neck or Hands. His Cloak appears as innumerable pieces of rags sown together, because of the divisions which rend apart their communities. He covers his heart with his hand, demonstrating his withholding and dissembling streaks in acts and words. He casts Prayer-books, Psalm-books and Catechisms at random, handling everything in the name of *Religious Freedom.* He stands near the bending Rush and Reed of the Immersers, clearly showing his humility, but not escaping the Proverb: *It worries the Reed that the Oak tree stands taller.* One can also observe his aversion to the Yoke of the Supreme Power, and the sword of War, both of which lie under the two grinding Millstones, the trademark of mutual Brotherly assistance and industry - two Mennonite Virtues which one can indeed praise and imitate. On his other side is seen a Beehive, showing both their growth and love of work, with a sack of Grain, ground by the Elders for the National Government; seeing that the People think more of sustinence than of Princely splendor, more about the Belly than of Honor. They, being Merchants, Burghers and Farmers, collect the things that Princes, Nobles and Soldiers dissipate. They are at peace with their condition, but the third or fourth member of the family smell even at the city hall, whenever they are inflated by the Money. In his Left hand he holds two things, a Mask, in order to appear fine, and his Purse - inseparable from both. A screeching Magpie, chattering frivolous gossip, sits on his Hand, with which he repudiates the Watershell of Baptism before the Years of Mature distinction in the Faith (L 108; Holl 673-736).

18. Jan van de Velde II, engraving in Starter, *Friesche Lust-hof* (Amsterdam [1623]), section 'Boertigheden', pp. C3^{v}-4^{v} (Holl 472) - UBA

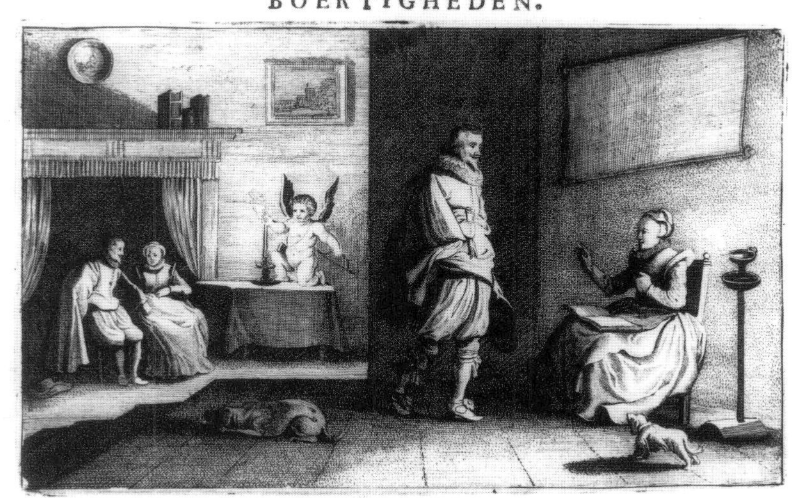

18 & 19a,b,c.
In his poem 'Mennonite Courtship,' Jan Jansz Starter depicts a 'Mennonite Sister' as the epidemy of hypocrisy. The accompanying engraving illustrates two scenes from the poem, which is found in the second edition of his *Friesche Lust-hof (Frisian Pleasure-garden)* (1623). Later, Pieter van Laer (Haarlem 1592-1642), painter of popular culture, sketched very tellingly the three main scenes of the poem in drawings that made up part of a manuscript with songs.

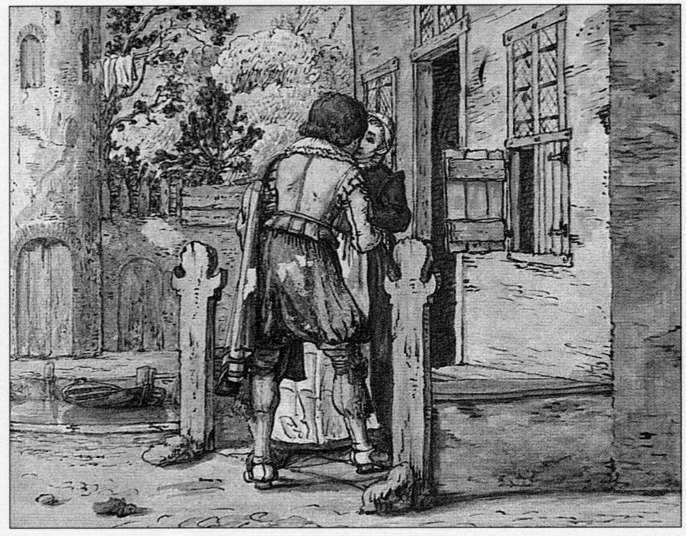

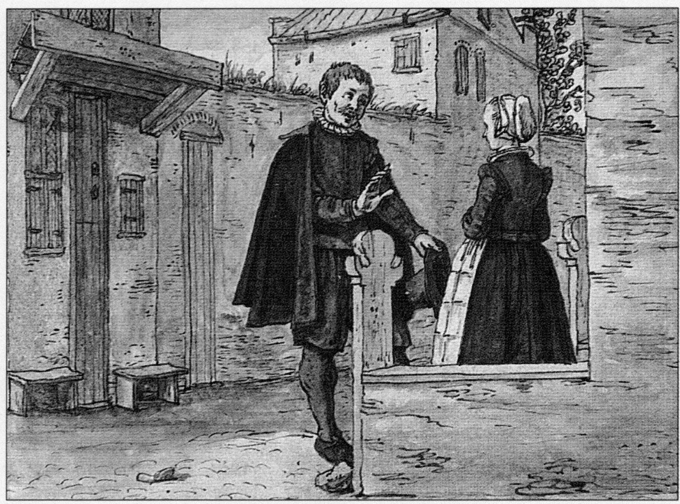

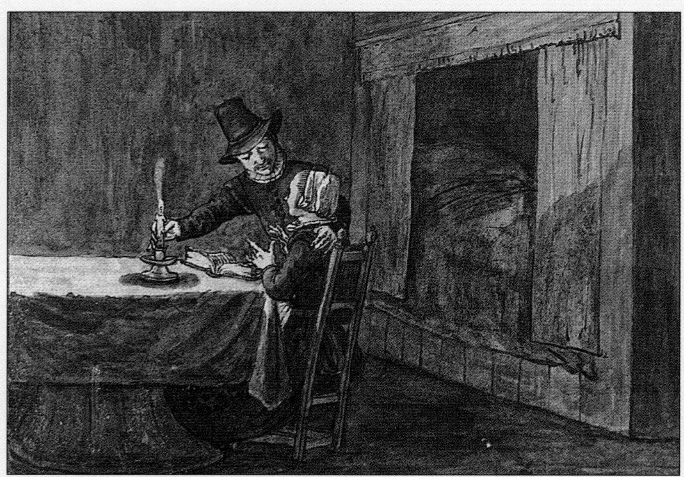

19a,b&c. Pieter Jacobsz van Laer,
washed pen drawings (1640) - AVS

Mennonite Courtship.

One time I courted a sweet Mennonite sister,
To whom I came with great hopes to greet with a kiss,
But what I did was wind, she says, with Yes and No,
This wooing offends my honor, I bid you, please go.
It is not allowable for us sisters to court
Except among the finest folk, by brothers in the Lord.
I lamented over my burning, I groaned over my pain,
I swore her love was mortared in my heart:
But what I did or suffered, I could not move her,
I could scarcely speak before she opposed me with Scripture,
And thus she propelled me like the wind blowing a feather,
For I knew none of it; she had it all under her thumb:
She had Moses in her head, she had consumed David,
She had built in her brain a cloister for the Prophets,
And all the Apostles lived in her body.
I thought: It is a fierce game with this woman.
She did not look at me; my appearance displeased her;
For my hair was too long, and my collar far too wide,
My sleeves too worldly wide, the starch much too blue,
Then my trousers too wide, my doublet much too narrow,
Each garter too long, and I had roses on my shoes:
In brief, she would commit a sin to kiss such a worldly man.
Well then, good evening young lady, I said, and she:
Go in the Lord's name, his wisdom abide with you.

It was not long afterwards, that I returned to her
Changed both in speech, in nature, and in clothes,
My cloak was entirely simple and black, my hair cut,
My white-stiffened collar as flat as a dinner-plate,
On all of my clothing was not a single adornment
And from my mouth came not a single unmannerly word.
Peace be to this house, I said, and I saw
As St. Steven did, Heaven laying open,
With the whites of my eyes lifted high;
I called her nothing but sister,
This seemed to put her heart somewhat at rest.
Immediately I read to her from a lovely Bible chapter,
And brought nothing but religious things to her ears:
Thus I crept into her goodwill; she seemed more cheerful,
And I became, with time, somewhat braver and more free.

One day I took her in my arms, and said, I will do it
By Yes and No, and gave her a Frisian kiss;
Then blushing for appearance's sake, she said, let that be,
One must be wary of the wagging of long-tongued people.
I swore to her, that I could keep it all very secret
Like the mid-night silence; and verily you must know
I will extinguish the candle. Oh please, do not swear!
Extinguish the candle so that you can keep your oath.
I cuddled around in the dark, until the time
I found a bed; I then took her to my side,
And swore: truly my love, here we will rest together
With all delights and joyful pleasures of the evening.
Are you swearing truly, she said? Have I admonished you so?
Oh Brother! If you had not given your sincerest oath
I would not for all the world have come with you;
But your boldness carried you away most badly.
So come then, I said. Yes, she replied, alhough I am in distress
I will come so that you could not break your oath.

20a, b & c.
In 1738 Cornelis Troost (1696-1750) painted four scenes from the comedy of Thomas Asselijn, *Jan Claasz of de gewaande dienstmaagd (Jan Claesz, or the maid-imposter)* (1682), three of which are shown here. The intrigue around a pair of lovers is enacted in the strange milieu of the Mennonites, who are satirically depicted as hypocritical, unfaithful and selfish. For this reason, at first, the piece was not staged, but between 1705 and 1736 it delighted audiences in more than thirty performances.

20a.
Daughter Saartje must be matched with the dull, virtuous Reinier Adriaansz. Two Mennonite brothers, who do not know what to do with their large hands, petition her parents successfully. However, the vivacious Saartje is in love with the dissolute Jan Claasz.

20b.
Saartje will have nothing to do with the clumsy advances of the sanctimonious Reinier. She resolutely spurns the ludicrous proposal of the meek Reinier, who finally has to leave without realizing his objective.

20c.
Saartje and Jan Claasz have contrived a plan with the knowledge of the neighbor women: Jan, disguised as a maid, will be ordered to sleep the night with Saartje in order to protect her chastity. Then 'a wedding was celebrated, though without any musicians.' The parents learn of the deception the following day and, to rescue the family honor, begrudgingly agree to a wedding (Buijsen pp. 54-59, nrs. 12-14).

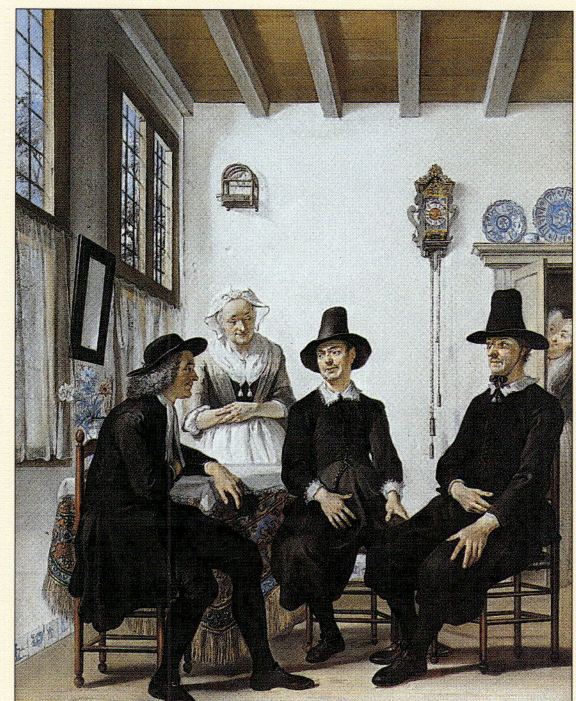

20a, b & c.
Cornelis Troost,
diverse techniques
on paper
(1738) - MHH

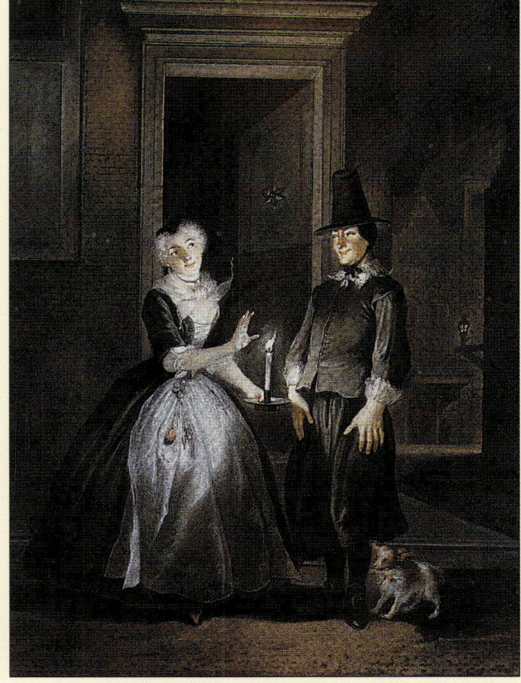

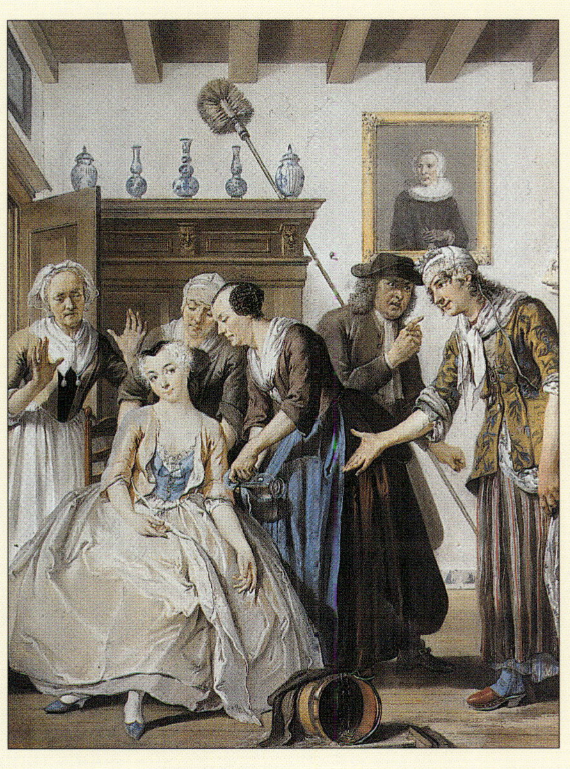

21.
In this caricature, the Mennonite community is literally ridiculed as 'full of crap' at a 'Mennonite wedding'. In the common parlance of the time, 'Mennonite wedding' was an expression for the nightly emptying of the chamberpot. The print shows how at a wedding, guests have mistaken 'purgative beans' (laxative fruits of the wonder-tree, *Ricinus communis*) for harmless sweets and are punished with mass diarrhoea. It is assumed that an historical incident formed the occasion for this print. There was even a ballet made of the *Purgeerboontjes* (*Purgative beans*). The rhymed caption, full of facile allusions, refers by number to the different scenes. Some of them are as follows:

1. This Show that I have begun
2. Yes Brother, but it is spun too course
5. I say to you, let me go, for I must also go drill
6. Brother, I follow you, as my rump also runs
9. I've wiped already but it comes again
   Upon this place I crap again
10. The sweet beans have done it
   That I have to keep crapping
14. I cannot crap
   Oh Sister, hold my head, for I must vomit it out.
15. Sister, how this will stink again
16. Yes Brother, that is true, but it will be performed in the Comedy Theater
22. Let us not reproach each other
23. That we crap in the Tub
24. If our brother Minno Simons could see us, he would be so amazed
   He should break strong winds, like the Münster Thundering
25. Which our brother Jan [van Leyden] and Knipperdol might hear
   They indeed have crapped from regret from St. Lambert's Spire

(M-his 3008; Wybrands 2, p. 55).

21. Anonymous, engraving: *Satire or Renewed Remembrance of the Purgative Beans* (ca. 1680) - UBA-DG

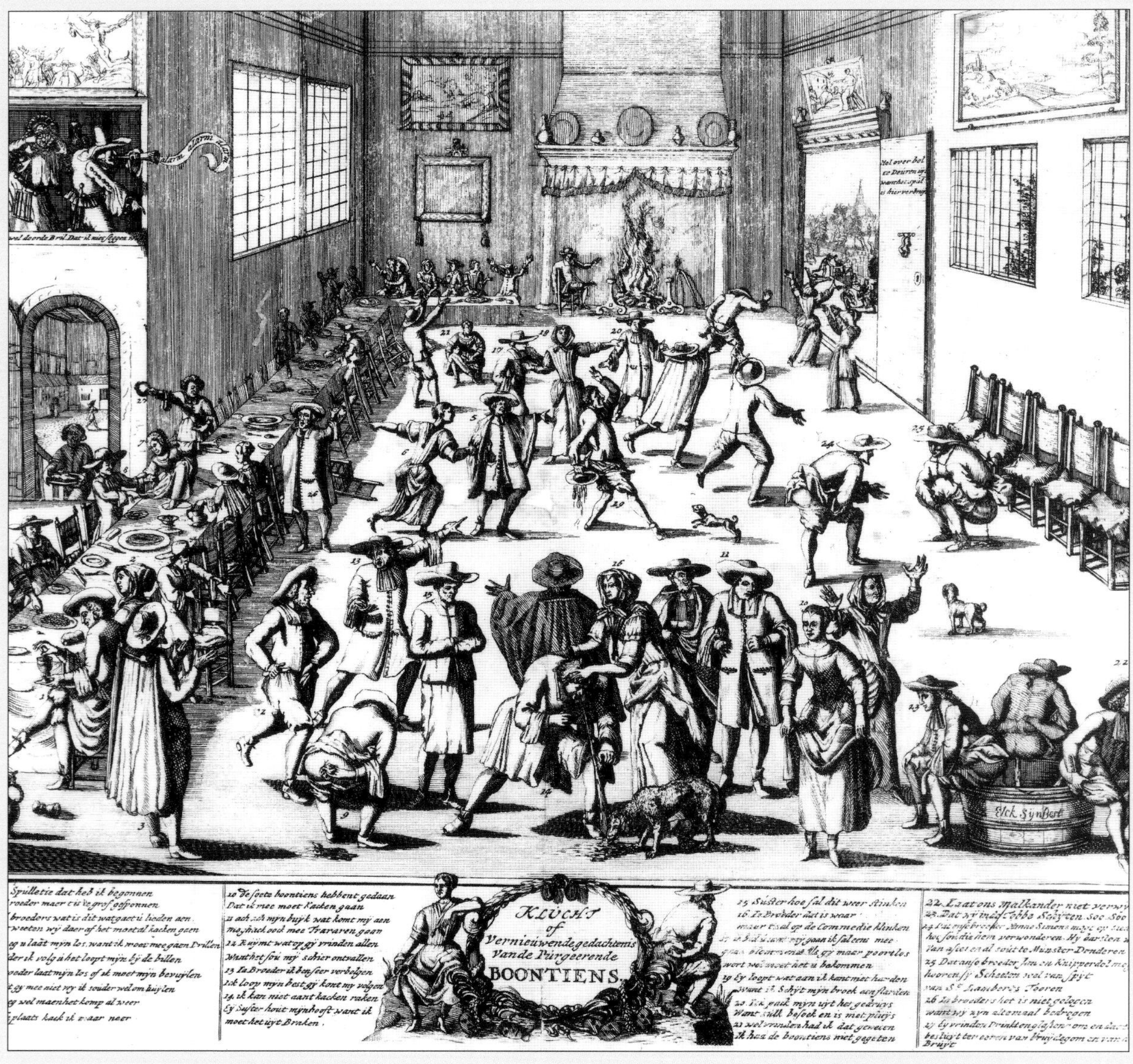

MENNONITE MEN:
MASTERS OF THE DIVIDED WORD

Strong personalities rather than strict, binding doctrine have characterized the history of the Mennonites. Dogmatics in the Protestant or Catholic sense is foreign to Mennonites; dogmatism much less so. The concept of the priesthood of all believers has meant that each person is free to read and interpret the Gospel. Spiritualists and literalists, liberals and orthodox alike were thus able to help shape a pluralistic community of faith, which to this day values church autonomy and individual freedom. The tragedy of Menno is that his peaceful and conciliatory message would ultimately result in a mature but severely fragmented denomination. In the Low Countries, this 'Anabaptist Babel' consisted of Waterlanders and High Germans; Young, Old, Groninger and Danziger Old Flemish; and Old and Young Frisians; as well as a number of local splinter groups. After various successful attempts at reunion in the course of the seventeenth century, a new conflict developed after 1664, leading to the dramatic split between Zonists and Lamists. Not until 1811 would most of the Dutch Mennonites be united in the Algemene Doopsgezinde Sociëteit (Dutch Mennonite Conference). On the American continent, fragmentation has been even more extreme. While the Hutterites and Amish form relatively homogeneous communities, Mennonites are divided into numerous groups – some with ethnic roots – such as the General Conference, Mennonite Brethren, Mennonite Church and Old Order Mennonites, to name but a few. In the Netherlands, the moderate Waterlanders formed a vanguard among the Mennonites for decades. They adapted the quickest to the surrounding society, or were the first to pay the price with their outward identity – judgement of their experience depends entirely on one's perspective. The fact is that Waterlander preachers were immortalized in portraits more often than those from other groups. The status of his office stipulated the minister's appearance. Although the non-academically educated *vermaners* (preachers), *leraren* (pastors), and *oudsten* (elders or bishops), the three hierarchical ranks, were not supposed to be distinguished in clothing from ordinary church members, most of them wore a simple cape or cloak and often a calotte, which emphasized their dignity and function as examples. As a result they scacely differed from their learned colleagues in the Reformed Church, whose gowns might have been more imposing with black silk collars often trimmed with fur.

The ministerial office was primarily volunteer work, held simultaneously with a worldly calling, although pastors sometimes received compensation for travel costs, living expenses or lost income. Along with the criteria of pastoral and rhetorical talent, economic status often contributed to the selection of ministerial candidates. While Mennonites dismissed the need for formal theological education for more than two centuries – the Mennonite Seminary would not be established until 1735 – a striking number of Mennonite intellectuals were doctors of medicine.

22.
After the death of Jan Matthijs on April 4, 1534, Jan Beuckelsz van Leyden became the leader in Münster. Ruling as an Old Testament king, he introduced involuntary community of goods and polygamy. On January 23, 1536, he was executed and, together with the bodies of Krechting and Knipperdolling, was placed in cages hung from the spire of St. Lambert's Church (ME III, pp. 77-78; Holl 88).

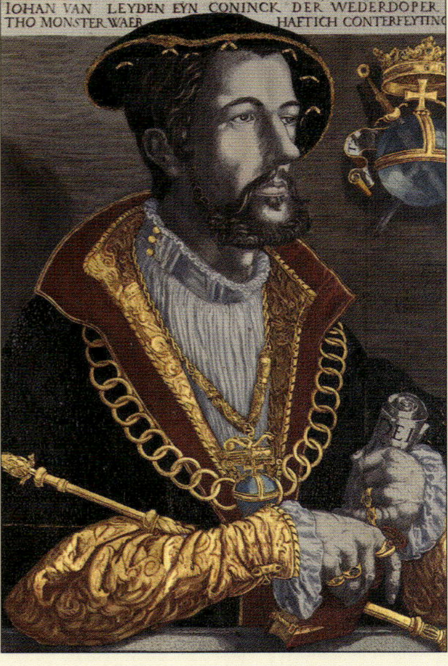

22. Jan Muller after Heinrich Aldegrever, engraving, printed by Clement de Jonghe (ca. 1670), colored and trimmed with gold by Dirck Jansz van Santen - UBA

23.
David Joris (ca. 1501-1556), glass painter from Delft, was one of the most important Anabaptist leaders besides Menno. Ca. 1538 he declared himself a prophet and became the leader of a despised mystical-spiritualistic sect. In order to escape persecution, he established himself in Basel under a different name in 1544. Of his more than 260 writings, the *Wonderboeck* (*Miracle Book*) (1542) is the most famous (ME II, pp. 17-19).

24. Frans van Mieris de Jonge after Michiel Jansz van Mierevelt (see 51), panel (ca. 1607) - AHM

24.
Lubbert Gerritsz (1534-1612), a weaver by trade, was from 1556 a minister of the Frisians at Hoorn and, after his excommunication in 1589, an elder of the Young Frisians. In 1591, under the name of 'Bevredigde Broederschap' (Satisfactory Brotherhood), these united with the High Germans and later also with the Waterlanders. Together with Hans de Ries, he framed the Waterlander Confession of Fatih (1610). This portrait has in the past been mistaken for Menno Simons (ME II, p. 505; Regteren pp. 161-162; Blankert p. 269).

25.
Hans de Ries (1553-1638), a bookkeeper from Antwerp of Reformed origin, was ca. 1576 baptized in De Rijp. From his home in Alkmaar, as an elder, he gave vision to the Waterlander Mennonites for more than half a century. At the same time, he enjoyed fame for his medical and alchemical expertise. This print with a laudatory poem by Joost van den Vondel (see 38) was copied from a painting by van Mierevelt (see 51) (ME IV, pp. 330-332; Holl 75).

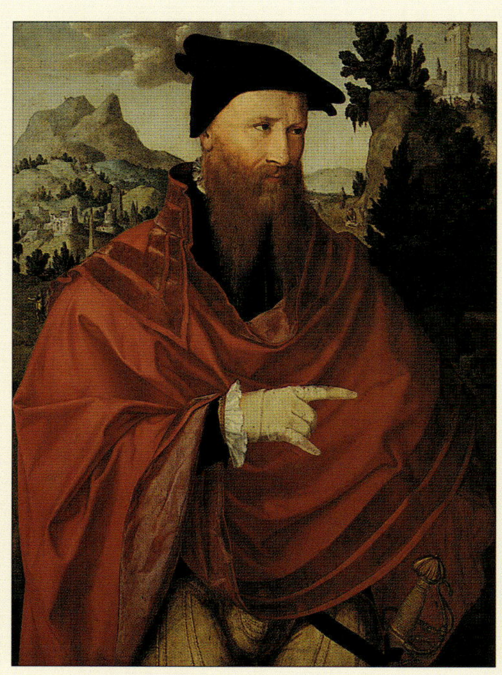

23. Frisian School, panel (ca. 1550-1555) - OKB (photo Martin Bühler)

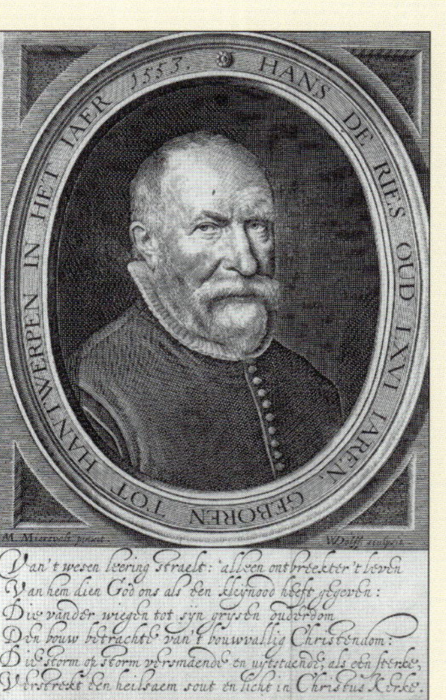

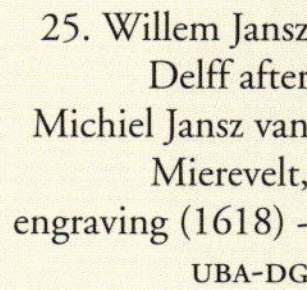

25. Willem Jansz Delff after Michiel Jansz van Mierevelt, engraving (1618) - UBA-DG

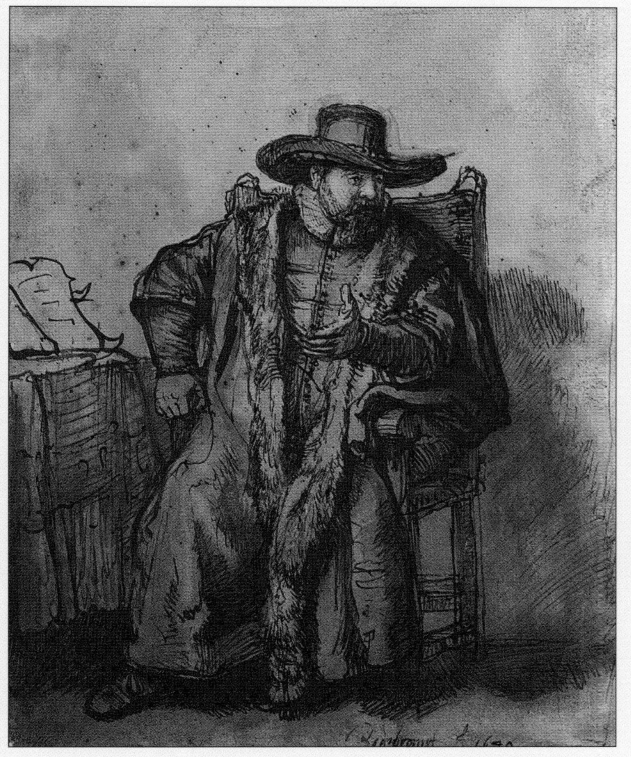

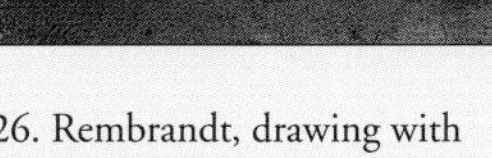

26. Rembrandt, drawing with chalk and pencil (1641) - MLP

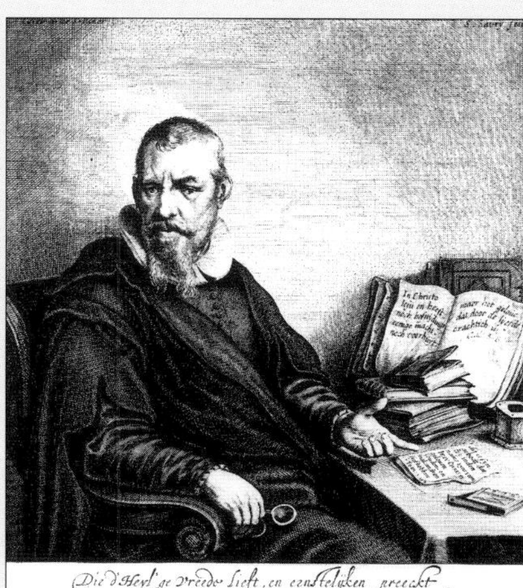

27. Salomon Saverij after Jacob Adriaensz Backer (see 52), engraving (ca. 1645) - UBA-DG

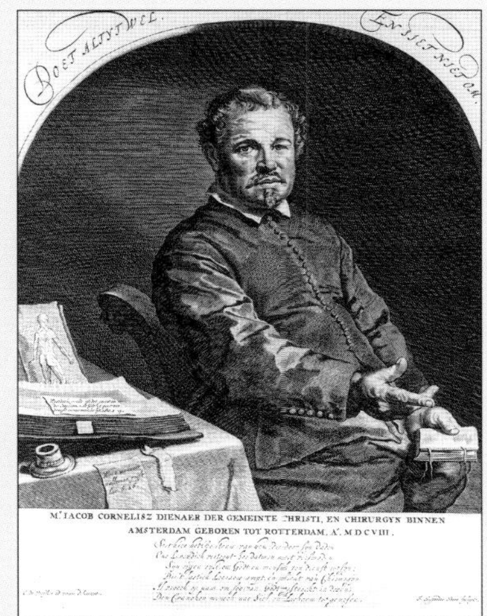

28. Frederik Hendrik van den Hoove after Cornelis Visscher II, engraving (ca. 1660) - UBA-DG

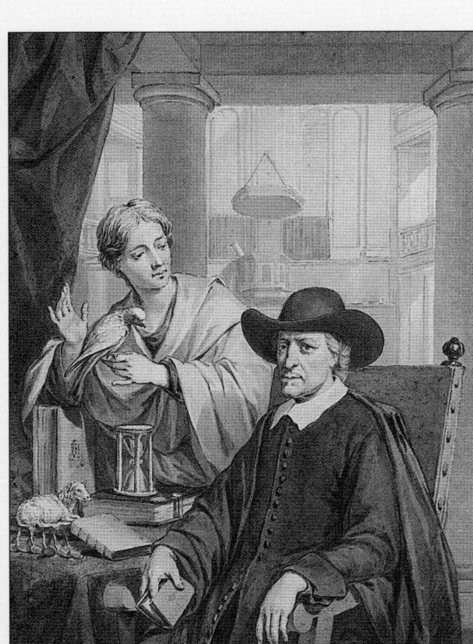

29. Nikolaes Verkolje, water color with chinese ink; page from the *Stamboek* of Joanna Koerten (ca. 1695; see 59) - P.C.5

26.
Cornelis Claesz Anslo (1592-1646), a prosperous silk and cloth merchant, was after 1617 preacher and later elder of the Waterlander Church of Amsterdam. Rembrandt made various portraits of him. This drawing is a preliminary study for the painting of Anslo and his wife (see 72) (ME I, p. 129; Schwartz pp. 217-218).

27.
Reynier Wybrandsz Wybma (1573-1645), of Frisian birth, was a glass painter in Hoorn and later merchant in Amsterdam. There in 1612 Lubbert Gerritsz (see 24) installed him as elder of the Waterlanders. From this time until his death, he kept a detailed 'Memoriael' (Minute-book), which contains a wealth of information about congregational life in Amsterdam (NNBW IX, 1294-1297; Holl 139[I]).

28.
The Rotterdammer Jacob Cornelisz van Dalen (1608-1664) was a surgeon and Waterlander preacher in Amsterdam. He wrote a number of books, among them *Oorciersel en Cieraet van de Godsalige Vrouwen (Ear Ornament and Jewellry of God Fearing Women)* (1652), wherein he sternly advocated modest and simple clothing. As a surgeon he enjoyed renown in the field of abcesses and tumors (ME II, p. 4; Holl 10).

29.
Galenus Abrahamsz de Haan (1622-1706), originally from Zierikzee, was a physician in Amsterdam. There the Flemish Mennonites *by't Lam* (their church was identified by an adjacent brewery at the sign of the Lamb) called him as minister in 1648. His prominent role with the Collegiants, a circle of Mennonites and Remonstrants who freely debated modernist theological questions, led in 1664 to the schism between 'Lamists' and 'Zonists'. The portrait is set in the Singel Church, with peace personified by a woman (ME II, pp. 431-435).

30. Cornelis van Dalen after Jasper Casteleyn and Rombout Uylenburgh (1616), engraving published by Gerrit van Goedesberg (ca. 1650) - UBA-DG

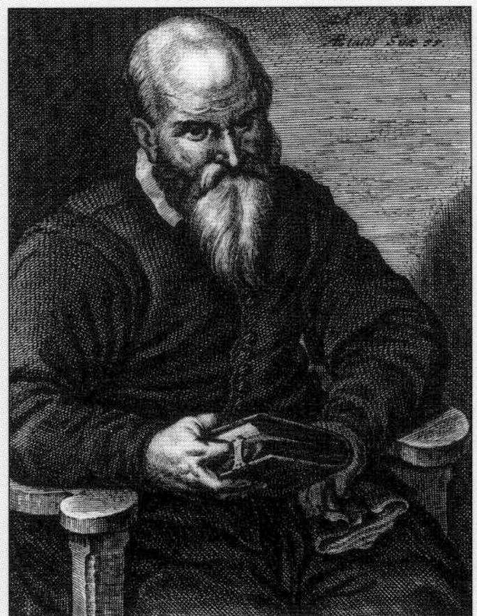

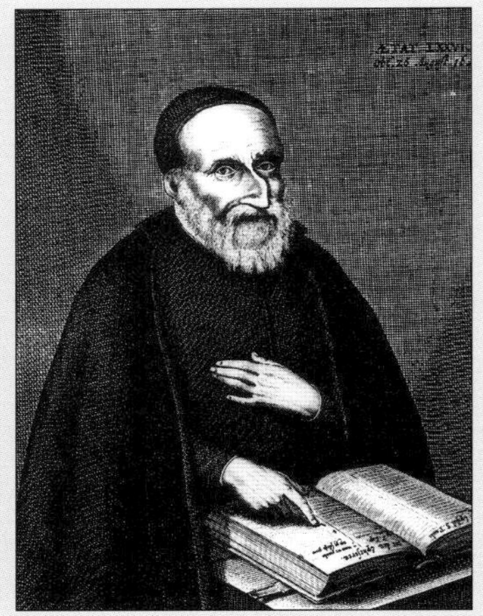

31. Cornelis van Dalen after J.J. van Collom, engraving published by Jan Rieuwertsz I (ca. 1650) - UBA-DG

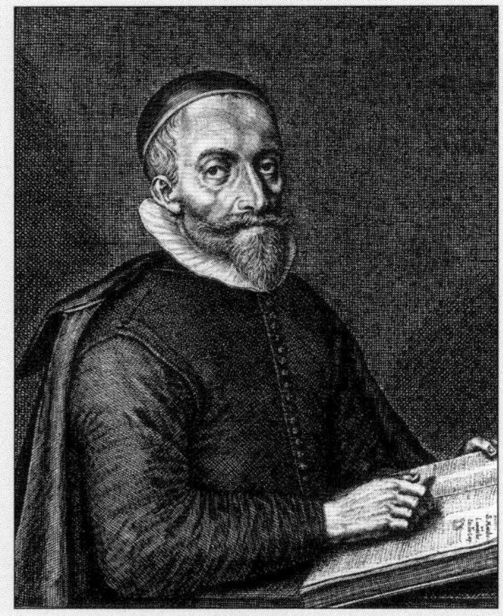

32. Anonymous copy after Crispijn de Passe II, engraving (1644) - UBA-DG

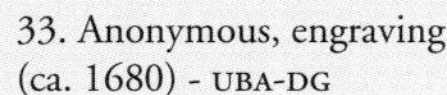

33. Anonymous, engraving (ca. 1680) - UBA-DG

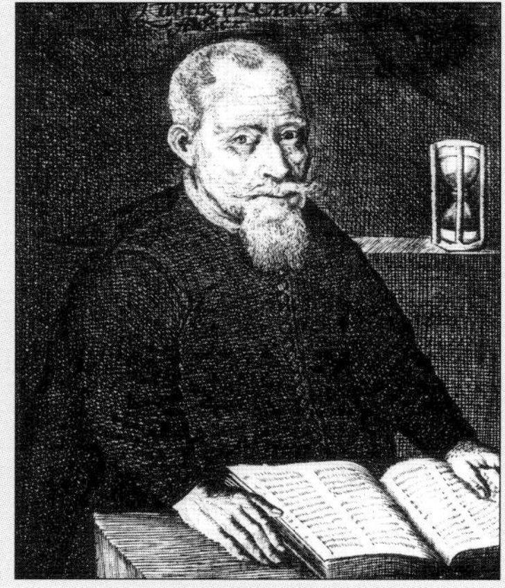

34a. Jacob Houbraken after Jacob le Blon and Jan Goeree, engraving (1730) - UBA-DG

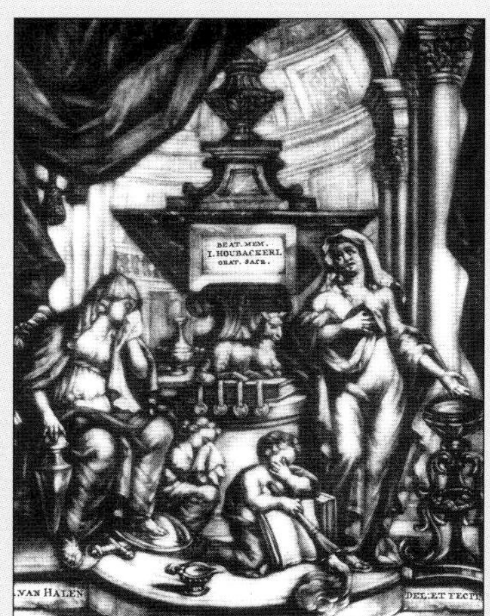

34b. Arnoud van Halen, mezzotint (1715) - UBA-DG

35. Jacob Houbraken after Henrietta van Peene, engraving (1727) - UBA-DG

30.
Jan Gerritsz van Emden (1561-1617) pastored the united Waterlander, Young Frisian and High German churches of Appingedam (1597), Haarlem (1606), Danzig (1607) and Marcushof (1612) in Poland. Painter Uylenburgh was a Waterlander active in Danzig (ME II, p. 504; M 1839; Holl 125).

31.
Aldert Volckertsz (1569-1645) was minister for more than forty years in the orthodox church of the Old Frisians or Jan Jacobs-minded in Amsterdam (Schijn III, pp. 77-80; M 2320; Holl 166).

32.
Joost Hendricksz (1592-1644) was pastor of the Flemish Mennonites in Harlingen (1626-1631) and Amsterdam. He was involved in many unification attempts and was engaged in a controversy with the Waterlanders and the Reformed. His *Stichtelijcke Predicatiën (Edifying Sermons)* (1646) was very popular (ME II, p. 703; M 2320; Holl 62).

33.
Lambert Claasz Aker (1616-1690) was a preacher for 46 years with the Old Frisians or Jan Jacobs-minded, first at Hoorn and thereafter at Harlingen (ME I, p. 28; M 50)

34a&b
Joannes Houbakker (1685-1715), pastor of the Amsterdam Lamists, began his training by Galenus Abrahamsz when he was only fourteen (see 29). His early death shocked the church. Mennonite artist van Halen (see 45-47) engraved this allegorical print of mourning (BWPGN IV, pp. 325-326; resp. M 2586 en 2589).

35.
Herman Schijn (1662-1727), medical doctor at Rotterdam and Amsterdam (1690), was one of the most influential leaders of the Zonists. His *Geschiedenis ... der Mennoniten (History of the Mennonites)*, expanded by Gerardus Maatschoen, is a monument of Anabaptist historiography. Through the 'Commission for Foreign Needs', he did a great deal to assist the emigration of Swiss and German Mennonites to America (ME IV, pp. 454-56; M 4892).

MENNONITE PATRONAGE: ALL THE WORLD'S A STAGE

Rare is the art museum in the western world that does not have a painting from the seventeenth-century Netherlands hanging on its walls. The Dutch spirit of business that sailed over the seas, a pragmatic political climate and, after the fall of Antwerp in 1585, capital brought by refugees from the Southern Netherlands – all of these created a period of unprecedented economic, intellectual and cultural achievement known as the Golden Age. The general public associates the Dutch Golden Age primarily with an artistic output of unequalled quantity and quality. While elsewhere in Europe nobles and clergy promoted the arts and literature, in the Protestant Low Countries bourgeois patronage by the regent and merchant classes reigned supreme.

This favorable climate fostered the gradual emancipation of the Mennonites. They came out from the dark wings and played not only economic, but also technological, intellectual and artistic roles on the world's center stage. Out of an ethically driven, almost artisanal mentality, emerged writers and poets, painters and engravers, bright minds and technical geniuses who contributed remarkable accomplishments as creative 'worker bees of the state'. Some placed their talents exclusively in the service of their own Mennonite circle. Most, however, worked for any potential client who was willing to furnish a commission, without regard for religious conviction. Some found Mennonite sobriety, often maintained by constricting social controls, too confining and sought salvation in roomier contexts.

'*In* the world, but not *of* the world' is supposed to characterize the Mennonites' relationship to culture. The country houses along the Vecht and Spaarne rivers, the 'Mennonite Heavens,' show just how irrelevant such a generalization can be. Here Mennonite élites allowed themselves a taste of the country life, be it always in a modest manner, from the mid-seventeeth century onward. A previous chapter has shown how the outside world reacted to the Mennonites' climb up the social ladder.

Poets and Writers

From the start, reading has been important to Mennonite culture. The Biestkens Bible, the *Offer des Heeren* with its martyr stories and a small volume of spiritual songs belonged to the standard package of almost every family. In this respect they differed from other religious persuasions. Illiteracy was found much less frequently among Mennonites than in the general population – at the very least, each member was expected to read the New Testament. Ironically enough, the development of the poetic arts benefitted from the proverbial Anabaptist zeal for schism. Often each new faction gathered its own new hymn repertoire, providing a training ground for poets and song writers. No other Protestant denomination has produced such a voluminous corpus of hymns.

In the wake of van Mander (see 36) and Vondel (see 38) many other greater and lesser talents threw themselves into the literary market and contributed to virtually all available genres. It is hard to identify 'Anabaptist authorship'. Indeed, it appears that the authors shared a common edifying message – then a requirement of the literary profession anyway. Mennonite authors tend to testify to the same essentials: a unity between biblical history, revelation of the Gospel and individual sanctification. Mennonite prosperity also promoted occasional poetry, poems for marriages and jubilees, from which some poets earned a tidy profit. Finally, the relatively high number of history writers in the circle of Mennonite authors is remarkable (MtM pp. 83-98 & 203-219).

36. Jan Saenredam after Hendrik Goltzius, engraving in Van Mander, *Schilder-Boeck* (Haarlem & Alkmaar 1604) - UBA

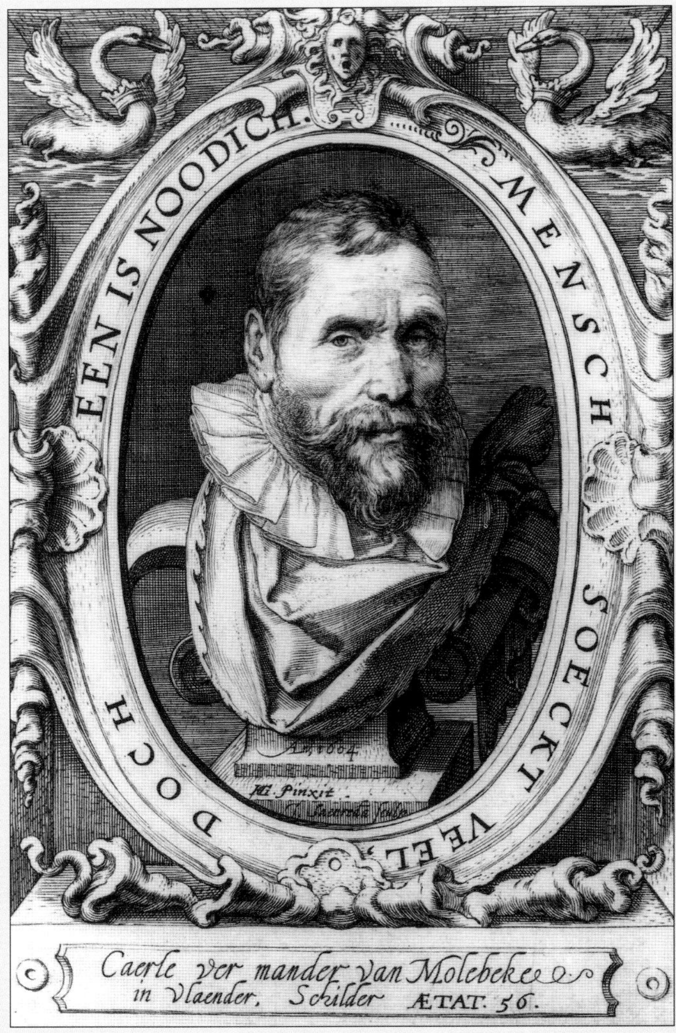

36.
The multifaceted Karel van Mander (1548-1606) was the most important Mennonite man of letters. This painter (see 50), writer and poet from Flemish origin, belonged to the conservative Old Flemish Mennonites of Haarlem. In spite of this, he was a pre-eminent Renaissance man. He holds an important place in Dutch literary history. His *Schilder-Boeck (Book on the Art of Painting)* (1604) is a formative work for art history. Under the motto 'Een is noodich' (One is necessary), besides prose and drama he wrote around 270 hymns, which were gathered together in 1605 by the Mennonite publisher Passchier van Wesbusch as *De Gulden Harpe (The Golden Harp)*. These songs, crafted in the style of the rhetoricians, have set their stamp upon the development of Mennonite hymnody in a way that should not be underestimated. Honored as a poetic hero from antiquity, van Mander was carried to his grave crowned with laurels (MtM pp. 83-87; Miedema pp. 11-168; NVA pp. 370-371).

37.
Jan Philipsz Schabaelje (1592-1656) was the most successful writer of edifying Mennonite literature. This Dutch John Bunyan spent the greatest part of his life in Alkmaar, where he was a preacher with the Waterlanders of Hans de Ries (nr. 25). A sexual lapse with the poet Judith Lubberts forced him to set aside his church office and to live quietly from his pen and capital that he had earned from the invention of a new milling technology. His volumes of biblical emblems, dialogues in prose and dozens of songs reflect the tolerant, mystical Waterlander sphere. His *Lusthof des Gemoets (Pleasure Garden of the Mind)* (1635) was reprinted more than 80 times in the Netherlands. In German translation there appeared since 1717 a further 24 reprints of this work and in English at least thirteen *(Die Wandlende Seele* and *The Wandering Soul,* respectively). The book was popular reading material for Mennonites and Amish, from Russia to America. Schabaelje died as a penniless book seller in Amsterdam (MtM pp. 99-109).

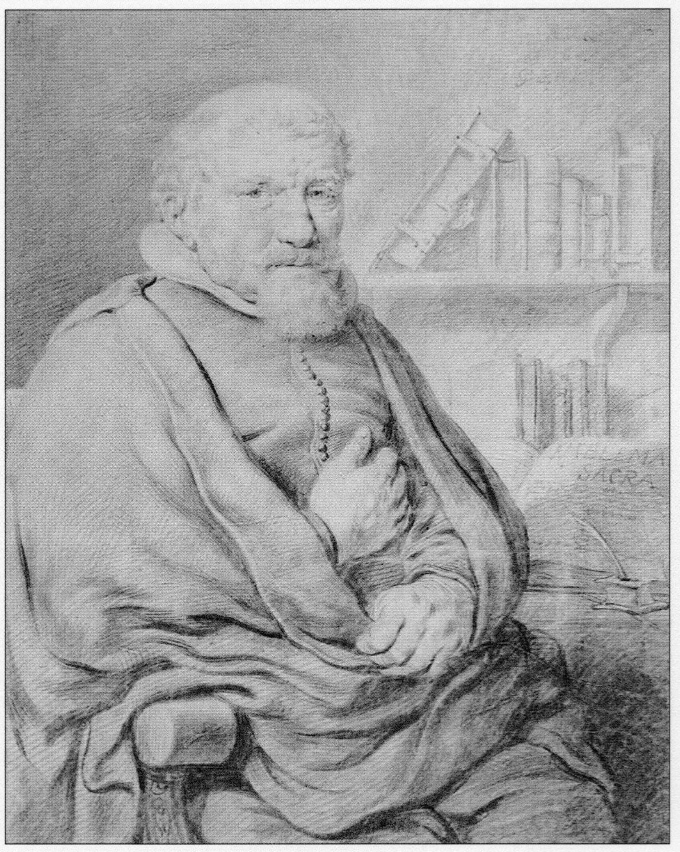

37. Gerbrand van den Eeckhout, chalk drawing: *Picture of an old Learned man* - PAW

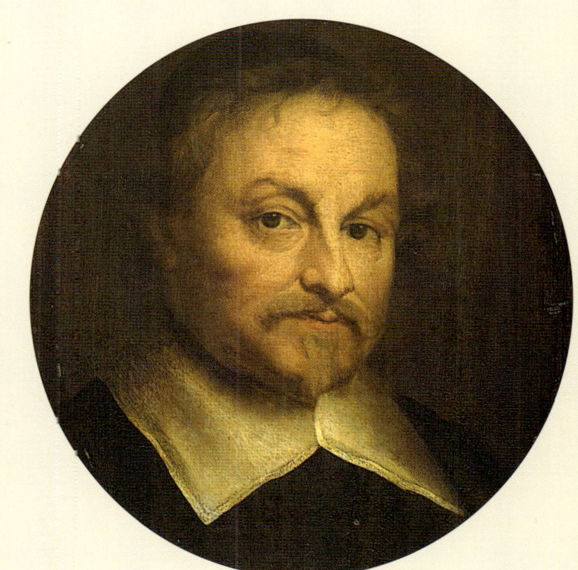

38. Govert Flinck (see 53), panel (1653) - AHM

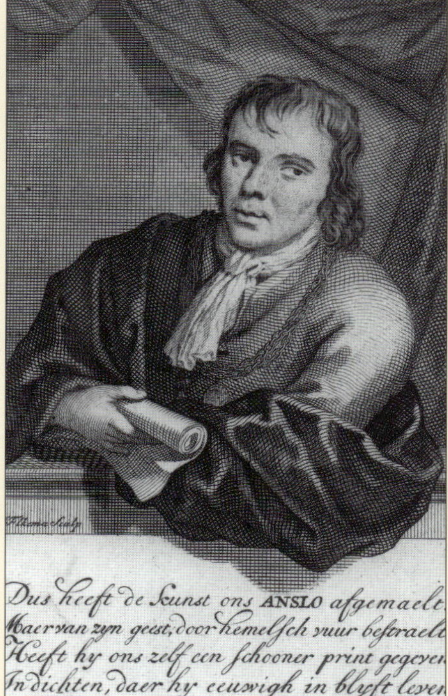

39. Jacob Folkema after Govert Flinck (see 53), engraving in Anslo, *Poezy* (Rotterdam 1713) - UBA

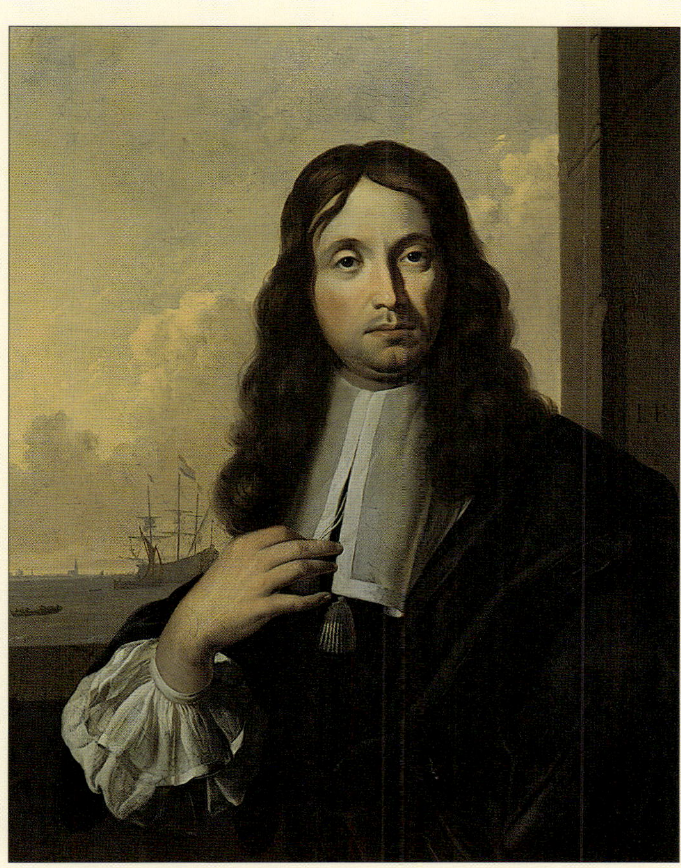

40. Ludolf Bakhuysen, canvas (ca. 1676) - UMA

38.
Joost van den Vondel (1587-1679) is the king of Dutch literature. He began his impressive poetry writing ca. 1605 while a shopkeeper of silk stockings. For four years he was a deacon with the Waterlanders at Amsterdam. After 1620 he withdrew more and more from the Mennonite world, until he became Catholic in 1641. His great talent brought him into the highest cultural circles. In 1638 his *Gysbreght van Aemstel* was performed for the opening of the new Amsterdam Theater - a tradition which, with some exceptions, endured every season until 1968. His immense oeuvre of poetry and drama fill more than 7,500 pages (NVA pp. 607-614; MtM pp. 87-91; Moltke 233; Blankert 155).

39.
Reyer Anslo (1626-1669), an ambitious nephew of Cornelis Anslo (see 26), attempted in his early poetical work to imitate and surpass the great Vondel. The epic poem of 1646, *Martelkroon van Steven den eerste Martelaar (Torture's Crown of Stephen, the First Martyr)*, was novel at the time because Jesus and the angel Gabriel made speaking appearances. His drama about St. Bartholomew's Day Massacre, *Parysche bruiloft (The Paris Wedding)* (1649), became a success. In 1649 he went to Rome and converted to Catholicism. He died as a priest in Perugia (NVA p. 50; MtM pp. 92-93; Knippenberg).

40.
Joannes Antonides van der Goes (1647-1684) was, like his father Anthony Janssen, a proficient poet. His tragedy *Trazil of overrompelt Sina (How Trazil took China by surprise)* (1666) evoked the admiration of Vondel in his old age. He became best known for his four-volume lauditory poem about Amsterdam, *De Ystroom (The Y River)* (1671). In 1674 he took a degree in medicine at Utrecht. In Rotterdam he became the doctor of the admiralty. In 1685 his father edited his collected poems, introduced by a short biography (NVA p. 51; NNBW IV, 54-57).

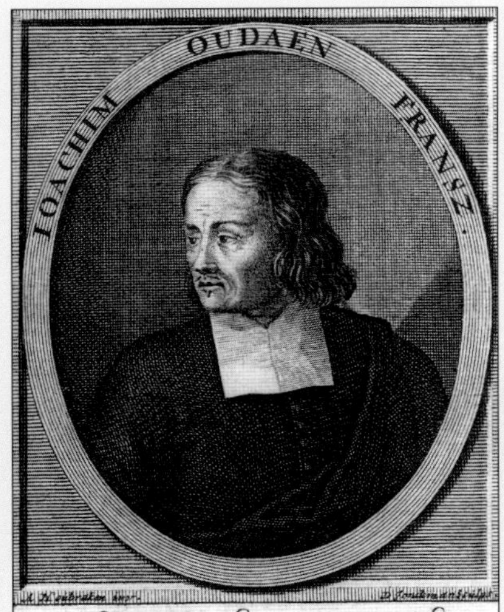

42. Dirk Jonckman after Arnold Houbraken, engraving in Oudaan, *Haagsche broedermoord* (1674) - UBA

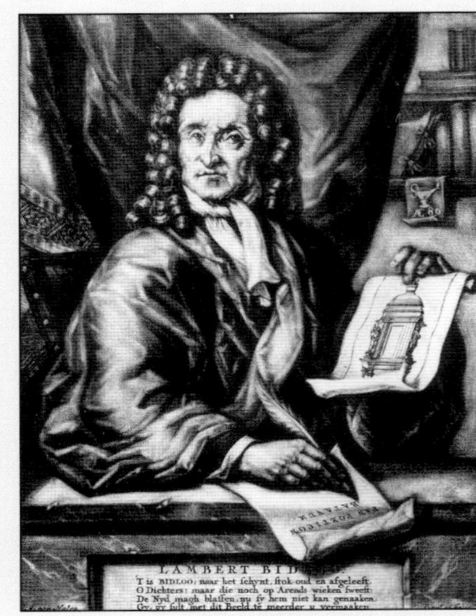

43. Arnoud van Halen, mezzotint (1720) - UBA-DG

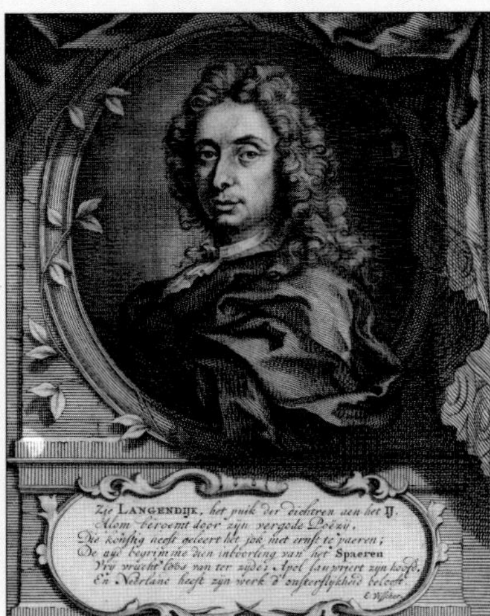

44. Johannes Houbraken, engraving (ca. 1725) - UBA-DG

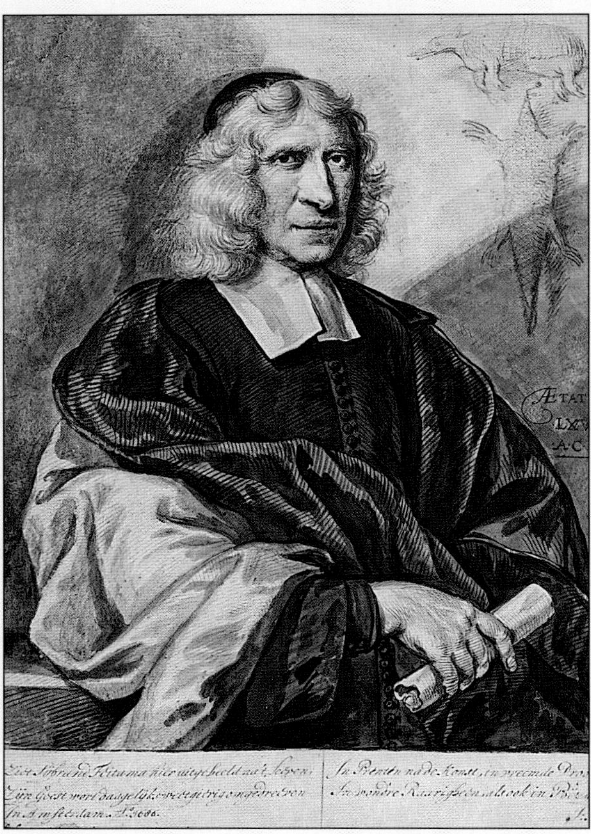

41. Jan van Somer, pen and pencil over black chalk (1685) - AHM

41.
Sybrand Feitama I (1620-1701), originally from Harlingen, was a merchant and druggist in Amsterdam. Although a second rank poet, his occasional poems were in great demand among the Mennonite élite. His greatest fame came as a collector of Dutch drawings and of taxidermied exotic animals preserved for display; an armadillo and the skin of a lizard decorate his portrait (NNBW I, 848-850; Wereld pp. 83-84).

42.
Joachim Oudaan (1628-1692) was a tile-maker at Rotterdam, deacon of the Waterlander church, enthusiastic Collegiant and highly esteemed poet. In 1648, as a Protestant counterpart to Vondel's Catholic play *Maria Stuart*, he wrote the drama *Johanna Grey of gemartelde onnozelheyd (... or tormented simplicity).* His political sympathies were expressed in a play about the murder of two governors, the brothers De Witt (NVA p. 429; MtM pp. 93-97).

43.
Lambert Bidloo (1638-1724), apothecary at Amsterdam and zealous member of the Zonists, was a skilled connoisseur of classical languages. As poet he achieved immortality with his *Pan-Poëticon Batavum* (1720), a biographical poem about the art collection of Arnoud van Halen (see p. 131). His brother Govert (see 66) wrote poetry as well; his son Nicolaas was personal physician to Tsar Peter the Great and founder of the first hospital in Moscow (NNBW IV, 146-147; ME I, pp. 338-339).

44.
Pieter Langendijk (1683-1756) began his career in Amsterdam, where he earned his keep by designing patterns for the silk and linen manufacturer, Anthony van Hoeck (see 76). From 1721 he lived in Haarlem. He received great acclaim for his French-classicist comedies in the style of Molière. In 1713 he exposed social differences between the Mennonites in the satirical poem *Zwitsersche Eenvoudigheid, klaagende over de bedorven zeden veeler Hollandse Doopsgezinden (Swiss Simplicity, Lamenting the Corrupt Manners of Many Dutch Mennonites)* (NVA pp. 342-343; MtM pp. 79-81).

Arnoud van Halen (1673-1732), art collector, painter and engraver, attended the Lamist church in Amsterdam. Via his second wife, he constituted part of the prominent Mennonite Rooleeuw family. He painted portraits of Dutch poets on small metal medallions (11 cm x 9.5 cm.). In 1720, Lambert Bidloo celebrated the collection when it stood at 200 portraits in his *Pan-Poëticon Batavum* (see 43). After van Halen's death, the collection came into the hands of the Lutheran merchant Michiel de Roode, who enlarged it by a further 113 portraits, most of them painted by Quinkhard. After a time in Leyden, the collection was finally sold in 1849 and dispersed. The Rijksmuseum at Amsterdam has 78 of these in its possession, some fifty of these by van Halen himself (NNBW VI, 684-686; Cat RM, pp. 723-736).

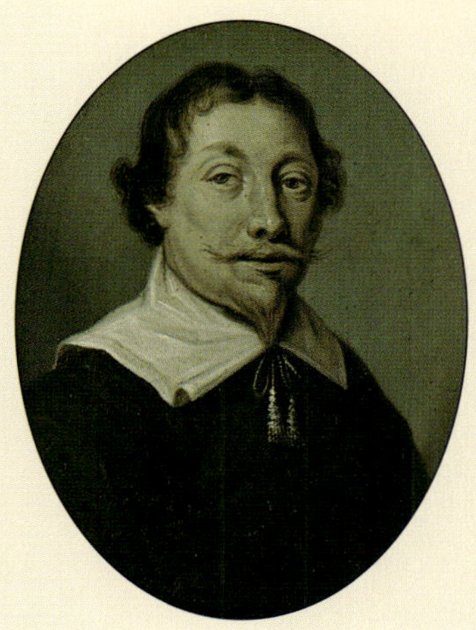

45. Arnoud van Halen - RMA

45.
Jan van der Veen (1578-1659), apothecary at Deventer and member of the Flemish church, became famous for his volume of emblems, *Zinnebeelden Oft Adams Appel (1642) (Allegories or Adam's Apple),* with prints by Salomon Saverij. In this work van der Veen 'reproved, ridiculed, lamented and abhored' human weaknesses, including the ostentatiousness of the Mennonites (OtO, pp. 36-37).

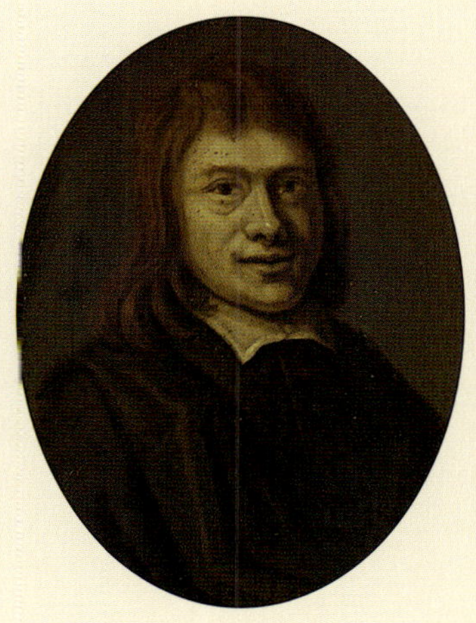

46. Arnoud van Halen - RMA

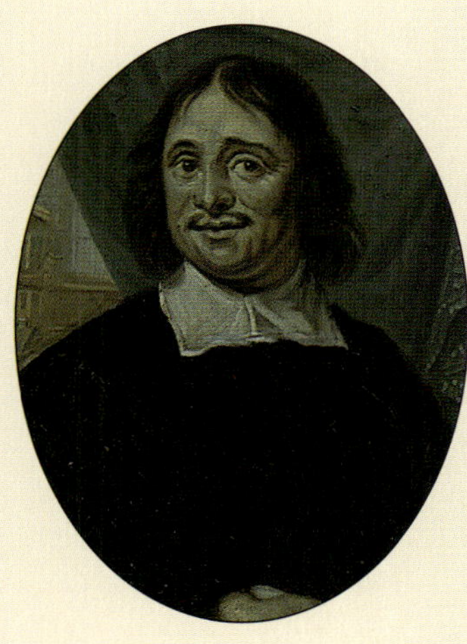

47. Arnoud van Halen - RMA

46.
Frans van Hoogstraten (1632-1696), from an artistic Mennonite family of Dordrecht (see 54), was a book seller in Rotterdam. He wrote poems and songs, as well as the emblematic *Voorhof der Ziele (Porch of the Soul)* (1668). He translated from Spanish and published a great deal of Catholic devotional literature (NNBW VIII, 883-884; Thissen pp. 71-88 & 144-173).

47.
Karel Verlove (1633->1695), weaver of cotton and silk, belonged to the Amsterdam Lamists. He moved in the non-conformist poets' circle of Jan Zoet and was friends with Jan Luyken (see 57) and the proto-communist Pieter Plockhoy. He wrote, among other works, the apostolic drama *Stefanus Eerste Khristen Bloedgetuyge (Stepen, the First Christian Martyr)* (1688) (OtO, pp. 43-44).

48.
Theodorus Velius or Dirk Seylemaker (1572-1630) came from a rich Frisian Mennonite family at Hoorn and studied medicine in Leyden and Padua (Italy). Although he also wrote occasional poetry, he made his reputation primarily as city historian with his *Chronijck van de stadt van Hoorn (Chronicle of Hoorn)* (1604) (ME IV, p. 509; RGN p. 485).

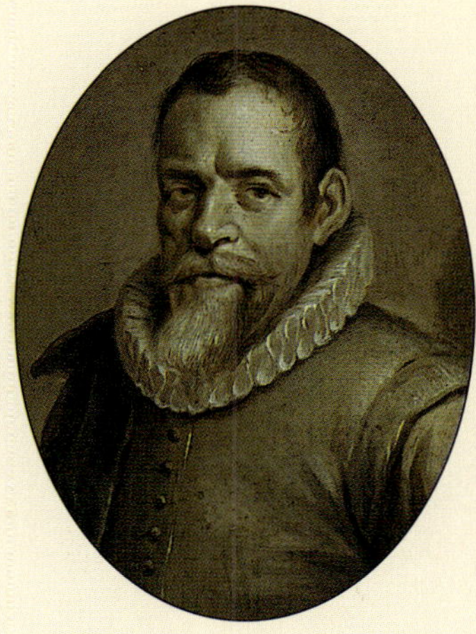

48. Jan Maurits Quinkhard - RMA

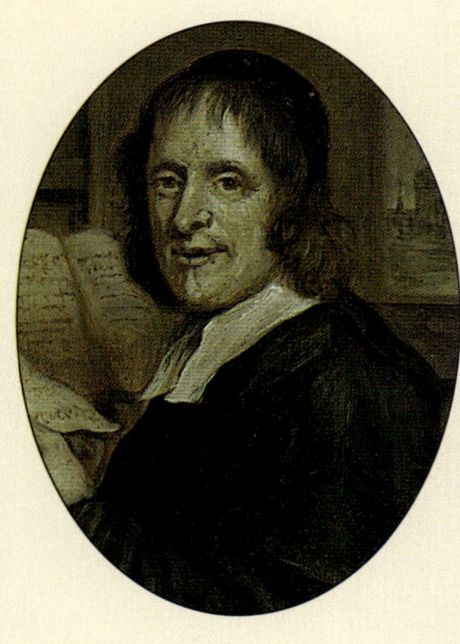

49. Jan Maurits Quinkhard - RMA

49.
Matthijs Jansz Balen (1611-1691), by calling a yarn winder and a Flemish Mennonite, belonged to the so-called Dordrecht school of poets, which also included the Van Hoogstratens (see 46 and 54) and the brothers Pieter en Tieleman Jansz van Braght (see 5). Many laudatory poems from this circle can be found in his voluminous *Beschryvinge der stad Dordrecht (History of Dordrecht)* (1677) (NNBW I, 230-231; RGN p. 25).

Painters, Engravers and Other Artists

In the century of Rembrandt, the grand master painter, a number of Mennonite artists availed themselves of the tremendous demand for paintings. In keeping with their religious-ethical principles, thoroughness stood at the forefront for Mennonite painters, and they applied themselves conscientiously to whatever their patrons, whoever they might be, desired. In Dutch Anabaptism there is almost no evidence of restrictions regarding the second commandment, that against making images. Anyone with objections toward cherishing portraits had to do so predominantly on artistic, not biblical, grounds. In the eyes of Karel van Mander (see 36 and 50) the painting of portraits, or 'counterfeiting' as it was called, earned a painter little honor. For van Mander, portraiture was merely one facet of history painting, the genre he regarded most highly. In his opinion, those who travelled this 'side road of the Arts' did so out of laziness or for profit only. Some years later, Samuel van Hoogstraten (see 54) echoed this view, at least when the portrait painter did nothing more than copy the 'eyes, noses and mouths always handsomely.' However, a painter could elevate portraiture to a higher level by seeking to capture the 'intellectual, rational soul' of the subject. The printer and engraver Salomon Saverij (ca. 1594->1664), an Amsterdam Waterlander, would immortalize many Mennonite faces in copper engravings. Like their colleagues in literature, some artists, who frequently moved in circles of the world's high and mighty, also found the Mennonite community too confining.

Among the rich Mennonites, especially of Amsterdam and Haarlem, there were several notable art collectors. One of the most famous was Rembrandt's associate and promoter, Hendrick Uylenburgh (ca. 1587-1661), an art dealer, who ran a prestigious painting school in Amsterdam. Famous collectors include the Amsterdam businessmen Cornelis Rutgers (1596-1638), Jan Pietersz Bruyningh (1599-1646) and Ameldonck Leeuw (1604-1647). Their collections do not reveal any true Mennonite preference, although they tended to acquire paintings in three categories: portraits, bibical histories and landscapes. This last genre, which the Flemish Mennonite Salomon van Ruysdael (ca. 1602-1670) of Haarlem excelled in, may have included an Anabaptist perspective. One could interpret his nature scenes with a lonely wanderer and a city in the distance as a spiritual landscape, the life of the pilgrim on the way to the heavenly Jerusalem. It seems that the very popular genre paintings, often refering to human lusts and vices, are strikingly absent.

The Golden Age furthered other art forms, now almost forgotten. Mennonites were notable in the art of calligraphy and *knipkunst* (the art of paper cutting) (Dudok 1; Falkenburg; OtO pp. 46-47).

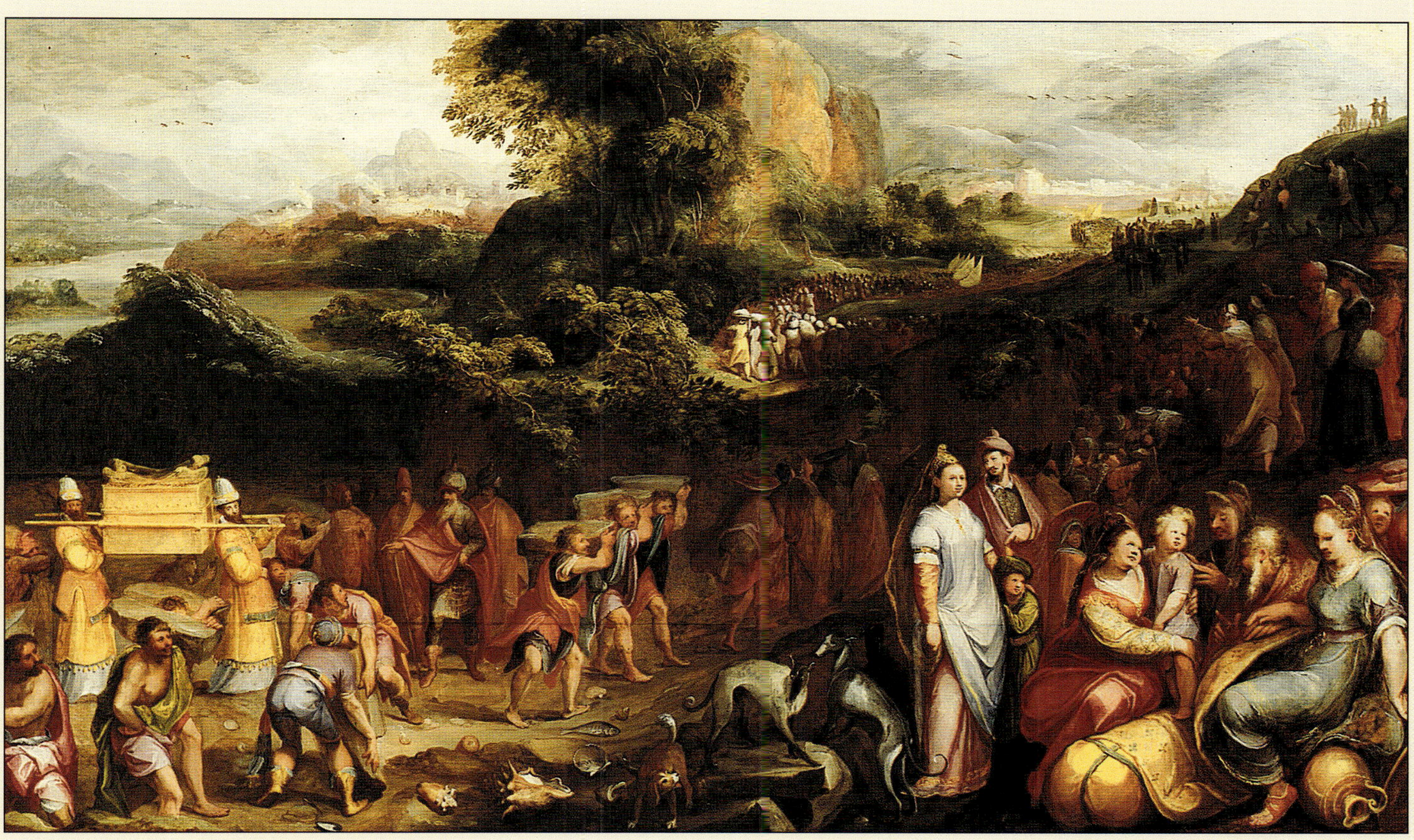

50.
Karel van Mander (see nr. 36), as a painter, did not leave behind a large oeuvre. For art theory and art history his *Schilder-Boeck* (1604) is of immense importance. It contains instructions for would-be artists and biographies of Italian, German and Dutch painters. His *Wtlegghingh op den Metamorphosis (Commentary on the Metamorphosis)* (1604) of Ovid was important for Renaissance art, which at that time was dependant on antiquity. Like so many of his Dutch contemporaries, van Mander had also studied the great classical models while on an art trip through Italy. The 1605 panel of the 'Passage through the Jordan' was based on Joshua 3-4, showing how the Israelites were able to cross over the dried-up Jordan into the Promised Land, thanks to the Ark of the Covenant. Joshua had twelve men take a stone out of the river bed, later used for a monument. The painting was commissioned by the wine merchant Isaäc van Gerwen (1580-1647) of Amsterdam, on the occasion of his marriage to Duyfje Roch. The married pair are depicted to the right of the middle foreground. On the left side, van Mander has painted himself as the foremost bearer of the Ark. For him this scene signified 'the way of all flesh to walk', or death, after which the 'kingdom full of sweet rejoicing' is expected (Miedema pp. 11-168).

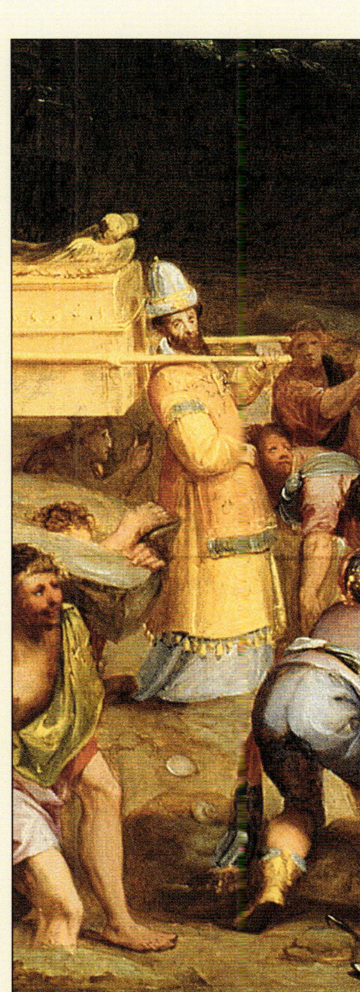

50. Karel van Mander, panel: *Passage through the Jordan* (1605) - MBB (foto: Tom Haartsen)

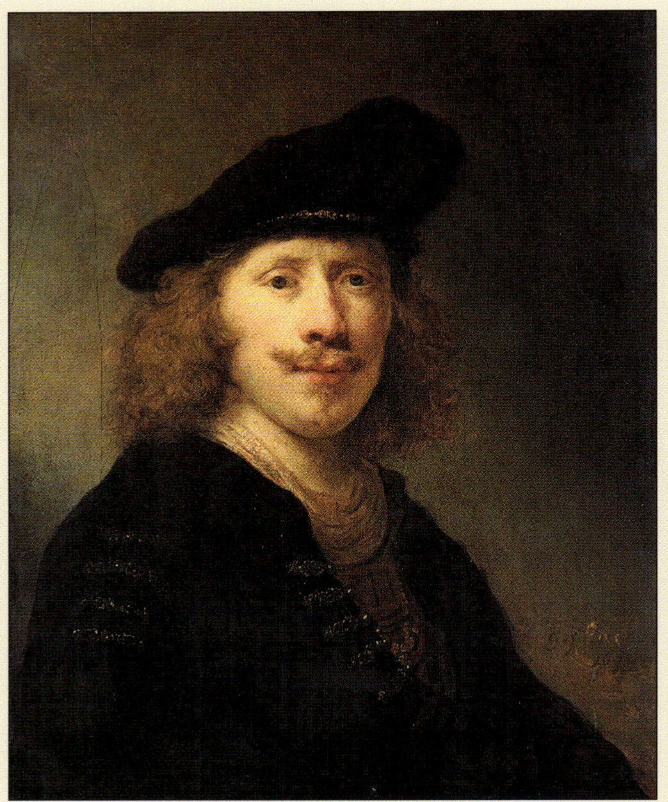

53. Self portrait in fancy clothing, panel (1639) - NGL

54. Self portrait with vanitas still life, panel (1644) - MBB

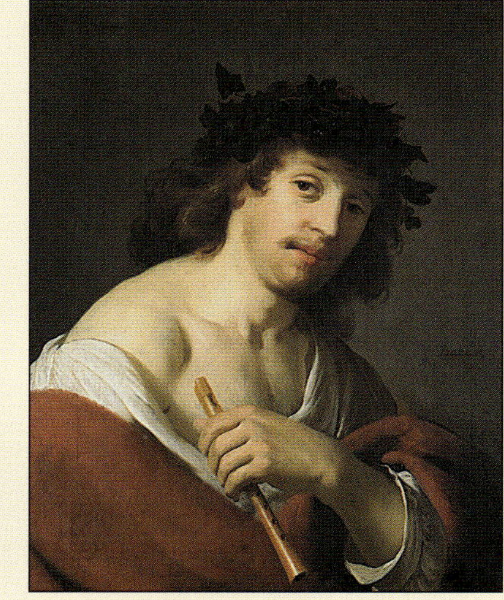
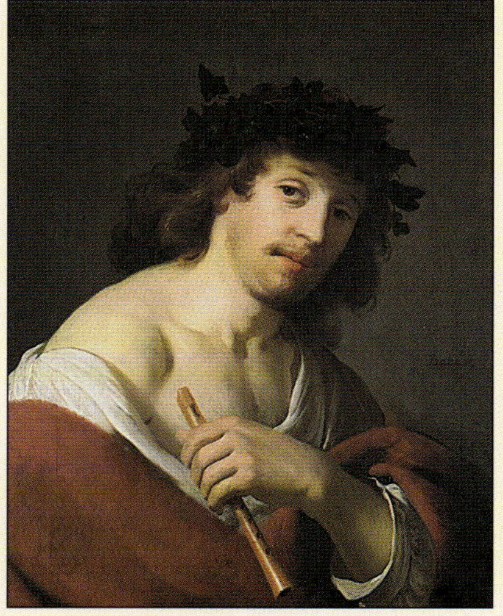

52. Self portrait as shepherd with garland and flute, panel (ca. 1633-1635) - FML

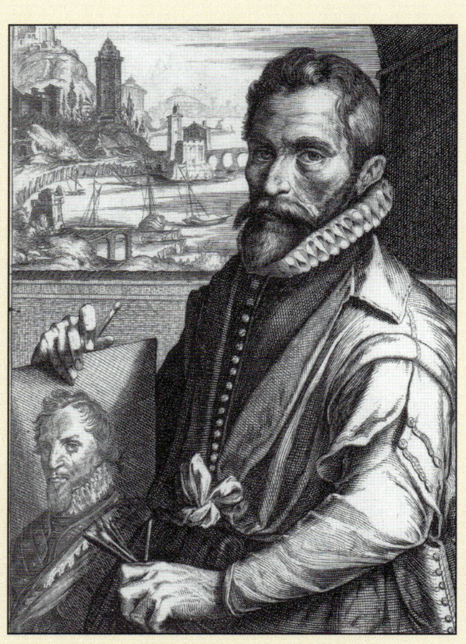

51. Hendrik Hondius I, engraving (ca. 1610) - RPA

51.
Michiel Jansz van Mierevelt (1567-1641) from Delft, presumably a Waterlander, was a very successful portrait painter. He has been compared to Holbein and Pourbus. He not only became the court painter of Prince Maurice, (shown here), but immortalized a number of foreign dignitaries in his Delft studio. Archduke Albrecht himself invited Mierevelt to the very Catholic court at Brussels 'on condition of freedom of Religion' (NNBW X, 628-630; Dawn pp. 310-311 & 592-593).

52.
Jacob Adriaensz Backer (1608-1651), a Harlinger by birth, grew up in Amsterdam. He went to Leeuwarden to study art under Lambert Jacobsz (ca. 1598-1636), who besides being a painter and art dealer was a Waterlander preacher. Around 1633, Backer worked for Rembrandt and Hendrick Uylenburgh. He painted for Amsterdam burgomasters and worked on the decoration of the palace Huis ten Bosch in The Hague. Just before his death in 1651, he joined the Remonstrant Church (Dudok 1, pp. 108-110; Dudok 2; NNBW II, 56-57).

53.
Govert Flinck (1615-1660), born in Cleves, also began his career with Lambert Jacobsz, Rembrandt and Uylenburgh. Like Backer, Flinck also became Remonstrant in 1651. Flinck achieved such skill in copying Rembrandt's style that it sometimes became difficult to distinguish between the two masters. Flinck beat out Rembrandt, his great rival, for the commission of twelve paintings in the new City Hall of Amsterdam, but his death hindered completion of the cycle (Dudok 1, pp. 109-110; Schwartz pp. 318-320; Moltke pp. 12-60).

54.
Samuel van Hoogstraten (1627-1678), brother of Frans (see 46), was an accomplished poet and painter. He worked in Vienna at the court of Ferdinand III and in London for the English élite. Because of his extravagent life style and his marriage to a Reformed niece of Matthijs Balen (see 49), he was banned by the Flemish church of Dordrecht in 1656. In 1678, following the footsteps of van Mander, he wrote a manual for the art of painting, the *Inleyding tot de Hooge Schoole der Schilderkonst* (Brusati pp. 16-51; Thissen pp. 52-106 & 175-192; Roscam 1).

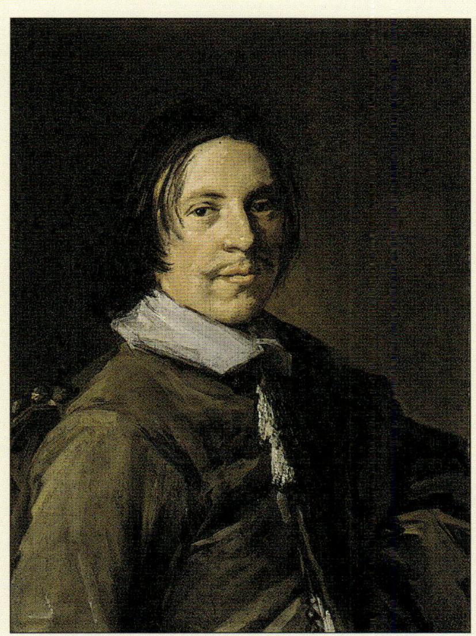

55. Frans Hals, canvas (ca. 1655-1660) - AGO

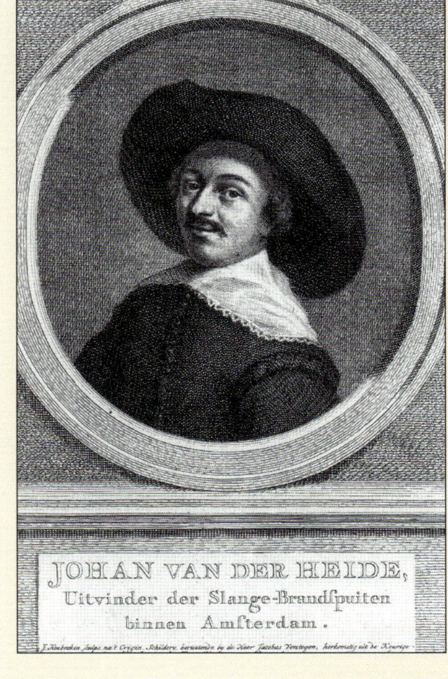

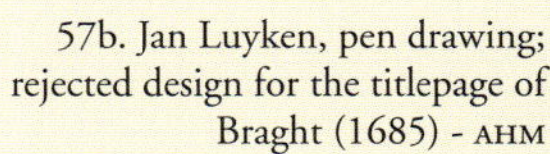

56. Jacob Houbraken, engraving after an unknown (self?)portrait (middle 18th century) - RPA

55.
Vincent Laurensz van der Vinne (1628-1702) was the progenitor of many artists, most of whom lived in Haarlem. Originally a physician with interests in the linen industry, he made his name primarily as a painter. He was trained by the renowned Frans Hals, whose style van der Vinne copied. The resulting still lifes and portraits were in great demand. Because he had the reputation of painting anything that brought in money - dishes, chests and ceilings - he became known as the Raphael of shop-sign painters. Originally Waterlander Mennonite, he followed his second wife to the Flemish Mennonites, where he spent many years as a deacon (Sliggers; Slive pp. 340-343, nr. 76).

56.
Jan van der Heyden (1637-1712) was an Amsterdammer with many talents. His invention of the fire pump in 1677 made him into a national hero, due partly to his own promotion and publicity campaign. As engineer of city lightings he had earlier gained some renown for his innovative system of street lamps. His still lifes, landscapes and above all the many cityscapes were in demand on account of the fine brush work and his eye for detail. He attended the Lamist church, where at various times between 1675 and 1701 he served deacon (Vries; ME II, p. 736).

57.
Jan Luyken (1649-1712) has gained an indelible place in Mennonite history as illustrator of van Braght's *Martyrs' Mirror* (1685). Following his baptism by the Collegiants in Beverwijk, he was after 1673 a member of the Amsterdam Lamist church. His ties to the Mennonite Church were very loose, however, because after his 'great conversion' in 1675, he bade the 'world' farewell and entered fully into the mysticism of Jacob Boehme. Debuting as a poet in 1671 with the very erotic volume *Duytse Lier (Dutch Lyre),* he left behind a large body of poetic works. His even more prolific graphic production, illustrations for more than 500 books, made him one of the most famous engravers of his time (Meeuwesse; Eeghen 2; vE&vdK p. 786, nr. A).

57b. Jan Luyken, pen drawing; rejected design for the titlepage of Braght (1685) - AHM

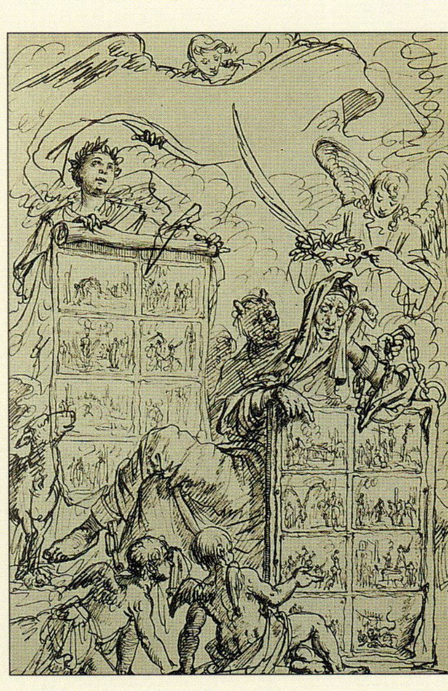

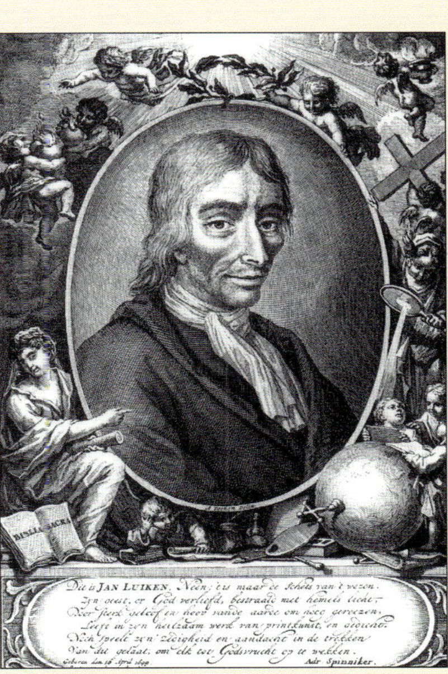

57a. Pieter Sluiter after Arnold Houbraken and Arnold Boonen, engraving in Luyken, *Schriftuurlyke Geschiedenissen* (1712) - UBA-DG

58a & b.
Lieven Willemsz van Coppenol (1598->1671) became known as the 'phoenix of all pens'. Originating from Haarlem, he established himself as a French schoolmaster in Amsterdam, where he worshipped with the Waterlanders. After 1650 he began to suffer the burden of mental illness. Because he could no longer teach, he dedicated himself to calligraphy. To the shame of his family and church, he began to frequent taverns and brothels. Nevertheless, between 1656 and 1658, he enjoyed his greatest success. Nearly all the great poets of the day praised his calligraphic work to the heavens. There were also a number of portraits made of him, among which are two etchings by Rembrandt. At a ripe old age, after a legal process on account of sexual debauchery, he was placed under curatorial care as a mad, lewd man. On this sheet from 1657 is a famous line of rhyme from Vondel (see 38): 'The World is a Stage, Each plays his Role and obtains his Part', with variants of this by Constantijn Huygens (Constanter) and from Eccl. 1:4 (Wijnman; Cat Rhuis p. 154).

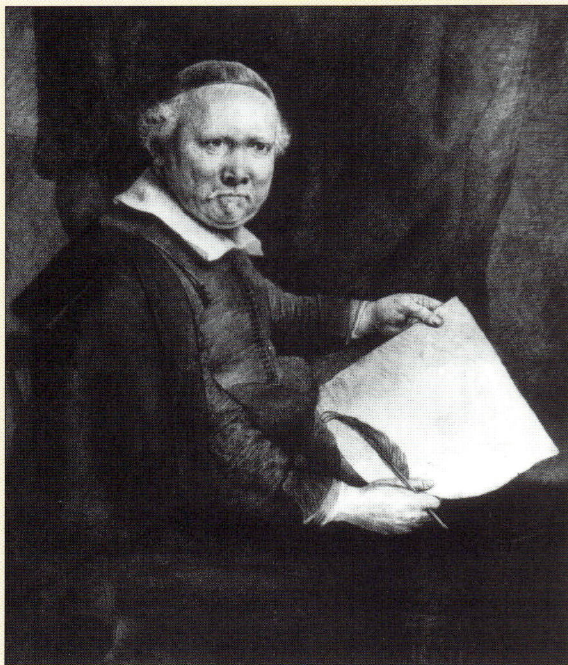

58a. Rembrandt, etching - MRA

59a & b.
Joanna Koerten (1650-1715), member of the Lamists in Amsterdam, was famous for *knipkunst* (the art of paper cutting). As a middle-aged woman, in 1691, she married the cloth merchant Adriaan Block. As a youth she learned embroidery, sewing, music, modelling and glasscutting. With paper and scissors, she produced for 4,000 guilders a magnificent flower arrangement for the German empress. Intricate scenes of classical and biblical subjects, a view of Amsterdam and many portraits made her collection one of the city's popular attractions. She collected the hundreds of reactions to her *knipkunst* in a *Stamboek* (*Register*), published after her death with the laudatory poems, *Gedichten op de overheerlyke papiere snykunst van wyle Mejuf-frouwe Joanna Koerten (Verses on the exquisite paper cut-work by the late Lady Joanna Koerten)* (1736). After 1762 the collection and also the *Stamboek* (see 29) were sold and dispersed. Displayed is Koerten's cut paper portrait of stadtholder William III (1672-1702), King of Great Britain and Ireland (1689-1702) (NNBW X, 478-481; Plomp; Holl 708[1]).

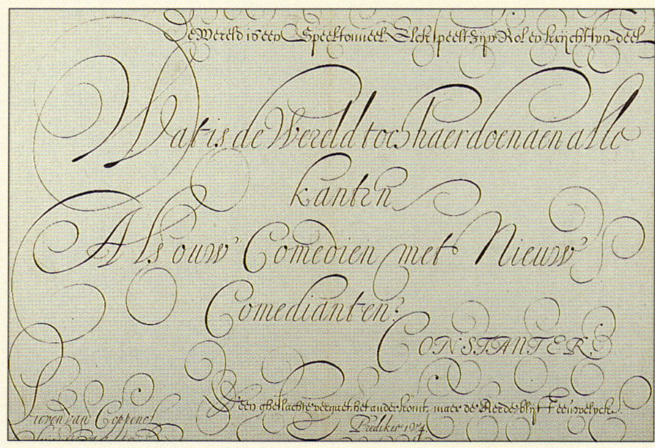

58b. Van Coppenol, pen work on parchment - UBA

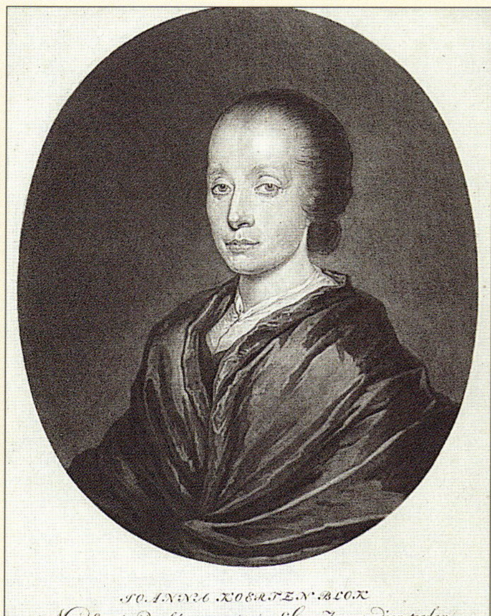

59a. Pieter Schenck after David van der Plaes, mezzotint (1701) - NOA

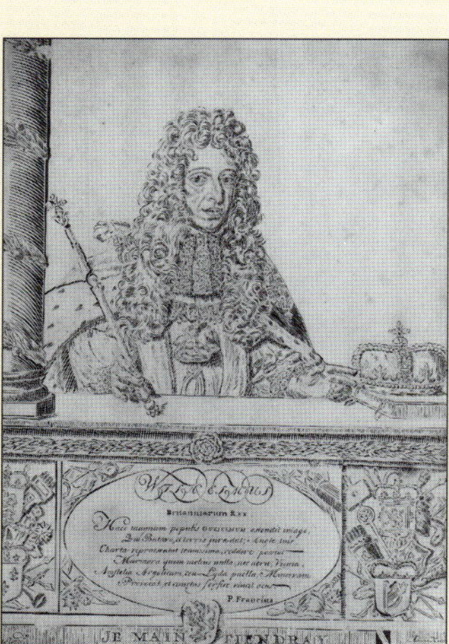

59b. Koerten, paper cutting on black background: Wilhelmus Britanniarum Rex (ca. 1700) - SML

Masters of Mechanics and Mathematics

With most doors closed to them in government and academia, Mennonites tended to develop their intellects in the areas where their economic interests were the greatest: trade, shipping and industry. Behind the important improvements in the once modern industrial technology of wind mills and horse mills stood the keen perceptions of early seventeenth-century Mennonites such as Salomon Ophey, Pieter and Jan Philipsz Schabaelje (see 37) and Pieter Pietersz. Sometimes their inventions were rewarded with patents, which usually ensured tidy profits. Wybe Adam, originally from Harlingen, participated in the land reclamation project in the Vistula Delta region of Poland. Around 1644 he won great fame for his 'Jacob's ladder', which helped to furnish the city of Danzig with a fortified wall. In the area of sailing, navigation and cartography, Mennonite contributions were even more remarkable. For example, in 1595 Pieter Jansz Lioren at Hoorn in 1595 developed the flute ship, modelled after Noah's ark, which required a smaller crew, could carry a larger cargo and thus added higher profits. Robbert Robbertsz le Canu (1563->1630), an intriguing personality, taught navigation and astronomy to great explorers such as Houtman, van Eck, Heemskerk and de Veer. Calculating and cosmopolite minded businessmen benefitted both from good instruction in accounting and knowledge of foreign languages. Waterlander Sybrandt Hansz Cardinael (1578-1647) was highly regarded as master of an accounting school in Amsterdam. The same held true in Haarlem with Jacob van der Schuere (1576->1643), who taught Italian bookkeeping, as well as French. Abraham de Graaf (1635-1717) became one of the most important mathematicians in the Dutch Republic. The illustrious Jan Theunisz (1569-ca.1637) taught Hebrew and Arabic in Amsterdam. In the book business of that time, which no less than the arts leant Golden-Age Holland its international allure, there were also active many Mennonites, especially in Amsterdam, Haarlem and Hoorn (Visser; Berkel pp. 23-28).

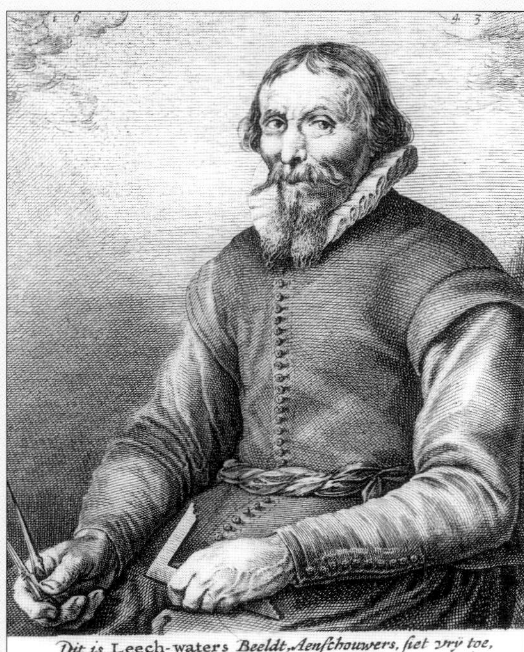

60. Salomon Saverij after Thomas de Keyser, engraving (1643) in: *Leeghwater, Kleyne Chronycke ... van Graft en De Ryp* (Amsterdam 1654) - UBA-DG

60.
Jan Adriaensz Leeghwater (1575-1647), a member of the Waterlander church at De Rijp, was a man of many talents. As engineer and mill builder, he became involved in land reclamation in Holland and Sleeswijk, but he also designed cabinets, clocks, bridges, locks, carillons and the town hall of De Rijp. He received great attention for his diving bell, in which he could remain underwater for three quarters of an hour. In 1641 he unfolded his plans to reclaim the enormous Haarlemmer Lake, a feat that would not be realized until the nineteenth century. (NNBW VI, 909-911; Roever; Holl 126[II]).

64. Theodorus Matham after Simon de Vlieger, engraving (ca. 1639) - UBA-DG

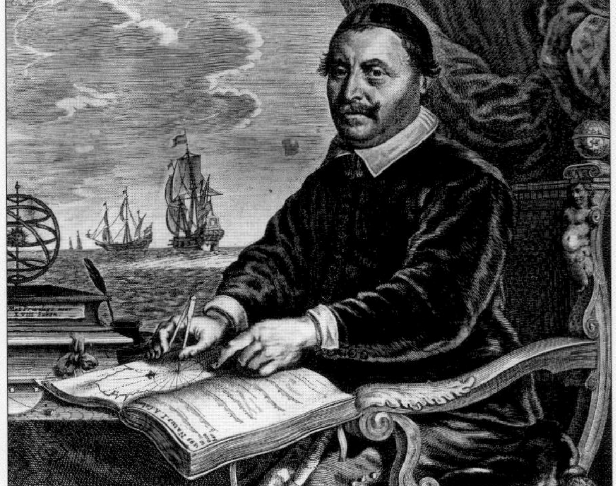

62. H.M., engraved frontispiece of van Nierop, *Nederduytsche Astronomia* (1658) - UBA

61. Christoffel van Sichem II, woodcut (1604) on the title-page of Drebbel, *Kort Tractaet van de Natuere der Elementen* (1632) - UBA

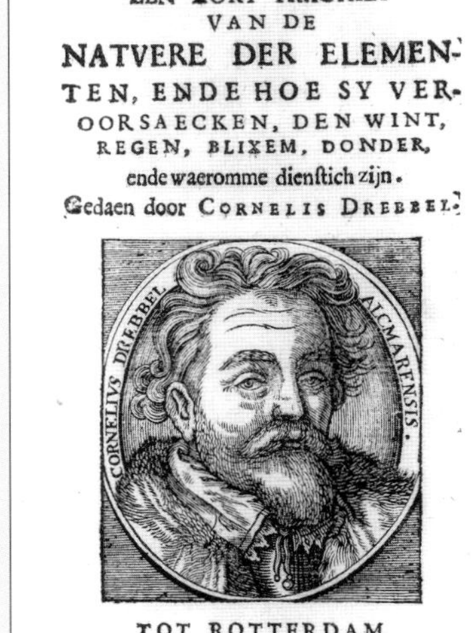

EEN KORT TRACTAET VAN DE NATVERE DER ELEMENTEN, ENDE HOE SY VEROORSAECKEN, DEN WINT, REGEN, BLIXEM, DONDER, ende waeromme dienstich zijn.

Gedaen door CORNELIS DREBBEL.

TOT ROTTERDAM,

By Jan van Waesberge Anno 1632.

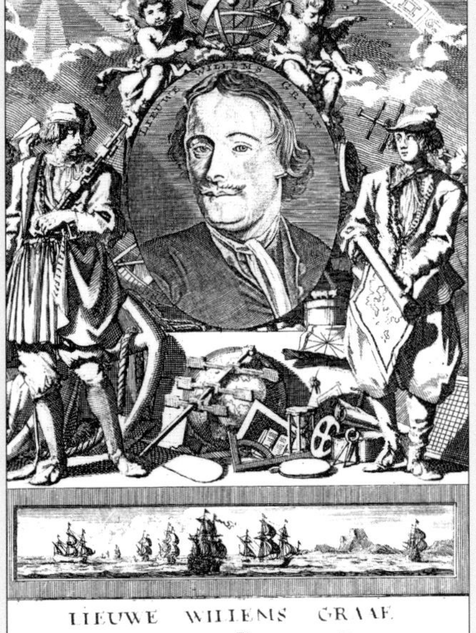

63. Anonymous, engraving published by Johannes van Keulen (Amsterdam, ca. 1690) - UBA-DG

61.

Cornelis Drebbel (1572-1633), originally from Alkmaar, trained himself in mechanics, physics and alchemy. He worked for a time at the magical, mystical court of Rudolph II in Prague. He made his name in England with King James I, where he received much attention for his perpetual motion machine and a sub-marine, which he navigated under the Thames. Despite his renown, he ended up as a poor proprietor of a London pub (NNBW VI, 451; Berkel pp. 27-28; cf. Holl 36).

62.

Dirck Rembrantsz van Nierop (1610-1682), a shoemaker at Nieuwe Niedorp, impressed many with his knowledge of astronomy, navigation, calendars, and mathematics. He published a number of writings, of which the *Nieropper Graedboeck (The Niedorp Book of Degrees)* (1656) and the *Nederduytsche Astronomia (Dutch Astronomy)* (1658) were the most famous. He corresponded with a number of scientists, such as Christiaan Huygens and Nicolaes Witsen (Smit; NNBW V, 373-374; vS 3881).

63.

Lieuwe Willemsz Graaf (1652-1704), a boatman in Harlingen, dedicated himself to the study of mathematics and astronomy. His work reached a climax with his discovery of the means of determining longitude at sea. Thanks to a patent and a subsidy of 2,000 guilders from the States General, in 1691 he was able to publish his theory, only to be disputed by academics such as Huygens, Fullenius and Abraham de Graaf. After this he began a school of navigation in Amsterdam, where he was also a preacher of the Old Frisian Mennonites (NNBW III, 485-487; ME II, p. 558; vS 2086).

64.

Jacob Aertsz Colom (1599-1673), a member of the Waterlanders, had a bookshop 'On the Water' (now the Damrak) in the center of Amsterdam. As a maker and publisher of sea maps, navigation books, atlases, and globes and celestial spheres, he was the greatest rival of his neighbor Willem Jansz Blaeu, *the* cartographer of the Golden Age, who was also of Mennonite descent. In addition, Colom also published Mennonite hymn books and tracts, as well as worldly plays. (NNBW IX, 156-160; Kölker pp. 13-23; Holl 79^{II}).

MENNO AND MERCURY:
THE PRIVILEGED UPPER CLASS

The Dutch Mennonites' rise in status is a remarkable phenomenon: a class of mostly simple artisans, once persecuted and displaced, was able to work its way up in society in just a few generations. The Mennonites, whose wings had been clipped by the heretic's sword and Menno's rejection of the world, received, thanks to the golden breeze of the Golden Age, the wings of Mercury. Mennonite capital helped lay the foundation for the erection of the Dutch East India Company in 1602. In De Rijp they dominated the herring fishery and later also the whaling business. Along the Zaan River, the oldest industrial region of the Netherlands and the unmistakable hinterland of Amsterdam's cosmopolitan harbor, were dozens of Mennonite mills grinding grain into flour and sawing logs into planks. Mennonites dominated the thriving ship-biscuit industry in Wormer and Jisp. In Haarlem, Amsterdam and soon also in Twente, their position in trade and manufacture of fine textiles such as linen, wool fabric and silk has to be recognized. In Rotterdam, Harlingen and Makkum, a number of Mennonite tile-makers were established. It was good to do business with the Mennonite businessman, for his yea was his yea and his nay was his nay.

The religiously-based ethic of industry, honesty and simplicity resulted in a sober bearing toward comsumption. As a result, dozens of Mennonites became richer and richer. By marrying within their own circles, families increased their capital. The lesser endowed brothers and sisters were also able to pluck the fruits of prosperity. The poorest – for while these did exist, all of the rich source material turns our attention primarily to the upper strata – could count on the support of congregational poor relief, orphan's and widow's chests, or work found through a Mennonite benefactor. The faith demanded that profit not be made for its own sake, but that business revenues be used for the good of the fellowship. So on the basis of Christian solidarity, a strong social consciousness came into practice, deeds were one with the Word. It was thus not without reason that often the most prosperous fulfilled the office of deacon.

Boards of Beneficence

It was generally a set matter of principle that Mennonites filled no positions in governmental organizations. When some did harbor such ambitions, they were rejected by the Reformed moralists. But sometimes the Mennonite squadron could not be turned away, and above all the Waterlanders did not find the burden of governmental office too heavy. When the Reformed church had but a finger in the political pie, the aforementioned ship builder Pieter Jansz Lioren could fulfill the office of alderman five times in Hoorn between 1597 and 1611. In 1612, Lioren, a member of the Young Frisians, was on the executive of the admirality and from 1614 to 1616 he was burgomaster of this important port city. In Westzaan until 1628 Waterlanders were in the college of aldermen, a body that adminstered justice, something Mennonites had earlier refused to do. In De Rijp until ca. 1650 they completely filled the political offices of the town council, to the great irritation of the Reformed minority. Thanks to a 'trick' by the national government in The Hague, an end was made of this hegemony; now new members of the council had to swear an oath of allegience, something which Mennonites refused to do on principle. In Amsterdam, with its tolerant authorities, Mennonites had opportunity to make a mark on city politics, even if these were exclusively quasi-governmental posts. Status was often more decisive than religious conviction. Thus Syvert Pietersz Sem (1560-1632) in the first quarter of the seventeenth century was named as regent of the Leper's House, along with three Reformed. But then Sem was not just anyone. In 1602, Sem was co-founder and administrator of the Dutch East India Company. He withdrew from this, along with several other brethren, when the Company decided in 1608 to equip its ships with cannon. Where the administrative work touched upon the professionally-bound organizations of the guilds, it was much simpler for the Mennonites, but often also much more profitable, for them to hold government positions.

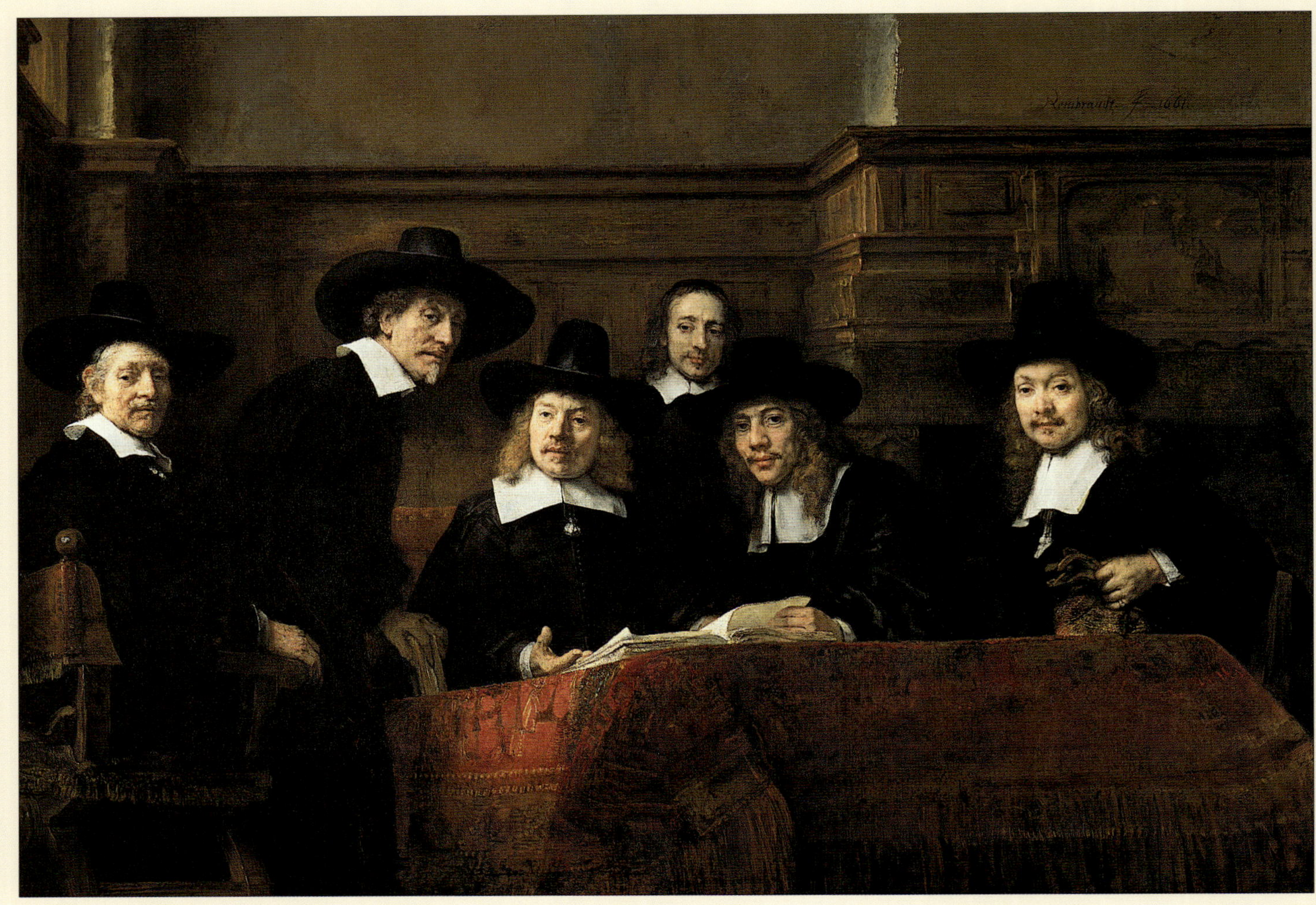

65. Rembrandt, canvas: *The Syndics* (1662) - RMA

65.
Next to the Nightwatch, 'the Syndics' is Rembrandt's most famous group portrait. This Amsterdam college of 'dignitaries of the cloth guild' formed the highest of the four city-named agencies that supervised cloth manufacture and trade.
The syndics were chosen from among the most prominent cloth merchants. Their task was to meet three times a week to check the quality of blue and black wool cloth. When Rembrandt immortalized the syndics, the board consisted of two Catholics, two Reformed and one Mennonite. The second man from the left (half standing), is the Old Frisian Mennonite merchant Volckert Jansz (ca. 1605-1681), who had joined the board in 1660. A bachelor, he lived in a large house on the Nieuwendijk, where he received visitors from far and wide who came to marvel at his renowned art and curiosity collection. His prominent position suggests that he commissioned the painting (Schwartz pp. 335-336; Eeghen 1, pp. 71-73).

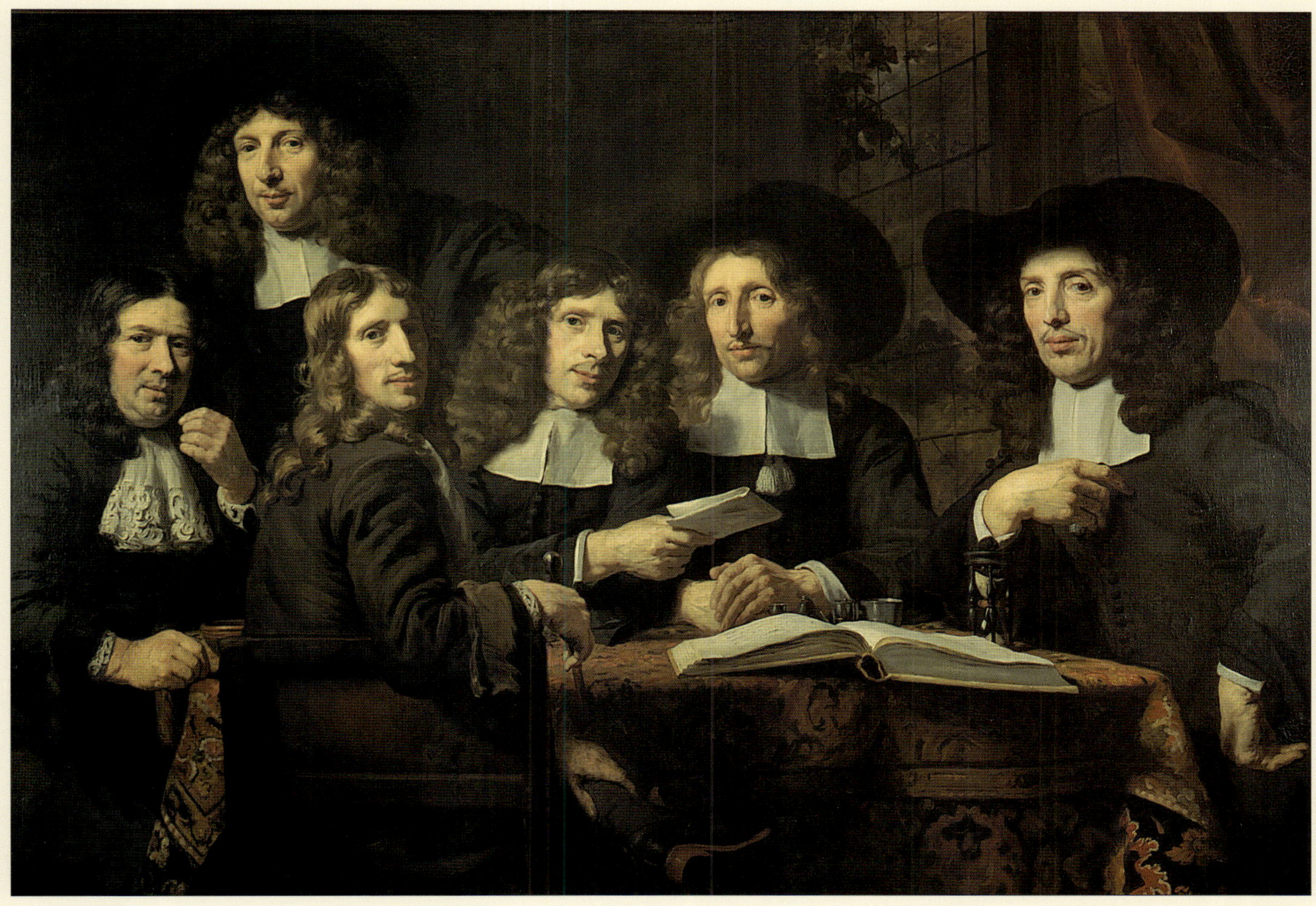

66. Nicolaes Maes?,
canvas: *Six Overseers of the Surgeon's Guild at Amsterdam* (1680-1681) - AHM

66.
Govert Bidloo (1649-1713), the younger brother of Lambert (see 43), was a talented man. He lived in Amsterdam where he attended the Lamist church and began his career as a surgeon, at that time regarded as a trade with its own professional organization. In 1680 he was one of the six overseers of the surgeon's guild; he is seated on the chair in the foreground. Two years later he earned his doctorate in medicine at Franeker and after practising in Amsterdam, he began in 1688 to give anatomy lessons in The Hague. There in 1690 he was named by King-Stadtholder William III as head of the medical staff of the Dutch and English armies. Later he would become William's personal physician. In the meantime he was also appointed professor at the University of Leyden. While in Amsterdam, Govert had made a name as a poet. His French-classicist dramas with ballets, novelties at the time, were very popular, but not with the critics. In 1685, he avenged himself on his critics, among them Philips de Flines (see p. 142), regent of the Amsterdam Theater, with a sensational play (NNBW VIII, 103-108; Worp pp. 140-142; Erenstein pp. 272-277; Blankert 260).

Throned in Humility

The art of portraiture might have been debatable on artistic grounds, but in economic respects it was a factor of great importance: in the seventeenth century there was hardly a more popular genre. Hundreds of patrons were immortalized. 'Faces' thereby became desirable objects for collectors. And what-ever generated a market was painted – heads were money.

The Mennonite upper stratum kept itself even less aloof from this mode. The pictures of patrons who had themselves and their wives immortalized on canvas and wood panels as pendant portraits, or together with their children, are legion. These portraits are not only interesting as a phenomenon of the unstoppable assimilation and emancipation of the Mennonites; they also depict their clothing, which likewise adapted gradually to the fashion of the day. In the older portraits, it is still quite easy to recognize Mennonites – not so much for their dark clothing, but mainly for the details such as simple flat collars, small cuffs and women's small caps. Some family portraits attract attention for their unusual setting, whereby the patrons intended to stress the Mennonite life-style. After the end of the seventeenth century, this all expression of humility in clothing and pose changed. Not surprisingly, Mennonites in the big cities usually bore themselves differently than their rural brothers and sisters. Although the townspeople clothed themselves in urban fashion the command of Rom. 12:2 still remained in 1659 an admonition for the Old Flemish Mennonites of Loppersum in Groningen: 'And be not conformed to this world – do not wear red cloth clothing, nor sleek satin; no stiffened bodices, gleaming aprons, sleekly ironed shirts and collarets; no shoes with high heels; no long hair and above all no coils and braids'. Their world would have stood at a great distance from that of a *mercator sapiens* such as the wealthy Amsterdammer Philips de Flines (1640-1700). He possessed a renowned art collection, with many Italian drawings. At his country house on the Spaarne at Haarlem, he laid out a beautiful orangery. And whenever in need of new inspiration, he travelled to Paris to view the treasures of fellow collectors (Schwartz pp. 57 & 146-149; Wybrands 2, pp. 35-42; Wereld pp. 132-133).

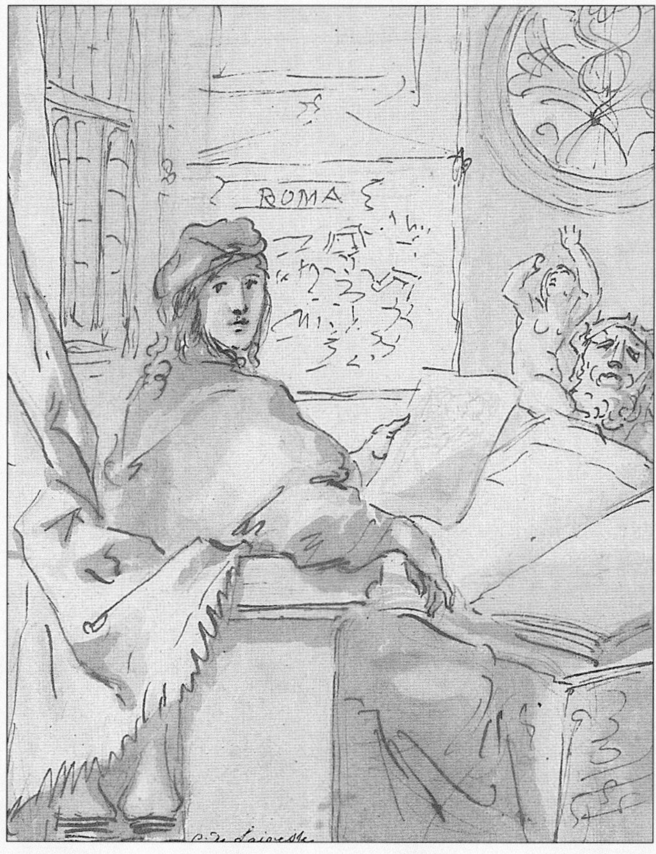

Gerard de Lairesse, washed pen drawing of Philips de Flines (ca. 1685) - RPA

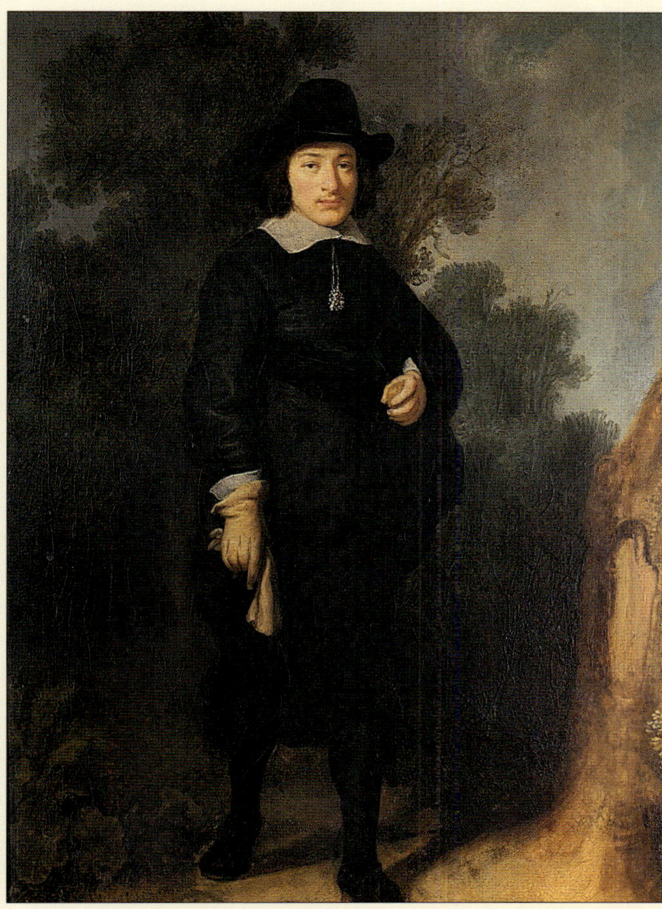

67. Govert Flinck, canvas (1636) - VDGA

67.
Dirck Jacobsz Leeuw (1614-1652), member of the Waterlanders at Amsterdam, was painted as a 22-year-old by his nephew Govert Flinck (see 53). In 1639 Dirck, along with his wife Maria Anslo, niece of Cornelis Claesz (see 26 and 72), joined the Remonstrant Church. This transfer did not occasion a breach with the family. Flinck placed Dirck, just as his cousin David (see 68), in a fanciful landscape. Dirck's hat originally had a broad brim; a later owner must have had this touched up to suit his own tastes. This painting previously hung in the Rijpenhofje, a house for old women, which from 1747 was governed by the diaconate of the church 'by't Lam' (Dudok 1, pp. 109-110; cf. Moltke 211: Jonas Jacob Leeuwen Dircksz).

68.
Flinck, who immortalized on canvas almost the entire Leeuw family, also painted Dirck's eight-year-old cousin David Leeuw (ca. 1632-1703). David was the son of businessman and art collector Ameldonck Leeuw. The Leeuws originally came from the Rhineland. David's grandfather had been an elder in Cologne. A number of descendants married into other well-to-do Mennonite families, such as de Bosch, Block, de Flines, Rutgers, van Lennep, van der Heyden and van Heyst. David's portion of the inheritence of his father's art collection stood at eighteen paintings and drawings, among them three Rembrandts. He would later marry Cornelia Hooft (see 78) (Dudok 1, pp. 119-120; Moltke 407).

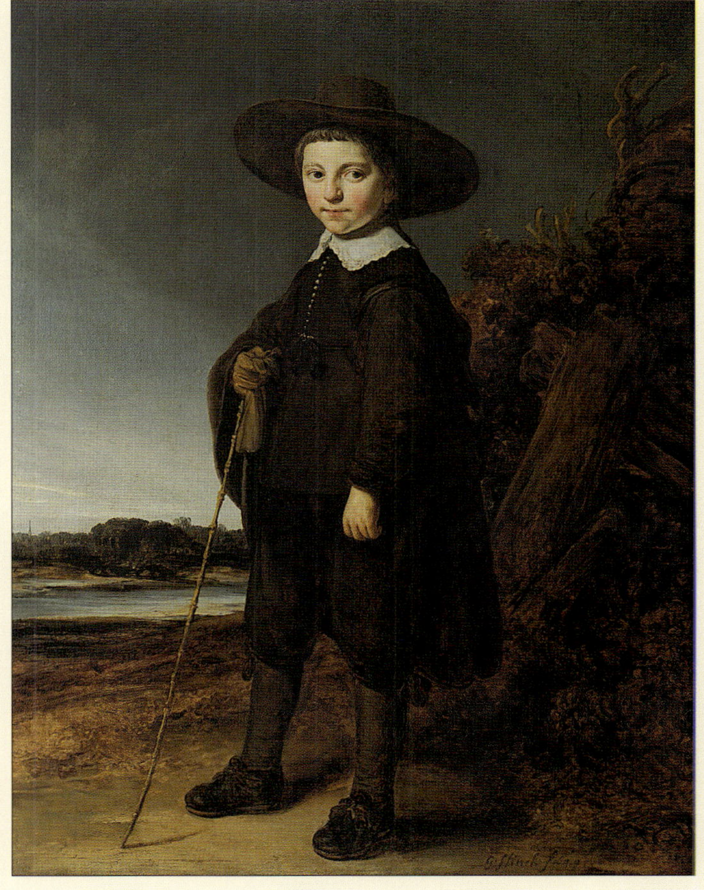

68. Govert Flinck, canvas (1640) - BIB

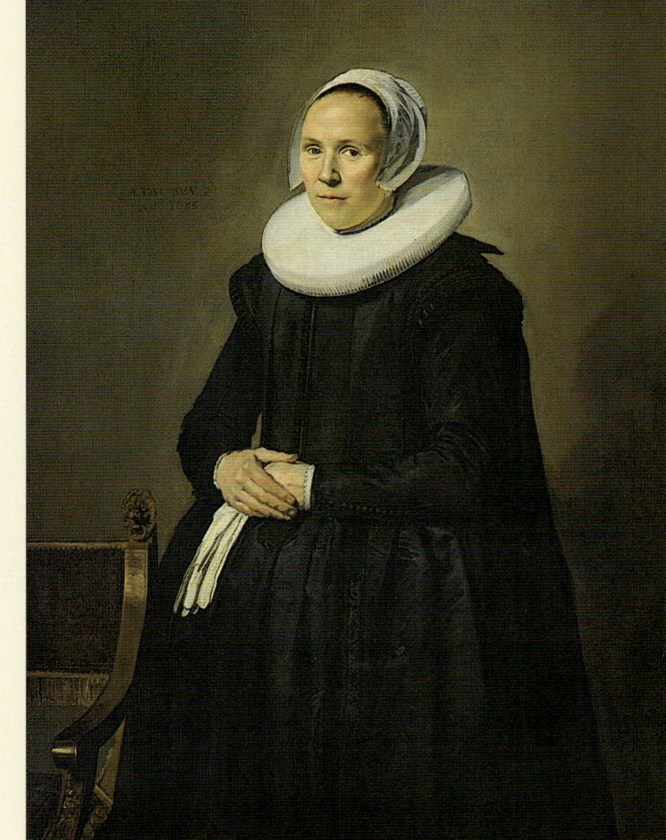

69a&b. Frans Hals, canvas (ca. 1635) - RMA

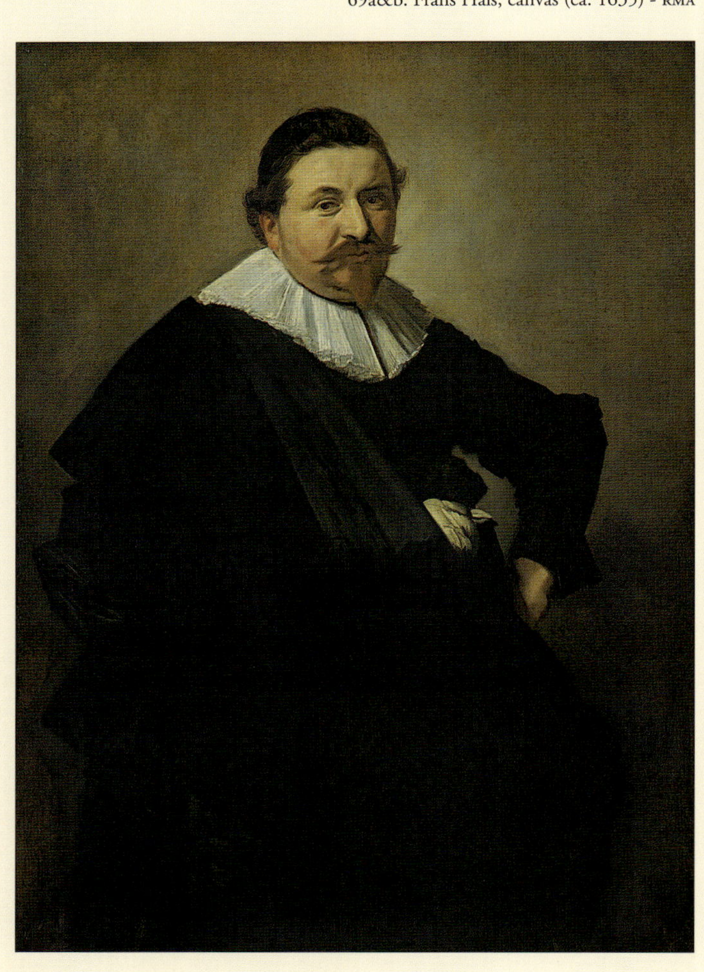

69.

Lucas de Clercq (ca. 1593-1652) and Feyna van Steenkiste (1603/04-1640) were married in 1626 at Haarlem and belonged to the church of the so-called *Vlaamse Block* of the Flemish Mennonites. Lucas was a rich merchant and had a linen bleaching operation outside of the city; Feyna was the daughter of a trader in potash, which was used for the bleaching. They were portrayed by the great Haarlem master Frans Hals. Their chic black clothing bespeaks the couple's well-to-do Mennonite origins, as do Feyna's small lace cuffs. Lucas' well-cultivated beard, their lace collars and white gloves lend an urban touch to their appearance. That they numbered among the élite, at least of the Mennonites, is evident from the great similarity in clothing with that of the Anslos (see 72). After Feyna's death, Lucas married Adriaentje Keyser; around 1645 they commissioned Pieter de Grebber to paint their portrait, which included the children from both marriages (Slive pp. 264-267; Clercq p. 4, VIb).

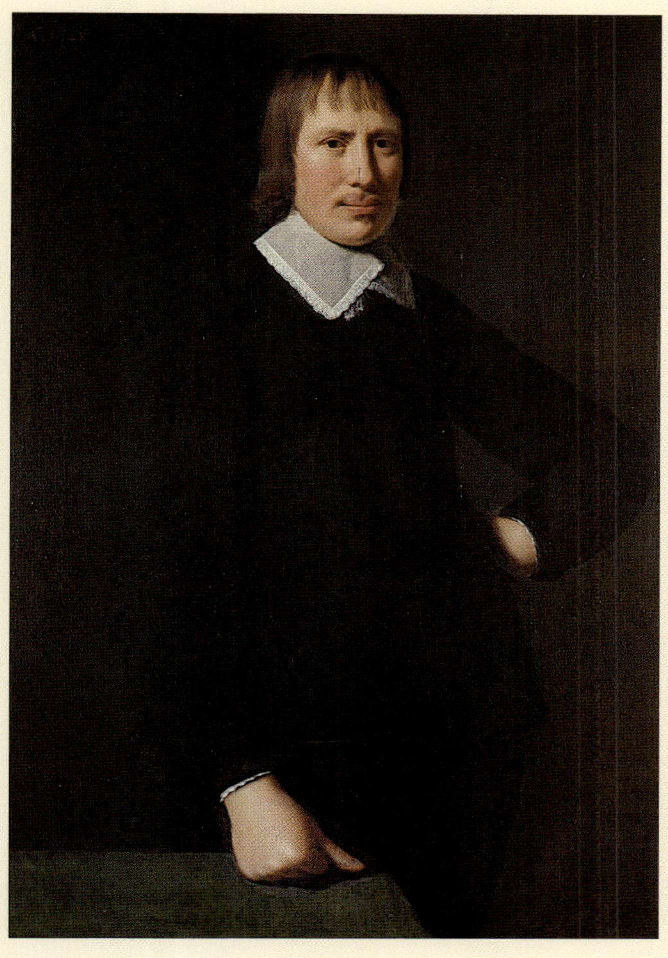

70a&b. Anonymous, canvas (1648) - GHH (photo: W.F. Proost)

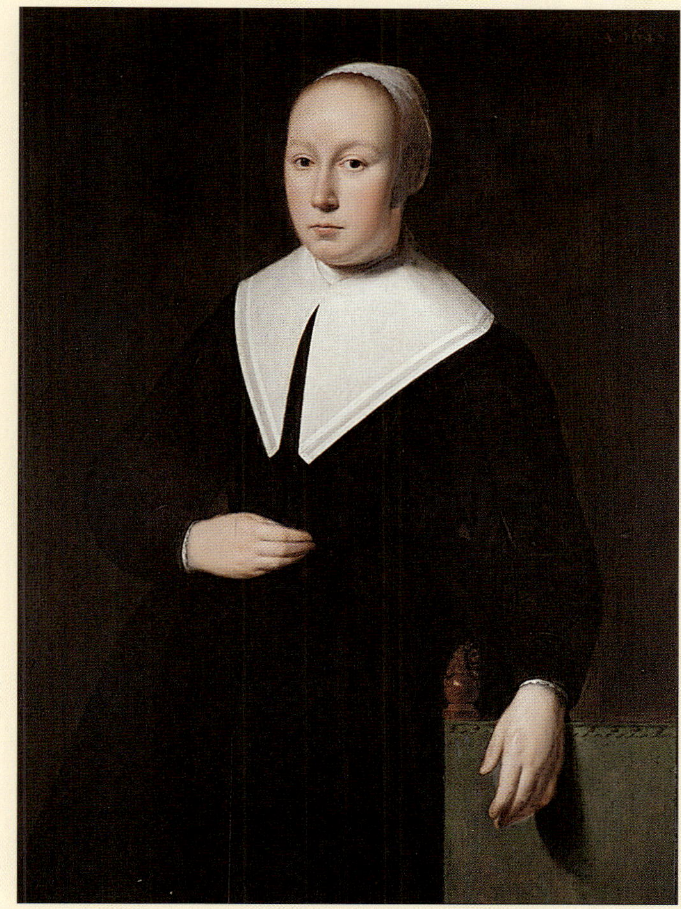

70.
Claes Jurjens Fontein (1616-1670) and his wife Antje Reijners Jeddema (1629-1660), belonging to the Mennonite élite of Harlingen, show clear differences in appearance from their Haarlem and Amsterdam contemporaries. Claes Fontein was a cloth merchant and both a deacon of the United Church of the Waterlander and Flemish Mennonites and an alderman in the city government. The small 'love knot chest' has been preserved from their marriage. At the betrothal the bridegroom gives a coin or pledge penny to the bride, who keeps it in the knot of a special cloth, in Frisian called the *knotte*, or 'love knot'. In the seventeenth century, silver 'love knot chests' to preserve the coin became the fashion among the richer families. The text engraved on the bottom says much about a particular 'Mennonite wedding':

> *Claes Jurjens Fontein on the 30th of March 1646 at the Town Hall of Harlingen married Antie Reiners Jeddema. He fetched her from Leeuwarden with the first 'treckschuit' (a passengers' barge pulled by horses) on March 29 Easter before the barges were moving. So the magistrate of Harlingen loaned him the 'treckschuit' and hired the horses for it himself. It was extremely nice weather and since there never in Friesland had been a similar barge the route from Leeuwarden to Deinum [ca. 6 km.] was full of people. This chest he has given her as a pledge.*

Until recently their pendant portraits were ascribed to Jacob Adriaensz Backer (Avest pp. 24-25; Boschma).

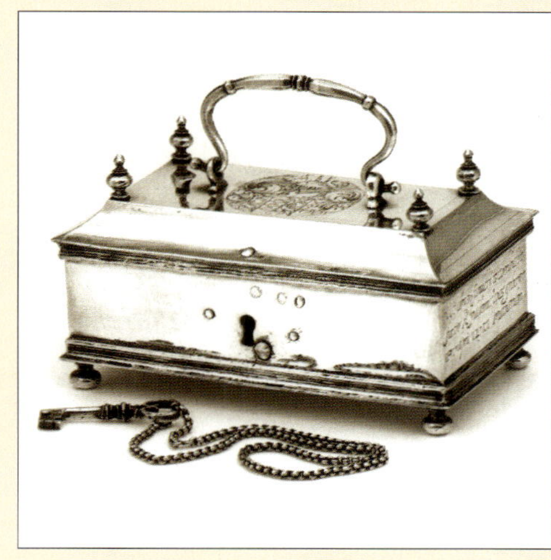

70c.Thomas Boogaert (Amsterdam 1641), silver love knot chest; on the cover are the family's coat of arms with the initials A.R.I. and C.I.F. - GHH(photo: W.F. Proost)

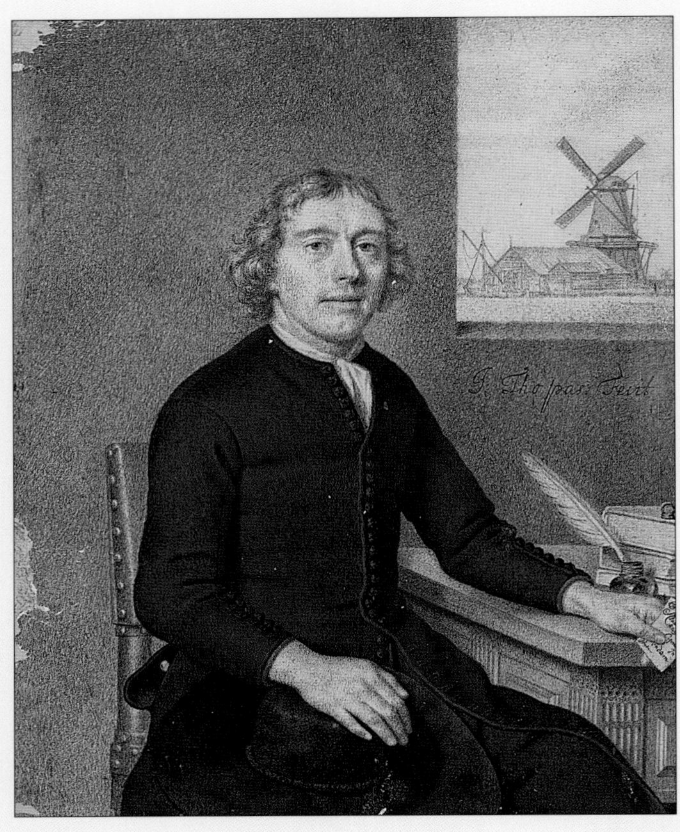

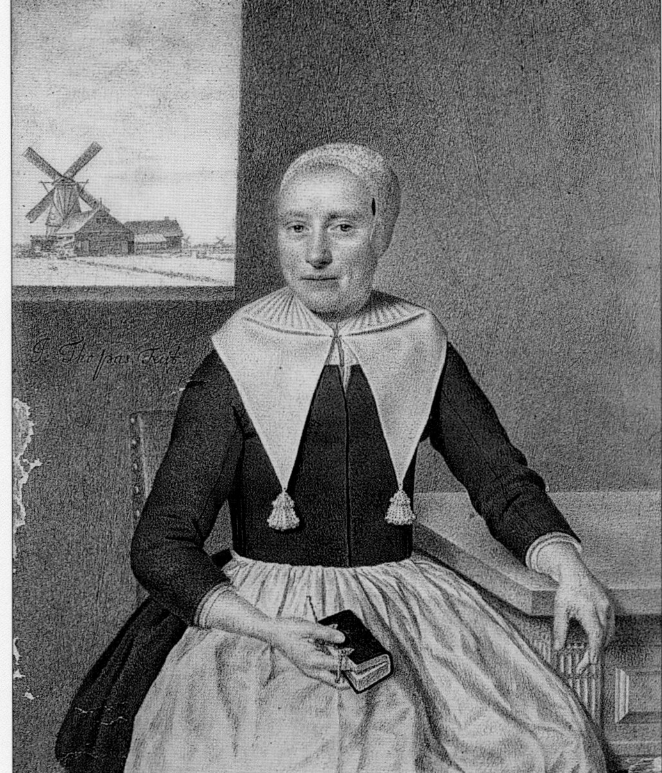

71a&b. Johannes Thopas, silver drawing on parchment (ca. 1685) - ZHM

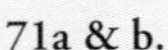

71a & b.
Claes Arisz Caeskoper (1650-1729) and his second wife Trijntje Gerrits Stock (1649-1709) were as Mennonites from the Zaan region literally and figuratively counterparts of their Amsterdam brothers and sisters. The many Mennonites along the bustling Zaan River, a district with its own traditions and costume, were averse to the urban bustle, although they often were no less rich. Claes began as a twelve-year-old apprentice at *Het Pink* (The Yearling), the oil mill of his father, at Koog on the Zaan and became a successful businessman. On his twenty-first birthday he married Hillegont Cornelis Swager, with 366 wedding guests at the ceremony. He was owner of the oil mill *De Reus* (The Giant), which is pictured in his portrait. His wife died at the birth of their second child. In 1680 he married Trijntje Gerrits Stock, daughter of a starch and paper manufacturer at the Koog, whose paper mill *De Koekuit* (The Cuckoo) is depicted next to her. The married couple were members of the United Flemish and Waterlander Church, where Claes was a deacon. He kept a diary for his entire life, the *Nootysye-Boeck (Notebook),* which possesses a treaure-trove of details over his business travels to Zeeland and Flanders, for example, where he bought rapeseed, or a number of pleasure trips by boat or by skates. The artist lived in Zaandam, where he was in high demand on account of his plain but chic silver technique (Honig pp. 74-94).

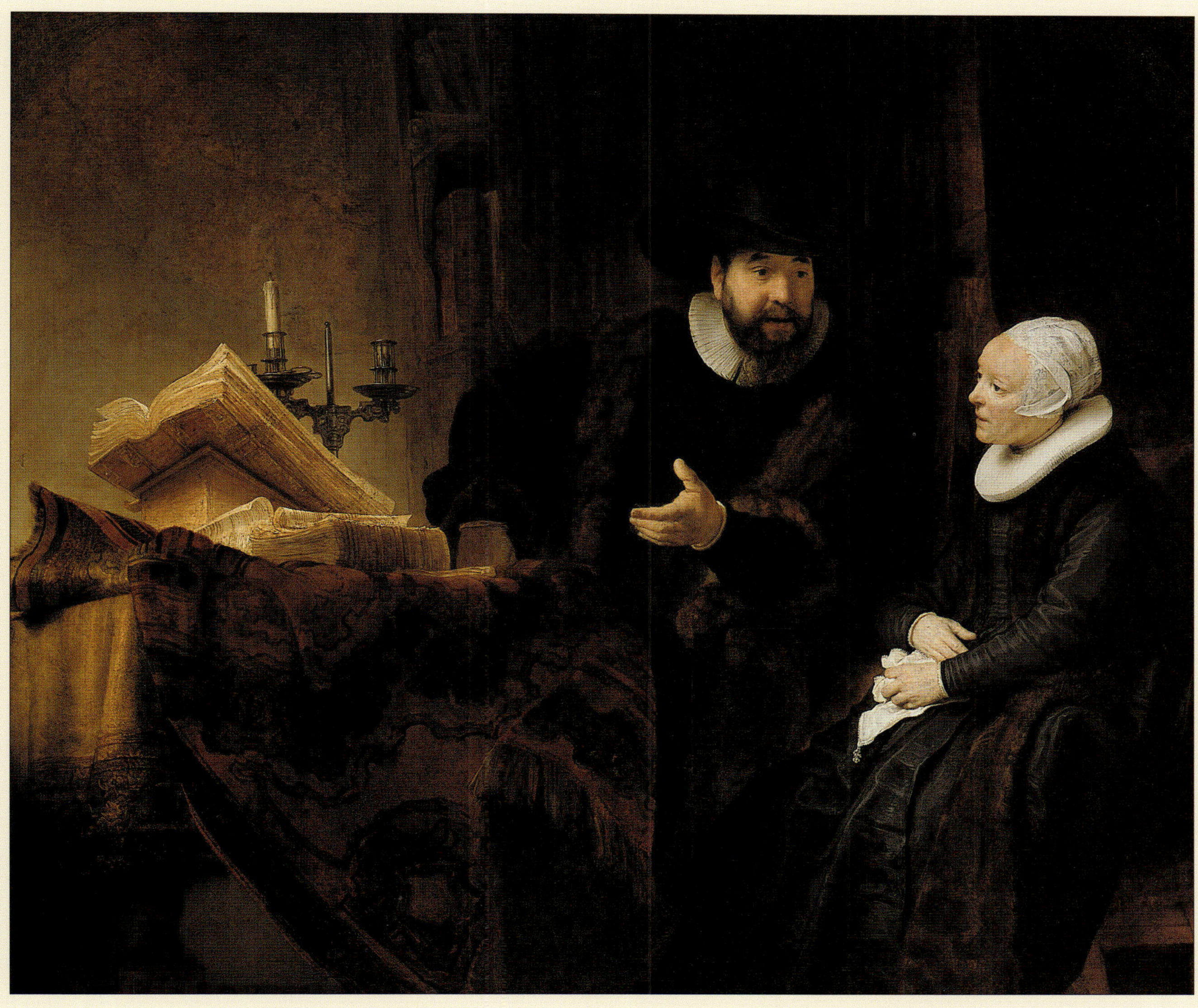

72. Rembrandt, canvas (1641) - SMB-PKG (photo: Jörg P. Anders)

72.
This immense double portrait (176 x 210 cm.) of merchant Cornelis Claesz Anslo (1592-1646) (see 26) and his wife Aeltje Gerrits Schouten (1598-1657) is one of the high points of Rembrandt's career. It seems, just as Vondel set it to rhyme, that Rembrandt attempted to capture Cornelis' voice in image:

Ay, Rembrandt, paint *Cornelis'* voice.
The visible part is the least of him
The invisible one knows only through the ears.
Who desires to see *Anslo*, must hear him.

Inimitably Rembrandt has caught the pious married couple in the intimacy of an admonition. Pointing with a rhetorical gesture Cornelis explains the words of the open Bible. Via his hand Aeltje's attention is completely on the Word. The candle snuffer on the drip plate under the candle also subtly suggests this theme. This pair of scissors was used to clip the wick when the flame became too high and the candle would drip excessively. With this the *correctio fraterna* is symbolized, the brotherly admonition for which the faithful must guard the soul from the superfluity of fat. The uncommon - for Mennonites - fur-wearing preacher and his wife, clothed modestly in a gleaming dress impress through their refined yet simple taste. The handkerchief in her hand reveals great prosperity. Rembrandt was a friend of Anslo's and a number of other Waterlanders. In April 1641, the year in which he painted the couple, he borrowed 1,000 guilders from Anslo's church using 150 etching plates as collatoral (Brown pp. 222-225; Schwartz pp. 217-219).

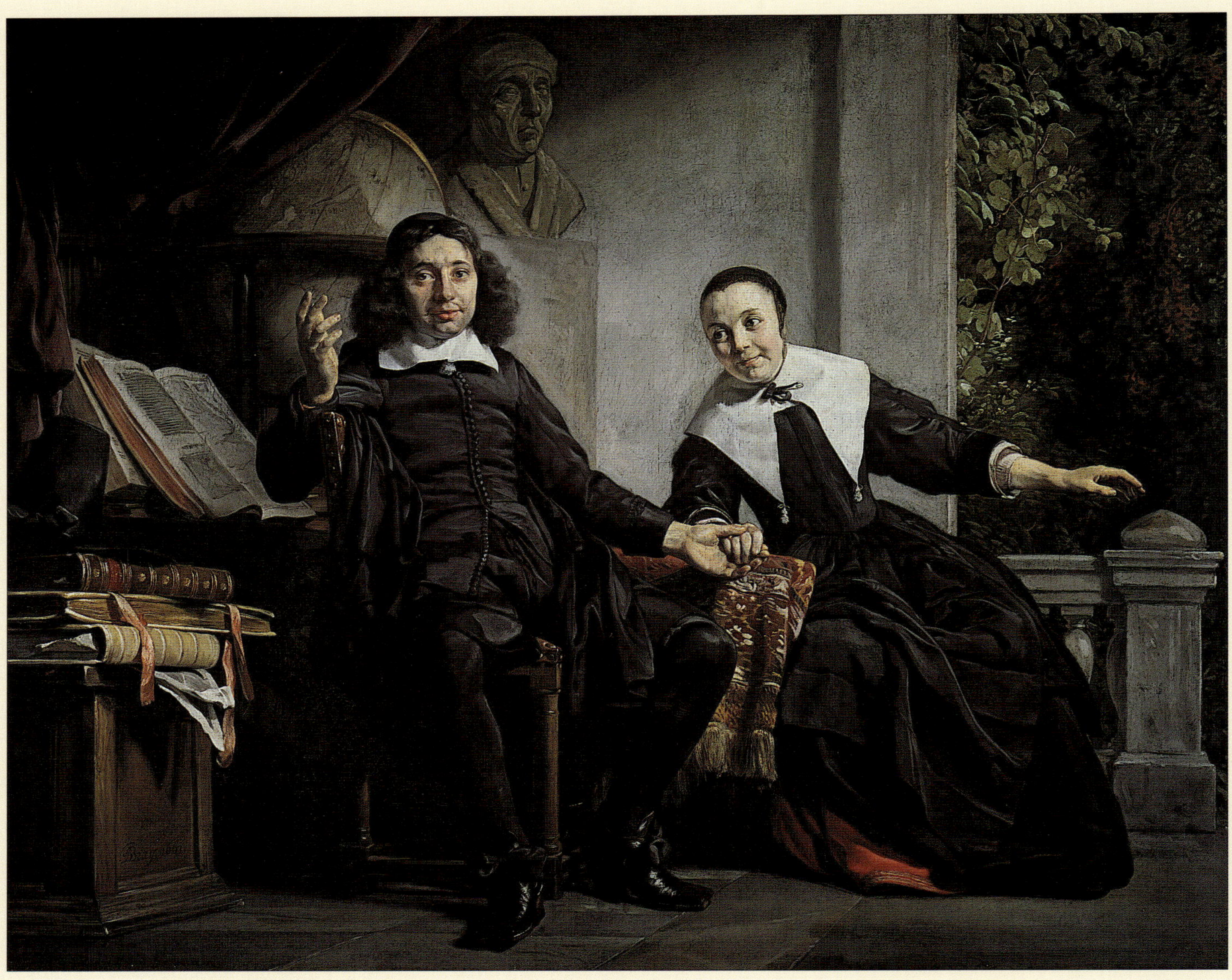

73. Jan de Bray, canvas (1663) - RMA

73.
Abraham Vincentsz Casteleyn (ca. 1628-1681) and Margaretha van Bancken (?-1693), Waterlander Mennonites at Haarlem, are depicted in something of an unusual pose. Abraham sits across the chair and appears to speak; Margaretha leans toward him with a suspended left hand. The couple radiate joyfulness and harmony in holding each other's hands. The decor with the books and the bust of the Haarlem hero Laurens Jansz Coster, who was at that time believed to have been the inventer of printing, points to the terrain where Abraham had his success. As son of a Flemish refugee book printer and publisher Abraham was trained, just as his three brothers and many more descendents, in the book business. In 1656 he began publication of the *Weeckelycke Courante van Europa (European Weekly)*, a newspaper which after 1664 would be called *Oprechte Haerlemsche Courant (Sincere Haarlem Newspaper)* and still exists today. Casteleyn's paper became, in contrast to its current format, famed as a newspaper of quality. This enterprising news agent built up an extensive network of correspondents, who supplied the news from all over Europe. The globe refers to this major activity. After his death Margaretha continued the business (NNBW IX, 132-134; Jongh 1, pp. 181-183).

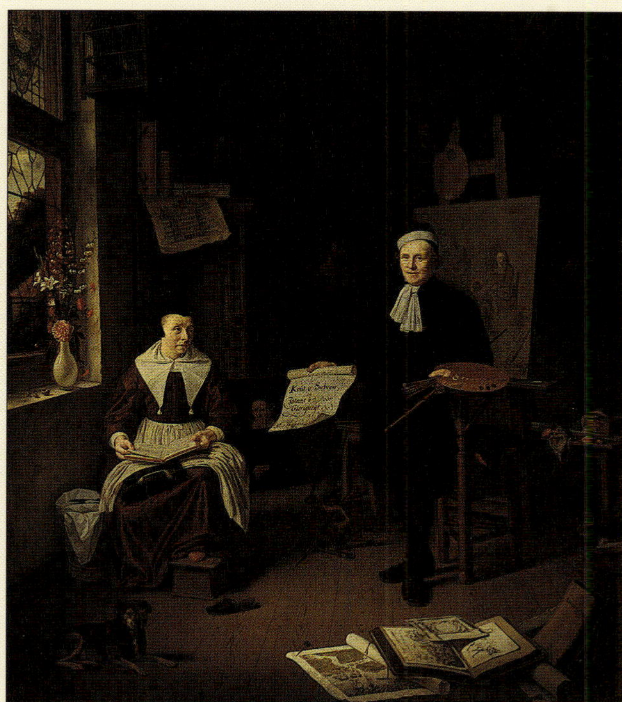

74. Michiel van Musscher, canvas (1669) - RMA

74.
The career of Michiel Michielsz Comans (ca. 1615-1687) is far from a 'glamour story'. A son of both a cabinet maker and preacher of the Flemish Mennonites at Rotterdam, Michiel from ca. 1645 was active as a cloth dyer at Amsterdam. Later in life he would practise the arts of calligraphy, engraving and painting, but practically without any success. After he established himself as a French schoolmaster in 1676 in Noordwijk, things improved for him, although at his death he left behind old debts of nearly 11,000 guilders. Together with Adam Boreel and Daniel van Breen, he was one of the initiators of the so-called 'free speech college' of the Amsterdam Collegiants. In connection with his third marriage in 1668 he had himself and his new partner Elisabeth van der Meersch painted in the studio, proudly displaying some works as hopeful signs of a new start (Thiel; Jongh 1, pp. 57-59).

75.
Grain merchant Cornelis Terwen (1621-?), Flemish Mennonite at Dordrecht, was portrayed together with his wife Segerina Lodewijcks Verbeeck (ca. 1612-?) and their two-year-old son Lodewijk, probably by Samuel van Hoogstraten (see 54), although the canvas has also been ascribed to Abraham Conincxvelt. The Terwens came from a distinguished business family that had fled from Flanders. Many male members served in the office of deacon. Cornelis' brother Abraham and Samuel van Hoogstraten were brothers-in-law; both were married with nieces of Matthijs Balen (see 49). Cornelis was married with the nearly ten-year-older Segerina in 1645. The couple, with expressions depicting their marital bliss, are posed rather stiffly for a romantic fanciful setting (Roscam pp. 63-64 & 97-98; Brusati p. 368).

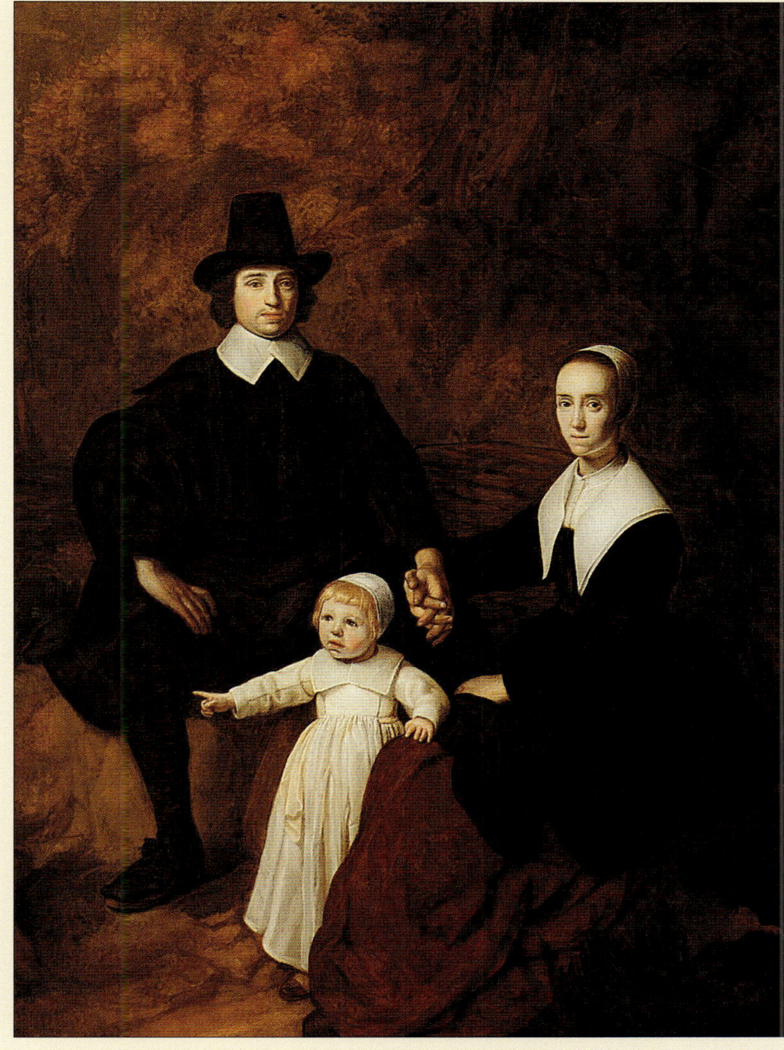

75. Samuel van Hoogstraten? / Abraham Conincxvelt?, canvas (ca. 1648) - CSA

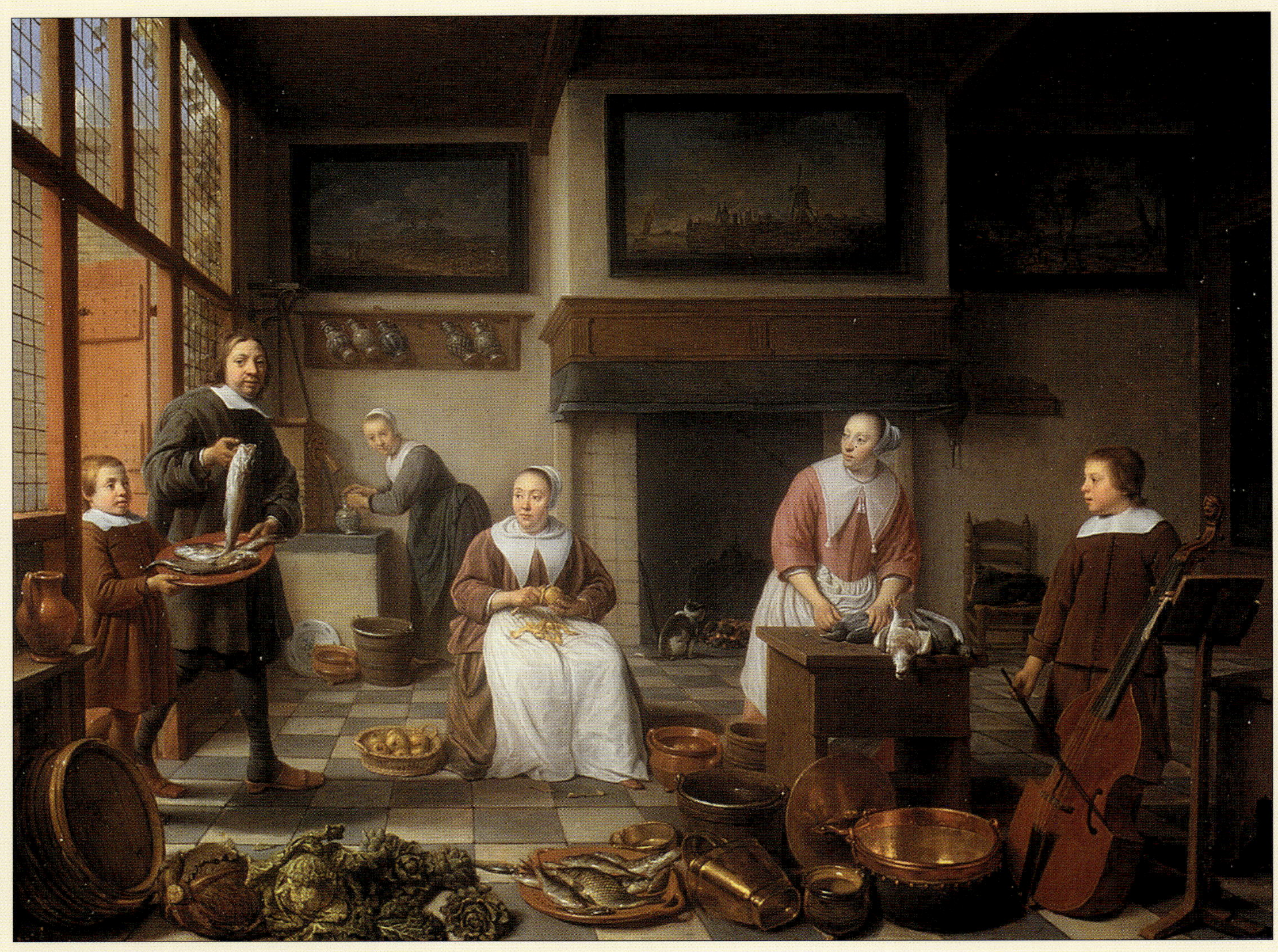

76. Hendrick Sorgh, panel (1663) - RBK

76.

The family portrait of the Amsterdam chamois merchant Jacob Abrahamsz Bierens (1622-1664) is one of the most remarkable of its kind. It was customary for a well-to-do family to be portrayed in its Sunday best, but here stands the family in the kitchen in their daily clothes, preoccupied with daily matters. Everyone watches as Jacob and his little son Anthony enter with fresh fish. His wife Cornelia, daughter of the silk merchant, art collector and Waterlander deacon Anthony van Hoeck, is paring apples; daughter Cornelia plucks pigeons; while Anthony plays the viola da gamba. The maid stands in the background washing a wine pitcher. Bierens appears to have expressed the Mennonite work ethic. Young and old work in a setting of simplicity, full of vigor (see the shining copper work) and in harmony (symbolized by the performing youth); the abundant gifts of God provided indispensable nourishment. They are distanced from delights and sensual pleasures (the cat which sits by the fire). The attention is directed to Jacob's 'amazing catch of fish', symbol of the success of the Christian businessman. This emphasis on the 'active life' refers to the 'contemplative life', wherein the person turns to God and enriches his soul with spiritual nourishment. The paintings on the back wall appear to strengthen this message: a city in the distance and two landscapes with wanderers, the human as a pilgrim on the way. Jacob, a son-in-law of Galenus Abrahamsz (see 29), would not taste the earthly pleasures much longer. A year after completion of the painting he died (Wybrands 2, pp. 36-37; Jongh 1, pp. 248-240).

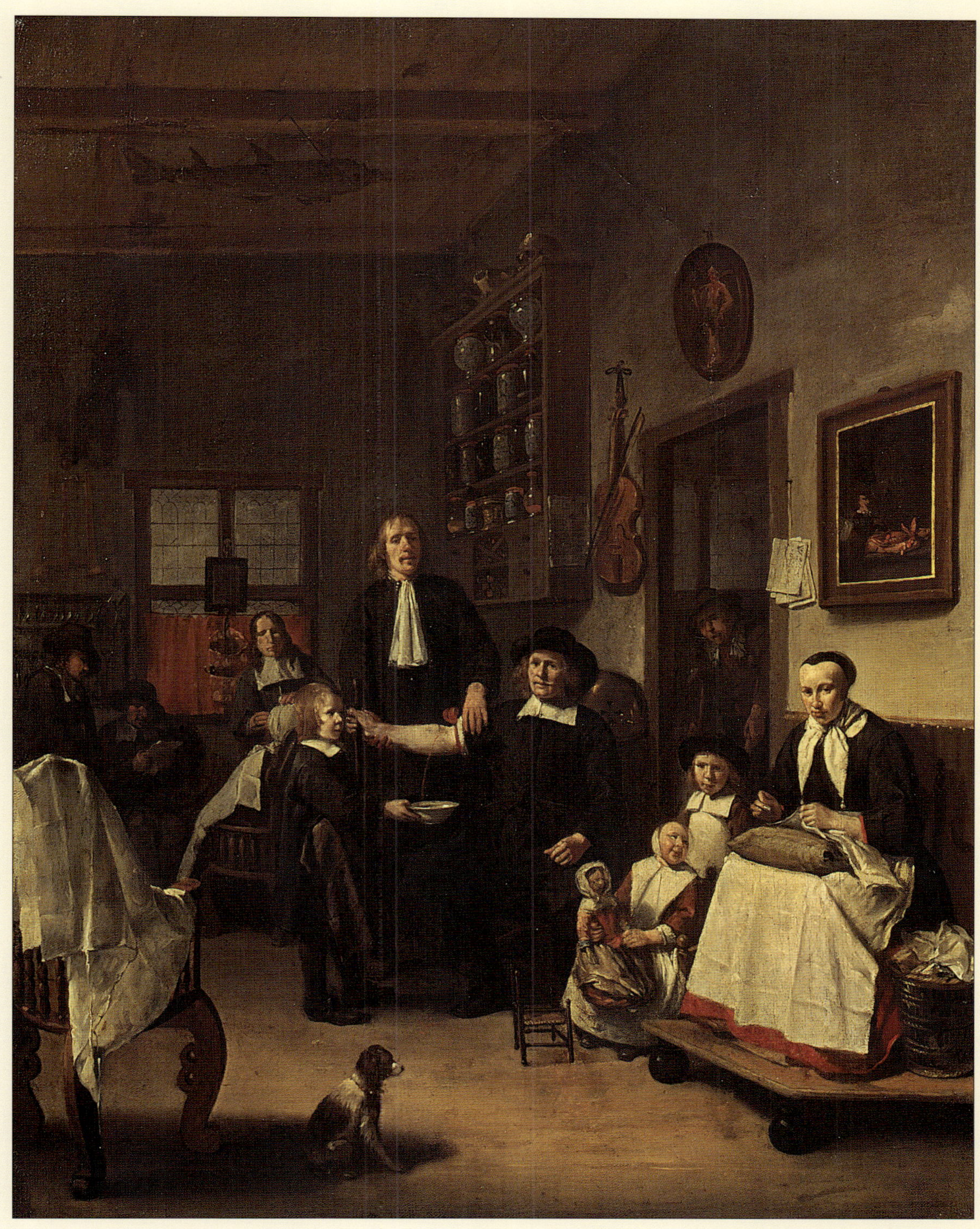

77. Egbert van Heemskerck,
canvas (1669) - AHM

77.
The painting of the Amsterdam barber-surgeon family of Jacob Fransz Hercules (ca. 1635-1708) also shows a Mennonite family together in activity. Jacob, assisted by his little son Thomas, is occupied with letting the blood of his older brother Thomas Fransz Hercules, who lived with them. His wife Anna Jans ter Burgh (ca. 1634-1707) sits on a small platform (to minimize the draft) doing needlework and mending, while her small son Frans and little daughter Francijntje play beside her. In the background the apprentice is shaving a client, while two others wait their turn. The man who is reading a newspaper or pamphlet, is the famous Socinian and Collegiant Jan Knol. In the door opening a sick man waits to be treated by Jacob. On the wall hang a chest filled with knives and pots, a violin and, above the door, a small oval panel with a Hercules figure, an allusion to the family name. The stuffed sawfish on the ceiling refers to Hercules' alchemical knowledge. The family Hercules stood lower on the social ladder than the family of Jacob Bierens. Nevertheless, at his death Hercules still left behind some paintings, among them two Rembrandts. Descendents donated this painting to the orphanage of the Collegiants, *De Oranje Appel* (The Orange Apple), from which it was sold in 1948 (Blankert 170; Jongh 1, pp. 257-258).

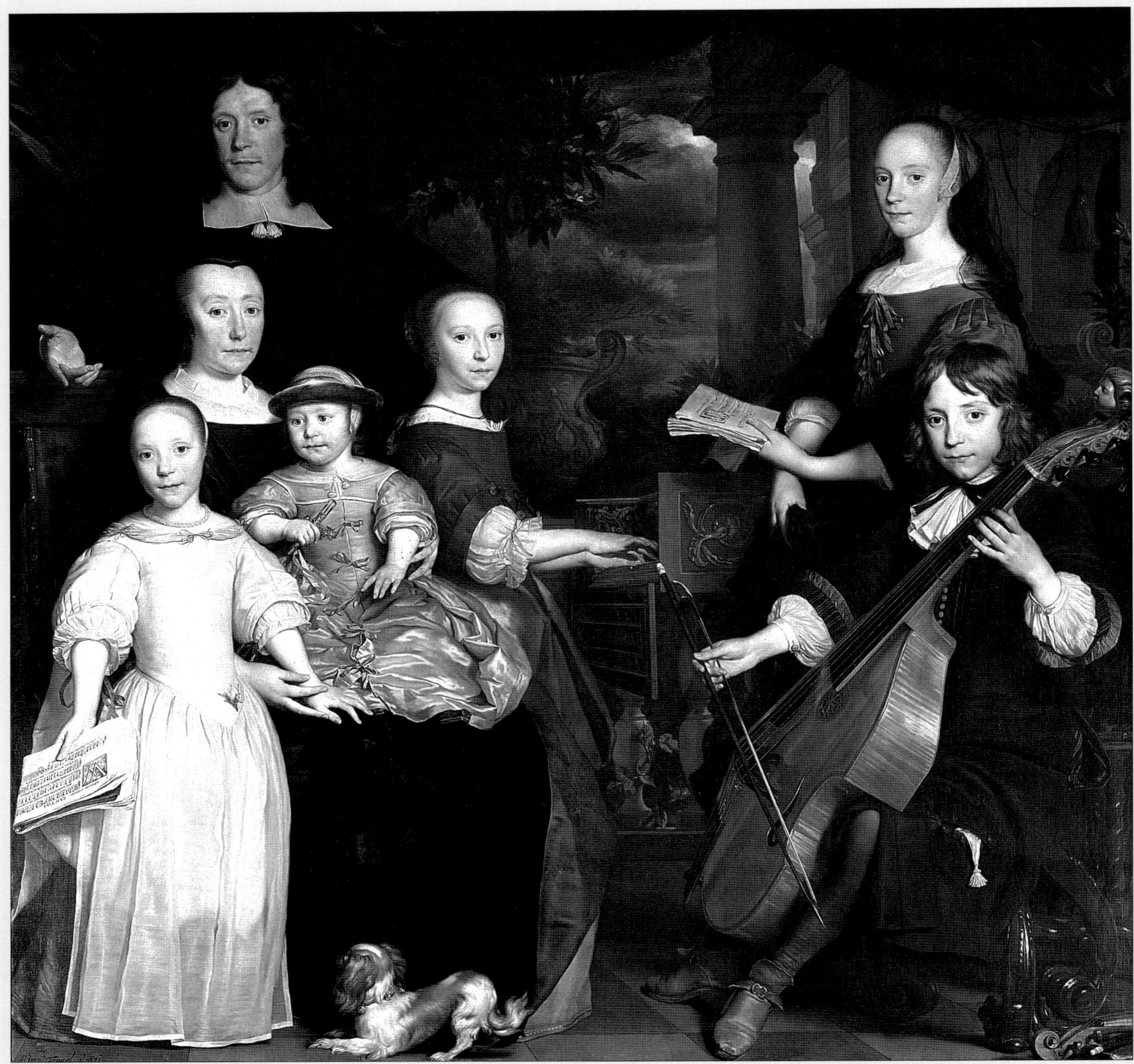

78. Abraham Jacobsz van den Tempel, canvas (1671) - RHM

78.

David Leeuw (ca. 1632-1703), whose portrait as a youth was painted by Flinck (see 68), is shown here with his musical family who lived in the house of his father, Ameldonck on the Rokin in Amsterdam. His wife Cornelia Hooft (1631-1708), whom he married in 1651, has on her lap her two-year-old daughter Suzanna, and next to her Cornelia (eight years old). Weyntje (twelve years old) plays the harpsicord, Maria (eighteen years old) sings and Pieter (fourteen years old) performs the viola da gamba. A number of Mennonite families were musical; especially among the Collegiants, singing in parts with musical accompaniment was very much appreciated. This musical staging naturally also refers to the harmony and unity in the family. In 1701, the married couple celebrated their fiftieth anniversary, something that hardly ever occurred. Adriaan Spinniker obtained the commission on that occasion to write a marriage poem. Similar to the urban regent patriciate, the family's clothing is not excessively luxurious, although substantially more modern than that of a generation earlier, as comparison with David's youthful portrait clearly shows. The painter Abraham van den Tempel, son of the Waterlander teacher and painter Lambert Jacobsz, originally worked at Leyden, but in 1660 moved to Amsterdam, where he was also active in the cloth trade (EeghenP 1; Cat RM pp. 534-535).

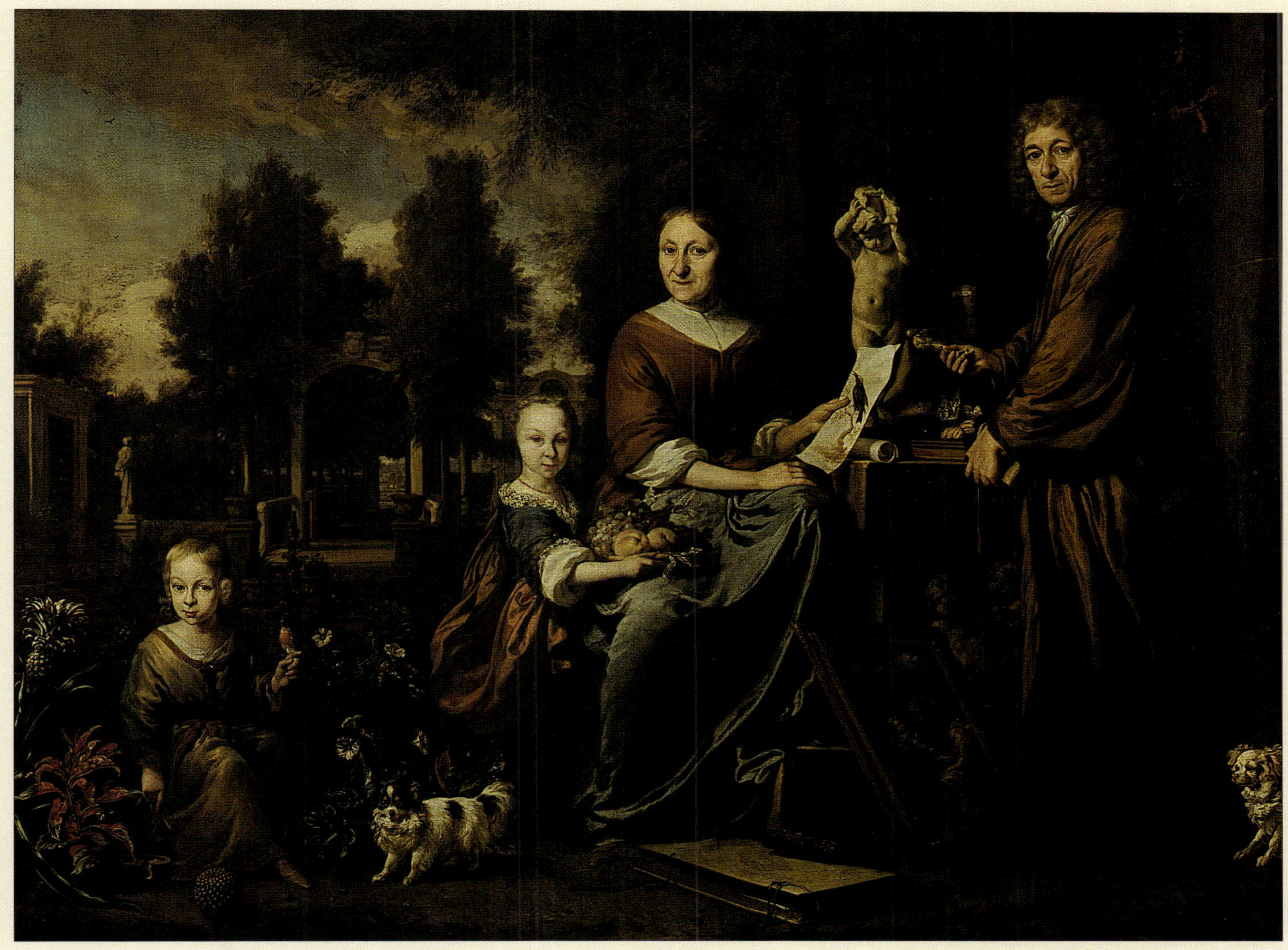

79. Jan Weenix, canvas (> 1674) - AHM

79.

Agnes Block (1629-1704) and Sybrand de Flines (1623-1697) were wed in 1674, a second marriage for both. Sybrand was a successful silk merchant at Amsterdam and deacon with the Waterlanders of the *Lam* and *Tooren* church. Their marriage remained childless. The two children depicted might have come from Sybrand's first marriage, but more plausibly they are a nephew and niece of Agnes, who made them heirs. That says a great deal about this woman, cousin and friend of Vondel (see 38), who dominates the painting. The great botanical knowledge of Agnes was known far and wide. She was in contact with both resident and foreign academics and cultivated all manner of exotic plants, among them the first Dutch pineapple. She commissioned many artists - among them the renowned Maria Sibylla Merian - to document her plants, flowers, birds and insects in drawings and water colors. She gained the nickname *Flora Batava.* Many prominent guests came to marvel at her nature and art collections at her country estate *Vijverhof* (Pond Garden) near Loenen on the Vecht River, in the so-called 'Mennonite Heaven', which she had bought in 1670. She painted and modelled clay and was very skilled in the art of paper cutting. Agnes was an emancipated woman, controlling her own capital and investments. She drew up a will at least eleven times, whereby she decreed that the *Vijverhof* remain in her family. All attributes of the painting point to her talents and interests. At the far left is the pineapple; the maiden by her lap may carry Agnes' fruits - the inheritence?. Sybrand, in 'Japanese cloak' and with modish French curls, stands literally and figuratively on the side (Graft; Jongh 1, pp. 265-267; Sprunger pp. 109 & 121-122; Blankert 499).

BIBLIOGRAPHY

PART I: SOURCES FOR THE INTRODUCTORY CITATIONS

1 ♦ Hans Alenson, *Tegen-Bericht Op de voor-Reden vant groote Martelaer Boeck* (Haarlem 1630), in: *Bibliotheca Reformatoria Neerlandica* [BRN] VII: S. Cramer, ed., *Zestiende-eeuwsche schrijvers over de geschiedenis der oudste Doopsgezinden hier te lande* ('s-Gravenhage 1910), p. 258

2, 3, ♦ Menno Simons, 'Renunciation of Rome' in: *Reply to Gellius Faber*, in: *The Complete Writings of Menno Simons c.1496-1561. Translated from the Dutch by Leonard Verduin and edited by John Christian Wenger, with a biography by Harold S. Bender* (Scottdale, Penn.. 1956), p. 668

4, 5 ♦ *idem*, p. 669

6, 7 ♦ *idem*, p. 670

8, 9, 10 ♦ *idem*, p. 671

11 ♦ Letter by the Frisian Court to governess Mary of Hungary, 19 May 1541, in: *Documenta Anabaptistica Neerlandica* [DAN] I: A.F. Mellink, ed., *Friesland en Groningen (1530-1550)* (Leiden 1975; Kerkhistorische Bijdragen VI), p. 63

12 ♦ Sentence of Syouck Haeyes, 14 November 1542, in: *idem*, p. 64

13 ♦ Menno Simons, *Brief and Clear Confession ... Concerning the Incarnation, in: The Complete Writings*, p. 424

14 ♦ Menno Simons, 'Renunciation' in: *idem*, p. 674

15 ♦ Menno Simons, *Confession of the Triune God*, in: *idem*, p. 489

16 ♦ Sentence of Claes Janszoon alias Brongers, 1 June 1549, in: *DAN* I, p. 84

17 ♦ Cassander, *Beati Vigilii Martyris Opera* (Cologne 1555), citation in *BRN* V: S. Cramer, ed., *Nederlandsche Anabaptistica (geschriften van Henrick Rol, Melchior Hoffman, Adam Pastor, De Broederlicke vereeninge)* (Leiden 1909), p. 323

18 ♦ *DAN* III: W.F. Dankbaar ed., *Marten Mikron, Een waerachtigh verhaal der t'zaamensprekinghen tusschen Menno Simons ende Martinus Mikron van der menschwerdinghe Iesu Christi (1556)* (Leiden 1981; Kerkhistorische Bijdragen X), p. 147

19 ♦ Menno Simons, 'Renunciation', in: *The Complete Writings*, p. 673

20 ♦ *idem*, p. 674

21 ♦ Hans Alenson, *Tegen-Bericht*, in: *BRN* VII, p. 258

22 ♦ V.P., *Successio Anabaptistica, Dat is Babel der Wederdopers* (Cologne 1603), in: *BRN* VII, p. 87

23 ♦ Hans Alenson, *Tegen-Bericht*, in: *BRN* VII, p. 258

PART 1: BIOGRAPHICAL SOURCES FOR THE CHRONOLOGY

♦ W. Bergsma & S. Voolstra (eds.), *Uyt Babel ghevloden, in Jeruzalem ghetogen. Menno Simons' verlichting, bekering en beroeping* (Amsterdam 1986)

♦ C. Bornhäuser, *Leben und Lehre Menno Simons'. Ein Kampf um das Fundament des Glaubens [etwa 1496-1561]* (Neukirchen-Vluyn 1973)

♦ G.R. Brunk (ed.), *Menno Simons: A Reappraisal. Essays in honor of Irvin B. Horst on the 450th Anniversary of the Fundamentboek* (Harrisonburg 1992)

♦ C. Krahn, *Menno Simons (1496-1561). Ein Beitrag zur Geschichte und Theologie der Taufgesinnten* (North Newton, KS, 1982[2])

♦ B. Rademaker-Helfferich (ed.), *Een leven vol gevaar: Menno Simons (1496-1561) leidsman der dopers* (Amsterdam 1996)

♦ K. Vos, *Menno Simons 1496-1561 zijn leven en werken en zijne reformatorische denkbeelden* (Leiden 1914)

PARTS I, II & III: ABBREVIATIONS OF THE REFERENCES

ADW ♦ *Algemeen Doopsgezind Weekblad* (1946-..)

Avest ♦ H.P. ter Avest (ed.), *Hoogaangeslagenen in Harlingen. Uit de nalatenschap van de gegoede burgerij* (Harlingen 1994)

B ♦ G.J. Boekenoogen, 'De portretten van Menno Simons', in: *Doopsgezinde Bijdragen* 53 (1916), pp. 3-106

B&H ♦ G. Braun & F. Hogenberg, *Civitates Orbis Terrarum* (Keulen 1572-1618) 6 vols.

Berkel ♦ K. van Berkel, *In het voetspoor van Stevin. Geschiedenis van de natuurwetenschap in Nederland 1580-1940* (Meppel & Amsterdam 1985)

Bircher ♦ M. Bircher, *Deutsche Drucke des Barock 1600-1720 in der Herzog August Bibliothek Wolfenbüttel. Abteilung B, Band 5* (München etc. 1986)

Blankert ♦ A. Blankert, *Amsterdams Historisch Museum: schilderijen daterend van voor 1800, voorlopige catalogus* (Amsterdam 1975-1979)

Boschma ♦ C. Boschma, 'Friese en Noordhollandse knottekistjes', in: *Antiek* 3 (1968/1969), pp. 559-566

Braght ♦ T.J. van Braght, *Het Bloedigh Tooneel, of Martelaers Spiegel der Doops-gesinde of Weereloose Christenen* (Amsterdam 1685; facs. ed. 1985) 2 vols.

Brown ♦ C. Brown et al. (eds.), *Rembrandt: De Meester & zijn Werkplaats-schilderijen* (Amsterdam & Zwolle 1991)

Brusati ♦ C.A. Brusati, *Artifice and illusion: the art and writing of Samuel van Hoogstraten* (Chicago 1995)

Buijsen ♦ E. Buijsen et al., *Cornelis Troost en het theater / and the Theatre of his Time: Tonelen van de 18de eeuw / Plays of the 18th Century* (Den Haag & Zwolle 1993)

BWPGN ♦ J.P. de Bie & J. Loosjes (eds.), *Biographisch woordenboek van protestantsche godgeleerden in Nederland* ('s-Gravenhage 1919-1949) 6 vols.

Cat Rhuis ♦ E. Ornstein-Van Slooten et al. (eds.), *Het Rembrandthuis: de prenten, tekeningen en schilderijen* (Zwolle & Amsterdam 1992)

Cat RM ♦ P.J.J. van Thiel a.o. (eds.), *All the paintings of the Rijksmuseum in Amsterdam. A completely illustrated catalogue* (Amsterdam & Maarssen 1976)

Clercq ♦ A.S. & W.A. de Clercq, *Familie-boek De Clercq* (Haarlem 1992)

Damhoudere ♦ J. de Damhoudere, *Practycke ende handbouck in criminele saeken* (Leuven 1555)

Dawn ♦ Ger Luijten a.o. (eds.), *Dawn of the Golden Age: Northern Netherlandish Art 1580-1620* (Amsterdam & Zwolle 1993)

Deventer ♦ Jacob van Deventer, *De kaarten van de Nederlandsche provinciën in de zestiende eeuw* ('s-Gravenhage 1941)

Dudok 1 ♦ S.A.C. Dudok van Heel, 'Doopsgezinden en schilderkunst in de 17e eeuw - Leerlingen, opdrachtgevers en verzamelaars van Rembrandt', in: *Doopsgezinde Bijdragen* 6 (1980), pp. 105-123

Dudok 2 ♦ S.A.C. Dudok van Heel, 'Het "schilderhuis" van Govert Flinck en de kunsthandel van Uylenburgh aan de Lauriergracht te Amsterdam', in: *Jaarboek Amstelodamum* 74 (1982), pp. 70-90

Eeghen 1 ♦ I.H. van Eeghen, 'De staalmeesters', in: *Jaarboek Amstelodamum* 49 (1957), pp. 65-80

Eeghen 2 ♦ I.H. van Eeghen, 'Jan Luyken en zijn bloedverwanten', in: *Doopsgezinde Bijdragen* 16 (1990), pp. 65-112

EeghenP 1 ♦ P. van Eeghen, 'Abraham van den Tempel's Familiegroep in het Rijksmuseum', in: *Oud Holland* 68 (1953), pp. 170-174

EeghenP 2 ♦ P. van Eeghen, 'Driehonderd jaar de stad uit', in: *Jaarboek Amstelodamum* 54 (1962), pp. 106-169

Erenstein ♦ R.L. Erenstein et al. (eds.), *Een theatergeschiedenis der Nederlanden. Tien eeuwen drama en theater in Nederland en Vlaanderen* (Amsterdam 1996)

Falkenburg ♦ R. Falkenburg, 'Landschapschilderkunst en doperse spiritualiteit in de 17de eeuw - een connectie?', in: *Doopsgezinde Bijdragen* 16 (1990), pp. 129-153

Graft ♦ C. van de Graft, *Agnes Blok, Vondels nicht en vriendin* (Utrecht 1943)

H ♦ I.B. Horst, 'De portretten van Menno Simons', in: *Doopsgezinde Bijdragen* 12-13 (1986-1987), pp. 169-172 + photo secton

Haskell ♦ Francis Haskell, *History and its Images. Art and the interpretation of the past* (New Haven & London 1993)

Holl ♦ F.W.H. Hollstein, *Dutch and Flemish etchings, engravings and woodcuts, ca. 1450-1700* (Amsterdam 1949-..)

Honig ♦ G.J. Honig, *Uit den Gulden Bijkorf. Genealogisch-historisch-economische studiën over Zaansche families* (Koog aan de Zaan 1952)

Hortensius ♦ L. Hortensius, *Van den Oproer der Weder-Dooperen* (Enkhuizen 1624)

Jongh 1 ♦ E. de Jongh, *Portretten van echt en trouw. Huwelijk en gezin in de Nederlandse kunst van de zeventiende eeuw* (Zwolle & Haarlem 1986)

Jongh 2 ♦ E. de Jongh, 'Van "vermakelijk bedrog" tot propagandistische "beelden-leughen", in: B. Kempers (ed.), *Beeldmanipulatie in de zeventiende eeuw, openbaring en bedrog. De afbeelding als historische bron in de Lage Landen* (Amsterdam 1995)

Knippenberg ♦ H.H. Knippenberg, *Reyer Anslo zijn leven en letterkundig werk* (Amsterdam 1913)

Kölker ♦ A.J. Kölker (ed.), *Jacob Aertsz Colom's Kaart van Holland 1639* (Alphen aan de Rijn 1979)

Koster ♦ S. Koster, *Van schavot tot schouwburg: vijfhonderd jaar toneel in Haarlem (Haarlem 1970)*

L ♦ John Landwehr, *Romeyn de Hooghe (1645-1708) as book illustrator. A bibliography* (Amsterdam 1970)

Lied ♦ P. Visser, *Het lied dat nooit verstomde. vier eeuwen doopsgezinde liedboekjes* (Den Ilp 1988)

M ♦ F. Muller, *Beschrijvende catalogus van 7000 portretten, van Nederlanders, en van buitenlanders, tot Nederland in betrekking staande* (Amsterdam 1853)

MB ♦ *Mennonitische Blätter* (1854-1941)

ME ♦ H.S. Bender a.o. (eds. vol. I-IV) & C.J. Dyck & D.D. Martin (eds. vol. V), *The Mennonite Encyclopedia. A Comprehensive Reference Work on the Anabaptist-Mennonite Movement* (Scottdale, PA & Waterloo, Ont. 1955-1990) 5 vols.

Meeuwesse ♦ K. Meeuwesse, *Jan Luyken als dichter van de Duytse Lier* (Groningen & Amsterdam 1977^{2})

Mellink ♦ A.F. Mellink, *De wederdopers in de Noordelijke Nederlanden 1531-1544* (Groningen & Djakarta 1954)

M-his ♦ F. Muller, *Beredeneerde beschrijving van Nederlandse historieplaten, zinneprenten en historische kaarten* (Amsterdam 1863-1882) 4 vols.

Miedema ♦ H. Miedema (ed.), *Karel van Mander. The lives of the Illustrious Netherlandish and German Painters* (Doornspijk 1995) vol. II

Moltke ♦ J. von Moltke, *Govaert Flinck 1615-1660* (Amsterdam 1965)

MtM ♦ P. Visser et al. (eds.), *From Martyr to Muppy. A Historical Introduction to Cultural Assimilation Processes of a Religious Minority in the Nederlands: the Mennonites* (Amsterdam 1994)

Münster ♦ S. Münster, *Cosmographei, oder Beschreibung aller länder, herschafften, fürnemsten stellen ... zum drittemal ... gemerct und gebessert* (Basel [1550])

NNBW ♦ P.C. Molhuysen & P.J. Blok (eds.), *Nieuw Nederlandsch Biografisch Woordenboek*, (Leiden 1911-1937) 10 vols.

Nissen ♦ P.J.A. Nissen, *De katholieke polemiek tegen de dopers. Reacties van katholieke theologen op de doperse beweging in de Nederlanden (1530-1650)* (Heerlen 1988)

NVA ♦ G.J. van Bork & P.J. Verkruijsse (eds.), *De Nederlandse en Vlaamse Auteurs. Van middeleeuwen tot heden met inbegrip van de Friese auteurs* (Weesp 1985)

OtO ♦ P. Visser, *Van Offer tot Opera: Doopsgezinden en kunst in de zeventiende eeuw - Catalogus UBA* (Amsterdam 1989)

Plomp ♦ M. Plomp, 'De portretten van het stamboek van Joanna Koerten (1650-1715), in: *Leids Kunsthistorisch Jaarboek* 8 (1988), pp. 323-344

Rademaker 1 ♦ B. Rademaker-Helfferich, *Een wit vaantje op de Brink. De geschiedenis van de Doopsgezinde gemeente te Deventer* (Deventer 1988)

Rademaker 2 ♦ B. Rademaker-Helfferich (ed.), *Een leven vol gevaar. Menno Simons (1496-1561) leidsman der dopers* (Amsterdam 1996)

Regteren ♦ I.Q. van Regteren Altena & P.J.J. van Tiel, *De portret-galerij van de Universiteit van Amsterdam en haar stichter Gerard van Papenbroeck 1673-1743* (Amsterdam 1964)

RGN ♦ E.O.G. Haitsma Mulier & G.A.C. van der Lem (red.), *Repertorium van geschiedschrijvers in Nederland, 1500-1800* (Den Haag 1990)

Roever ♦ J.G. de Roever, *Jan Adriaensz Leeghwater. Het leven en werk van een zeventiende-eeuws waterbouwkundige* (Amsterdam 1944)

Roscam ♦ M. Roscam Abbing & P. Thissen, *De schilder & schrijver Samuel van Hoogstraten 1627-1678. Eigentijdse bronnen & oeuvre van gesigneerde schilderijen* (Leiden 1993)

Schijn ♦ G. Schijn & G. Maatschoen, *Geschiedenis Dier Christenen, Welke in de Vereenigde Nederlanden onder de Protestanten Mennoniten genaamd worden* (Amsterdam 1743-1745) 3 vols.

Schwartz ♦ G. Schwartz, *Rembrandt zijn leven, zijn schilderijen. Een nieuwe biografie met alle beschikbare schilderijen in kleur afgebeeld* (Alphen aan de Rijn 1984)

Sliggers ♦ B.C. Sliggers & D.F. Goudriaan, 'De Haarlemse kunstenaarsfamilie Van der Vinne', in: *Jaarboek van het Centraal Bureau voor Genealogie* 41 (1987), pp. 148-207

Slive ♦ S. Slive a.o. (ed.), *Frans Hals* (Londen etc. 1989)

Smit ♦ J. Smit, *Dirck Rembrantsz van Nierop 1610-1682. Het leven en werk van een beroemd Sterrenkundige, Meester in de Wiskonst en een uitmuntend Onderwijzer voor Schippers en Stuurlieden* (Winkel 1992)

Sprunger ♦ M.S. Sprunger, *Rich Mennonites, Poor Mennonites: Economics and Theology in the Amsterdam Waterlander Congregation during the Golden Age* (Urbana, IL, 1993 - dissertation)

Thiel ♦ P.J.J. van Thiel, 'Michiel van Musscher's vroegste werk naar aanleiding van zijn portret van het echtpaar Comans', in: *Bulletin van het Rijksmuseum* 17 (1969), pp. 3-36.

Thissen ♦ P. Thissen, *Werk, netwerk en letterwerk van de familie Van Hoogstraten in de zeventiende eeuw. Sociaal-culturele achtergronden van geletterden in de Republiek* (Amsterdam & Maarssen 1994)

vE & vdK ♦ P. van Eeghen & J.H. van der Kellen, *Het werk van Jan en Caspar Luyken* (Amsterdam 1960-1978) 2 vols.

Visser P. Visser, 'De artes als zinnebeeld: over doopsgezinden en hun relatie tot kunst en wetenschap', in: *De zeventiende eeuw* 5 (1989), pp. 92-102

vR ♦ G. van Rijn, *Atlas van Stolk. Katalogus der historie-, spot- en zinneprenten betrekkelijk de geschiedenis van Nederland* (Amsterdam 1895-1833) 10 vols.

Vries ♦ L. de Vries, *Jan van der Heyden* (Amsterdam 1984)

vS ♦ J.F. van Someren, *Beschrijvende Catalogus van gegraveerde portretten van Nederlanders. Vervolg op Frederik Mullers Catalogus van 7000 portretten van Nederlanders* (Amsterdam 1881-1891) 3 vols.

W ♦ A. von Wurzbach, *Niederländisches Künstler-Lexikon auf Grund archivalischer Forschungen bearbeitet* (Wien & Leipzig 1906-1911) 3 vols.

Wereld ♦ E. Bergvelt & R. Kistemaker (ed.), *De wereld binnen handbereik. Nederlandse kunst- en rariteitenverzamelingen, 1585-1735 - Catalogus* (Amsterdam 1992)

Wijnman ♦ H.F. Wijnman, 'Mr. Lieven van Coppenol. Schoolmeester-Calligraaf', in: *Jaarboek Amstelodamum* 30 (1933), pp. 92-187

Worp ♦ J.A. Worp, *Geschiedenis van den Amsterdamschen Schouwburg 1496-1772. Uitgegeven met aanvulling tot 1872 door J.F.M. Sterck* (Amsterdam 1920)

Wybrands 1 ♦ C.N. Wybrands, *Het Amsterdamsche Tooneel van 1617-1772* (Utrecht 1873)

Wybrands 2 ♦ C.N. Wybrands, 'Het Menniste Zusje', in: *Jaarverslag [van het Koninklijk Oudheidkundig Genootschap] in de vijf-en-vijftigste Algemeene Vergadering* (Amsterdam 1913), pp. 29-107

ABBREVIATIONS OF THE LOCATIONS

& ORIGINS OF THE ILLUSTRATIONS

The following abbreviations indicate the various locations of the prints, maps, paintings, books and photographs, as well as the origins of the reproductions. All illustrations are reproduced in respect of the conditions concerning publication and with the approval of the institutions and individuals listed below.

AGO ♦ Art Gallery of Ontario, Toronto (Can.): III 55
AHM ♦ Amsterdam Historical Museum (Neth.): III 3a, 3b, 7a, 24, 38, 41, 57b, 66, 77, 79
AVS ♦ Atlas van Stolk Foundation, Rotterdam (Neth.): I 3d; II 3, 61; III 10, 19a, 19b, 19c,
BIB ♦ Barber Institute of Fine Arts, Birmingham (Eng.): III 68
CCU ♦ Museum Catharijne Convent, Utrecht (Neth.) III 11, 14
CSA ♦ Six Collection, Amsterdam (Neth.): III 75
DGS ♦ Mennonite Seminary, Amsterdam (Neth.): II A9, A18
EMS ♦ Eastern Mennonite Seminary, Harrisonburg, VA (V.S.): II A4
EVW ♦ Esther van Weelden, Amsterdam (Neth.): I 1a, 2a, 3a, 4c, 5b, 6a, 6d, 7b, 8d, 9a, 9b, 10b, 11a, 12d, 13d, 13e, 14a, 14b, 15b, 15c, 16a, 16b, 16c, 17a, 17d, 17f, 18a, 18c, 19a, 19d, 20c, 21a, 21g, 22a, 23a, 23b
FHM ♦ Frans Hals Museum, Haarlem (Neth.) III 12
FML ♦ Frisian Museum, Leeuwarden (Neth.): I 1b, 2c, 2e, 4a, 4d, 5a, 5d, 9e; II 7.4, 7.5, 11.1, 11.2, 25.1, 31.4, 34.1, 38.1, A1; III 52
GAH ♦ Municipal Archives, Haarlem (Neth.): II 7.1
GHH ♦ Municipal Museum Het Hannemahuis, Harlingen (Neth.): III 70a, 70b, 70c
IBH ♦ Iconographical Bureau, The Hague (Neth.) : II 54
KBH ♦ Royal Library, The Hague (Neth.): II 67
L.U. ♦ Location unknown: II 12.1, 12.2, 18, 35, 42, 43.2, 51
MBB ♦ Museum Boymans-Van Beuningen, Rotterdam (Neth.): III 50a, 54
MFW ♦ Mennonite Research Institute, Weierhof (Germ.)
MHH ♦ Museum Het Mauritshuis, The Hague (Neth.): III 20a, 20b, 20c
MHL/GC ♦ Mennonite Historical Library, Goshen College, Goshen, IN (USA)
MLP ♦ Louvre Museum, Paris (Fr.): III 26
MMR ♦ Maritime Museum Prins Hendrik, Rotterdam (Neth.): II 27
MRA ♦ Museum Het Rembrandthuis, Amsterdam (Neth.): III 58a
MSHL/EMU ♦ Menno Simons Historical Library, Eastern Mennonite University, Harrisonburg, VA (USA): II 37, 69, 74, A10, A11,
NGL ♦ National Gallery, London (Eng.): III 53
NOA ♦ Nederlands Openluchtmuseum, Arnhem (Neth.): III 59a
OKB ♦ Oeffentliche Kunstsammlung, Kunstmuseum, Basel (Sw.): III 23
PAW ♦ Pinakotek, Graphische Sammlung Albertina, Wien (Aus.): III 37
P.C.1 ♦ Private collection Voolstra, Landsmeer (Neth.): II A2, A17
P.C.2 ♦ Private collection Pol-Visser, Ruinen (Neth.): II A19
P.C.3 ♦ Private collection Gleysteen, Goshen, IN (USA): II A3
P.C.4 ♦ Private collection Forum Antiquarian Booksellers, 't Goy (Neth.): II 30.4
P.C.5 ♦ Private collection Bierens de Haan, Arnhem (Neth.): III 29
RBK ♦ Rijksdienst Beeldende Kunst, The Hague (Neth.): III 76
RMA ♦ Rijksmuseum, Amsterdam (Neth.): III 45, 46, 47, 48, 49, 65, 69a, 69b, 73, 74, 78
RPA ♦ Rijksprentenkabinet Rijksmuseum, Amsterdam (Neth.): II 1a, 7.2, 8.1, 30.1, 30.2, 33, 39, 45.1; III 51, 56, p. 134
RPL ♦ Rijksprentenkabinet, University of Leyden (Neth.): II 44.2
SMB-PKG ♦ Staatliche Museen zu Berlin - Preußischer Kulturbesitz Gemäldegalerie, Berlin (Germ.): III 72
SMK ♦ Statens Museum for Kunst, Kopenhagen (Den.): II 8.2
SML ♦ Municipal Museum De Lakenhal, Leyden (Neth.): III 59b
UBA ♦ University Library, Amsterdam (Neth.): I 1b, 2b, 2d, 3e, 3f, 5c, 5e, 6b, 8a, 8b, 9c, 9f, 10f, 13a, 14c, 14f, 15a, 16d, 16e, 18b, 18d, 19b, 20e, 21c, 21f, 22d, 23c; II 19, 20, 22, 30.3, 47, 55, 63, 64; III 1, 2, 4, 15, 17, 18, 22, 36, 39, 42, 58b, 61, 62
UBA-DG ♦ University Library - Mennonite Historical Library, Amsterdam (Neth.): I 3b, 3c, 4b, 4e, 6c, 6e, 7a, 7c, 7d, 7e, 8e, 9d, 10b, 10c, 10e, 11b, 11c, 11d, 11e, 12a, 12b, 12c, 12e, 12f, 13b, 13c, 13f, 14d, 14e, 15d, 16f, 17b, 17c, 17e, 18e, 18f, 18g, 19c, 20a, 20b, 20d, 21b, 21d, 21e, 21g, 22b, 22c, 22e; II 1b, 2, 4.1, 4.2, 5, 6, 7.3, 9a, 9b, 10, 11.3, 13, 14, 15, 16, 17, 21, 23, 24, 25.2, 26, 28, 29, 31.1, 31.2, 31.3, 31.5, 32, 34.2, 35, 36, 38.2a, 38.2b, 40.1, 40.2, 41, 43.1, 43.3, 44.1, 45.2, 46, 48, 49, 50, 52.1, 52.2, 53, 56, 57, 58, 59, 60, 62, 65, 66.1, 66.2, 68, 70, 71, 72, 73, 75, 76, 77, 78, 79, 80, A5, A6, A7, A8, A12, A13, A14, A15, A16, A18.1, A20, A21; III 5, 6, 7b, 8, 9, p. 113, 13, 16, 21, 25, 27, 28, 30, 31, 32, 33, 34a, 34b, 35, 43, 44, 57a, 60, 63, 64
UMA ♦ University Museum De Agnietenkapel, Amsterdam (Neth.): III 40
VDGA ♦ United Mennonite Church, Amsterdam (Neth.): III 67
ZHM ♦ Zaan Historical Museum, Zaandijk (Neth.): III 71a, 71b

INDEX OF NAMES

COLOPHON

The book has been compiled on occasion of the fifth centennial of Menno Simons' birthday in 1996 and published simultaneously in Canada, the United States of America, Germany and The Netherlands.

INITIATIVE
Kees Knijnenberg, Krommenie, The Netherlands

DESIGN AND TYPESETTING
Esther van Weelden and Sher Doruff, Amsterdam

TYPEFACE
Garamond

PAPER
80 lb. /100 lb. Luna matte

COVERMATERIAL
Rainbow 2

PAPER DUSTCOVER
100 lb. Luna gloss

COLORSCANS
PrePress Center, Assendelft, The Netherlands

PRINTING AND BINDING
Friesens, Altona, Manitoba, Canada

CIRCULATION
6.750
(English edition 3,500, Dutch edition 2,500 and German edition 750)

♦ TABULA ♦ GRATULATORUM

♦

A

E. Aartsen-König, Hoorn, NL
Ethel Abrahams, USA
Adirondack Mennonite Heritage Association, USA
Walter V. Adrian, USA
Henk Akkerman, Utrecht, NL
Henry Albrecht, CAN
Russell L. Alderfer, USA
Algemene Doopsgezinde Sociëteit, Amsterdam, NL
William J. Allan, USA
Harmen en Nel Ament, Alkmaar, NL
The American Book Center, Amsterdam/Den Haag, NL
Jim & Lorraine Stutzman Amstutz, USA
David & Sonia N. Araujo, USA
Archiefdienst Westfriese Gemeenten, Hoorn, NL
C.S. Arendz, Groningen, NL
Ir. Menno Arendz, Boijl, NL
Ulrike Arnold, Redaktion Brücke, Bad Soden-Salm, D
Nico A. Aten, Amsterdam, NL
Brent Auernheimer, USA
David W. Augsburger, USA

B

Gerhard Bachmann, CAN
Rufus F. Baehr, USA
Nelson D. & Kathryn A. Baer, USA
Gerald Baerg, USA
Rev. Henry R. & Anne Baerg, USA
Peter Baerg, CAN
A.A. Bakker-Olthof, Den Burg, NL
A.H. Bakker, Giethoorn, NL
A.Th. Bakker-Joustra, Ouderkerk a/d IJssel, NL
C.D. Bakker, Den Burg, NL
Jacob en Akkie Bakker, Hollum, NL
Ing. Joh. Bakker, Den Burg, NL
Drs. M.G. Bakker-van Kampen, Oenkerk, NL
Menno, Henk, Joke en Marja Bakker, Heiloo, NL
Prof. dr. ir. W. Bakker, Enschede, NL
Wessel en Cornelia Bakker, Heiloo, NL
Wijntje Bakker, Workum, NL
Prof. dr. W. Balke, Werkhoven, NL
Jennifer Balmer, USA
A.M. Balt, Elst, NL
Drs. Th. Balt, Drachten, NL
Gabe Bangma, Boazum, NL
Carl & Marjorie Friesen Bangs, USA
E. Robert & Elva M. Bare, USA
Manfred Bärenfänger, Pastor i.R., Münster, D
Verna Janzen Bargdill, USA
Carolyn Barkley, USA
P. Bart, Haarlem, NL
Gerhard Bartel, CAN
Jan-Hendryk Bas, Norderney, D
Orpha Elizabeth Amstutz Basinger, USA
Catherine Bast, CAN
Glenn Baughman, USA
Aden M. Bauman, CAN
Blaine E. Bauman, USA
Charles Bauman, USA
Alice Ann Beachy, USA
Alice-Ann Beachy, USA
Jim & Pam Beachy, USA
Elton Bechtel, CAN
Ervin Beck, USA
Hasso Becker, Lüchow-Kolborn, D
J.C. Beekhuis, Haarlem, NL
Eint Beekman Ockels, Sprang-Capelle, NL
Mr. E.V.F. Belinfante RA, Bergen, NL
H. & M. Jsert Bender, CAN
Paul Bender, USA
Ross T. Bender, USA
Sanford & Joy Bender, CAN
Mr. Ch.J. van Benten, Barneveld, NL
Cheryl Berg, CAN
Colin Berg, CAN
Orrin & Ruby Berg, USA
Wesley & Selma Berg, CAN
A. van den Berg-de Jong, Baflo, NL
C.J. van den Berg, Utrecht, NL
Drs. J.P. van den Berg, Baflo, NL
Henry W. Bergen, CAN
Karl Bergen, CAN
Laurie & Shelby Bergen, CAN
Margaret Bergen, CAN
Menno I. Bergen, CAN
Curtis & Esther Bergey, USA
Lorna L. Bergey, CAN
Jan en Trienke Bergsma, Zwaagwesteinde, NL
J. Bes, Bleiswijk, NL
Bethel Collega Mennonite Church Library, USA
Jack van Bethlehem, Sneek, NL
Jacob Beuker, Beetsterzwaag, NL
P.A. Beun, voorzitter A.D.S., Haarlem, NL
Drs. C. Bianchi, Amstelveen, NL
Gosse Bierma, Voorst, NL
Gerald & Susan Biesecker-Mast, USA
Drs. H. van Bilderbeek, Sneek, NL
Dr. Willem T. Binnerts, Renkum, NL
Fred J. Birza, Haren, NL
J. Russell Bishop, USA
Thomas R. & Trinda H. Bishop, USA
David W. & Marjorie Bixler, USA
John W. & Rebecca Troyer Bixler, USA
Richard & Arlee Blackburn, USA
H.J. Blanksma, Aerdenhout, NL
P.C. Blanksma, Heerenveen, NL
Jan Blauw, Groningen, NL
Y.H. Blauw, Wageningen, NL
C.J. Bloem, Meppel, NL
Geertje Bloemsma, Amsterdam, NL
Ds. L.C.M. Blomjous-Maillette de Buy Wenniger, Aerdenhout, NL
Donald W. Blosser, USA
Harold Blosser, USA
H. Boddéus-Oosterbaan, Ommen, NL
Anja Boegborn-Dam, Maarssen, NL
Drs. G. Boekhoff, Apeldoorn, NL
G. de Boer, Aalsmeer, NL
G.H. de Boer, Castricum, NL
J. de Boer, Drogeham, NL
Mr. K.Y. de Boer, Roden, NL
Arthur Boers, CAN
D. Boersma, Holwer, NL
John & Tina W. Bohn, USA
Lisa Bohnert, USA
Lyle & Carol Bohnert, USA
Dra. J.G. Boiten-du Rieu, Amsterdam, NL
B.A. Bokma, Waddinxveen, NL
Ton Bolland, Amsterdam, NL
J.J. Bolt, Onstwedde, NL
Gerbrand Boltjes, St. Jacobiparochie, NL
Mr. C.M. van Bommel, Havelte, NL
Tjitske Bongers, Veenwouden, NL
John Bontrager, USA
Harold Bontreger, USA
M. Boogaard, Aalsmeer, NL
P.A. Booij, Koog a/d Zaan, NL
Griet Boomsma-Knol, Holwerd, NL
Prof. dr. Rudolf Boon, Amsterdam, NL
W.F. Boon, Sliedrecht, NL
F. Boonstra en J.M. Boonstra-Duijf, Zwaagwesteinde, NL
T.R. Boonstra, Zeist, NL
Jacob & Hilda Born, CAN
Wilhelmina F. Bos, Amsterdam, NL
Drs. A.M. Bosch, Amsterdam, NL
F. Bosch-Kuipers, Drachten, NL
Jozef van den Bosch, Bonheiden, B
Erwin Boschmann, USA
T. Bosma-Zoethout, Veenwouden, NL
Dr. J. Bouterse, Vlaardingen, NL
Han en Henk Bouwman-Koopal, Apeldoorn, NL
Family Bowers, USA
Bine D. Braam-Bierma, Hoorn, NL
R.P. Brands, Gorredijk, NL
Ernest N. Braun, CAN
Gilbert Braun, CAN
A. Breet, Amersfoort, NL
P. Breeuwer, Alblasserdam, NL
P. Breeuwer, Heerenveen, NL
Drs. K.A. Bremer, Amsterdam, NL
James E. & Terri J. Brenneman, USA
Paul G. Brenneman, M.D., USA
Virgil J. Brenneman, USA
G. Brinkman, Uitgeverij Kok Kampen, NL
J.A. Broere, Aalsmeer, NL
Leendert Broere, Den Burg, NL
Mr. drs. Th.W.C. Brok, Utrecht, NL
H. Bronkhorst, Alkmaar, NL
A.J. Brouwer, Vlissingen, NL
Rev. F. & A. Brouwer, Fennel Bay, N.S.W., AUS
Ila & Merle Brubaker, USA
J. Mark & Beryl Brubaker, USA
Romkje van Bruggen-Oosterhof, Rottevalle, NL
Familie P. Bruijn, Twisk-Abbekerk, NL
Drs. N.W. Bruinsma, Amsterdam, NL
Gerald R. Brunk, USA
J. Bruntink, Amstelveen, NL
J.P. Bruntink, St. Pancras, NL
C.F. Brüsewitz, Den Haag, NL
Jaap en Lucie Brüsewitz, Leiden, NL
John Bueckert, CAN
John & Anna Bueckert, CAN
Gerhard R. Buhr, USA
John Buhr, USA
G.E. Buijn, Heemstede, NL
L. Buiskool-Sijtsma Poll, Grijpskerk, NL
H. Buiter-Wouda, Assen, NL
Arlin & Maretta Buller, USA
Harold W. Buller, USA
Irvin D. & Ruby E. Buller, USA
John S. Buller, USA
Victor D. Buller, USA
J.G. Burema van Veen, Zeerijp, NL
Dick van Buren, Harderwijk, NL
Prof. dr. Christoph Burger, Vrije Universiteit Amsterdam, NL
A.N.C. Burggraaf, Oisterwijk, NL
Drs. M.G.A. van der Burgt, Schagen, NL
Ranier W. Burkart, USA
James Burkett, USA
Sheldon W. & Janis S. Burkhalter, USA
J.R. & Susan Burkholder, USA
Lawrence Burkholder, USA
Dan & Janice Bylsma, USA

C

Calico Rock Mennonite Fellowship, USA
Canadian Mennonite Bible College, CAN
Carpenter Park Mennonite Church, USA
Center for Mennonite Brethren Studies, Fresno, USA
Center for Mennonite Brethren Studies, Tabor College, USA
Central Christian High School, USA
Centre for M.B. Studies, CAN
R.A. Chaudron en R.J.F. van der Wal, Den Haag, NL
Chesley Mennonite Fellowship, CAN
J. David Chittick, USA
John Chittick, USA
Tony & Barbara Chmiel, USA
Anne Chrisman, USA
David J. Christner, US
Jörg Cibis, Isernhagen, D
Meribeth N. Claassen, USA
Wilmer & Darlene Classen, USA
James E. & Angela D. Clemens, USA
Michael Clemens, Neustadtgödens, D
D.C. de Clerq, Amsterdam, NL
Pieterdiena A. Clevering-Allersma, Warffum, NL
David & Vivian Coffman, USA
John Coffman, CAN
A. Cohen-Drent, Terneuzen, NL
Columbia Bible College, CAN
Concord College Library, CAN
Carol W. Condon, USA
Conestoga Christian School, USA
Conestoga Mennonite Church, USA
P. Coolman, Haren, NL
T.A. Coomans, Ouddorp, NL
John F. Cooper, USA
Donald Cooprider, USA
Drs. R. Cordes, Bloemendaal, NL
Erwin Cornelson, CAN
Louise Cornies, CAN
Lewis & Mary Coss, USA
B. Cuperus, Den Haag, NL

D

E. Daalder, Hilversum, NL
Ds. Albert A. van Daalen, Kortenhoef, NL
Kees en Sally Dalmeijer-Handrich, Hoorn, NL
R. Dalmeijer-Nijland, Amsterdam, NL
Mabel Nickel Danenberg, USA
E. Dankmeijer-van Eijkern, IJmuiden, NL
Neva M. Danner, USA
Hinderikus Dassel, Gorssel, NL
Michael & Susan Wolfgang Davis, USA
A.C. DeFehr, CAN
Drs. L.J. Degenaar, Heiloo, NL
L. Dekker, Villa Park, IL 60181, USA
M.M. Dekker-Hoek, Emmastad, Curaçao, NA
H.E. Dekkers-de Kok, Zwijndrecht, NL
Mr. Delp & Mrs. R. Lee, USA
Hermine Denz, Amsterdam, NL
John D. Derstine, USA
Paul Dick, CAN
William O. Dick, USA
John G. Diegel, CAN
Daniel Diener, USA
Kees Dijk, Ternaard, NL
Folkert Jelger van Dijk, Hoorn, NL
S. van Dijk, Santpoort, NL
H.G. Dijkerman, Schiedam, NL
Nelly Dijkman, Krommenie, NL
Klaas P. Dijksma, Drachten, NL
A. Dijkstra, Groningen, NL
Y. en M. Dijkstra, Heerenveen, NL
Elisabeth Dirkmaat, Broek op Langedijk, NL
J. Dirkmaat, Hoogeveen, NL
Dirk Dobber, Heerhugowaard, NL
J.H.J. Docter-de Vries, Santpoort-Zuid, NL
Milford Doell, USA
J.C.L. Donkel, Haarlem, NL
G. Donker-Peenstra, Laag Soeren, NL
Willemien van den Dool-Winkel, Wageningen, NL
Doopsgezind Seminarium, Amsterdam, NL
Doopsgezinde Bibliotheek, UB, Amsterdam, NL
Doopsgezinde Gemeente Almelo, NL
Doopsgezinde Gemeente Ameland, NL
Doopsgezinde Gemeente Breda, NL
Doopsgezinde Gemeente Deventer, NL
Doopsgezinde Gemeente 's-Gravenhage - 'De Boekerij', NL
Doopsgezinde Gemeente Groningen, NL
Doopsgezinde Gemeente Haren, NL
Doopsgezinde Gemeente IJlst, NL
Doopsgezinde Gemeente Leeuwarden, NL
Doopsgezinde Gemeente Middelstum, NL
Doopsgezinde Gemeente Noord-West Veluwe Flevoland, Putten, NL
Doopsgezinde Gemeente Sneek, NL
Doopsgezinde Gemeente Ternaard, NL
Doopsgezinde Gemeente Utrecht, NL
Doopsgezinde Gemeente Veenwouden, NL
Doopsgezinde Gemeente Wageningen, NL
Doopsgezinde Gemeente Zeerijp-Zijldijk, NL
Doopsgezinde Gemeente Zeist, NL
Doopsgezinde-Remonstrantse Gemeente, Hoorn, NL
Doopsgezinde Vredesgemeente in Nederland, Oosterbeek, NL
P. Doves, Zaandam, NL
Mr. W. Downer, Leiden, NL
M. Doze, Winschoten, NL
Eibert Draisma, Pijnacker, NL
Sadie Draper, USA
Dale Driedger, CAN
Diane Driedger, CAN
Leo Driedger, CAN
Margaret Driedger, CAN
A. Drost-Smit, Roden, NL
Dr. G.W. Drost, Rijswijk, NL
Brian Drudge & family, CAN
Neil Drudge & family, CAN
Chr. Duhoux-Rueb, Wassenaar, NL
H. van Duinen, Vught, NL
Dr. H. Duits, Hilversum, NL
Ds. E.L. van Dunné-de Bi ll Nachenius, Dordrecht, NL
G. van Duren-Rolie, Sliedrecht, NL
D.F. Durnbaugh, USA
Ab van Duuren, Den Haag, NL
Anna Dyck, CAN
Arthur K. Dyck, CAN
B. Harry & Lois Dyck, USA
Cornelis J. Dyck, USA
Dan Dyck, CAN
Ernest G. Dyck, CAN
Gerald & Lee Dyck, CAN
Greg Dyck, USA
Harold & Alfrieda Dyck, USA
Henry Dyck, CAN
Rev. Jack W. Dyck, CAN
John Dyck, CAN
John & Ellie Dyck, CAN
Korey Dyck, CAN
Leonard & Anne Dyck, CAN
Marwood W. Dyck, USA
Dr. Michael Dyck & Lisa Bueckert, CAN

E

Eastern Mennonite High School, USA
Richard L. Ebersole, USA
Ed & Eva Eby, USA
Gerald Ediger, USA
Ing. W.J. Eek, Hoorn, NL
T.K. Eendhuizen-Vos, Zeerijp, NL
Wilhelmina Geertruida Eendhuizen-Boerma, Zuidlaren, NL
L.E. Egberink, Uithoorn, NL
Mr. & Mrs. Allan Eicher, USA
F. van Eijkern, Den Helder, NL
W.C. Eijssen-Harms, Arnhem, NL
Betty en Gerben Elzinga Alkmaar, NL
R.D. 'Dick' Emerson, USA
Emmaus Mennonite Church, CAN
E.D. van den End, Woerden, NL
Art & Mary Enns, CAN
Ed & Bert Enns, CAN
Gerhard (George) H. Enns, CAN
Walter John Enns, CAN
Abram E. Ens, CAN
Henry G. Ens, CAN
Anthony R. Epp, USA
Betty S. Epp, USA
Henry P. Epp, CAN
Jerry A. Epp, USA
Peter Epp, CAN
K.J.B. Erné, Apeldoorn, NL
J.M.C. Ernsting-Schaly, Z.O. Beemster, NL
Elbert & Zola Esau, USA
Elma E. Esau, USA
John A. Esau, USA
John H. Esau, USA
Floyd & Donna Esch, USA
Europäische Mennonitische Bibelschule, Liestal, CH
Darl W. Evans, USA
Alana Ewy, USA
Daniel & Frances Becker Ewy, USA

F

Faculteit der Godgeleerdheid UvA, Amsterdam, NL
Bibliotheek Faculteit der Godgeleerdheid en Godsdienstwetenschap, Rijksuniversiteit Groningen, NL
George H. & Florence Fadenrecht, USA
James & Jean Fairfield, USA
Jean Longenecker Fairfield, USA
Dr. Heinold Fast, Norden, D
John & Barbara Fast, USA
Kathi Fast, CAN
Peter G. Fast, USA
Werner Fast, CAN
Dale & Laura Fehr, CAN
G. Feijen, Hoofddorp, NL
A. Feitsma, Grou, NL
F.R. Fennema, Groningen, NL
G.R. Fennema, Meppel, NL
R. Fennema, Oosterbeek, NL
Mrs. Richard L. Ferguson, USA
Sarah Voth Ferris, USA
Hermien Fictoor Kamp, Heemskerk, NL
First Mennonite Church of Champaign, USA
First Mennonite Church of Christian, USA
First Mennonite Church (Edm.), CAN
First Mennonite Church Library, Berne, USA
First Mennonite Church Library, Reedley, USA
Mrs. Jacob A. Flaming, USA
T. Fledderman, Nijmegen, NL
Gordon Flickner, USA
David Flynn, CAN
Anna Bonnie Folkertsma, Kûbaard, NL
James & Lynn Forbes, CAN
Herbert & Mary Fransen, USA
Ken Fransen, USA
Werner Klassen Fransen, USA
Frazer Mennonite Church, USA
Donald L. Frederick, USA
Stanley L. Freed, USA
Freeman Heritage Archives, USA
Marc Freligh, USA
J.G. Frerichs, Beverwijk, NL
Dr. L.L. Frerichs, Edam, NL
Bruce L. Fretz, CAN
Joseph H. Fretz, USA
Gwen Frey, USA
James & Fannie Frey, USA
Willard Frey, USA
Friese Doopsgezinde Sociëteit, Leeuwarden, NL
Abraham & Gerry Friesen, USA
Dave & Esther Friesen, USA
David Friesen, CAN
Delbert Friesen, USA
Donald H. Friesen, USA
Edward H. Friesen, CAN
George Friesen, CAN
Isaac L. Friesen, CAN
Dr. John K. Friesen, CAN
Kay Friesen, CAN
Leonard & Elenor Friesen, CAN
Marlin Friesen, USA
Rudy P. Friesen, CAN
Verda Eck Friesen, USA
Walter Friesen, CAN
Walter & Margaret Friesen, CAN
William & Doris Friesen, USA
Willem Frijhoff, Rotterdam, NL
A. Frijling-van Buren, Bolsward, NL
G. Frijling, Grouw, NL
Th.R. Frijling, Dronrijp, NL
Harry & Letha Froese, USA
Jake Edwin Froese, CAN
Kevin Froese & Heide Kanning, USA
Peter Froese, Amsterdam, NL
Gerald Funk, CAN
Melvin & Frances Funk, USA
Randy & Kaethe Funk, CAN

G

R. Gaaikema, Heemstede, NL
John & Mary Gaeddert, USA
Menno Gaeddert, USA
Harold Gaede, USA
Garden Valley Church, USA
B. Gardenier-Wiegersma, Veenwouden , NL
Joseph & Barbara Gascho, USA
A.H. Geertsema-Frieling, Winsum, NL
Gehman Mennonite Church, USA
Ds. Willy Geijlvoet, Heerenveen, NL
Irvin L. Geiser, USA
Peter & DeLores Gade Geiser, USA
W. Geldorp, Amsterdam, NL
Gemeente Wûnseradiel, Witmarsum, NL
Abraham Gerber, USA
John Gerbrandt, USA
Susan Gerbrandt, CAN
Robert & Joyce Gerhart, USA
J. Gerlofs, Arnhem, NL
Germantown Mennonite Historic Trust, USA
J. Gerrits-Broekman, Den Burg, NL
Anna Gerritsen, Sneek, NL
Lawrence Giesbrecht, CAN
Gilbert Gingerich, USA

Lester Gingerich, USA
Ray & Wilma Gingerich, USA
Velma F. Gingerich, USA
J. Lloyd Gingrich, USA
G. Glaudé, Amsterdam, NL
Gerrie Gleijsteen, Goshen, Indiana, USA
Jan Gleysteen, Goshen, Indiana, USA
Jan & Barbara Gleysteen, USA
Amy Susan Glick, USA
Daniel M. Glick, USA
Ervie & Mary Glick, USA
Melvin Glick II, USA
Harold B. Gochnauer, USA
Jacob D. Goering, USA
Wayne M. Goering, USA
Helen Goertzen, CAN
Hilde & Peter Goertzen, CAN
Jacob & Olga Goertzen, CAN
James M. Good, USA
Kie Goudsmit-Schootman, Wolvega, NL
B. de Graaf, Nieuwkoop, NL
Joute en Eke de Graaf-Gulmans, Sneek, NL
Familie J.W. de Graaf, Twello, NL
M. en A.C. de Graaf-Uidam, Ochten, NL
Pieter de Graaf, Sexbierum, NL
Dr. Tjeerd de Graaf, Paterswolde, NL
Tineke de Graaf-Nauta, Sexbierum, NL
Willem de Graaf, Zaandam, NL
Kenneth E. Graber, USA
Martha F. Graber, USA
O'Ray & Edith E. Graber, USA
Grace Community Church, USA
Anna Mae Graybill, USA
Y. Greebe-Haaksma, Boekelo, NL
Dr. Louis Peter Grijp, Driebergen-Rijsenburg, NL
W.N. Grimme, Lisse
Ing. Meine Groeneveld, Den Helder, NL
A.C. de Groot, Sappemeer, NL
Prof.dr. Cornelis J. de Groot, Amsterdam, NL
Joh.Th. de Groot, Jorwerd, NL
Leonora de Groot, Utrecht, NL
R.J.M. de Groot, Spijk, NL
Prof. dr. E.K. Grootes, Haarlem, NL
Joel & Karen Gross, USA
J. Grupstra, Santpoort-Noord, NL
James H. Gungoll, USA
Neill & Edith von Gunten, CAN
Ronald W. Guth, USA

H

Fokje Haak-Oosterhof, Drachten, NL
H.C. de Haan, Harlingen, NL
Hedzer en Marnel de Haan-Tas, Aalsmeer, NL
Geesje Hack-Wardenier, Schoorl, NL
Ray K. & Agnes R. Hacker, USA
E.M.J. Hageman, Heerhugowaard, NL
A.K. Hagen-Fast, De Bilt, NL
Elly Haleber-Kok, Santpoort, NL
James Halteman, USA
Hamilton Place Bible Study Group, USA
Rex E. Hamilton, USA
A. Hamm, CAN
Andrew S. Hamsher, USA
Hanley Mennonite Church, CAN
Jacob D. Harder, CAN
Willmar T. Harder, USA
C.J.H. Haremaker, Burgum, NL
G. Lester & Lucille Franz Harms, USA
Geoffrey & Diane Burkett Harms, USA
Gordon & Paula Goering Harms, USA
Hugo Harms, CAN
James O. & Elaine Harms, USA
Kelly & Veronia (Isaak) Harms, CAN
Menno Harms, USA
Timothy Paul & Susan K. Harrison, USA
C. van der Harst-Hendrikse, Son, NL
H. de Hart-Kuijn, Middenbeemster, NL
P. de Hart, Grootschermer, NL
Maarten J. 't Hart, Aalsmeer, NL
Jerry E. & Vicki Hols Hartness, USA
Ralph W. Hartzler, USA
Patricia Haverstick, USA
S.S.F. Hazewinkel, Haren, NL
Roy & Donna Heatwole, USA
J.H. Heeres, Oosterend, NL
Horst Heidebrecht, Münster, D
R. van der Heijde-Groen, Enkhuizen, NL
Klaas Heijers, Assen, NL
E.D. Heijnis-Renssen, Arnhem, NL
Dr. Willem Heijting, Zevenhoven, NL
Marvin & Mary Helen Hein, USA
Bert Heinrichs, CAN
Elfrieda Heinrichs, CAN
Ruth Heinrichs, CAN
K.C. van Helbergen-Vaandrager, Bussum, NL
Mr. & Mrs. Jake Helfer Jr., USA
Anneke Hellinga, Leeuwarden, NL
Loren & Maivi Helmuth, USA
Patricia S. Helton, USA
Ir. R.N. Hemmes, Zwolle, NL
F. Hendriks, Drachten, NL
Carolyn Lehman Henry, USA
F.F. den Herder-Vriend, Utrecht, NL
D. Heres-Torenbeek, Groningen, NL
J.G. Heres Diddens-Wischmeyer, Nijeholtwolde, NL
H. Ralph & Elizabeth Hernley, USA
Timothy L. Herr, USA
Harry Hersh, USA
Bernard M. & Neva Lou Hershberger, USA
Truman V. Hershberger, USA
Hiram & Mary Jane Lederach Hershey, USA
James & Shirley Hershey, USA
Joanne Hershey, USA
Lester T. Hershey, USA
Donnie & Jean Hertig, USA
C. Richard & Mary Ann Hess, USA
Drs. C.C. Hesselink-Melchior, Vaassen, NL
J.C. Hesselink-Janzen, Santpoort-Zuid, NL
A.T. Hiddema, Bentveld, NL
Rein Hiddema, Stadskanaal, NL
Wâtse Hiddema, Franeker, NL
Allen & Lois Hiebert, USA
Erwin N. Hiebert, Harvard University, USA
Frances & Paul Hiebert, USA
G.J.J. van Hiele, Wageningen, NL
J.G. Hijmans-de Vries Reilingh, Sleeuwijk, NL
Ernie Hildebrand, CAN
J.W. Hilverda, Amsterdam, NL
Daniel E. Hochstetler, USA
Ken & Sue Hochstetler, USA
Peter H. van der Hoek, Makkum, NL
A.G. Hoekema, Haarlem, NL
Ds. G.G. Hoekema, Aalsmeer, NL
W.K. Hoekstra, Rottevalle, NL
E. Hofenk, CAN
Beno Hofman, Groningen, NL
Drs. M.M. Hofman, Zoetermeer, NL
Ds. R. Hofman, Bilthoven, NL
Gabe Hofstra, CAN
H.T. Hofstra, Kootstertille, NL
Piet Hofstra, Waddinxveen, NL
Sippy Hofstra, Franeker, NL
Tette Hofstra, Roden, NL
G. Hogeterp-Okkema, Uithoorn, NL
Ir. A. Hoitsma, Reeuwijk, NL
Scott Holland, USA
L.J. den Hollander, Hoofddorp, NL
Janet Hollingsworth, CAN
Jim Holm, USA
Jerry L. Holsopple, USA
B.K. Homan, Enkhuizen, NL
Gerlof D. Homan, USA
C.A. Homburg-Hagel, Arnhem, NL
Home Street Mennonite Church, CAN
F.G. Hommes en C. Hommes-Schermer, Wijk aan Zee, NL
Magda Hommes, Heiloo, NL
G. Honig-Vink, Sint Pancras, NL
G.J. Honig, Wormerveer, NL
J.C. Honig, Ede, NL
H. v.d. Honing, Roden, NL
Art & Vicky Hoock, CAN
Ron & Linda Hoock, CAN
Steve & Val Hoock, CAN
F.J. Hoogewoud en R.M.M. Hoogewoud-Verschoor, Haarlem, NL
D.E. de Hoop, Wommels, NL
Annemarie van Hoorn, Amsterdam, NL
C. van Hoorn, Groningen, NL
Pieter van Hoorn, Groningen, NL
Ds. S.J. van Hoorn-Dantuma, Groningen, NL
Tammo van Hoorn, Scheemda, NL
Th. Hoornstra, Purmerend, NL
M.O. Hoornwegvanrij, Oranjewoud, NL
Amos B. Hoover, USA
H.C.M. Hordijk en C.W. Kooper, Zevenhuizen, NL
R. William Horrisberger, USA
Elam B. Horst, CAN
Galen Horst-Martz, USA
Irvin B. Horst, Heemstede, NL
Eldon E. Hostetler, USA
Marian Hostetler, USA
Philip M. Hostetler, USA
Stan & Iona Hostetter, USA
Lodewijk Houthakker, Amsterdam, NL
Dr. J. Houtzager, Apeldoorn, NL
G. Hovinga-Zijlstra, Assen, NL
Harold & Vida Huber, USA
Marijse Huber-Spaans, Neftenbach, CH
John H. Huebert, USA
Vie & Merle Huebner, USA
Jerry & Carolyn Huffman, USA
H. Huibers, Arnhem, NL
Egbert en Tineke Huijing-Zijlstra, Roodkerk, NL
Drs. W. Huizing, Aalsmeer, NL
Mr. H.Ch. Hulshoff, Den Haag, NL
J.M. Hulshoff-Hulshoff, Doorwerth, NL
Fulco Y. van Hulst, Groningen, NL
Rev. Alex Hunfeld, CAN
Walter E. Hurst, USA
B.W. Hylkema, Dordrecht, NL

I

J.F.A. Idema en T. Idema-Hilberts, De Wijk, NL
Former Jans Idsardi, Holwerd, NL
T. Iedema-Schat, Burgum, NL
Ph. IJntema, Nieuweschoot, NL
J. Inja, Peize, NL
Paul Isaak, USA
F. Iwema-Schipper, Purmerend, NL

J

Drs. Simon de Jager, Heiloo, NL
Art & Katherine Jahnke, CAN
J. Jansen-Span, Vlaardingen, NL
Hugo W. Jantz, CAN
Mr. & Mrs Joe Jantz, USA
Leola Jantz Epp, CAN
Anne & Carl Jantzen, USA
Eric Jantzen, USA
Irene Jantzen, CAN
Mark Jantzen, USA
Paul & Elaine Jantzen, USA
Douglas & Karen Jantzi, USA
Ruth & Ken Jantzi, CAN
Irma Janzen, CAN
John M. & Reinhild Kauenhoven Janzen, USA
Louis & Jean Janzen, USA
Peter P. Janzen, CAN
Richard Janzen, USA
Rod & Deborah Janzen, USA
Royce & Carol Janzen, USA
Vernon & Genevieve Janzen, USA
William Janzen, CAN
G. Jaspers, Hilversum, NL
Johannes Jaspers, Leiden, NL
P. Jellema, Haaksbergen, NL
J. Jepma, Beilen, NL
Marlin Jeschke, USA
A.C. Jesse, Amsterdam, NL
Barry & Janeen Bertsche Johnson, USA
Mr. & Mrs. Douglas Jones, USA
Anna en Geert de Jong, Assen, NL
Anne de Jong, Schoorl, NL
Drs. Anne S. de Jong, Hilversum, NL
Arnold de Jong, Breda, NL
Auke F. de Jong, Bussum, NL
D. de Jong, Leusden, NL
G. de Jong-Gerling, Leiden, NL
Hielke & Siegelinde de Jong, CAN
I.R. de Jong, Dokkum, NL
Dr. J.A. de Jong, Zeist, NL
N.M.W. de Jong-Jongkind, Hoofddorp, NL
Dr. O.J. de Jong, Amsterdam, NL
Piet J. de Jong, Wormer, NL
Theo de Jong, Joure, NL
Ds. Willemke de Jong, Bussum, NL
Drs. A.D. de Jonge, Rotterdam, NL
Popko de Jonge, Emmeloord, NL
W.K. de Jonge, Zwolle, NL
M.J. en J. Jongens-Loon, Tolkamer, NL
H.B. de Jonghe, Den Helder, NL
Elizabeth Jongsma-Velda, Damwoude, NL
Els Jonk, Leiden, NL
Jan Jonk jr., Leiden, NL
Wim Jonker, Koog a/d Zaan, NL
L. Jonkman, Warga, NL

Ir. J.N. Joustra, Rotterdam, NL
Peggy Joyner, USA
M.P.A. van Juchem-Lamme, Breda, NL

K

Kenneth Kahler, USA
A.J. Kalkman-Krottje, Den Helder, NL
Drs. J.S. Kalkman, Nijmegen, NL
L.G. Kalma, Heerhugowaard, NL
Kalona Mennonite WMSC, USA
J. van Kampen, Leeuwarden, NL
Walter Kampen, CAN
Ing. I. Kanbier, Haarlem, NL
J.J. Kanis, Zaandam, NL
Jess R. Karber, USA
Katholiek Lyceum in het Gooi, Hilversum, NL
Adeline Kauffman, USA
Charles & Jennie Kauffman, USA
Elroy W. Kauffman, USA
Howard Kauffman, USA
Nyle Kauffman, USA
Regina B. Kauffman, USA
Roger & Rachel Kauffman, USA
Virgil Kauffman, USA
Angie S. Kaufman, USA
Ken & Joyce Kaufman, USA
Waldo W. Kaufman, USA
A.J. Kavelaars-Westbroek, Ten Boer, NL
Dorothy Showalter Keener, USA
Fred Kemper, Amsterdam, NL
Arthur J. Kennel & Lois Ruth, USA
Ezra L. & Viola Kennel, USA
Kurt A. & Betty Lew Kennel, USA
Rev. Nancy Kerr, CAN
Mr.F.W. van Ketwich Verschuur, Doorn, NL
Ds. H.R. Keuning, Drachten, NL
A.F. Keuter, Krommenie, NL
L.M. Keuter jr., Koog a/d Zaan, NL
N. Keuter-Visser, Koog a/d Zaan, NL
John D. Kiblinger, USA
Sanderijn C.A.F. Kiel, Amsterdam, NL
Sieb Kiestra, Rottevalle, NL
Drs. A.C. Kik, Amstelveen, NL
Hanneke Kik, Blokker, NL
P. Kik, Blokker, NL
P. Kik en C. Kik-van Gils, Blokker, NL
Harold M. Kilheffer, USA
C. Kinderman, Grootegast, NL
Walter & Miriam King, USA
Wendell & Esther King, USA
Akke Kingma, Velsen, NL
Willard L. Kinzie, CAN
Da. Nanny Klaasen, Drachten, NL
Gerhard Klaassen, CAN
Randolph A. Klaassen, CAN
Victor E. Klaassen, USA
Drs. ds. J.E. Klanderman, Beverwijk, NL
Arthur & Milly Klassen, USA
Benno & Frances Klassen, CAN
Clarence Klassen, USA
Clifford & Virginia Klassen, CAN
Garry Klassen, CAN
John L. Klassen, CAN
Loyal & Bertha Klassen, USA
Paul Klassen, CAN
Peter J. Klassen, USA
Jeanne Kleijn-Seijffer, Heiloo, NL
M.L. Kleisen, Enschede, NL
W. van Klingeren-Reedijk, Velsen Zuid, NL
Donald & Linda Klippenstein USA
Lawrence Klippenstein, CAN
Ds. G. ten Klooster, Hollum, NL
Ing. J. Kluft, Woerden, NL
H.J. Klugkist, Uithuizermeeden, NL
Peter W. Knapp, USA
Annette Knijnenberg, Alkmaar, NL
Annie en Kees Knijnenberg, Heiloo, NL
C.N. Knijnenberg-de Jong, Krommenie, NL
Coert Simon Knijnenberg, Heiloo, NL
Marianne Knijnenberg, Muiden, NL
Marlies Knijnenberg, Rotterdam, NL
Willy Knijnenberg, Oostwoud NL
J.P.J. Knipscheer, Workum, NL
Ds. L.D.G. Knipscheer, Den Burg, NL
Atie & Huib Knottnerus, Zuidvelde, NL
Thomas & Bernice Koehn, USA
T.S. Koevoets, Beverwijk, NL
Familie Kok, Den Burg, NL
H.J. Kok-Weg, Meppel, NL
Anton Kollen en Jantje Kollen-Vos, Giethoorn, NL
Aurelia G. Koning-van Reenen, Roden, NL
Koninklijke Bibliotheek, Den Haag, NL
E.Kooistra-v.d. Galiën, Damwoude, NL
Pieter Kool, Missisanga, Ont., Can
Helen Koop Johnson, CAN
Peter Albert Koop, CAN
A. Koopmans-van Nes, Middelburg, NL
Hermine J. Koornneef, Bergen, NL
J.W.E. Korsten, Utrecht, NL
Theodore Koslowsky, CAN
Henk B. Kossen, Amersfoort, NL
Jakob Kraan, Veendam, NL
Robert & Ellen Krabill, USA
Russell & Martha Krabill, USA
Ivan Kraemer, CAN
O.H.M. Kragt, Harlingen, NL
George P. Krahn, CAN
Marcus R. Kramer, CAN
Ernest & Eunice Kraybill, USA
Andrew & Katie Kreider, USA
J. Robert and Virginia S. Kreider, USA
S. Krijtenburg-Smeding, Zwolle, NL
G.C.H. Krist-Haremaker, Veenwouden, NL
Ernie Kroeger, CAN
Henry Kroeker, CAN
Marvin E. Kroeker, USA
N.J. (Elisabeth) Kroeker, CAN
Wally & Millie Kroeker, CAN
Walter & Madeline Kroeker, CAN
Wes & Elaine Kroeker, USA
O.W. Krommenhoek, Krommenie, NL
Idske Kroon-de Jong, IJlst, NL
James L. Kropf, USA
Levi Kuepfer, CAN
John W. Kuhl, CAN
Henderika Kühler, Leiderdorp, NL
M.C.P. Kühler-Köhlen, Oegstgeest, NL
R.J. Kuijpers, Wormerveer, NL
Drs. F.C.J. Kuiken, Harlingen, NL
Yme Kuiper, Leeuwarden, NL
J. Kuipers, Drachtster Compagnie, NL
J. Kuis, Amersfoort, NL
S.R. Kuit en G. Kuit-Veerman, Krommenie, NL
R.S. Kuitse, Amsterdam, NL
A.E. Kunst-Gaaikema, Amsterdam, NL
Drs. W. Kunze, Den Haag, NL
Sjoerd & Betty Kupeerus, USA
D. Kuperus Man, Nijmegen, NL
Becky Kurtz, USA
Bishop Paul S. Kurtz, USA
Elam & Orpah Kurtz, USA
Eldon Kurtz, USA
Kevin & Beth Kurtz, USA
Maynard & Hilda Kurtz, USA
Michael & Karen Kurtz, USA
L. Kuurstra, De Bult, NL
B. Kuyt, Koog a/d Zaan, NL

L

J.W. Laan en A. Laan-Boogaard, H.I. Ambacht, NL
L. Laan-Roggeveen, Midwoud, NL
D. van der Laan-IJbema, Koog a/d Zaan, NL
Theo van der Laan, Apeldoorn, NL
Marijke Laane, Almere, NL
Jac.J. v.d. Laarse, Rijsenhout, NL
Ruud Lambour, Amsterdam, NL
Lancaster Mennonite High School, USA
Henry & Jane Landes, USA
Drs. G.M. Landheer, Rotterdam, NL
Darryl Lynn Landis, USA
Herb Landis, USA
John G. Landis, USA
Christian Lang, Worms-Ibersheim, D
Jan Lucas de Lange, Eindhoven, NL
Richard Langill, USA
Langley Mennonite Fellowship, CAN
M.N. Lansdorp, Heemstede, NL
K. en M. Lantinga, Heiloo, NL
Andrew Lapp, USA
Arlin & Janet Lapp, USA
Jonathan Lapp, USA
Dr. Joseph L. Lapp, USA
LeRoy G. Lapp, USA
Michael Lapp, USA
N. LeRoy & Catherine Lapp, USA
J.A. Lasco Bibliothek, Emden, D
D. Latenstein van Voorst, Haarlem, NL
Huibert Latenstein, Koog a/d Zaan, NL
Drs. E.L.T. Laterveer RA, Baarn, NL
Leo Laurense, Zutphen, NL
J. Lavooij, Oostzaan, NL
J.J. Lawant, Alkmar, NL
J. Welby Leaman, USA
Marvin D. & Shirley C. LeBlanc, USA
Geertruida A. Leendertz, Haarlem, NL
K. van Leersum-den Hartog, Bergen, NL
G. van Leerzem, Veenwouden, NL
Ds. Barrie Lees, Falmouth, UK
J. van Leeuwen, Aalsmeer
Harold & Ruth Lehman, USA
John E. Lehman, USA
Marion A. Lehman, USA
Milton Lehman, USA
Mary L. Lemke, USA
Naomi Lepp (Reimer), CAN
Arnold G. Leppke, USA
Peter Letkeman, CAN
C.D. van Leyden-Windhouwer, Leusden, NL
Richard J. Lichty, USA
Russel & Marjorie Liechty, USA
Wayne J. Liechty, USA
N.C. Ligteringen Verstegen-Swenne, Heiloo, NL
H.J. van Lijnen Noomen, Enkhuizen, NL
Cliff & Hope Lind, USA
Louise Lind, USA
Line Lexington Mennonite Church, USA
Allen R. Linscheid, USA
Lititz Area Mennonite School, USA
Betty T. Livengood, USA
Ken Loewen, CAN
Ted Loewen, USA
Lois Marie Peters Loflin, USA
London Mennonite Centre, UK
Rebecca H. Longenecker, USA
A.A. Lont, Leiderdorp, NL
J. Lont Jzn., Hippolytushoef, NL
Jaap Lont, Amsterdam, NL
Marieke Lont, Groningen, NL
P.C. Lont, Diepenveen, NL
Joachim Löper & Frau Dorothea Löper, Bad Salzuflen, D
J. Los, Schermerhorn, NL
Pearl Loucks, USA
A.F.H. Lourens-Schagen, Wenum/Wiesel, NL
Lowville Mennonite Church Library, USA
Darvin Luginbuhl, USA
D.R. de Lugt en H.M. de Lugt-Timmerman, Haarlem, NL
Mr. Menno Luikinga, Haarlem, NL
David Luthy, CAN
Chris Luursema, Hoorn, NL

M

Drs. K. Maarse jr., Leiderdorp, NL
Dr. Chris L. Maas, Utrecht, NL
Drs. W.J.J.A. Mahieu, Breda, NL
Ds. J. Mantel, Grou, NL
R.J. Mantel, Falmouth, UK
Dirk Mantje, Ferwerd, NL
Em. pred. R.E.H. Marcus, Amersfoort, NL
J.A. Marseille, Aalsmeer, NL
Lois Weidner Marshall, USA
B. Martens, CAN
Mrs. & Mrs. C. Martens, CAN
Gert Martens, CAN
John W. Martens & Janice L. Vansickle, CAN
Arvid Martin, USA
Earl S. & Vera L. Martin, CAN
Greta Martin, USA
Katie Martin, USA
Larry L. Martin, USA
Leo Martin, USA
Thelma L. Martin, USA
Martinsburg Mennonite Church Library, USA
Mary Miller Library, USA
Austin Mast, USA
Daniel Z. Mast, USA
Earl Elam Mast, USA
Elizabeth Z. Mast, USA
Horace & Bertha Mast, USA
J. Lemar & Lois Ann Mast, USA
Kathy Z. Mast, USA
Mildred R. Mast, USA
Vicki Mast-Wilson, USA
Ron & Carol Ann Maust, USA
Esther Diller McCoy, USA
David A. & Dena B. McGlothin, USA

G. v.d. Meer, Sexbierum, NL
F.K. van der Meer, Meppel, NL
Joh. van der Meer, Amsterdam, NL
Pim van der Meer, Aalsmeer, NL
Ds. Sybout van der Meer, Haarlem, NL
Arend Meester, Edam, NL
J.G. Meester, Harlingen, NL
Sj. Meester-Bruinsma, Grou, NL
A. Meiboom, Heiloo, NL
Ank Meihuizen, Amsterdam, NL
F. en E. Meihuizen-Gerver, Hilversum, NL
Dr. L.S. Meihuizen, Hengelo, NL
R.M. Meihuizen, Deventer, NL
Anneke R. Meijer, Almelo, NL
C.D. Meijer, Zeist, NL
J.Z. Mellema-Toppinga, Loppersum, NL
H.J. Mennens, Havelte, NL
Menno Mennonite Church, USA
Menno Simons Historical Library, USA
Mennonite Central Committee, USA
Mennonite Heritage Collection Public Library, USA
Mennonite Historians of Eastern Pa., USA
Mennonite Memorial Home, USA
Mennonite Post, CAN
Mennonite Your Way, USA
Mennorode, vakantie-en konferentieoord, Elspeet, NL
Mr. G. Mesdag, Haren, NL
Em. pred. P. Messie, Breda, NL
Robert & Lois Messner, USA
H.E. Metselaar en M.G. Haarsma, Krommenie, NL
Carl & Doris Metzler, USA
Henriette J. de Meulder-Tjalsma, Hoofddorp, NL
C. van der Meulen, Tolbert, NL
Jacob van der Meulen, Damwoude, NL
Klaas van der Meulen, Gorinchem, NL
Jocele Meyer, USA
Dr. C.W.C. Middelhoven, Amsterdam, NL
Mick & Marne Mierau Friesen, CAN
Ray & Doreen Mierau, CAN
Andy Miller, USA
Brian Miller, USA
Chris Miller, USA
D. Paul & Anna Miller, USA
Edward E. Miller, USA
Ellen M. Miller, USA
Ernest C. & Ruth Ann Miller
Floyd & Edith Miller, USA
George T. Miller, USA
Glen E. & Marily J. Miller, USA
H.N. Miller, USA
John K. Miller, USA
Mr. & Mrs. Joseph Miller, USA
Keith Graber & Ann Miller, USA
Kenneth C. & Doris F. Miller, USA
Levi Miller, USA
Liana Miller, USA
Rich & Jan Wooster Miller, USA
Roy Miller, M.D., USA
Sarah J. Miller, USA
Stan & Marianne Miller, USA
Susan Fisher Miller, USA
W. Molema-Graalman, Santpoort-Nrd, NL
Jan IJsbr. Molenaar, Leusden, NL
F. Mollema, Haarlem, NL
A.T. Moussault, Amsterdam, NL
J. Harold & Rosemary Moyer, USA
T. Mud, Veenwouden, NL
Ted & Berneil R. Mueller, USA
H. de Muinck Keizer-ten Cate, Bilthoven, NL
John C. Murray, USA
John F. Murray, USA

N

Mr. & Mrs. George F. Nachtigall, USA
Ralph L. & Judith F. Nafziger, USA
A. van Neck-Almekinders, Haarlem, NL
J.E.W. van Neck, Haarlem, NL
Drs. W.J. van Neck, Zeerijp, NL
A. Neervoort-Zeylstra, Den Haag, NL
E.H. Nesbitt, CAN
Wil en Henk Nessen, Heiloo, NL
Harry Neuenschwander, USA
Stefan te Neues, Krefeld, D
Arnie Neufeld, CAN
Elmer Neufeld, USA
Hannah Neufeld, USA
Jacob Neufeld, CAN
James K. & Velma R. Vogt Neufeld, USA
Nancy Neufeld, USA
David Neuhouser, USA
Paul Neustaedter, CAN
Niagara United Mennonite Church, CAN
Alvin L. Nickel, M.D., USA
Hans & Hertha Nickel, CAN
Menno & Ruth Nickel, CAN
Prof. dr. J.T. Nielsen, Leeuwarden, NL
Susie Niemeyer, CAN
R.J. Nienhuis, Haren, NL
Anna Niessen, CAN
Prof. dr. ir. J.G. Niesten, Eindhoven, NL
E.A. Nieuwenhuijzen Kruseman, Haarlem, NL
Ds. S.G. Nijdam, Koog a/d Zaan, NL
Prof. dr. Willem Nijenhuis, Haren, NL
Jan H. Nijntjes, Koog a/d Zaan, NL
J.M. Nijntjes-Lispet, Heiloo, NL
P.W. Nijntjes, Castricum, NL
Agnes Nikkel, CAN
Beulah Nisly, USA
Weldon & Marg Nisly, USA
Prof. dr. Peter J.A. Nissen, Den Bosch, NL
A.C. Nobel, Hollum, NL
Ed & Carol Nofziger, USA
Tom & Carolyn Nolan, USA
James K. Nolt, USA
Steven M. & Rachel S. Miller Nolt, USA
A.J. Noord, Gouda, NL
J. Noordraven, Noordwijk, NL
North Goshen Mennonite Church, USA
Northgate MB Church, CAN
John Edward Nunemaker, USA

O

W.E. Obbes-Hoogenstraaten, Rotterdam, NL
John Jacob & Becky Oberholtzer, USA
J. Oele, Amersfoort, NL
Thomas & Brenda Oelschlager, USA
Co Oerlemans, Enschede, NL
C.A. Olij-Spaan, Amsterdam, NL
Mr. dr. G.G. Oly, Amsterdam, NL
Drs. Jitske T. Oortman Gerlings-de Jong, Ilpendam, NL
Huibert Oortwijn, Breda, NL
Drs. A. Oosterbaan, Amsterdam, NL
J.A. Oosterbaan, Heemstede, NL
Willard R. Opdycke, USA
Oregon Mennonite Archives and Library, USA
Elizabeth Jane Oswald, USA
Cheryl Ours, USA
Verle Oyer, USA

P

Paul & Marianne Paetkau, CAN
J. Pama, Utrecht, NL
Dave S. Pankratz & Janet P. Schmidt, CAN
Ernest Pankratz, CAN
Henry & Elsie Pankratz, USA
Anna van Panthaleon van Eck-Kampstra, Rotterdam, NL
Park View Mennonite Church Library, USA
F. Jim & Janice Parks, USA
Helen Rose Pauls, CAN
Henry & Ingrid Pauls, USA
Jacob Pauls, CAN
Jacob & Marianne Pauls, USA
James & Marian Payne, USA
Chet & Ruthann Peachey, USA
Evelyn Peifer, USA
Betty Penner, USA
Doug & Raylene Hinz Penner, USA
Dr. Hartmut Penner, Neunkirchen, D
Herb Penner, CAN
Dr. Horst Penner, Kirchheimbolande, D
Karen L. Penner, USA
L. Penner, Den Haag, NL
Mel & Anita Penner, CAN
Paul Penner, CAN
Anne Peters, CAN
David C. Peters, USA
Herbert J. Peters, CAN
J. Peters, Oosterhout, NL
Margaret Peters & David Froese, CAN
Mildred Peters, USA
Virgil F. Peters, USA
Peters-Fransen, CAN
Florence E. Petersen, CAN
Carroll Peterson, USA
Ank Pfister-Sluis, Amsterdam, NL
Drs. W.F.H. Pilaar, Voorschoten, NL
Frank Pister, Erzenhausen, D
Kenneth J. & Eloise T. Plank, USA
Wayne Plenert, CAN
Delbert F. Plett, Q.C., CAN
Henry Poettcker, CAN
Jan Pol, Ruinen, NL
A.R. Poortinga, Gaastmeer, NL
Klaske en Bé Poppens-de Groot, Groningen, NL
Esther Porter, USA
Piet Post, Wormerveer, NL
Dr. N.M. Postema, Minnertsgea, NL
Dr. G.H.M. Posthumus Meyjes, Oegstgeest, NL
Hilligje Posthumus, Wolfheze, NL
J.F. Postma, Den Haag, NL
M.A. Postma, Hamburg, D
Ds. Tj. Postma, Terneuzen, NL
T.S. Postma, Molenend, NL
B.P. Postmus, Wormerveer, NL
P. Postmus, Wormerveer, NL
J.A.J. Praastink Wessel en D.H.J. Bontius, Deventer, NL
Dr. A.M.L. Prangsma-Hajenius, Bilthoven, NL
Drs. N.M. Prangsma, Leiden, NL
Predikfonds Ver. Doopsgezinde Gemeente Haarlem, NL
Lois Thieszen Preheim, USA
Louise & Vic Price, CAN
Derk Jan Prins, Leeuwarden, NL
Klaas Prins en Aattje Kuiken, Steenwijk, NL
A. Pronk, Scharwoude, NL
Dr. W.F. Prud'homme van Reine, Leiden, NL
Pulaski Mennonite Church, USA
D. Purmer RA, Ruurlo, NL

Q

Roma Quapp, CAN
Dorothy Franz Quillin, USA
David Menno & Suzanne Quiring & family, CAN
Eric & Doris Quiring & family, CAN

R

Drs. B. Rademaker-Helfferich, Deventer, NL
Guenter & Jutta Rahn, CAN
Howard Raid, USA
Howard D. Raid, USA
Rainbow Mennonite Church, USA
William Todd Rainey, USA
Kenneth & Virginia Ratzlaff, USA
Calvin & Freda Redekop, USA
Fred Redekop, CAN
Isaac & Margaret Redekop, CAN
Edwin Redekopp, CAN
Elsa-Maria Redekopp, Karlsruhe, D
P.J. Reede, Leusden, NL
N. Reedijk-Visser, Veenwouden, NL
Harold & Alice Reesor, CAN
Wes & Beth Georzen Regehr, USA
William & Maurine Regehr, USA
Mr. Regier, USA
Elmer Regier, CAN
Elmer & Agnes Regier, CAN
Frank A. Regier, USA
Hilda Regier, USA
Jacob Regier, CAN
Robert W. & Vernette Regier, USA
Regionaal Archief Alkmaar, NL
William, Magaret & Nathan Reid, USA
Henry A. Reier, CAN
Joke Reijntjes-Vonk, Amersfoort, NL
K.M. Reijsenbach de Haan-Binnerts, Eindhoven, NL
Abram Jacob Reimer, CAN
Bill & Ellen Reimer, CAN
David Reimer, USA
Delmer J. & Geraldine L. Reimer, USA
Paul Reimer, USA
Victor Reimer, CAN
Ds. G.A. Reinhold-Scheuermann, Utrecht, NL
Christopher Reist, USA
Anne J. Reitsma, Leeuwarden, NL
C.J. Reitsma, Bosch en Duin, NL
Jaap Rem, Nijkerk, NL
Abram E. Rempel, CAN
Averno M. Rempel, USA

Leo Rempel & Heather Martens Rempel, CAN
Henry D. Remple, Ph.D., USA
Drs. H.C. van Renselaar, Teheran, Iran
F. Renssen, Paterswolde, NL
Daniel J. Reschly, USA
Jake Retzlaff, CAN
C.G. Rezelman, Middelburg, NL
Rollin R. Rheinheimer, USA
Rose Allen Rhodes, USA
Jeffrey & Michelle Riegsecker, USA
Joel & Cynthia Riegsecker, USA
Marlin & Nancy Riegsecker, USA
Timothy & Jacob Riegsecker, USA
Evan Riehl, USA
Drs. T.G. Rienksma, Groningen, NL
J. Rietbergen-Bruijn, Delfgauw, NL
Drs. A.A. Rijken, Oosterhout, NL
B.F. Rispens-Hoekstra, Roden, NL
Dr. A.R. Ritsema, De Bilt, NL
Maria Francisca Ritsema, Groningen, NL
Lindsey Robinson, USA
J.H. Roelvink, Middelburg, NL
Thomas B. Roep, Alkmaar, NL
Maarten Roeper, Den Burg, NL
Anne Marie Rogalsky, CAN
C.J. Rogge, Lisse, NL
Margreet en Marius Romijn-Banga, Zaandam, NL
J.J. Roosma, Buitenpost, NL
Rosedale Bible Institute Library, USA
Gloria Horst Rosenberger, USA
David M. Ross, USA
Gene M. Ross, USA
Kenneth & Naomi Ross, USA
Richard F. Ross, USA
Richard L. Ross, USA
Stanley W. Ross, USA
Westly J. Ross, USA
Donald W. Roth, USA
Loren P. Roth, USA
Paul S. Roth, USA
Roy D. Roth, USA
Willard & Alice Roth, USA
Evelyn I. Rouner, USA
J.J. Ruitenberg, Den Haag, NL
Charles L. Rupp, USA
John & Roma Ruth, USA
John Rutt, M.D., USA
Willemien Ruygrok, Amsterdam, NL

S

L.G. Saalmink, Amsterdam, NL
H. Sabel-Dijkman, Koog a/d Zaan, NL
K.W. Sabel, Heiloo, NL
Marlin W. Sala, USA
Salem Mennonite Church, USA
Sandy Hill Mennonite Church, USA
Elda Santoro, USA
Rod & Lorna Sawatsky, USA
Wes Sawatsky, CAN
Walter Sawatsky, USA
John Sawatzky, CAN
Peter C. & Hilde Sawatzky, CAN
A. Schaafsma-Vellinga, Zwaagwesteinde, NL
Guda Schaap, Heiloo, NL
Ir. G.J.A. Schaap, Sleeuwijk, NL
H.A.J.O. Schaap, Edam, NL
Gudrun Schafer, D
A.J.H. Scheeuwe, Amsterdam, NL
De heer en mevrouw van Scheijen-Dijkema, Doorwerth, NL
Rosella Meriam Schell, USA
Jack Schellenberg, CAN
F. Schellinger, Oudeschild, NL
Barbara Schiere-Slusarczyk, Maarn, NL
P. van Schieveen en C.M. van de Pol, Broek in Waterland, NL
A.H. Schilthuis-van Bruggen, Rotterdam, NL
Mr. G.J.C. Schilthuis, Middelstum, NL
Drs. Pieter G. Schipper, Leusden, NL
David W. Schlabach, USA
Martin Schlabach, USA
M.P.A. Schlecht, Amsterdam, NL
Dr. mr. J.A. Schlette, Purmerend, NL
John & Lydia Schmid, USA
F. Vernon Schmidt, USA
Gordon & Diena Schmidt, USA
Hilda & Carl Schmidt, USA
John W. Schmidt, USA
Orville & Sandra Kroeker Schmidt, USA
Ted P. Schmidt, USA
Norbertus Scholma, Uithuizen, NL
C.H. Schoone, Wormerveer, NL
H.C. Schoone, Sliedrecht, NL
N.J. Schoone, Wormerveer, NL
W.J. Schoone, Dokkum, NL
J.M.M. Schopenhauer-Kortlandt, 's-Heerenberg, NL
A. Schottmann-Keizer, St. Annaparochie, NL
W.E. Schotvanger-Kemper, Hoofddorp, NL
Dale E. Schrag, USA
Robert M. Schrag, USA
Harry Schram, Baarn, NL
Dellis & Twila Schrock, USA
Rob Schrock, USA
William Schrock, USA
Anna Schroeder, CAN
David & Mildred Schroeder, CAN
Duane D. Schroeder, USA
Karl V. Schultz & Pauline C. Pilar, USA
Wilmer F. Schultz, USA
P.B. Schuringa, Hollum, NL
Mr. O. Schutte, Den Haag, NL
Seattle Mennonite Church, USA
D.H. van Seijst en A.M. van Seijst-ten Hoorn, Den Ilp, NL
H.G. van Seijst en N.S. van Seijst-Zweepe, Landsmeer, NL
Robert Senner, USA
Ivan Z. Sensenig, USA
Jan en Hennie van Setten-Veenstra, Stiens, NL
Shalom Mennonite Fellowship, USA
Anna B. Shank, USA
David A. Shank, USA
Robert & Judy Shantz, CAN
Eugene Shelly, USA
Maynard & Griselda Shelly, USA
Richard W. Shertzer, USA
Ralph Shetler, USA
Arlin & Esther Shisler, USA
Lowel E. Short, USA
Bernard Showalter, USA
Welby C. Showalter, USA
Dj.E.W. Sicama, Zorgvlied, NL
L.H. Siebeling, Zeist, NL
Marvin Siebert, USA
J. Donald & Joanne Siegrist, USA
Charlotte Siemens & David Sprunger, USA
Tena Siemens, CAN
Dr. E. Sietsma, Werkhoven, NL
D. Sijpkens Schuiling, Ulrum, NL
Onijdes en Jantsje Sijtsma-Anema, Berlikum, NL
P.J. Simonides-Weg, Zwolle, NL
Jacob Simons, Bergen, NL
S.R. Simons, Amsterdam, NL
S.IJ. Sinnema, Buitenpost, NL
Richard & Carole Skinner, USA
Goldie Slagell, USA
F.A. Slikker, Velserbroek, NL
E. Sluijters-Voûte, Warnsveld, NL
Em. pred. A.J. van der Sluis, Wijchen, NL
Carl L. Smeltzer, USA
Doris Metzler Smeltzer, USA
A. Smit-Wagtho, Veenwouden, NL
Annabel Smit, Amsterdam, NL
F. Smit, Oldemarkt, NL
Henk Smit, Amsterdam, NL
Walter L. & Leanne M. Smith, USA
Art Smoker, USA
Levon R. Smoker, USA
Mark L. Smucker, USA
Ds. A.J. Snaaijer, Kortehemmen, NL
Ds. H.V.A. Snoeker-van Dunné, Nieuwe Niedorp, NL
C. Arnold Snyder, CAN
James A. Snyder, USA
Willis Snyder, USA
Donald Sommer, USA
James T. & Susan L. Sommer, USA
Keith F. Sommer, USA
Otto I. Sommer, USA
Ralph Sommer, USA
Arthur Sommerfeld, CAN
Elvin R. & Patty Souder, USA
N.M. Spaan-Visser, Scheveningen, NL
Wayne Speigle, USA
E.A. Spigt-Poortman, Santpoort-Nrd, NL
M.K. Spoel-van der Sluijs, Etten-Leur, NL
J. Sprenger-Steenhoek, Vught, NL
Ben Sprunger, USA
Keith & Aldine Sprunger, USA
Philip Sprunger & Elizabeth Yoder, USA
Stads- of Athenaeumbibliotheek, Deventer, NL
Stadsbibliotheek Haarlem, NL
Antje Stallinga, Den Haag, NL
Harry Stauffer, CAN
Merv & Helen Stauffer, USA
H. Stavenga-de Jager, Veenwouden, NL
Steinbach Bible College Library, CAN
Steinbach Mennonite Church Library, CAN
Steven R. Steiner, USA
Tj. en C. Stelwagen-de Haan, Heerenveen, NL
B. Stenvers-de Boer, Amsterdam, NL
Philip & Laura Stephenson, USA
Mark A. Stevanus, USA
Stichting Kultuer en Toerisme yn Fryslân, Leeuwarden, NL
Gerda Stieva-Alderden, Aalsmeer, NL
Ott-Heinrich Stobbe, Oldenburg, D
F. Stoel-Hoekstra, Bolsward, NL
Conrad Stoesz, CAN
Dale K. Stoltzfus, USA
Dave & Rose Stoltzfus, USA
Douglas A. Stoltzfus, M.D., USA
Lorna C. Stoltzfus, USA
Vernon Stoltzfus, USA
A.A. Stolp-Simons, Middenbeemster, NL
Tiny en Ed van Straten, Leidschendam, NL
Lewis Strite, USA
Anneke T. Struijf, Zaandam, NL
Roland & Elaine Stucky, USA
Gerald C. Studer, USA
R. Stuiver-Wouda, Burgum, NL
Ervin & Bonita Stutzman, USA
F.J. Stuurman, Den Dolder, NL
J.A. Stuurman, Den Haag, NL
J.G. Stuurman, Amsterdam, NL
Elmer F. Suderman, USA
Harold J. Suderman, CAN
A.J. Surink-Paré, Leeuwarden, NL
Surrey Mennonite Church, CAN
John & Ruth Suter, USA
J. Swaan-Lamme, Bloemendaal, NL
A.P. Swarte-Gorter, Oudeschoot, NL
William L. Swartley, USA
Edward A. Swartz, USA
Keith Swartzendruber, USA
Loren & Pat Swartzendruber, USA
W. Swartzendruber, USA
Alvin & Rosanna E. Swartzentruber, USA
Wilmer D. Swope, USA

T

Tabor Mennonite Church, USA
Hiroshi Takeda, CAN
Y. Tarnsma-Faber, Schoorl, NL
Al en Els Tas, Aalsmeer, NL
N. Tas, Aalsmeer, NL
M.P. van der Tas-Kühler, Eindhoven, NL
John & Anna Taves, CAN
Glenn E. Taylor, USA
Abram & Olga Teichroeb, CAN
J.C. Terluin, Beetsterzwaag, NL
Arthur D. Thiessen, USA
Bernhard Thiessen, Hamburg, D
Harold Thiessen, CAN
Howard Thiessen, USA
Harold D. Thieszen, USA
Jon H. Thieszen, USA
J.A. Thimm-Richardson en A.A. Thimm, Haarlem, NL
Paul F. en Akke-Clara Thimm-Stelwagen, Heemskerk, NL
David N. Thomas, USA
Duane R. Thomas, USA
Lillie K. Thomas, USA
James E. & Helen Thurmond, USA
Walter & Wileta Tieszen, USA
P.H.A. Tillema, Diepenveen, NL
E.J. Timmerman, Beets, NL
C. Tjalsma, Sneek, NL
Willem Tjerkstra, Sneek, NL
Dave Toews, CAN
Geoffrey Bernard Toews, CAN
Gregory Ryan Toews, CAN
Paul Toews, USA
Boekhandel J.P. van den Tol, Dordrecht, NL
Ing. A.C. Tolsma, Assen, NL
Dr. D.K.J. Tommel, Amersfoort, NL

J.C. van der Toorn-van Eldik Thieme, Zeist, NL
J.J.E. Touw-ter Kuile, Hengelo, NL
Chr. Toxopeus, Haren, NL
J.K. Toxopeus, Groningen, NL
Dr. Jeanine Treffers-Daller, Istanbul/Amsterdam, TR/NL
Nine Treffers-Mesdag, Amsterdam, NL
Thaddeus J. Trenn, CAN
Trenton Mennonite, USA
Trinity Western University, CAN
David Troyer, USA
Donald & Beth Troyer, USA
Matthew J. Troyer, USA
Maynard & Dorothy Troyer, USA
W.N. Tuijn, Nijmegen, NL
D. Tuinstra, Appingedam, NL
Em. pred. E. van Turnhout-Dijkstra, Emmeloord, NL

U

P.E. en E.P. Uidam-de Jong, Ermelo, NL
Elton E. Ulrich, USA
Drs. Y.J.E. Ulrich-van de Vijver, Oegstgeest, NL
Ed & Elfi Unger, CAN
Peter A. Unger, CAN
United Mennonite Educational Inst., CAN
Judith Unk, Enschede, NL
Walter D. Unrau, USA
William E. Unrau, USA
Darrell & Judith Unruh, USA
Ervey A. Unruh, USA
LeRoy & Elaine Unruh, USA
Joe & Carolin Urich, USA

V

Martha Vander Werf, USA
Gerry J. Vandeworp, Rev., USA
J.A. Veen, Steenwijk, NL
C.T. van der Veen-Osinga, Den Haag, NL
Wicher Veen, Amsterdam, NL
D.H. Veenstra en F.M. Veenstra-Vis, Rottevalle, NL
R. Veenstra, Groningen, NL
Ilse van der Veer-Stas, Hoofddorp, NL
Catrien en Henk van der Vegt, Austerlitz, NL
J.A. Vegter-Hiddema, Castricum, NL
Nel en Henk op den Velde, Heiloo, NL
Maaike van der Velden-Bos, Soest, NL
Hessel Veldstra, Raerd, NL
Jac. Velt, Hilversum, NL
Prof. dr. P.E. Venekamp, Landsmeer, NL
A.E. van der Vennip, Zaandam, NL
Vereenigde Doopsgezinde Gemeente Haarlem, NL
Vereniging van Vrienden van Fredeshiem, De Bult, NL
J.G. Verkoren, Veenendaal, NL
W.M. Vermeulen-Maarse, Terneuzen, NL
Wilhelmina Verweij, Rotterdam, NL
Eileen L. Viau, USA
Daniel L. Villanueva, USA
Vincent Mennonite Church, USA
Ds. S.A. Vis, Westerhoven, NL
Anne-Marie Visser, Amsterdam, NL
Dirk Visser, Amsterdam, NL
J. Visser, Enkhuizen, NL
Piet Visser, Zaandam, NL
J.M. Vissinga, Rijswijk, NL
Drs. Nicolaesz Vlaming, Zaandijk, NL
T.C. Vlas-v.d. Vlies, Den Burg, NL
J.A. v.d. Vlies-Frijling, Noordwijkerhout, NL
D.H. van Vliet, Krommenie, NL
W. Vlug-zur Kleinsmiede, Dordrecht, NL
H. Vogelesang, Haarlem, NL
J.Th. Voltelen, Zaandam, NL
Prof. dr. S. Voolstra, Landsmeer, NL
Janet Voth, USA
Waldo O. Voth, USA
A. Vreken, Aalsmeer, NL
Dr. Oebele Vries, Westergeest, NL
A. de Vries, Drachten, NL
A. de Vries-van Dijk, Zutphen, NL
Drs. H.G. de Vries, Schiermonnikoog, NL
Mr. J. de Vries, Den Haag, NL
K.J. de Vries, Dokkum, NL
T.G. de Vries-van Lijnen Noomen, Hoorn, NL
U.W. de Vries, Veenwouden, NL

W

C.E. Waal, Amsterdam, NL
Donald Wagler, CAN
Henry Wagler, USA
Lorne & Dora Wagler, CAN
Drs. R.J.F. van der Wal, Den Haag, NL
T. Walda, Groningen, NL
Delmer & Linda Wall, CAN
Leroy J. & Helen Wall, USA
Derrold Waltner, USA
Everett Waltner, USA
John & Neta Warkentin, CAN
John H. Warkentin, M.D., USA
Ken & Linda Warkentin, CAN
Paul & Ina Warkentin, Reichenhall, D
Kurt A. Warschauer, Bilthoven, NL
J. Wassenaar-Langhout, Winsum, NL
Waters Mennonite Church, CAN
David Z. Weaver, USA
J. Denny Weaver, USA
Laura H. Weaver, USA
Robert L. Weaver, USA
William Weaver, USA
Vernon Weber, CAN
I. Weerman-de Haan, Haarlem, NL
Elfrieda Weier, CAN
Herman F. Weits, USA
G. en A. Welsing-Boogert, Heeze, NL
Russell Welty, USA
John A. Wenger, USA
Robert B. Wenger, USA
Drs. J.F.M. Wentholt, Den Haag, NL
Klaas van der Werf, Buitenpost, NL
Orpha Wertz, USA
Drs. J.M. van Wesel-Hulshoff, Holten, NL
H. Wesselius, Workum, NL
E.A.C.M. Wessels, Oosterhout, NL
West Union Mennonite Church, USA
West Zion Mennonite, USA
G.F. Westendorp, Heemstede, NL
A. Westerhof, Aalsmeer, NL
M.G. Westerhuis, Roodeschool, NL
Westgate Mennonite Collegiate Library, CAN
Ds. H. Wethmar, Rotterdam, NL
Ing. N. van Wettum, Ulvenhout, NL
Evan Whitesell, USA
Marjorie Wideman, USA
J. Glen Widmer, USA
John R. & Mabel A. Widrick, USA
Adina B. Wiebe, USA
David & Lorma Wiebe, USA
Dietrich Wiebe, Stocksee, D
Dwight & Margot Stauffer Wiebe, USA
Edwin Wiebe, CAN
Henry Wiebe, CAN
John H. Wiebe, CAN
Linda Wiebe, CAN
Lydia Wiebe, CAN
Roland J. Wiebe, USA
Werner I. Wiebe, CAN
William & Lorraine Wiebe, USA
A. Wiebenga, Amsterdam, NL
Ir. H.R.C. Wieberdink, Oranjewoud, NL
Anne H. Wieler, CAN
Arthur N. Wiens, USA
Gordon & LeAnna Wiens, USA
Henry & Helen Wiens, CAN
Jeryl J. Wiens, USA
Jeryl J. Wiens, USA
John Wiens, CAN
John A. Wiens, CAN
Mark Allan Wiens, USA
Martha Wiens, CAN
Martin D. Wiens, USA
Martin D. Wiens, USA
Ted & Emma Wiens, CAN
Trevor Wiens & Brenda Tiessen-Wiens, CAN
C.J. Wierenga-te Hennepe, Groningen, NL
Ds. J. Wieringa, Nijmegen, NL
J.A. Wieringa, Roden, NL
Eije Wiersema, Lemmer, NL
William M. & Thelma L. Bartel Wiest, USA
Louise E. Croyle Wigle, USA
Janke van Wijland, Dordrecht, NL
Bas Wijnands, Nieuwehorne, NL
Getty de Wilde-Grimm, Doorn, NL
Em. pred. M.C. de Wilde-Mulder, Zutphen, NL
Phoebe A. Wiley, USA
Bob & Lucille Willems, USA
Kathleen Brouse Williams, USA
E.A. van der Willigen-Binnerts, Hilversum, NL
Mary M. Willis, USA
Ardith Schertz Wilson, USA
Larry J. Wilson, USA
H. Wind-de Vos, Eindhoven, NL
J. Winkler Prins, Assen, NL
J.A. Winkler Prins, Assen, NL
Esther Winsemius, Amsterdam, NL
Femke Winsemius, Amsterdam, NL
Hessel C. Winsemius, Amsterdam, NL
Ruth Winsemius-Oosterbaan, Amsterdam, NL
C.W. de Wit-Ovinge, Eindhoven, NL
F.W. de Wit, Zoetermeer, NL
J.H. de Wit, Zaandijk, NL
Maartje de Wit Jd., Westerland, NL
H.J. Witteveen, Deventer, NL
H.D. Woelinga, Uithoorn, NL
Darrell W. Woelk, USA
G.M. van de Woestijne, Haarlem, NL
C. de Wolf-Pel, Grou, NL
Kathryn Wolfer, USA
Drs. M.I. Wolff-Craandijk, Rozendaal, NL
Lydia Arlene Sitler Woods, USA
Ds. R.B. Workel, Veenwouden, NL
Eva E.J.W. Wouda-Hageman, Markelo, NL
F. Wouda, Beetsterzwaag, NL
F. Wouda, Drachten, NL
Jan Wouda, Harich, NL
Erica R. Wouterloot, Zoetermeer, NL
N.M. Wouterloot, Maarssen, NL

Y

Katherine Yamada-Peters, USA
John A. Yeakel, USA
Ds. R.P. Yetsenga, Groningen, NL
Al Yoder, USA
Dr. Carl J. Yoder, USA
Conrad G.T. Yoder, USA
David Yoder, USA
Emerson David Yoder M.D., USA
Ervin C. Yoder, USA
Gene E. & Fern Yoder, USA
Gilbert L. & Joyce B. Yoder, USA
Henry & Mildred Yoder, USA
Ida Yoder, USA
Jonathan David Yoder, USA
Joseph Yoder, USA
Lamar Yoder, USA
Levi M. & Colleen Yoder, USA
Lonnie & Teresa Boshart Yoder, USA
Mark & Alice Yoder, USA
Paul R. Yoder Jr., M.D., USA
Samuel & Lillian Yoder, USA
Stanley J. Yoder, USA
Vernon & Dolores Yoder, USA
John & Shirley Yukich, USA

Z

Henry & Edna Zacharias, CAN
Leslie V. Zacharias, CAN
J.W. Zantema, Leeuwarden, NL
M. van Zee, Deventer, NL
Th. van der Zee, Beetsterzwaag, NL
Evan S. Zehr, USA
K. Warren Ziegler, USA
Dr. S. Zijlstra, Groningen, NL
Mr. A. van der Zijpp, Oosterbeek, NL
E.N. van der Zijpp-Stuker, Zwolle, NL
Jetske van der Zijpp, Arnhem, NL
John W. Zimmerly, USA
Raymond G. Zimmerman, USA
Zion Mennonite Church Library, USA
Zoar Mennonite Church, CAN
Freerk Zoethout, Den Haag, NL
Jan Zoethout, Leeuwarden, NL
J.W. Zondervan, Vlissingen, NL
Dr. Herman van Zonneveld, Tervuren, B
Floyd & Betty Zook, USA
Merlin W. Zook, USA
Warren H. Zuercher, USA
E. v.d. Zwaag, Den Ham, NL
W.A.J. Zwart-Heslinga, Haren, NL
A. Zwartendijk, Den Haag, NL
R.H. Zweep, Zwolle, NL

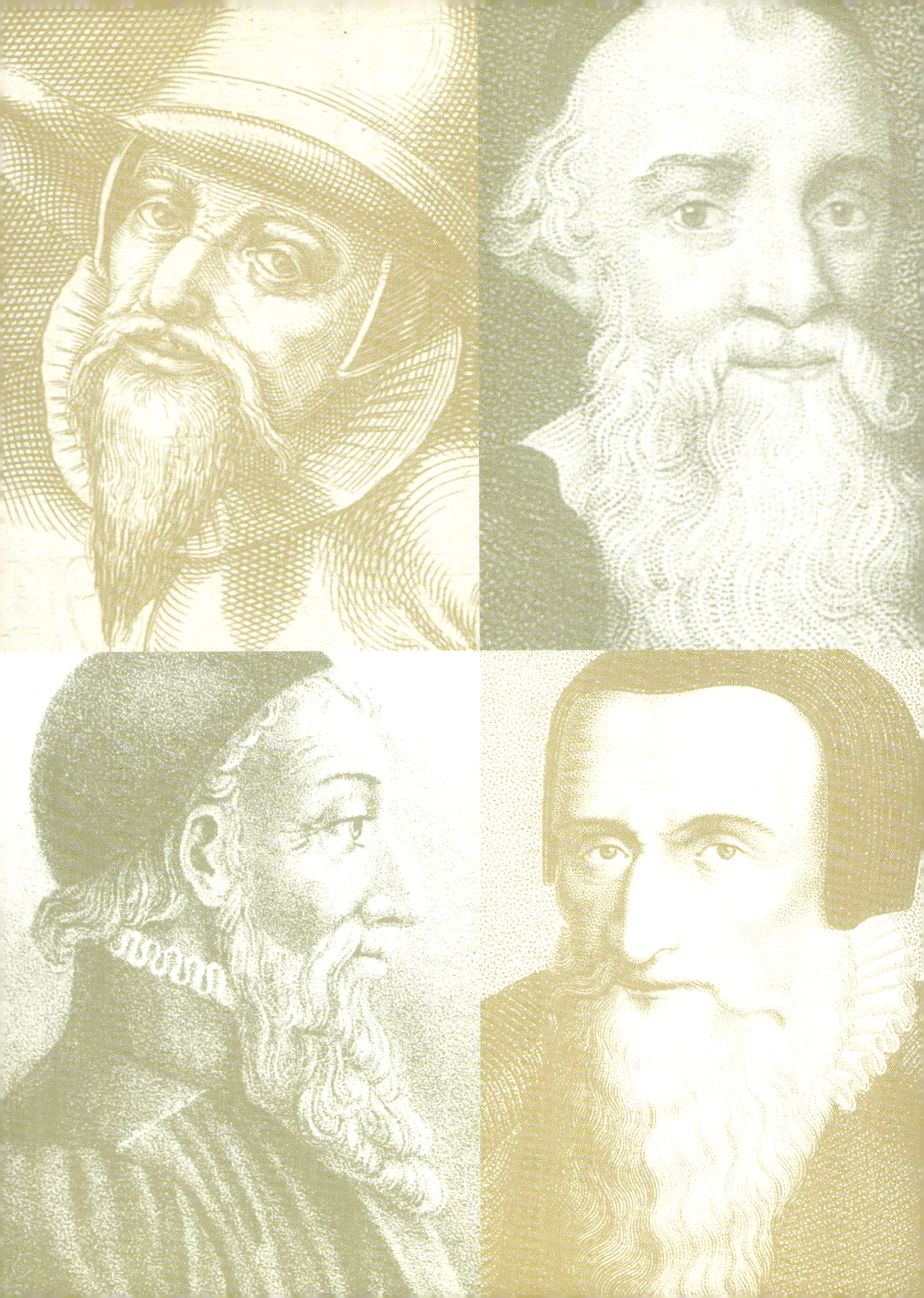